Victorian Sewing And Crafts

Program Guide For Public TV Series-200

by Martha Campbell Pullen, Ph.D.

May God Bless You

Martha Pullen

Book Team

Book Design: *Ann Le Roy*; Color, *Leighann Simmons*

Contributing Sewing Designers: *Kathy Brower, Kathy McMakin, Claudia Newton, Sue Pennington, Gail Settle and Margaret Taylor*

Construction Consultant and Editor: *Kathy McMakin*

Illustrated By: *Kathy Brower and Angela Pullen*

Other Sewing Contributors: *Louise Baird, Dody Baker, Westa Chandler, Suzanne Crocker, Kathy Ghorashi, Kathy Harrison, Mary Penton, Susie Price, Esther Randall, Patti Smith, Rhonda Smith, Mary Soltice, Laura Jenkins Thompson and Susan York*

Photography: *Jack Cooper Photography, Huntsville AL.*

Photo Stylist: *Amelia Johanson*

Printed By
The C.J.Krehbiel Company
Cincinnati, Ohio

Published And Distributed By
Martha Pullen Company, Inc.

518 Madison Street
Huntsville, Alabama 35801-4286

Phone 205-533-9586
Fax 205-533-9630

"Library of Congress Catalog Card Number" 94-93993

ISBN 1-878048-04-X

Dedication

To John Houston Crocker and his family; Susanne, Sarah Joy, and Rebekah Anne.

Sometimes God creates a person that is destined for doing His work. My youngest son, John Houston Crocker is one of those individuals. Looking at me with those big chocolate brown eyes was enough to melt me from the very beginning. My Daddy loved to baby sit John because he would sit in his lap for literally hours on end and "talk to" his "Gangy," the boys' pet name for my Daddy. Listening to books for hours at a time was his favorite activity; actually as long as he was in someone's lap, he would sit for hours and just coo and smile. John is a gentle giant and always was.

John's creativity began very early in life. His first grade teacher in Gainesville, FL. was Mrs. Losch. That started his successful school career which has just led go the completion of a seminary degree. Mrs. Losch would call me occasionally to tell me the adorable things John had said in class. He really liked show and tell and anything that had to do with speaking. In the second grade, his teacher, Mrs. Palmer, called me one day and said that since John had won the first two story writing contests, he would be ineligible for the next several competitions. She lovingly read me his latest winning entry, "Mickey Mouse's Birthday Party." John always liked school and was very fortunate to have good teachers who loved him.

Moving to Huntsville in the middle of the third grade was wonderful. I remember John exclaiming that we now had a real bathtub which we could fill with bubbles. Our previous apartment only had a shower! John always loved participating in many activities. The fifth grade found John as a patrol person opening car doors each morning and afternoon for the parents when they picked up the children. Huntsville Middle School was another good place for John, and he excelled at all he attempted. In the tenth grade, he transferred to The George School in Newtown, PA for three exciting years in his school career. He studied the usual subjects as well as drama.

During the first semester of his freshman year at the University of Arizona, he was called into the ministry. After being baptized on October 28, 1984, he decided that he wanted to transfer to a Christian university; therefore, he came back to Alabama to attend Samford University the second semester. At Samford, he was called to the foreign mission field, specifically, Africa. While at Samford, he was very active in and president of the MA's which is the Ministerial Association. During his college days, he served in Panama City and in Israel as a summer missionary.

Through his MA activities, he met a beautiful young woman, Suzanne Laramore. As a child, Suzanne's family spent seven years in Guatemala with the Southern Baptist Mission Board. When Suzanne was three years old, she told her mother that she wanted to be a missionary nurse when she grew up. After her freshman year in college, she went to Zimbabwe, Africa to serve as a summer missionary at Sanyati Baptist hospital. Suzanne and John were MA friends and even wrote letters while they were in Israel and Africa. Later that year, the friendship turned to love and they married December 17, 1988, after they had graduated from college. Their first missionary trip as husband and wife was a seven month term in Togo, West Africa. While they were there, they realized that John needed to finish seminary; they returned to Memphis where he entered Mid America Baptist Theological Seminary.

When John was in seminary, the Lord blessed them with two beautiful daughters, Sarah Joy and Rebekah Anne. It seemed that God had given them everything. God still had more joy to bring to John and Suzanne when the Southern Baptist Foreign Mission Board appointed them to go back to Togo for the ISC program when John graduated. On February 1, 1995, John, Suzanne, Sarah Joy and Rebekah left for Kara, Togo, West Africa to serve the Lord with the ISC program of the Southern Baptist Foreign Mission Board. What a thrill it is to me and my family to see their absolute joy in having been chosen by God to return to the same city where they served 5 years ago. I thank God that He chose our children for this most critical task of serving the people in this poverty stricken, third world country. John's job title is church planter apprentice; he will be working under the direction of The Reverend Ray Eitelman, who has been in West Africa for over 20 years. The Reverend Eitleman has been instrumental in starting over 30 churches. Suzanne tells me that his wife, Patsy, is a gifted seamstress and has used sewing classes to help women learn how to support their families. Many people have come to know Christ through her sewing ministry.

John's responsibilities primarily are assisting 15 local congregations with evangelism. His main role is to inspire local congregations and their leaders to reach out to unevangelized areas. This will be done by precept and example. In addition he will be helping and playing an important part in strengthening implanted congregations through regular visits, preaching, and participating in organized evangelistic activities.

I dedicate this book and this 200 series of *Martha's Sewing Room* to John, Suzanne, Sarah Joy and Rebekah Anne. Suzanne has done some absolutely beautiful sewing for several aspects of my business including *Martha's Sewing Room*. It was a joyous event for me the day John was born. Little did I know when I looked into my beautiful baby's face that someday God would call him and his family to serve Him halfway across the world. I love them, and I thank them. ❧

Acknowledgments

"For with God nothing shall be impossible." Luke 1:37

Developing a television series for public television has been a dream of mine for many years, and without the help of God, my family, friends and staff, it would never have happened. I am forever grateful to the following people:

My mother and father, Anna Ruth Dicus Campbell and the late Paul Jones Campbell were my first and greatest teachers. Their example of living a Godly, decent, and hard-working life certainly formed my attitude toward life and what should and could be accomplished. I love them and I thank them.

My children, Camp and Charisse, John and Suzanne, Mark and Sherry Ann, Jeff and Angela and Joanna have always loved me and believed in me. I love them all, and I am so proud of them.

My grandchildren have to be the most beautiful, the smartest, the cutest, and the most creative in the world! Isn't that spoken like a true grandmother? To Campbell, Morgan Ross, Sarah Joy, Rebekah, Marshall and Bradley—I love you dearly, and I thank you for coming into my life bringing such pure joy!

My sisters and brothers-Mary, Dottie, Cliff, and Robin-and their families are beautiful individuals whom I love very much. Brothers and sisters are gifts from God who grow more precious with every year.

The University of Alabama has been a real cornerstone in my educational life. My first degree was awarded from this institution in 1965. In 1972, the College of Education offered me enough money for an assistantship making it possible for me to return to my alma mater to attend graduate school full time. I received my Ph.D. in 1977. To have "my" university as my partner in this television series demonstrates that once more, this great institution was there to help me achieve my goals. I am grateful for all that the University of Alabama means to me and my family.

Tom Rieland, Director, Center for Public Television, Alabama Public Television at the University of Alabama, returned my call very quickly when I contacted several states about the possibility of filming a public television series about sewing! Without his vision, this series and this book would not have been possible. Tom, you certainly started this dream on the track of possibilities.

Dwight Cameron, Program Director, University of Alabama Center For Public Television, was there to hear my ideas when we first visited Tuscaloosa with two suitcases full of clothing, quilts, and projects. Dwight is unshakable and very creative. Dwight, thanks for believing in me and in creative sewing.

Mike Letcher, Production Manager, University of Alabama, Center For Public Television, has been uplifting and helpful in the meticulous planning of this series. He carefully explained the necessity of sitting down and planning every minute of 26 shows two months before filming.

Bill Teague of the University of Alabama Theatre Department has worked long and hard building the wonderful set which will house *Martha's Sewing Room*. I love the stairs which lead to Martha's Attic. I've been talking about Martha's Attic all these years; now I even have one on my television show.

Dawn Leach and Vince Pruitt, graphics designers with the University of Alabama Center for Public Television, have captured the essence of *Martha's Sewing Room* with their graphics to introduce and close each show and to divide the sections of the show. Their research into the "feel" of heirloom sewing is greatly appreciated.

I am appreciative to the Southern Educational Communications Association (SECA) for choosing to air *Martha's Sewing Room* on their satellite. I am especially grateful to the SECA President, Skip Hinton and to the SECA Program Director, Chuck McConnell. Because of Chuck's advice to me a couple of years ago, I believe my performance on this television series is much better than it would have been if he hadn't taken the time to give me an honest evaluation.

Judy Stone and Henry Bonner of Alabama Public Television have offered nothing but encouragement about *Martha's Sewing Room*. They have done everything possible to share the joy of *Martha's Sewing Room* with other television networks. APT was the first television network in the U.S. to air the series and I thank them for being great partners.

My business could not be a reality without the talents of many people. I have dedicated staff who has helped me produce this show and write this book. I love them and I appreciate them.

Leighann Simmons, Kathy Pearce, Toni Duggar, Lakanjala Campbell, Angie Daniel, Westa Chandler and Camp Crocker have kept the business running while others worked on this book!

Patti Smith has always been available to sew clothing for all of our publications. She works with great creativity, speed and enthusiasm even when we ask her to sew 40 things in two days.

Susie Price stitched several of the beautiful dropped waist dresses with great flair and speed. Her designs are gorgeous.

Kathy Harrison designed and stitched some of the dropped waist dresses for the series. Kathy's ideas twinkle under the sewing machine needle.

Louise Baird creates such gorgeous things with a sewing machine. She always helps us sew and plan, never complaining about deadlines.

Seeley's Doll Company gave us permission to use their doll bodies for the pattern drafting section of this book. They have been wonderful to work with.

Tom Azuma made the gorgeous dolls which you see on *Martha's Sewing Room*. Of course, they have a Seeley's body!

The Bernina, Elna, Pfaff, and Viking sewing machine companies have been with me from the beginning of *Sew Beautiful* magazine. They have invited me to teach at their national and international conventions, they have always advertised in the magazine, they have sent in hundreds of sewing machines for my schools here in Huntsville, they have sent educators to teach with us, they have planned for our traveling schools with their dealers over the world, and they have opened many doors for me. We appreciate their willingness to allow us to use their machines alternately on this television series. I consider this to be the ultimate in co-operation among companies. Each one of these companies is as wonderful as their machines, and I am very grateful not only to the corporate offices but also to the wonderful dealers around the world who have supported me and my business.

Susan York, Patti Smith, Rhonda Smith, Laura Jenkins Thompson, Kathy Ghorashi, Mary Soltice, Louise Baird, Dody Baker, Mary Penton, Gail Settle, Sue Pennington, Westa Chandler, Claudia Newton and Margaret Boyles loaned us garment after garment for our beautiful clothing for the introductory section of each show. Each of them have helped this endeavor in so many different ways.

Susan Clanton designed the appliqué and shadow appliqué for the dropped waist dress collars. Her creativity is brilliant.

Westa Chandler traveled with us to Tuscaloosa and spent hours ironing, organizing, and doing general "everything" to help us. She also stitched some of the beautiful silk ribbon embroidery.

My daughter, Joanna Pullen, modeled for the wedding show and was very patient during the fittings. She was the original inspiration for this whole business and she has been a vital part of all aspects.

Gail Settle designed and made pillows and crafts with such flair. Her work is so exciting and fresh.

Claudia Newton's work at a sewing machine is unbelievable. She's made clothing and pillows that take my breath away.

Louise Baird stitched the shadow applique squares and constructed the whole quilt. She has become a great little television star and demonstrates techniques like no one else can.

Esther Randall traveled from Provo to demonstrate wool embroidery so masterfully. I also thank Esther for being one of the national underwriters.

Margaret Boyles has been teaching with me for over 12 years. It is such a pleasure to have her demonstrate shadowwork embroidery for the viewing audience.

Sue Pennington designed doll dresses, pillows, garments and "story boards" for the series. She stitched until all hours of the night helping us meet deadlines. I truly don't know what I would do in this business without her.

Suzanne Crocker stitched quilt squares with great mastery. She took Kathy Brower's designs and embellished them with love and beauty.

Jack Cooper's photography is professional and creative. He has such patience in working with little people.

Angela Pullen's drawings add life and magic to all of our books. Her illustrations have great depth, detail, and creativity. She always meets deadlines and never complains about the boxes of work that we send her.

Amelia Johanson's photo styling of the color section adds so much to the aesthetic enjoyment of this book.

Ann LeRoy's book design is creative and lends a professional touch to all of the sections. It is not an easy task to take hundreds of drawings and computer disks of information and create a book out of it. To have an element of style and beauty in addition to correctness of directions and pictures is quite a feat. It overwhelms me to think of all the decisions which she had to make concerning the layout of this book.

Margaret Taylor stitched the heirloom quilt, wrote directions on several sections, prepared items for the television show "how-to" portions and in general helped with everything. Margaret is always there with her talent in many different areas. I also think she is a great television teacher.

Kathy McMakin's pattern drafting, construction ideas, technical writing skills and designing/sewing ability make her invaluable to every aspect of this business. She literally helped with every part of this book from direction writing to sewing and serging. Her contributions to this television series program guide are vast. Now her talents include television teaching and she does a great job of it all.

Kathy Brower's designing ability, writing ability and drawing ability for the "how-to" sections absolutely amaze me. Not only are her illustrations gorgeous, she knows how to draw everything in the construction sequence by just looking at the craft. She designed and constructed many of the items for this book, illustrated nearly all of the "how-to" sections, wrote part of the directions including the entire silk ribbon directions and in general acted as the foreman for the sewing of this book. I also think she is a wonderful "T.V. Star" when she teaches her silk ribbon segments.

There is one person to whom I am especially grateful. Next to God, he has been my faithful advisor, my financial partner, my idea person, and my mentor. My husband, Joe Ross Pullen, has always believed in me more than I believe in myself. He is a wonderful dentist and has been one of the worldwide pioneers in implant dentistry. He is a wonderful Christian husband and father, and God blessed me beyond my wildest imaginations the day that Joe asked me to marry him. He is my best friend and my partner; I love him, and I thank him.

A number of years ago, I gave this whole business to God. He took it, figured out what to do next, and has given the guidance for moving in the directions in which we are moving. All the credit and glory for any success that we have had in the sewing industry go to Him and Him alone. The path has not been nor is it now an easy one. I don't think He promised us an easy trip through life. He did promise to be with us always and I can testify that He has never failed me. ▓

Special Thanks To Our Underwriters

Dreaming of producing a television series for PBS has been in my mind for many years. Having that dream come true is a blessing from God! So many people helped this dream come true. Four of those "people" are actually companies who believed in this series before they had anything but a lot of ideas from me. I thank them, and I believe in their products or I wouldn't have asked them to be the underwriters. I feel very humbled that I only mentioned underwriting to five companies and four of those accepted.

I have known Clotilde nearly as long as I have been in this business. Her catalogue will forever be a boost to the sewing industry and her enthusiasm is unending. She helped me spread the word about *Sew Beautiful* magazine to millions of people through her catalogue. She has sold thousands of books from us, and I have bought lots of notions from her. She has always been there for me for friendship and for business advice. She and Don even furnished the place for my son Camp and his bride Charisse to go for their honeymoon. Thanks Clotilde!

Esther and Dan Randall of YLI have been good friends for ever so long. My first trip to Utah was to teach for them in one of our traveling schools. I have enjoyed a long and exciting relationship with both them and their children, Nancy, Scott and Esther. Esther Randall is responsible for reviving the art of silk ribbon embroidery and spreading it to the world. She is now importing the lovely New Zealand wools to bring back the art of wool embroidery.

Barbara Parsons Massey loves heirloom sewing and is a new shop owner in Arkansas. When I first told my school in February about the new television series, she came to me immediately and said, "Martha, who are your underwriters going to be?" After I replied that I didn't know yet, she said, "Well, I want Parson's Cabinets to be one." After putting me in touch with Bud Massey, we worked out the arrangements. Parsons wasn't a new company to me. I had sold their wonderful Cabinets when I opened my first retail store. It is a pleasure to be working with them again and to have them on board.

My relationship with Fiskars Scissors company first came about when I purchased a pair of their "arthritis" scissors. After seeing the absolutely perfect quality of these lightweight scissors, I had to have several more pairs. I have enjoyed working with Kevin Phays and Sandra Cashman in telling them about our dreams and in sharing with them how completely sold I was on Fiskars.

To Clotilde, YLI, Parsons Cabinets, and Fiskars, I hope you love the programs as much as we do. Since your products are the very best, I know our viewers will be anxious to purchase them. I also know the readers and viewers who love *Sew Beautiful* magazine and *Martha's Sewing Room* will also appreciate your making this program possible, in part. Our readers and viewers tend to be very loyal individuals, and I feel assured that they will give your products every consideration. ▓

Table of Contents

If fine laces, batiste and heirloom sewing supplies are not available locally, call 1-800-547-4176 for Martha Pullen Co., Inc. retail catalogue. Martha Pullen Co., 518 Madison, Hunstville AL 35801

Foreword To This Program Guide

To say that we have loved planning this program guide to go along with our 200 series *Martha's Sewing Room* would be an understatement! We have had so much fun putting together exciting and creative projects and developing the technique instructions to go along with them. I love to sew and I can bet that most anyone who is reading this foreword loves to sew also. The joy of heirloom sewing is overwhelming to me and the delight at seeing new fabrics, new garments, new ideas is just as great today as it was about 17 years ago when I saw my first French sewn dress. I have loved smocking since I was in college when my mother made me the most wonderful pale green smocked dress. Let me tell you something very sad. That beautiful dress made from a McCall pattern was the only garment that I ever had stolen from my college clothing. I guess even a dishonest person can recognize beauty.

Some of my newest sewing excitement is the recreating of details on antique clothing using today's modern sewing machines. Once again at the end of each show, I go to my attic and share with the audience garments from my vintage clothing collection. I only wish that I knew who made these garments and the exact date of their origination. I really believe that the smocked and French garments that are being created today will be the museum clothing for tomorrow. Please as you create your masterpieces, use the alphabet on your machine and stitch in the names of the wearer, the sewer, the date, the city and the occasion if there is a special one such as an Easter dress or birthday dress.

We love for Martha Pullen books to be an extraordinary value for our readers. With this in mind, we have included in this book, a dropped waist girl's pattern sized 4-12 and lots of variations and collars. The collars, in all sizes, are round portrait collar, V-collar, shaped collar, square collar, long square collar, and double square collar. I believe if you or I were to buy a multi-sized dropped waist pattern with many collar variations from any commercial pattern book, the patterns would cost well over the price of this book.

Sewing for the home is one of the largest areas of home sewing today. The home decorating section offers heirloom ideas for pillows. Beautiful pillows are among the most appreciated and creative gifts you can give to almost everyone on your Christmas list. They always fit and they will be a gift which can't be purchased at the store. I believe some of these pillows fall into the decorative arts masterpiece category. You enjoy them and have fun practicing your techniques!

I know how many sewers are also doll makers. Those little dolls need gorgeous clothing and many of our porcelain masters have become perfection heirlooms sewers. It is rumored that doll collecting, dressing, and making is second only to stamp collecting in this country. Seeley's Doll Company has the most complete line of composition bodies that I have seen. This company was generous in loaning us their bodies for French Body, German Body, and Modern Body so we could size and cut a major pattern collection for each of these popular doll sizes. Included here are patterns and directions for 12 styles to fit 13 sizes of Seeley's bodies. Several companies make very popular "play with" vinyl dolls in the 18" size. The pattern sizes in this book which comes closest to fitting these 18" dolls is MB160 or FB17. The skirt lengths will have to be changed; just measure your doll to see how long you want your dress to be. If you want to make the gift of a lifetime for someone you love, dress a doll with an entire wardrobe.

The craft section is just plain fun. Most of the projects are so easy to make and I really believe that we have something for everyone in this section. We enjoyed demonstrating the "how to" on the television series, and this guide includes directions for every project. Some of them are purely hot glue gun projects which have an elegant and Victorian flair. Others require a little bit of easy sewing. This great section will help you plan gifts for any occasion.

This series has two quilts; the shadow appliqué memory quilt and the sampler quilt. I love quilts but I haven't learned to piece and hand quilt, yet. I need quilts which can be made quickly and easily. The sampler type quilt is the answer. This type of quilt takes almost no time to construct and it is as pretty as a traditional pieced quilt. Even if you have never quilted, watch Margaret Taylor's segment on the television show or just read the directions in this book, and you will be inspired to make lovely quilts for a baby, your king-sized bed or wherever you want an elegant quilt.

Silk ribbon embroidery has to be the most exciting news to come along in a long time. With Kathy Brower's showing you how on the television series and with her wonderful directions in this book, you should have no trouble learning. Silk ribbon embroidery, like shadow embroidery, is terribly easy and even a beginner can make gorgeous things. Wool embroidery is enjoying a comeback in the heirloom sewing circle. Wool embroidery is ever so lovely on wool bears, baby blankets, pillows and other items for the home. Esther Randall demonstrates some wool embroidery stitches and the directions are included in this book.

This program guide would not be complete without beginning through advanced French sewing techniques. Our techniques have become world famous for being easy and readable. Many women have created very elaborate christening dresses or other garments by using only the written directions in our books. The directions are written in easy to understand terms accompanied by professional illustrations.

You will find patterns, patterns, and more patterns in the fold out section as well as in the back of this book. We have tried to include some of the smaller patterns in the regular sized pages; the large templates and patterns are on the fold out pattern section. All of the pattern pieces and templates you will need to make all the exciting projects pictured are either in the back of the book or on the fold out section.

We are so excited about *Martha's Sewing Room*. The response from public television stations all over this great United States has been fabulous. If you don't have *Martha's Sewing Room* in your area, please call your local public television station and request it. Tell them that *Martha's Sewing Room* is broadcast to the stations via the SECA satellite system out of South Carolina. In closing, I hope that you enjoy this program guide and these patterns as much as we have enjoyed creating them for you. We are excited about this hard cover book; we have created the finest product for you that we know how to create. Without your interest and enthusiasm, we couldn't bring *Martha's Sewing Room* into your home. We appreciate you and we thank you! ❈

Introduction To Pillows

Sewing for the home is becoming one of the top areas of sewing in the world today. In heirloom sewing, we make beautiful pillows for every room of the house. I don't know if you have been "pillow shopping in decorator shops" recently but I have. To find lovely pillows in the $100-$300 price range for one pillow is not uncommon. Look in any decorator magazine and I think you will find the most gorgeous assortment of decorator pillows on the beds. Hardly a magazine has a "naked" bed anymore. Using the techniques on this television program and in this book can give you a whole new outlet in life— pillow making. Speaking of new outlets in life, at one time I said that I needed another hobby like I needed a hole in the head; however, if your little ones aren't at the age to wear the lovely heirloom clothing, then it is time to redecorate your bedrooms.

After making your heirloom quilt, then I give you permission for the next number of years, to make pillows to decorate that bed with the quilt on top. Recently I attended a tea given by the Huntsville Symphony Orchestra to benefit our youth orchestra and I was thrilled to be able to tour not only the downstairs of this UNBELIEVABLE historic home in Huntsville, but also the bedrooms. On every bed whether it was a tailored masculine bedroom or a little girl's bedroom or the master bedroom, this home had designer heirloom type pillows. She even had an antique tiny pillow on her mantle which had a verse of scripture printed by sticking pins in the writing and the floral decoration around this "pin sticking" was done with tiny nails poked into the pillow. The pillow was stuffed with something hard so that the pins and the nails stayed in properly. The pillow had lovely fringe around the whole pillow. I had never seen anything like this at all. In the tailored wing chair in the master bedroom there was an antique lace pillow for decoration. Even in the son's bedroom, there were cross stitch pillows on his very masculine and tailored bed. I think pillow time has arrived in a bigger way that ever before in the home decorating industry.

The gift of a pillow is truly one to be desired. I cannot think of any lovelier presents than one I received from a friend in Florida which had my initials stitched in shadow work embroidery amongst rows of lace, ribbons and batiste. Suzanne made Joanna a beautiful heirloom pillow for her bedroom a couple of years ago. Joanna treasures that pillow so much. Please try an heirloom pillow as a present for someone very special on your list; however, we have a rule to give hand made gifts only to someone who will appreciate your love and time in this type of present.

Making a pillow or a quilt square before you tackle a dress is always a good idea. Pillows are the perfect way to practice and then have something to be treasured from your first effort. In this section we have some traditional heirloom pillows as well as some which aren't heirloom at all.

The Diamond Braid Pillow is for your living room or your den. Two baby pillows-Lace Shaped Baby Pillow and Crazy Patch Baby Pillow- are masterpieces for the new baby that you love. The Lace Shaped Baby Pillow can be made before the baby comes. You will have to wait to enter the birth details on your sewing machine for the Crazy Patch Baby Pillow. Either one will be sure to please the new mother, I promise. What a thrill the Heart Puffing Pillow is to the eye! The Lace Heart Demi Pillow is equally as sweet in a much less complicated way. Celtic Boudoir Pillow is easy and quick to make. A treasure for any wedding is the Crazy Patch Wedding Pillow. You can individualize it is any way you want. For a living room or a bedroom is the Appliquéd Rose Pillow. The Woven Basket Pillow is so sweet using the lace shaping tape and the Peach Madeira Appliqué Pillow with Cameo Pin is a Victorian dream. The ever popular Shark's Teeth Pillow will certainly be a favorite of everyone who sees it.

Have fun making your pillows and using all of your favorite techniques from this television series. I think your bedroom, living room, den or other favorite room of your house will be much more beautiful with hand made pillows plopped all around. If you give one of the pillows for a gift, please let me know what the reaction was from the lucky recipient. I think you will find the pillow styles will lend themselves to any of your favorite techniques in any type of sewing so you have my permission to use these pillow ideas for any type of your sewing. Let your imagination be the only guide to using this section for many hours of very happy sewing. Isn't that what sewing is all about? ❈

Heart Puffing Pillow

Touches of 1-1/4 inch puffing, shadow work embroidery, surface embroidery, clear crystal beads, and ecru French laces all combine in a delicate pillow which I think anyone would love! The heart puffing nearly covers the whole pillow and it is edged with ecru French insertion also curved in a heart shape. Gathered French edging is stitched to the front of the pillow as an outline of the heart. A machine entredeux stitch with a wing needle catches the insertion and the gathered French lace edging. Gathered French edging is used to trim the outside of the pillow also. The colors in the embroidery are burgundy, blue, and green. The finished measurements of the pillow are 14 inches by 14 inches. This would be a beautiful pillow for a ring bearer to carry and the embroidery could be in the colors of the bridesmaid's dresses. It would also be beautiful in a bedroom, on a sunporch or in any Victorian decorated room.

Materials Needed

- ✄ 5/8 yd. Swiss batiste Nelona
- ✄ 6 yds. edging lace 1" wide 5/8" wide
- ✄ 2-1/2 yds. of lace insertion
- ✄ Floss for shadow work embroidery and surface embroidery
- ✄ Crystal beads
- ✄ Polyester fiber filling
- ✄ Light weight sewing thread
- ✄ Wing needle
- ✄ Paper stabilizer (Stitch N Tear)

I. Making The Top Of The Pillow

1. Cut three pieces of batiste 15" by 15". One piece will be used for the pillow top. One piece will be used for the pillow top lining and one will be used for the pillow bottom.

2. With a washout marker, trace the template onto the top piece. The template is on the centerfold of this book.

3. Cut three pieces of fabric 2-1/4" wide by 45". Stitch these strips together using a 1/4" seam to form one long strip for the puffing. Trim the seam allowance to 1/8" and overcast the edges with zigzag.

4. To create the puffing either run two gathering rows on each long side of the long strip at 1/4" and 1/2" or gather using a gathering foot, placing the stitching at 1/2" on each side (**fig. 1**).

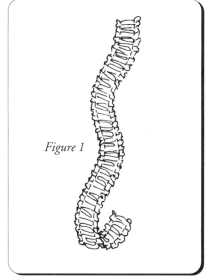

Figure 1

5. If rows of gathering are used, pull the bobbin threads of the stitching to gather each side to form the puffing.

6. Place the fabric with the traced template on a lace shaping board.

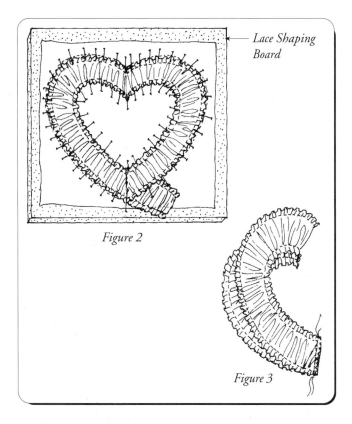

Lace Shaping Board

Figure 2

Figure 3

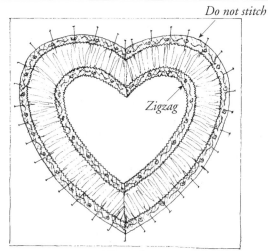

Do not stitch

Zigzag

Figure 4

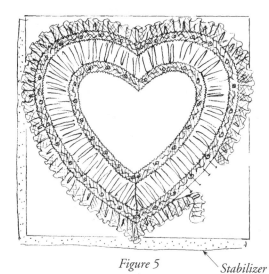

Figure 5

Stabilizer

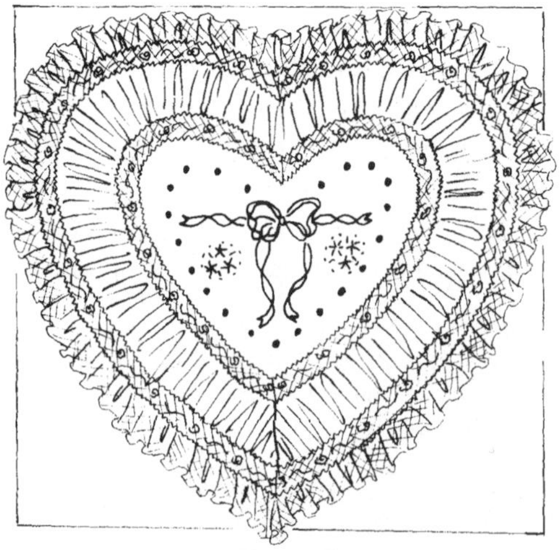

Figure 6

7. Shape the puffing on the heart, placing the pins in the outer edge of the puffing strip. Allow for a 1/4" seam at the bottom of the heart (**fig. 2**). Trim away the excess puffing strip. Starch and press lightly. Remove the puffing heart from the board and stitch the ends together with a 1/4" seam. Overcast the seam allowance with a zigzag (**fig. 3**). Place puffing back on the pillow top in the designated area. Pin in place.

8. Shape the lace insertion along the puffing outside and inside the heart following the template lines. Refer to the heart lace shaping directions in this book. Pin laces in place. Starch and press lightly.

9. Using a small zigzag, stitch along the inside and outside edges of the inner lace heart and along the inner edge of the outer lace heart (**fig. 4**).

10. Gather 2-1/2 yards of edging lace to fit the outer edge of the lace heart. Pin in place. Place your stabilizer (stitch-n-tear or other stabilizer) underneath this heart of lace shaping, and stitch the laces to the fabric (**fig. 5**). Here is the perfect place to use your wing needle/pinstitch or entredeux stitch on your sewing machine if you have this stitch. If you don't, a tiny zigzag with a regular needle will do just fine.

11. Trace the embroidery design in the center of the heart. Complete the embroidery in desired colors (**fig. 6**).

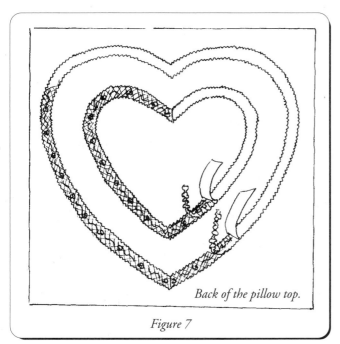

Back of the pillow top.

Figure 7

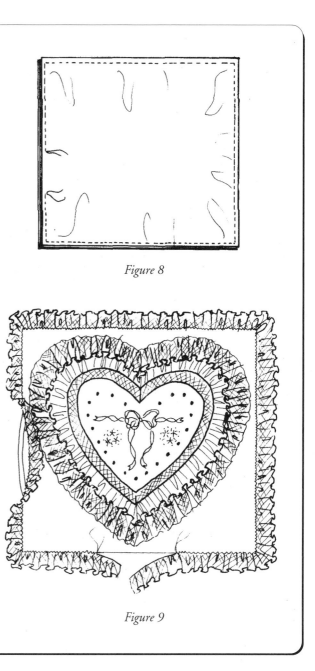

Figure 8

Figure 9

12. Carefully trim away the fabric and puffing edges under the lace insertion hearts (**fig. 7**).

II. Finishing The Pillow

1. Place a second piece of fabric on the wrong side of the pillow top for the lining. Pin in place and treat the pillow top and lining as one layer of fabric.

2. Place the pillow back to the top right sides together. Stitch together using a 1/2" seam, leaving a 3" opening in one side. Trim the seam allowance to 1/4" (**fig. 8**).

3. Turn the pillow to the right side. Gather the remaining edging to fit the outer edge of the pillow. Butt the edging to the pillow edge and zigzag in place allowing the zigzag to catch the edging and the pillow edge (**fig. 9**).

4. Stuff the pillow. Stitch closed the opening used for stuffing the pillow. ▨

Lace Heart Demi-Pillow

This little pillow is only 7 1/2 inches across and is ever so sweet. Four ecru French lace hearts touch in a circle and there is a piece of ribbon 21 inches long which is stitched to the pillow in the middle. The ribbon ties in a pretty little bow. Narrow French insertion is zigzagged to French edging to make a wider piece of lace to gather to the outside circle of the pillow. Although this pillow is a demi pillow, it would be absolutely beautiful used as a pin cushion also. If this were 1900 I think this pillow would be used for hat pins and if you by chance collect hat pins, this pillow would be perfect for displaying your antique treasures. I can also see this pillow as a perfect place for holding broaches, either antique or new. Whatever its use, this is one delicate and pretty item for your home. Wouldn't this be a sweet gift for a bride to give her bridesmaids?

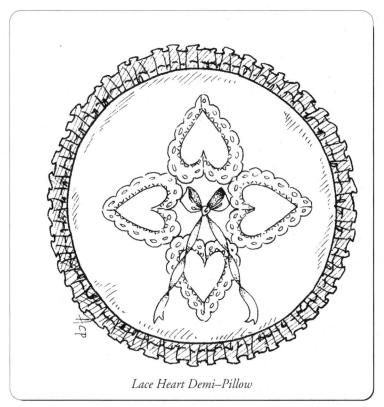

Lace Heart Demi–Pillow

❋ *Materials Needed* ❋

- ❋ 1/4 yd. batiste for pillow
- ❋ 2-1/2 yds. French edging 1/2" wide
- ❋ 1-1/3 yds. French insertion 3/8" wide
- ❋ 3/4 yd. 3/8" ribbon
- ❋ Polyester fiber filling
- ❋ Light weight sewing thread

I. Shaping The Lace Edging Hearts

1. Cut out two circles with an 8" diameter of the pillow fabric.

2. Using the template given on the next page, trace the four hearts on the pillow front.

3. Pin the lace edging so that the scalloped side of the lace edging is on the outside and the straight heading of the lace is on the inside. Then, you can pull the inside string of the heading to shape the hearts.

4. Shape all four of the lace hearts. Refer to the heart lace shaping directions in this book. Straight stitch the hearts to the pillow on both the outside and the inside (**fig. 1**). Do not cut away the fabric from behind these hearts.

5. Center the ribbon to the exact center of the pillow. Stitch in place with a tiny zigzag. This will be tied into a bow upon the completion of the pillow (**fig. 2**).

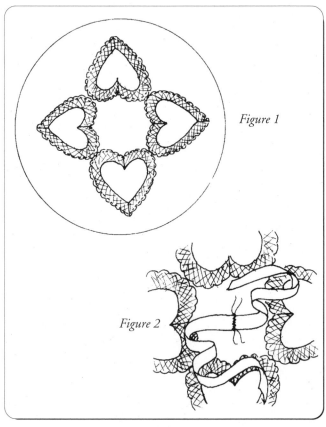

Figure 1

Figure 2

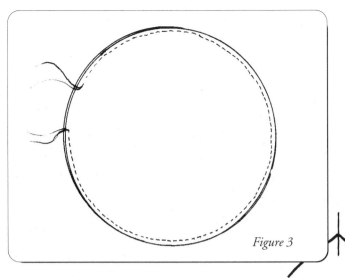

Figure 3

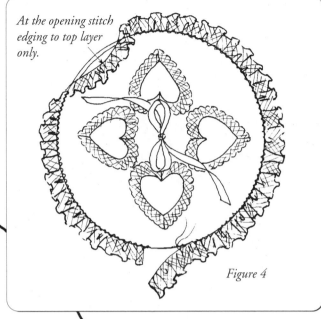

At the opening stitch edging to top layer only.

Figure 4

II. Constructing The Pillow

1. Place the pillow top and bottom, right sides together. Stitch using a 1/4 inch seam. Leave a 1-1/2 inch section unstitched (**fig. 3**). Turn right side out and press.

2. Zigzag the lace insertion to the lace edging to make a wider piece of edging or use one, 3/4" wide piece of edging. Pull the gathering thread in the heading and gather the lace.

3. Distribute this gathered lace edging to fit the pillow edge. Butt this gathered piece up to the outside edge of the pillow. Pin in several places and zigzag the gathered lace to the finished the pillow (**fig. 4**). To finish the ends turn one end under and overlap the other end. You may also unpin the lace, stitch a seam in the ends and pin again to finish stitching.

4. Stuff the pillow. Stitch closed the section you used to turn the pillow. ▨

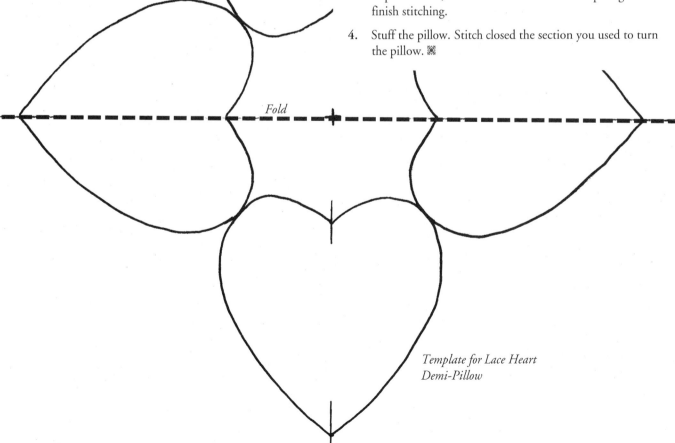

Fold

Template for Lace Heart Demi-Pillow

Crazy Patch Baby Pillow

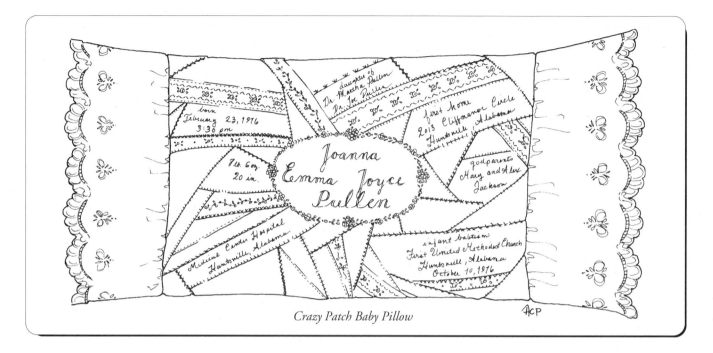

Crazy Patch Baby Pillow

Encircled in a machine stitched, silk ribbon oval is the name "Joanna Emma Joyce Pullen." Using the crazy patch technique, we stitched pieces of ribbon, Swiss handloom, Swiss white embroidery, netting, and plain batiste together to form this beautiful baby pillow. The colors are pink, blue, green and darker pink. The threads are all white on the crazy patch portion of the pillow. Lots of machine decorative stitches are used to embellish the crazy patch portions. Embroidered on the white batiste sections is the following information: Daughter of Dr. Martha Pullen and Dr. Joe Pullen; first home, 2013 Cliffmanor Circle, Huntsville, AL; godparents, Mary and Alex Jackson; Infant baptism, First United Methodist Church, Huntsville, Alabama, October 10, 1976; Medical Center Hospital, Huntsville, Alabama; and 7lb. 6oz. 20 inches. The machine stitched letters for the information is embroidered in a medium shade of pink since Joanna is a girl. I would use blue for a boy. A wide machine scallop has been stitched in the back of the pillow. It has 5 tiny pearl buttons which button in the buttonholes made in the overlap. This back closing reminds me of French and Italian antique linen pillowcases which button at the end to keep the pillow from coming out.

Materials Needed

※ 1/2 yd. white batiste (backing and crazy patch backing)

※ Assorted laces, Swiss trims for crazy patch

※ Scraps of pink and blue batiste for crazy patch

※ Pink, blue, green silk ribbon

※ White thread

※ 1-5/8 yd. Swiss or American embroidered 5 1/2" edging

※ Assorted pieces of ribbon in pink, blue and white for crazy patch

※ Pink or blue machine embroidery thread for machine lettering

※ 13" by 17" piece of Solvy or water soluble stabilizer

※ Polyester fiber filling

I. Making The Top Of The Pillow

1. Cut or tear a piece of fabric 13-1/2" by 17". The top of this pillow can be larger or smaller depending on your preference. Trace the outline of the oval template onto the center of the fabric. Template on page 317.

2. Work patchwork over the entire piece of fabric, including the oval (for specific instructions refer to the crazy patch section in this book). If words will be written on some of the patches, do the writing on rectangles of fabric which will then be used to make patches. Be sure that none of the writing is inside the oval, or it will be lost.

3. When all of the patchwork is in place, topstitch with decorative stitches over the seams.

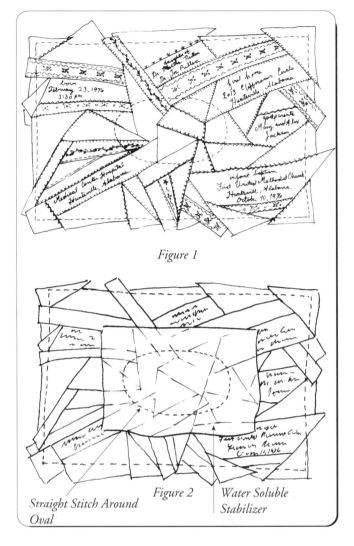

Figure 1

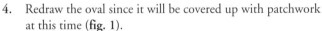

Straight Stitch Around Oval   *Figure 2*   *Water Soluble Stabilizer*

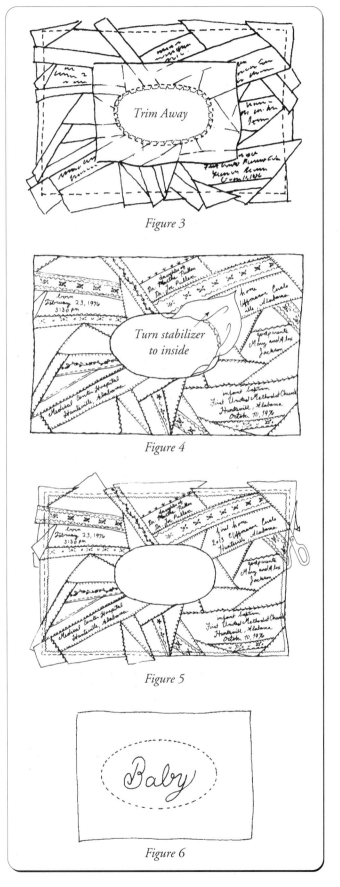

Figure 3

Figure 4

Figure 5

Figure 6

4. Redraw the oval since it will be covered up with patchwork at this time (**fig. 1**).

5. Place a piece of water soluble stabilizer (Solvy) over the oval. Stitch on the oval template line with a straight stitch (**fig. 2**). Trim away the inside of the oval leaving a 1/4" seam allowance. Clip the seam allowance (**fig. 3**).

6. Turn the stabilizer to the inside, creating an oval shaped hole (**fig. 4**). Press the seam. If you must press on the stabilizer side, use a press cloth.

7. Zigzag 1/4 inch inside the outer edge of the pillow to finish the crazy patch edges and trim off the excess patches along the edge (**fig. 5**).

8. Trace the oval shape onto a piece of the batiste fabric. Monogram or decorate the inside of the oval. On this baby pillow, Joanna's full name is stitched by machine (**fig. 6**). Baby template on page 317.

9. Place the patchworked pillow top over the monogramed oval center section, with both pieces right side up. Stitch the two pieces together around the edges of the oval, using a blanket stitch or tiny zigzag (**fig. 7**).

10. On the back side, trim away the extra fabric and stabilizer (**fig. 8**).

II. Embellishing The Pillow Top

1. Work embroidery around the edges of the oval, or trim the edge with lace. You may want to use silk ribbon embroidery by machine.

III. Silk Ribbon Embroidery By Machine Directions-Feather Stitch

1. To make a featherstitch wind 2 mm silk ribbon onto a bobbin. To wind a bobbin with silk ribbon either wind it by hand or hold it out with your fingers and run the machine. You do not thread the ribbon through anything in order to wind it onto a bobbin.

2. Bypass the bobbin tension by pulling the ribbon through the bobbin case slit only (**fig. 9**). Another good way is to use an extra bobbin case, loosen the bobbin tension screw on the case (**fig. 10**). Mark this bobbin case, so that you do not confuse it with your regular bobbin case.

3. Thread the top of the machine with embroidery thread to match the ribbon; tighten the top tension about 2 steps.

4. Using the largest settings possible, work a feather stitch around the oval, sewing with the wrong side of the pillow up facing you.

5. When you come back to the beginning, thread the ribbon and the thread tails into a large eyed needle and carry the needle to the back. Tie a knot in the ribbons and threads to hold in place.

IV. Silk Ribbon Embroidery By Machine Directions-Flowers

1. Drop the feed dogs.

2. Using embroidery thread and sewing from the top, make a small to medium zigzag in place until the thread starts to mound up; tie-off; this is the center; you may move the fabric slightly forward to make a larger center.

3. Wind 4mm silk ribbon onto a bobbin.

4. Thread the top of the machine with embroidery thread and tighten the top tension about two steps.

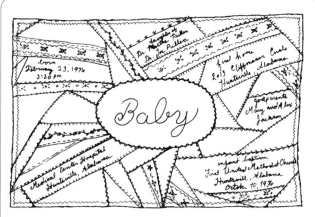

Figure 7

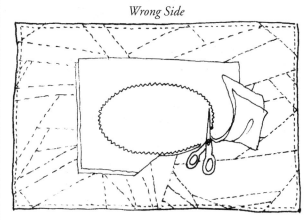

Wrong Side

Figure 8

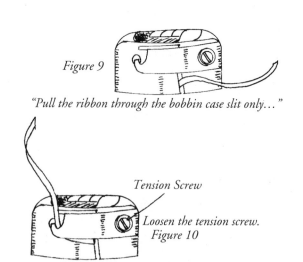

Figure 9

"Pull the ribbon through the bobbin case slit only…"

Tension Screw

Loosen the tension screw.
Figure 10

5. Sewing with the wrong side up, set the machine for a medium to wide zigzag.

6. Your flower will have 3 to 4 sides; begin at one corner and take three stitches in place (**fig. 11**).

7. Pivot with the needle in the fabric, and make three more stitches on the next side.

8. Continue to pivot and stitch until you are back at the beginning (**fig. 12**).

9. Use a needle to thread the silk ribbon and thread tails to the back side and tie a knot.

10. Work these large flowers at the circles on the template.

11. Work French knots at the dots on the template; they are made the same as the centers, but with a narrower stitch; use embroidery thread and sew from the right side.

12. Leaves can be worked like French knots, but with a wider stitch; use embroidery thread and sew from the right side.

V. Finishing The Pillow

1. Cut a piece of pillow fabric 2" longer than the pillow top and wide enough to be a little over 1/3 the pillow width when folded in half. Approximately 17" by 12". Fold the fabric in half; starch and press. This will be the top portion of the pillow back, the one with the buttonholes.

2. Stitch a row of scallops about 1" from the folded edge. Trim the folded edge away from the scallops (**fig. 13**). Center the scalloped edge over the pillow and trim ends even with the pillow edge. Be sure that one of the scallops is in the center, because a buttonhole will be worked here.

3. Work 5 buttonholes in this scalloped top part of the back of the pillow (**fig. 14**).

4. Cut a piece of pillow fabric 17" by 20". Fold it in half to 17" by 10". Starch and press. This will be the bottom portion of the pillow back, the one with the buttons. Place both pieces on the pillow and line up the edges, be sure that the folded edge is under the scalloped edge and mark under the buttonholes. Sew on the buttons.

5. Place the pillow back and the pillow front, right sides together; stitch along the two long sides of the pillow (**fig. 15**). Turn right side out. Baste stitch across the ends with a 1/4" seam. (fig. 16).

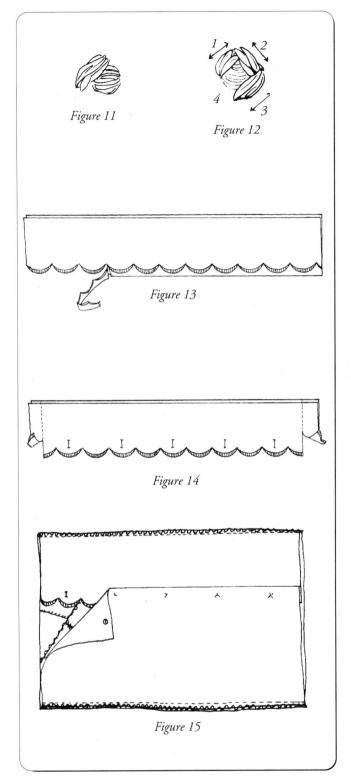

Figure 11

Figure 12

Figure 13

Figure 14

Figure 15

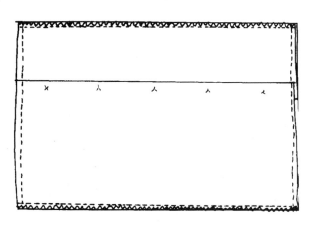

Figure 16

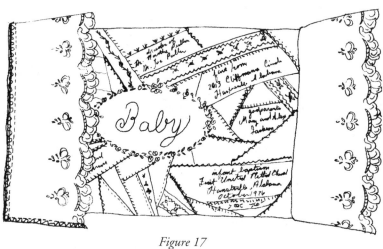

Figure 17

6. Measure across the ends and double this measurement. Cut two pieces of wide Swiss or American embroidered edging to this measurement plus 1/2" for a seam. Place the short ends of each embroidery piece together to form two tubes. Stitch together using a 1/4" seam. Overcast the edges with a zigzag or serger. Place the tubes to the ends of the pillow, right sides together. Stitch across the ends of the pillow top using a 1/4" seam. Overcast the seam allowance with a zigzag (**fig. 17**). Flip tubes to the right side.

7. Stuff the pillow through the opening created in the pillow back or make an inner pillow to be placed in this beautiful pillow cover. ✤

Celtic Boudoir Pillow

Pale robin's egg blue Nelona is the fabric for this circular pillow for your bedroom. The Celtic lace design has eight little loops of a narrow ecru French lace insertion. Gathered ecru French lace trims the edge of the pillow. The finished size of the circular pillow is 11 inches in diameter. This Celtic design would be pretty on a much larger pillow also made of velveteen or silk dupioni or patchwork for other rooms of your home.

Materials Needed

- ❈ 1/4 yd. robin's egg blue Swiss batiste Nelona
- ❈ 1/4 yd. robin's egg blue material for lining the pillow
- ❈ 2 1/2 yds. 1/4" ecru French insertion
- ❈ 2 yds. 1 1/4" ecru French edging
- ❈ One 12" circle of stitch-n-tear or other stabilizer
- ❈ Polyester fiber filling

I. Constructing The Front Of The Pillow

1. Cut two 11 1/2" circles of the Swiss batiste for the pillow top and bottom.

2. Cut two 11 1/2" circles of the fabric you are going to use for the lining of the pillow.

3. Trace on the top of the Swiss batiste circle with a water soluble pen or pencil the Celtic template design, page 317.

4. Place this circle on a lace shaping board. Using glass head pins, begin shaping the lace insertion along the design lines. Refer to the lace shaping techniques in this book. Lightly spray starch and press the lace shaping into place.

5. Remove the pins from the board, and pin the Celtic lace design in enough places so that it won't slip when you go to the sewing machine to stitch it.

6. Place your stabilizer (stitch-n-tear or other stabilizer) underneath this circle of lace shaping, and stitch the laces to the fabric. Here is the perfect place to use your wing needle/pinstitch or entredeux stitch on your sewing machine if you have this stitch. If you don't, a tiny zigzag will do just fine (**fig. 1**).

Celtic Boudoir Pillow

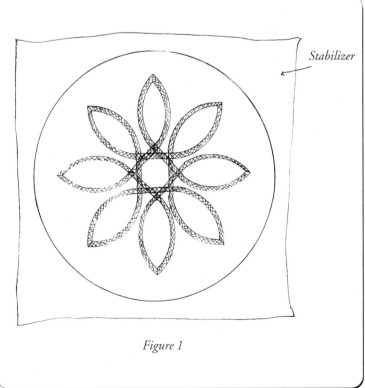

Stabilizer

Figure 1

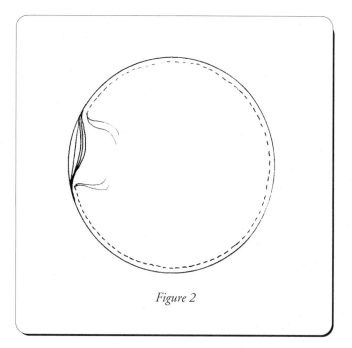

Figure 2

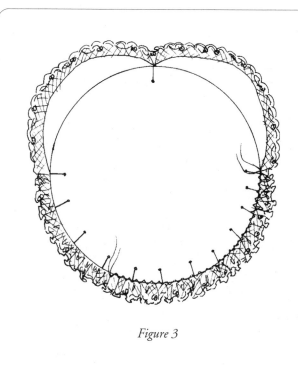

Figure 3

7. Remove the stabilizer, press, and pin your lining circle to the back of this pillow top.

8. Pin the lining material to the pillow back. Place the pillow front circles to the pillow back circles, right sides to right sides, and stitch them together using a 1/4" seam allowance. Leave enough space to turn the pillow right side out (**fig. 2**). Turn the pillow and press.

II. Finishing the Pillow

1. Stitch the ends of the ecru French edging lace together. Mark the lace at the quarter points and pin to the quarter points of the pillow. Pull the gathering thread in the heading of the lace circle.

2. Distribute the gathers as evenly as you can around the finished pillow. Butt the gathered lace to the edge of the pillow and zigzag the lace to the pillow edge (**fig. 3**). Pull the bottom two layers out of the way. Turn the top two layers under and zigzag the lace to the folded edge (**fig. 4**).

3. Stuff the pillow and stitch the hole closed.

4. Using a permanent marking pen, sign and date your pillow if desired. ▩

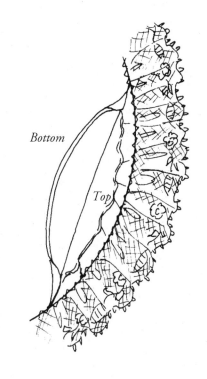

Bottom

Top

Figure 4

Crazy Patch Wedding Pillow

Weddings seem like the perfect time to sew special items for reminiscence. This particular wedding pillow was created to celebrate the wedding of Martha and Joe Pullen. We included the wedding, December 30, 1974; the church, First United Methodist Church, Huntsville, AL; the honeymoon, Gulf Shores, AL; our fraternities, Delta Tau Delta and Chi Omega; and some showers which we actually didn't have. I included an engagement party, a rehearsal dinner, an ornament shower, a bridal tea, a 24 hour shower and a lingerie shower. Since I only had 3 hours notice that Joe intended for us to marry that day, I didn't have time for any parties. I had told him that I would marry him as soon as I finished my Ph.D. in about 6 months. He said that his accountant told him that he needed to marry before the end of the year for tax purposes. I looked at him and said, "Joe, I can't marry you. I don't even know you that well." He replied, "Don't worry honey, when you get to know me you're going to like me a lot." He was right since we have just celebrated our twentieth wedding anniversary! Now about this pillow; I just made up some stuff so it would be interesting. If you had a "normal" wedding with all of the parties and other special times please put them on your pillow. Or you can do like I did and just make them up. One hundred years from now, who will know about the number of teas and showers great grandmother Martha had. My ancestors will think that Joe and I had the world's largest wedding. Little will they know that we married in the chapel with only the two of us and the preacher! I thank God every day that I had the good sense to go on and marry Joe so he could get that tax deduction!

Now, back to this gorgeous pillow! The information was created with crazy patch pieces, entredeux, ecru ribbon, covered buttons (like would have been on a wedding dress if I had one), love birds stitched from a sewing machine, antique brownish lace, and other Swiss trims all stitched together and cut out in the shape of a heart. The information was stitched in from a sewing machine, of course! Slightly gathered lace was stitched around the heart. The background of the pillow is linen with beautiful flowers and ribbons stitched into the linen with straight stitches. There is a "P" stitched in at the top of the heart. Two rows of antique lace, one insertion and one edging,

Crazy Patch Wedding Pillow

are stitched together and gathered for the lace edging around the outside of the pillow. The square pillow closes in the back with a casing which laps over the other side; Three satin covered buttons and buttonholes are present. Machine decorative stitching also decorates the top of the closing.

Materials Needed

- ❉ 1/2 yd. handkerchief linen
- ❉ 1/2 yd. of Solvy or water soluble stabilizer
- ❉ 1/3 yd. white batiste
- ❉ 3/4 yd. of 3/4 inch ecru satin ribbon
- ❉ 8 3/8" buttons to cover with satin ribbon
- ❉ Scraps of entredeux, lace for inside patchwork
- ❉ Ecru thread for machine embroidery
- ❉ 5-3/4 yds. 1 inch wide ecru edging
- ❉ 4 yds. of 1-3/4" wide lace insertion
- ❉ Polyester fiber filling

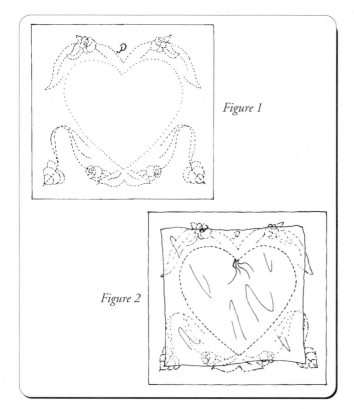

Figure 1

Figure 2

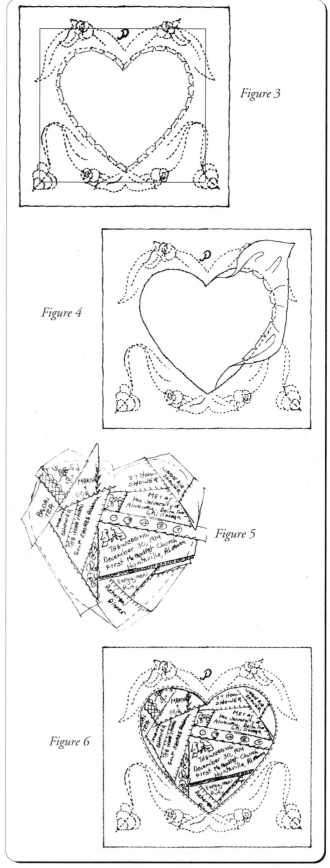

Figure 3

Figure 4

Figure 5

Figure 6

I. Preparing The Pillow Front

1. Cut out a 17" square of linen.

2. Trace along the heart stitching line and the decorative lines. Template on center pull out.

3. Stitch along the decorative stitching lines, using a reinforced straight stitch, a saddle stitch or tiny zigzag (**fig. 1**).

4. Cut out a 17" square piece of Solvy. Place the square of Solvy on top of the decorated square. Stitch the Solvy to the pillow top along the heart template line (**fig. 2**).

5. Trim the center out of the heart, leaving a 1/4" seam allowance (**fig. 3**).

6. Turn the Solvy through the hole to the wrong side; press the seam, creating a heart-shaped hole (**fig. 4**).

II. Making The Patchwork Wedding Memories

1. Stitch your information on white batiste scraps using machine stitching.

2. Cover the buttons if desired for one decorative strip.

3. Stitch your patchwork pieces onto a piece of batiste about 1/2 inch larger than the heart (**fig. 5**).

4. Place your heart patchwork underneath the pillow front lining up the edges. Straight stitch your patch work piece to your heart outline (**fig. 6**).

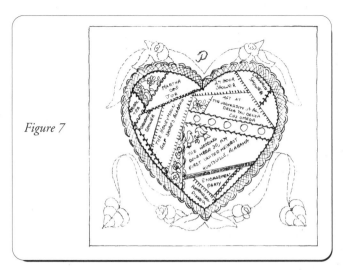

Figure 7

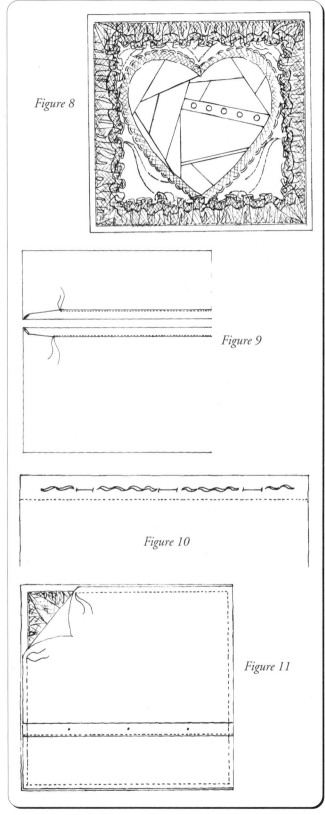

Figure 8

Figure 9

Figure 10

Figure 11

III. Finishing The Pillow Front

1. Place the pillow onto a lace shaping board. Cut about 1-1/2 yds. of lace edging. Using the instructions for making lace hearts, shape the lace edging flat to the edge of the heart, mitering at the top and bottom of the lace shaping (**fig. 7**).

2. If your machine has an entredeux stitch, machine entredeux catching the edge of the patchwork and the edge of the curved lace edging heart. If you don't have this feature, simply zigzag the lace edging onto the front of the heart.

3. Create a wide lace ruffle by zigzagging insertion and edging laces together. Pull the top thread of the lace insertion to gather the lace ruffle. Right sides together, baste the ruffle to the pillow top along a 1/2" seam line on all four sides of the pillow top; turn the lace edges under or stitch them together where the ruffle ends meet (**fig. 8**).

4. Cut one piece of linen 9" by 17" for the pillow back underlap; cut one piece of linen 13" by 17" for the pillow back overlap.

5. Along one 17" edge of each piece, turn under 1" and press; turn under 1" again and press; this makes a double hem. Stitch the hems in place on each piece (**fig. 9**).

6. On the larger piece, work 3 buttonholes; work a decorative stitch on either side of and between the buttonholes. This is the pillow back top flap (**fig. 10**).

7. Mark and sew buttons in the hem allowance on the pillow back bottom underlap.

8. Overlap the two pillow back pieces with right sides up; button the buttons. Baste the two pieces together at the sides.

9. Place the assembled back on top of the pillow front, right sides together; pin, then stitch together along the ruffle basting line on all four sides (**fig. 11**). Unbutton and turn the pillow right side out through the back opening.

10. Stuff the pillow through the opening created in the pillow back or make an inner pillow to be placed in the pillow cover. ▓

Appliqued Rose Pillow

What an elegant way to use applique! One usually thinks of applique on children's clothing, on sweat shirts, or on denim! Well, think again. This beautiful pillow is elegant enough for any room in your home. The base fabrics are ecru and pink Nelona. The outside border of the design is pink Nelona as is the back of the pillow. The inside of the design which is the background for the rose applique is ecru Nelona. The rose is made of three shades of pink with green leaves. The interesting appliqued shape which joins the background ecru and the border pink is a deep pink. The applique thread of each of the sections is done in the same color as the fabric. A beautiful ecru rayon braid trims the outside of the pillow. This is another pillow which would be just as pretty done in dark fabrics, water stained taffeta, crazy patch or velveteen for other rooms of your home. The finished size of this pillow is 11-1/2" by 9-1/2".

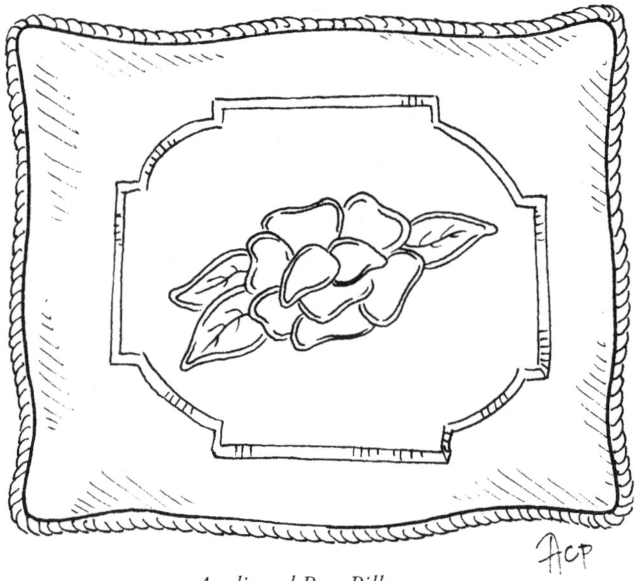

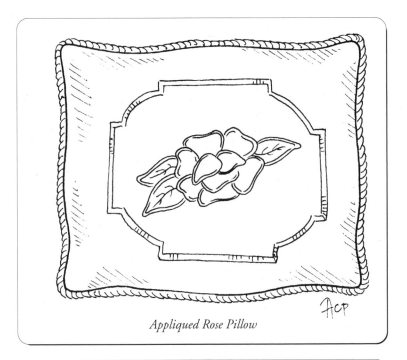

Appliqued Rose Pillow

Materials Needed

- 3/8 yd. base fabric (ecru Nelona Swiss batiste)
- 3/8 yd. border fabric (pink Nelona Swiss batiste) and pillow back fabric
- 3/8 yd. unbleached muslin (if base fabric is sheer)
- Small pieces of three colors for rose
- Small pieces of green for leaves
- 1/2 yd. of cord with an attached seam tape
- Polyester fiber filling

I. Making The Pillow Top

Note: Use the applique directions in this book as a reference when stitching the applique.

1. Cut out a piece of the Swiss batiste (or whatever base fabric you choose) 10" by 12". On our pillow the base fabric is Ecru Nelona and the border and back of the pillow are made of pink Nelona. Cut out a piece of the border fabric also 10" by 12" to be used for the back of the pillow.
2. Trace rose petals and leaves on the paper side of paper backed fusible web. Iron onto correct fabric color and cut out rose petals and leaves (**fig. 1**). Template on page 314.
3. Trace border of the pillow the same way and cut out.
4. Remove paper and iron the border on the base fabric (**fig. 2**).
5. Either stabilize this pillow front or put it in a hoop before stitching. Satin stitch around the inner edges of this

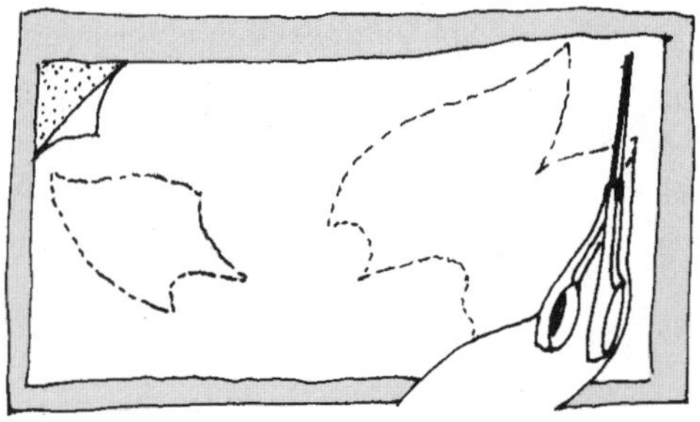

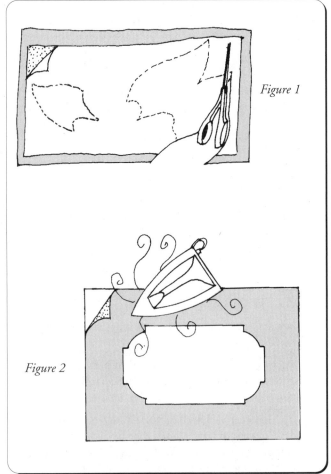

Figure 1

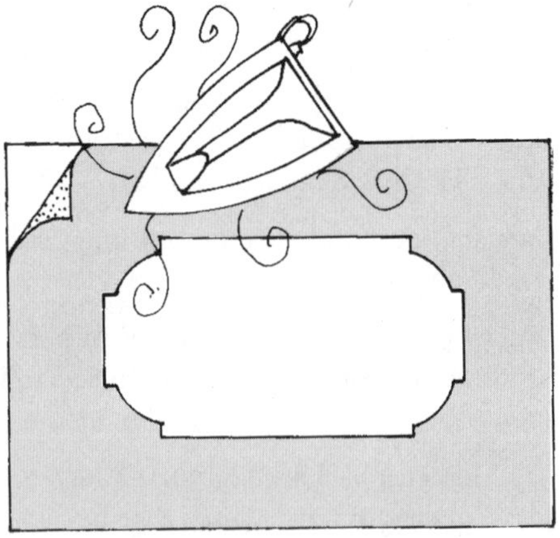

Figure 2

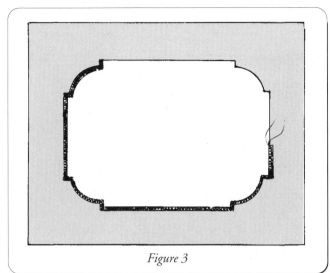

Figure 3

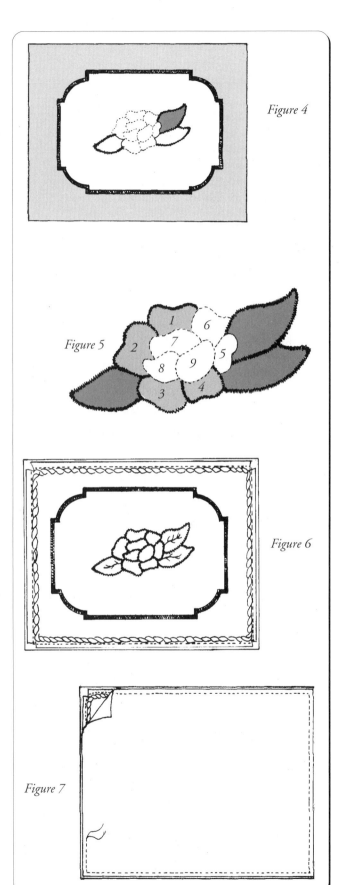

Figure 4

Figure 5

Figure 6

Figure 7

border in a color of thread to match the rose in the center. We used a medium pink machine embroidery thread (**fig. 3**).

6. Trace the rose design onto the center of this center section. Place the leaves on first. Iron on. Satin stitch around the outer edges of the leaves (**fig. 4**).

7. Place the rose petal #1. Iron and satin stitch around outer edges.

8. Place rose petal #2. Iron and satin stitch around the outer edges.

9. Do the same for petal number #3 and on until you finish the rose sections (**fig. 5**).

10. Either trace or free hand with a pencil or water soluble pen, the veins in the leaves. To embroidery the veins in the leaves you can either free motion if you are comfortable with that technique or just straight stitch the designs in the traditional sewing way.

II. Finishing The Pillow

1. When the pillow top is finished, place a piece of un-bleached muslin behind the top. This is so the batting doesn't show through when you stuff the pillow.

2. Stitch the cord around the edge of the pillow top (**fig. 6**).

3. Using your pink pillow back , stitch the back to the front, right sides together, leaving an opening to turn the pillow right side out. Turn the pillow. Press. Stuff with fiberfill. Stitch opening closed (**fig. 7**).

4. Sign the back of the pillow with a permanent ink and date, if desired. ▓

Woven Basket Pillow

Unusual would be the best word to describe this breathtaking little pillow. Actually, I've never seen anything exactly like this pillow. The beautiful border is attached using the shadow applique technique. The basic pillow is peach Nelona with the border's being a medium blue. Shadow applique by machine white flowers are trimmed with the same technique in yellow centers of the flowers. Green leaves have the same shadow applique by machine technique used. Gray lace tape was used to weave a sweet little basket and to curve the top of the basket. The handle of the basket is this lace tape twisted over and over and tacked by hand down to the pillow. Shades of peach, gray, yellow, green and blue make this a true work of art. Once again, this center treatment could be used on darker fabrics or on fabrics more suitable for a formal living room or a den. The little pillow is a 9 inch square; however, you could make it as large as you wanted to make it.

Materials Needed

✷ 1/3 yd. batiste fabric (peach Nelona Swiss batiste)

✷ 1/3 yd. batiste fabric (white Nelona Swiss batiste)

✷ 1/3 yd. batiste fabric (blue Nelona Swiss batiste)

✷ Small pieces of green fabric for leaves

✷ Small pieces of white broadcloth for flower petals

✷ Small pieces of yellow fabric for flower centers

✷ Thread to match applique fabrics and lace tape

✷ 3 yds. grey lace tape

✷ 4" by 4" piece of Wonder Under

✷ Polyester fiber filling

I. Making The Top Of The Pillow

1. Cut the following 10" by 10": Two pieces of peach batiste, one piece of blue batiste and two pieces of white batiste.

2. Trace the applique design and border on one piece of white batiste. Template on page 313.

3. Applique the design by placing the colored fabric under the white batiste, stitching around the design lines with a tiny zigzag or a tiny blanket stitch and then trimming away the excess colored fabric from behind. Applique this design in the following order: blue border, yellow flower centers, white flowers and green leaves. Refer to the shadow applique directions in this book (fig. 1).

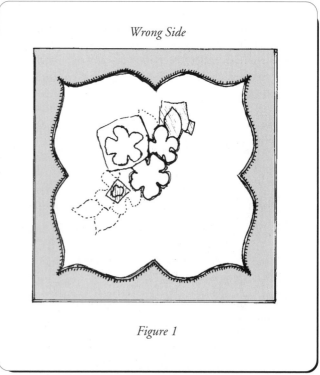

Wrong Side

Figure 1

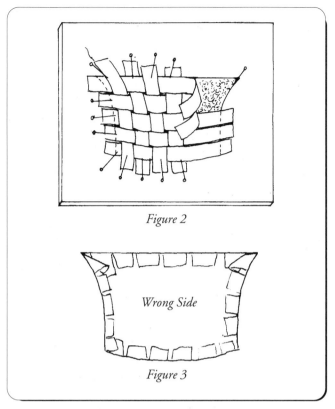

Figure 2

Wrong Side

Figure 3

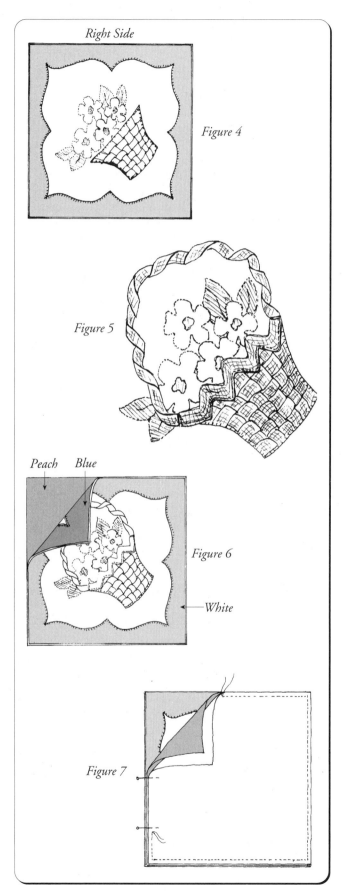

Right Side

Figure 4

Figure 5

Peach   Blue

Figure 6

White

Figure 7

4. Woven basket - cut out basket from the Wonder Under. Place the paper side of the Wonder Under basket down on a lace shaping board. Shape lace tape strips on top of the Wonder Under horizontally across the basket pattern leaving 3/8" extended on the edges. Shaping the tape to curve can be achieved by pulling a thread in the outer edges. Weave tape strips vertically in and out of the horizontal strips leaving 3/8" extended on the edges (**fig. 2**). Once the basket pattern has been covered with the tape, press. Remove from board and peel off the paper backing. Fold all ends under (**fig. 3**). Pin basket to the pillow top in the correct position. Stitch in place with a small zigzag or blanket stitch (**fig. 4**). Tack the twisted ribbon to the pillow top as a handle. Shape the lace tape into a rick rack shape, fold the ends under and stitch to the top of the basket with a straight stitch along the lower edge (**fig. 5**).

5. Place one piece of peach fabric under the pillow top to complete. Treat all layers of fabric as one layer (**fig. 6**).

II. Finishing The Pillow

1. Place one white square to the pillow top, right sides together. Place the peach square on top of the white square. Pin all layers together.

2. Stitch using a 1/2" seam, leaving a 3" opening (**fig. 7**).

3. Turn the pillow to the right side and stuff.

4. Stitch the opening closed. ▧

Peach Madeira Applique Pillow
with Cameo Pin

The colors for this pillow were inspired by the dark peach and ecru cameo adorning the center. The Madeira applique border is in peach as is the center section onto which the cameo is attached. The cameo on this pillow is glued in position. A glued piece of small gold braid conceals the edges of the cameo. The center scalloped section is of ecru Nelona. The edges of the pillow are ecru entredeux with a wonderful heavy braid attached flat to the entredeux trim. The edges of the trim and entredeux are mitered. A Madeira applique is used around the scalloped border of the ecru piece and around the center circular piece. The colors on this pillow, in combination with the antique looking cameo, make a beautiful design statement. This pillow would also be a beautiful place to display an antique cameo broach. Sometimes I think we keep our jewelry hidden in jewelry boxes and we might enjoy some pieces more if they could be on display on pillows or in translucent boxes. Just an idea for some of you who love to collect antique jewelry.

Materials Needed

- 1/2 yd. ecru Swiss batiste Nelona
- 1/2 yd. peach Swiss batiste Nelona
- Ecru light weight sewing thread
- Cameo
- 1/4 yd. small gold braid
- 2 yds. entredeux
- 2 yds. edging
- 15" by 13" water soluble stabilizer (WSS)
- Polyester fiber filling

I. Construction Of The Pillow Front

1. Cut two pieces of peach batiste 15" by 13". One piece will be used for the pillow top border. The other piece will be used for the bottom of the pillow.

2. Cut three pieces of ecru batiste 15" by 13". One piece will be used for the pillow top. One piece will be used for the pillow top lining. The other piece will be used for the bottom lining of the pillow.

3. Trace the Madeira template on one piece of peach batiste. Template on page 316.

4. Place the water soluble stabilizer (WSS) on top of the peach batiste. The traced pattern should be seen through the water soluble stabilizer.

5. Stitch, with a straight stitches, around the Maderia template lines (**fig. 1**).

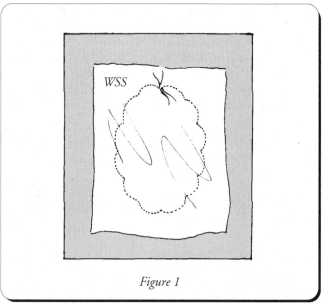

Figure 1

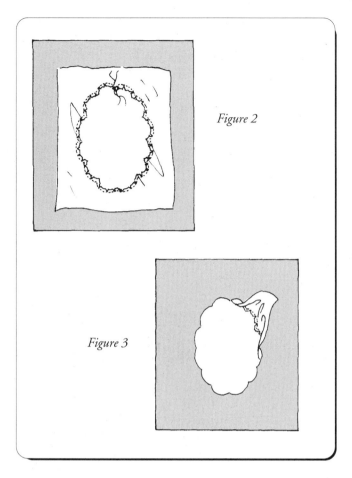

Figure 2

Figure 3

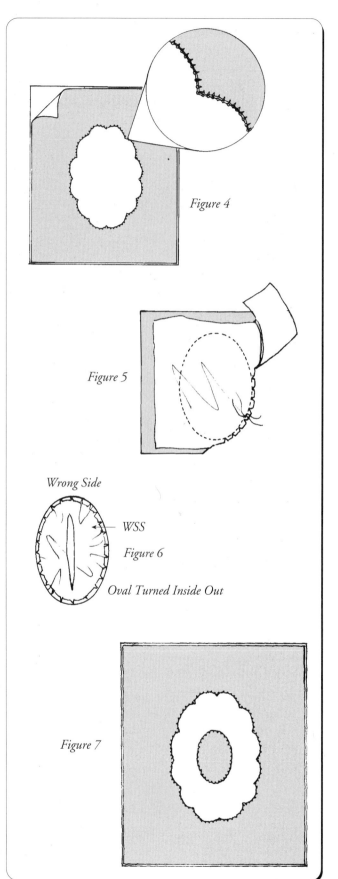

Figure 4

Figure 5

Wrong Side

WSS

Figure 6

Oval Turned Inside Out

Figure 7

6. Trim peach batiste and WSS, 1/8" away from the template stitching lines. Clip and/or notch the curves corners and points. Remove the center (**fig. 2**).

7. Turn the WSS to the wrong side of the peach batiste. The WSS will act as a facing for the applique border making the inside edges easy to turn under. Use a point turner to ensure sharp points (**fig. 3**). Press well.

8. Pin the border on top of one piece of ecru batiste. Press and pin in place. Use a pinstitch or other desired stitch to attach inside edge of the border to the ecru batiste (**fig. 4**).

9. Trace the oval on the peach batiste. Place a piece of WSS on top of the traced oval. Straight stitch along the oval template lines. Trim the seam allowance to 1/8". Clip the curves (**fig. 5**). Place a slit in the WSS and turn the oval through the slit (**fig. 6**). Use a point turner to ensure a neat edge. Press.

10. Place in the center of the pillow top. Pin in place and press. Stitch in place with a pinstitch or other desired stitch (**fig. 7**).

11. Place a second piece of ecru under the pillow top as a lining. Pin all layers together, border, pillow top and pillow lining. Treat all layers as one layer of fabric.

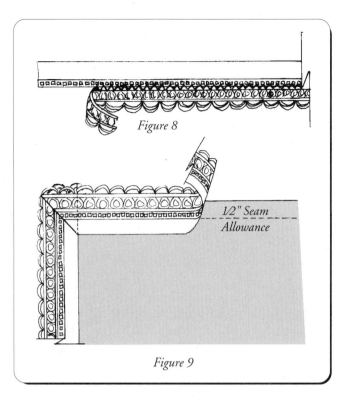

Figure 8

1/2" Seam
Allowance

Figure 9

Figure 10

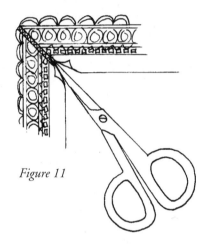

Figure 11

II. Finishing The Pillow

1. Trim one fabric edge of the entredeux. Place the edging along this edge and zigzag together. Refer to the technique lace to entredeux (**fig. 8**).

2. To miter the corners, first place the edge of the entredeux along the 1/2" seam line of the pillow top with the edging facing outward (**fig. 9**). Pin the miters and stitch. Trim the excess edging from behind each mitered corner.

3. Place the edging back onto the pillow top, this time with the edging facing inward (**fig. 10**). To do this, clip the fabric to the entredeux at each miter (**fig. 11**). Stitch about 1/8" from the entredeux edge.

4. Next, place a piece of peach batiste on top of the pillow top and the edging. Place a piece of ecru on top of the peach batiste as the back pillow lining. Pin in place.

5. Stitch the pillow top to the pillow bottom/lining using the edging stitching lines as a guide. Stitch inside the edging lines nest to the entredeux edge. Leave a 3" opening along one side (**fig. 12**). Turn the pillow through the opening.

6. Stuff the pillow. Stitch the hole shut.

7. Glue the cameo in the middle of the oval. Glue small gold braid to the outer edge of the cameo, if desired.

8. Using a permanent marking pen, sign, and date your pillow if desired. ❊

Figure 12

Bi-Directional Shark's Teeth Pillow

I think everyone loves shark's teeth. This is a fabulous technique for any type of tailored heirloom elegance. This pillow has eight tucks on one side and eight on the other. The pillow is made of ecru Nelona with a lavender pillow on the inside which peeks through to make a pastel lavender and ecru pillow. There is a sweet ecru Nelona ruffle on each end with entredeux and fringe stitched on the edge. This little pillow would be the perfect size for a ring bearer's pillow as well as for a very special gift.

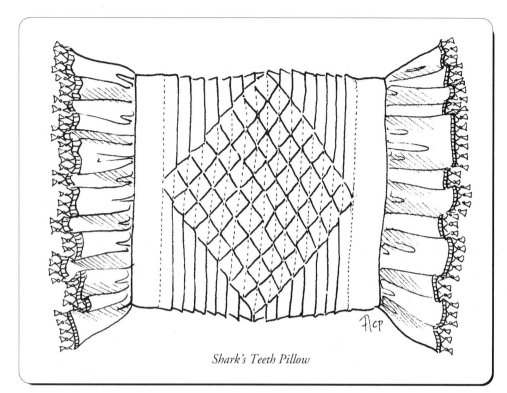

Shark's Teeth Pillow

Materials Needed

※ 1/3 yd. ecru Swiss batiste Nelona

※ 1/4 yd. lavender batiste (lining)

※ 1-1/4 yd. ecru entredeux

※ 1-1/4 yd. ecru tassel trim

I. Making The Pillow Top

1. Cut one piece of fabric 8-1/2" by 27". Fold the fabric in half and mark the center with a washout pen.

2. Use the tucking guide found in the pull out section of this book. Mark eight tucks above the center line and eight tucks below the center line (**fig. 1**).

3. Fold and stitch tucks 1/2" from each fold line (**fig. 2**). Starch well and press tucks toward the center.

4. Using the shark's teeth template found on page 312, center the template and mark the slash lines on the tucks. Clip each slash line to the stitching on the tuck (**fig 3**).

5. To complete, follow the directions given for "Shark's Teeth" in the technique section of this book.

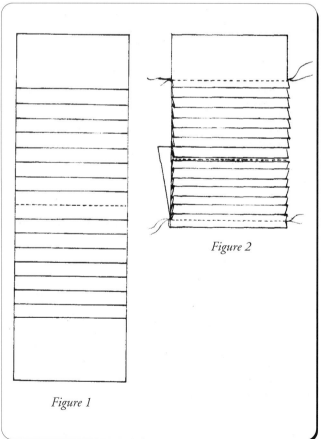

Figure 2

Figure 1

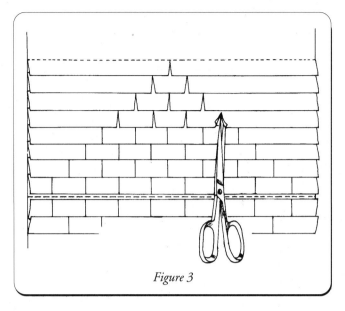

Figure 3

II. Finishing The Pillow

1. Cut a fabric piece for the pillow back to the measurement of the pillow top and two pieces of lavender fabric to this same measurement. Place one piece of lavender fabric to the wrong side of the pillow top. Pin together and treat as one layer. The lavender side is now the wrong side. Set aside.

2. Place the second piece of lavender fabric on the wrong side of the pillow back. Pin together and treat as one layer. The lavender side is now the wrong side.

3. Cut two pieces of fabric 3" by 22". Attach entredeux to one long side of each piece using the technique entredeux to fabric (fig. 4). Trim off the remaining fabric edge of the entredeux and attach the tassel trim to the entredeux using a zigzag (**fig. 5**).

4. Fold the short sides of the ruffle pieces to the back 1/8" and 1/8" again. Stitch in place to finish the edge (**fig. 6**).

5. Gather the ruffles to fit the short sides of the pillow moving in 1/2" on each side. Place the ruffles to the pillow, right sides together. Baste in place (**fig. 7**).

6. Place the pillow bottom on top of the ruffle/pillow top, right sides together or ecru side together. Pin in place and stitch using a 1/2" seam leaving a 3" opening (**fig. 8**). Be careful not to catch the ruffle in the long sides of the pillow. ▧

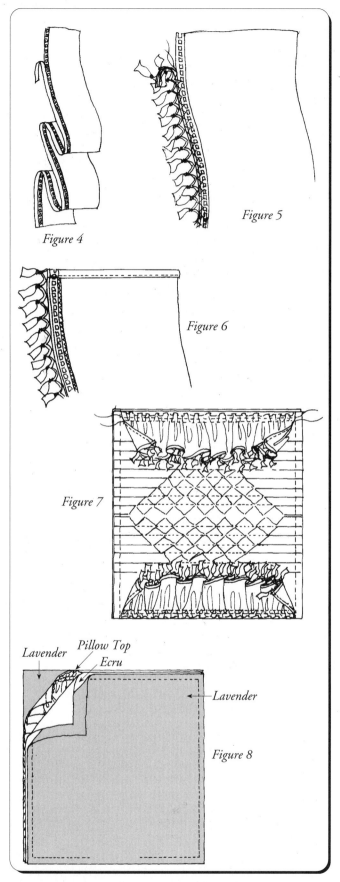

Figure 4

Figure 5

Figure 6

Figure 7

Figure 8

Lavender

Pillow Top

Ecru

Lavender

Australian Windowpane Pillowcase

Australian Windowpane Pillowcase

While in Australia several years ago, I purchased a blouse with the technique which we later named "Australian Windowpane" because it looked exactly like a windowpane to peek through. The organdy "windowpane or "peek-a-boo" technique exhibits just how elegant machine embroidery and applique can be on a museum-quality garment or pillow. This pillowcase features not only the Australian technique but also shadow applique by machine. With the advent of today's wonderful machines, entredeux can be made when used in combination with a wing needle. This is how we stitched the curly design above the flower. Machine embroidery, the built in variety, further demonstrates the simplicity of creating lovely heirlooms entirely on the machine; notice the little teardrops. The lace and the bows are stitched using a machine pin stitch or tiny blanket stitch. My all time favorite technique is lace shaping; in this pillowcase, a sweet little circle houses the lovely floral design. To finish the inside of the flower and the leaves, place organdy behind the fabric and simply follow the design with a light zigzag stitch . Then cut away the fabric on top and satin stitch over the previous zigzag.

— *I. Materials Needed For Pillowcase* —

NOTE: 2/3 yd. of batiste 45" wide will make two pillowcases.

⚹ One piece batiste 22 1/2" wide by 24" long.

⚹ 50" lace edging (1/2" wide or wider) for the edge of the ruffle.

⚹ 30" lace insertion (1/2" wide) for the lace shaped circle.

⚹ 30" entredeux (optional, since you will have directions for making wing needle entredeux on your sewing machine)

⚹ Thread to match lace and material for shadow applique fabric underneath the bow.

⚹ 8" hoop

⚹ One 9" square piece of organdy

⚹ 1 9" square piece of colored fabric to go underneath bow

⚹ Water soluble fine point pen, Dixon water soluble pencil, or #2 pencil.

⚹ Fabric board or piece of cardboard.

⚹ Glass head pins.

⚹ Tear Away stabilizer or tissue paper: 10" by 10" or larger.

⚹ Glue Stick (optional) to use to glue the fabric to the pillowcase before you do the shadow applique.

Materials Needed for pillow to use to stuff your pillowcase

⚹ 1 piece of lining material 24" by 17" to make the pillow for the pillowcase.

⚹ Stuffing material for the pillow.

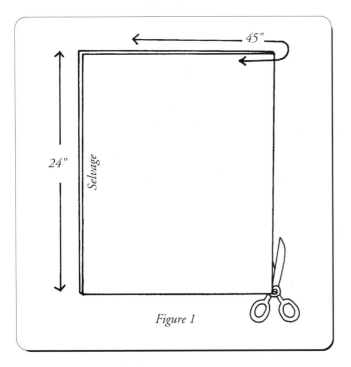

Figure 1

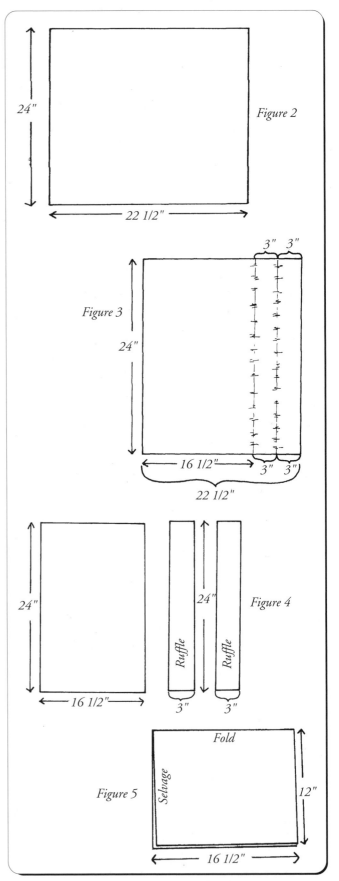

Figure 2

Figure 3

Figure 4

Figure 5

II. Cutting Out The Pillowcase and Ruffles

1. Cut a piece of batiste 24" by 22 1/2" (**fig. 1**). This is for one pillow. If you have 2/3 yds. of fabric cut your pillow-case out in the following manner. You will have enough fabric to make two pillowcases if you have 2/3 yd. of fabric.

2. Two thirds of a yard measures 45" by 24 inches (**see fig. 1**). Fold selvage edge to selvage edge (the 24" edge).

3. Pull a thread and cut the folded center portion. This will give you two pieces of batiste 24" long and 22 1/2" wide (**fig. 2**).

4. From the 24" cut edge of fabric (not the selvage edge) pull a thread and cut two ruffles 3" wide by 24" long (**fig. 3**).

5. You now have one piece of batiste 24" long by 17" wide and two ruffles 3" wide by 24" long (**fig. 4**).

III. Marking Your Designs On Your Pillowcase

1. Fold the large piece of batiste in half, matching the selvage edges. Your folded piece of fabric now measures 12" by 16 1/2 inches. Press this fold (**fig. 5**).

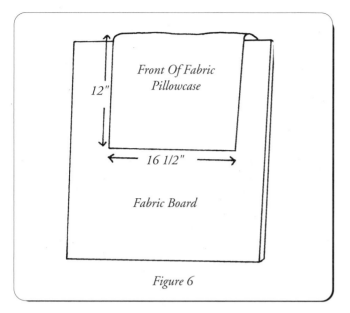

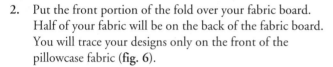

Figure 6

Figure 7

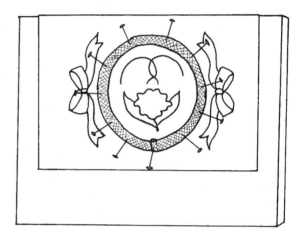

Figure 8

2. Put the front portion of the fold over your fabric board. Half of your fabric will be on the back of the fabric board. You will trace your designs only on the front of the pillowcase fabric (**fig. 6**).

3. Trace the outside line only of the circle where your lace will be shaped later.

4. Trace a bow on either side of your circle.

5. Trace the teardrops, the outside of the leaves and the outside only of the flower. Later, you will trace the inside of the leaves and the flower (**fig. 7**). Template on page 315.

IV. Shaping The Lace Circle And Stitching It To The Pillow

1. Pin the lace insertion around the lace circle, sticking the glass head pins into the outside only of the lace. Let the overlap be in the lower center portion of the circle. When you have pinned the circle, gently pull the inside thread so the lace will lay flat into a circle (**fig. 8**). Remove the pins from the fabric board, and pin the lace circle flat to the pillowcase front in about 4 places.

2. Put your 10" by 10" piece of stabilizer underneath the pillow.

3. Using a plain zigzag stitch or a wing needle entredeux stitch, stitch both sides of the lace insertion to the pillow. You will stitch through both the lace, the pillowcase and the stabilizer.

4. Go ahead and stitch your entredeux curls above the flower while you have your machine set and your wing needle in (**fig. 9**). Tear away the stabilizer.

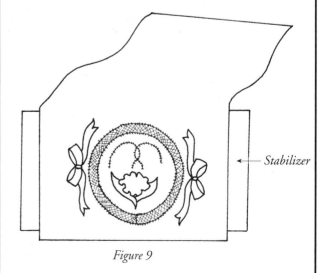

Stabilizer

Figure 9

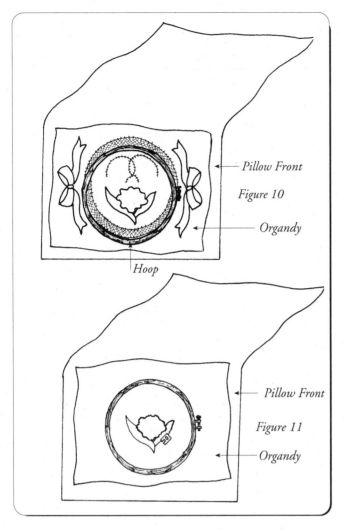

Pillow Front

Figure 10

Organdy

Hoop

Pillow Front

Figure 11

Organdy

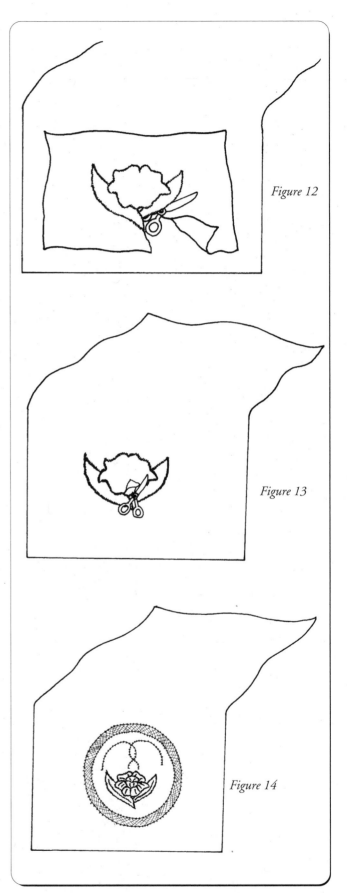

Figure 12

Figure 13

Figure 14

V. Stitching The Australian Windowpane Flower And Leaves

1. You have traced the outside of the leaves and the outside of the large flower onto your pillowcase.

2. Position your 9" by 9" piece of organdy on top of the pillowcase and place the pillowcase and the organdy into a hoop (**fig. 10**).

3. Using a small zigzag (L=1,W=1), stitch around the outer edges of both the leaf and the flower design (**fig. 11**).

4. With sharp scissors, trim the organdy from the **outside** of the design (**fig. 12**).

5. Turn the pillowcase over to the back side and trim the pillowcase fabric batiste away from the **inside** of the design (**fig. 13**).

6. Put the hoop back on the pillowcase on the front side. You are now ready to trace the two veins on the leaves and the inside petals and cup of the flower. You will be drawing only on the organdy since the batiste is cut away (**fig. 14**).

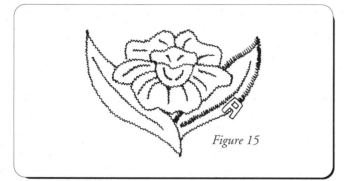

Figure 15

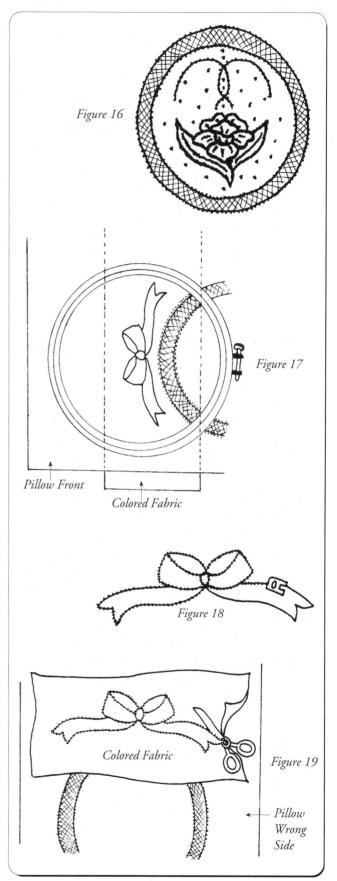

Figure 16

Figure 17

Figure 18

Figure 19

Pillow Front

Colored Fabric

Colored Fabric

Pillow Wrong Side

7. Working on the right side, use a medium width satin stitch (L=.5 to 1; W=2), stitch around all the petals and leaves working from the background to the foreground. Stitch once again around your original stitching line around the outside of the leaves and the flower. The veins in the petals and leaves are made with a stitch width of 1 at both ends, increasing gradually to a width of two in the center. Be sure to secure the threads at both ends of the veins (**fig. 15**).

VI. Stitching The Machine Embroidered Teardrops

1. While the fabric is still in embroidery hoop, zigzag in the little teardrops. Some machines have a stitch already programmed in the machine which is similar to these teardrops (**fig. 16**).

2. If you prefer to take the pillowcase out of the hoop, then use tear away stabilizer behind the tear drops while stitching.

VII. Stitching The Shadow Applique By Machine

1. Cut the 9" x 9" colored fabric in half.

2. Place one 9" by 4 1/2" piece of colored fabric behind the drawn bow on one side of your lace circle. Place the pillowcase and the fabric square into a hoop. The colored fabric is on the bottom, the pillowcase on top (**fig. 17**).

3. It is prettier to use the same color thread as the colored fabric behind your bow. Stitching from the pillowcase side, stitch around the bow using a narrow zigzag setting (W=1/2 to 1: L= 1/2 to 1) (**fig. 18**).

4. Carefully trim the excess colored fabric from the wrong side. Trim closely to the stitching without cutting the stitching (**fig. 19**). This leaves a raw edge on the back; that is correct. Nothing else is done to finish the back. You are finished with the shadow applique. Now, stitch the other bow on the opposite side, using steps 2-4 above.

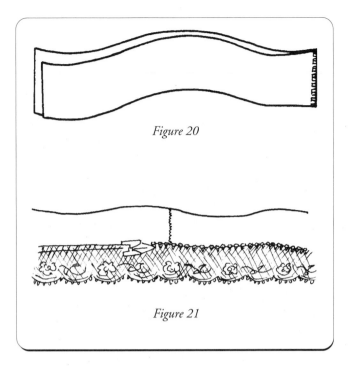

Figure 20

Figure 21

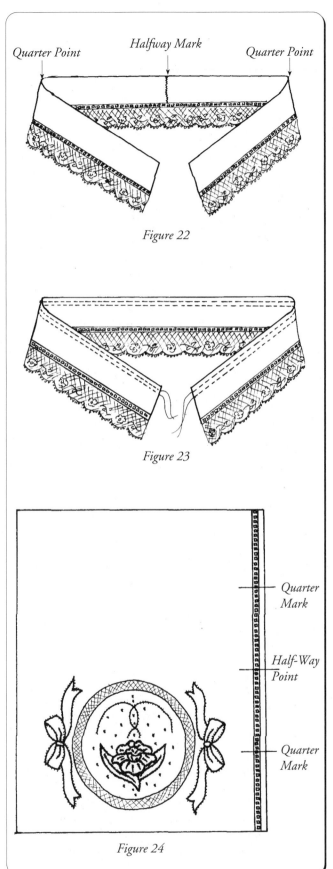

Figure 22

Figure 23

Quarter
Mark

Half-Way
Point

Quarter
Mark

Figure 24

VIII. Making the Ruffle and Attaching It To The Pillowcase

1. Seam the two ruffle pieces together at one end only, using a French seam, a regular seam plus an overcast, or a serger (**fig. 20**).

2. Place the lace edging right side up, on the right side of the ruffle. Using the wing needle/entredeux stitch on your sewing machine, attach the lace to the ruffle by stitching in machine made entredeux (**fig. 21**). Or using the technique, Lace To Fabric, stitch the lace edging to the bottom of the ruffle.

3. This seam is the half way point of the ruffle. Fold the ruffle once again so you can mark the quarter points (**fig. 22**).

4. Machine Entredeux Stitched Into The Pillowcase Method

a. Stitching 1/2" from the long edge of the pillow, using a wing needle and the machine entredeux setting on the machine, stitch a row of entredeux.

5. Using purchased entredeux place the piece of entredeux on the long side of the pillow. Using the method, entredeux to flat fabric, or the serger attach the entredeux to the pillow.

6. Mark, with a fabric marker, the half way point and quarter points of the pillow along the entredeux edge (**fig. 23**).

7. Run two rows of gathering threads in the top of the ruffle; one 1/4" from the edge, the other 1/2" from the edge (**fig. 24**).

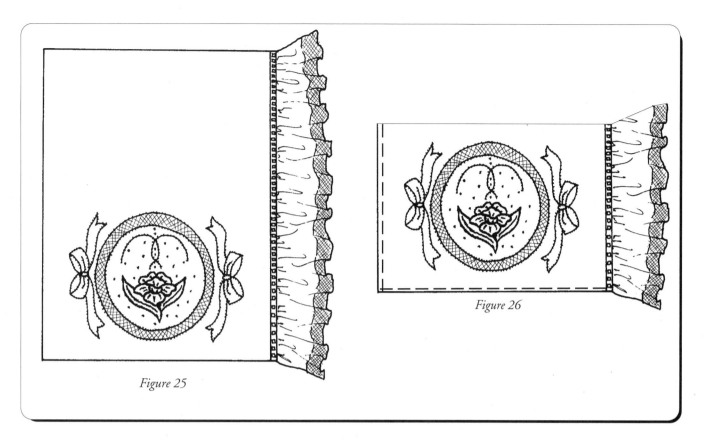

Figure 25

Figure 26

8. Using the technique, Entredeux To Gathered Fabric, attach the ruffle to the pillow. Stitch in the ditch, trim and zigzag (**fig. 25**).

X. Finishing the Pillowcase

1. Turn the pillowcase right sides to right sides and stitch the side and the long end, using a 1/4" seam allowance. Stitch all the way through the ruffle and to the end of the lace. You can serge this seam closed also (**fig. 26**).

2. Turn the pillowcase right side out and enjoy!

3. Using your 17" by 24" piece of lining material, fold it to a 12" by 17" rectangle.

4. Stitch around the three raw sides leaving a space large enough to stuff filling fiber into the pillow.

5. Stuff the filling into the pillow and whip shut. ▨

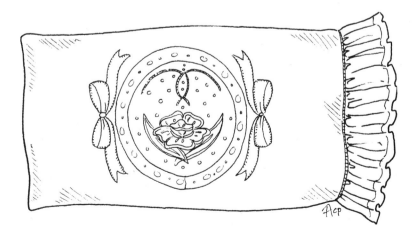

Lace Shaped Baby Pillow

The uniqueness of this sweet little blue broadcloth pillow is that the "Baby" on the front is lace shaped with tiny (1/4" wide) tea dyed French edging rather than the traditionally used insertion. The border of the pillow is embellished with coffee dyed French beading and there is a very full 1-3/4" ruffle of French edging all the way around the outside of the pillow. This pillow is precious for a baby done in blue, pink or white. Actually, you could take the colors of any nursery and adapt this pillow to more contemporary baby colors as well. I think for a shower where the sex of the child is unknown, a white pillow with ecru or coffee dyed laces would be elegant. And as my friend Margaret Boyles has said to me on so many occasions, "Martha, there is nothing more elegant than white on white."

Materials Needed

- ✖ 1 1/2 yds. 1/4" wide French lace edging
- ✖ 1 1/2 yds. French beading
- ✖ 2 1/2 yds. 1 3/4" wide French edging
- ✖ 1/3 yd. broadcloth
- ✖ Fiberfill for stuffing

I. Constructing The Front Of The Pillow

1. Cut two pieces of broadcloth, 13" by 10". One is the pillow top, the other is the bottom.

2. Using a lace shaping board or a piece of cardboard, put the pillow top on the board. Draw the "Baby" onto the top of the pillow using a water soluble pen or a pencil. Template on page 316.

3. Using glass head pins, shape the lace "Baby" sticking the pins into the scalloped side of the lace. The straight side will be on the inside. Pull the thread in the lace heading (straight edge) in order to shape the curves.

4. Lightly spray starch, remove the pins, repin the "Baby" in enough places to hold it into place, and straight stitch both sides of the "Baby" lace shaping (**fig. 1**). You can zigzag the straight side of the lace if you want too;

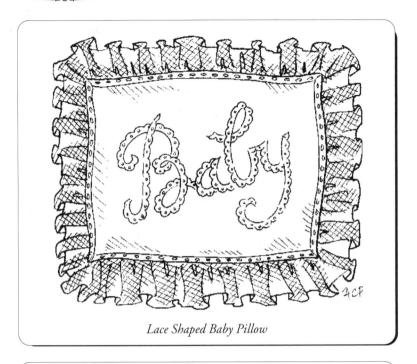

Lace Shaped Baby Pillow

Figure 1

however, I think it is prettiest to straight stitch the scalloped side of the lace. Do not cut away the fabric from behind the lace shaped "Baby."

Figure 2

5. Shape the lace beading around the outside edges of the pillow leaving a 1/4" seam allowance. Miter the corners. Zigzag the beading onto the pillow (**fig. 2**).

II. Finishing The Pillow

1. Right sides to right sides, place the pillow top and bottom together. Using a 1/4" seam allowance stitch them together, leaving enough unstitched to turn the pillow right side out (**fig. 3**). Turn right side out and press.

2. Stitch the ends of the lace edging together to make this long piece a circle. Pull the gathering threads in the heading of the lace and gather the laces.

3. Distribute the lace gathers as evenly as you can around the four sides of the pillow. Butt the gathered laces to the edge of the pillow and zigzag to the pillow (**fig. 4**). Be sure to pull the back side of the opening out of the way when stitching the edging to the pillow top.

4. Stuff the pillow and stitch the opening shut.

5. Using a permanent pen and ink, sign and date your pillow, if desired. ▩

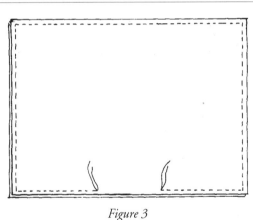

Figure 3

Figure 4

Diamond Braid Pillow

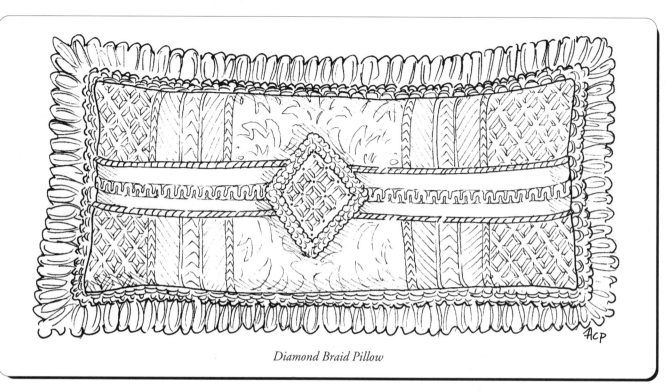

Diamond Braid Pillow

Breaking the rules of sewing is one of my favorite things to do. Using the heirloom technique of lace shaping, we substituted traditional upholstery braid and fabrics to do some pretty fancy footwork on a beautiful pillow for your living room, your den, or any other room in which you want traditional upholstery fabrics. We used an upholstery brocade with three different prints in the brocade. We simply rearranged the border and used it as a strip on both sides of the brocade. That way you have "matching" fabrics without having to buy three different prints. Three different gold braids were combined in this pillow. The flat gimp braid was used to shape a diamond in the middle of the pillow around the edges of a fabric diamond. Another type of braid was used for the center trim. Loopy fringes were used all the way around this rectangular pillow for the perfect finish. Of course, you can make this type pillow any size you want for your home.

Materials Needed

- 5/8 yd. upholstery brocade with three different "prints" in that one piece of fabric
- 2 yds. loopy fringe
- 1-1/4 yds. cord with heading
- 5/8 yd. gimp braid (serpentine style)
- 1/2 yd. different gimp braid (for diamond)
- Fiberfill to stuff pillow

I. Making The Pillow Front

1. Piece brocade if necessary to get the proper size that you want. Our finished/pieced pillow front measures 19" by 9 1/2 inches. Make one for the front and one exactly like it for the back of the pillow. We have stitched two border design pieces to both sides of the brocade piece.

2. Stitch serpentine gimp to one side of cord with fabric heading. Stitch another strip of cording on the other side the same distance apart (**fig. 1**).

3. Place this piece horizontally in the center of the pillow top and pin in place.

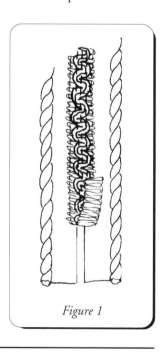

Figure 1

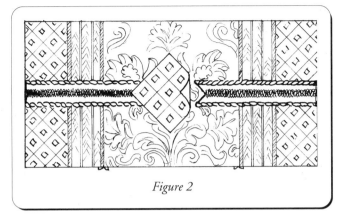

Figure 2

Figure 3

4. Make a diamond shaped about 3-1/4" out of the upholstery fabric. Pin in the center of the center panel (**fig. 2**). Diamond Template on page 316.

5. Mark placement lines on the horizontal braid and trim away from under the diamond shape so that you don't have that bulky portion underneath your diamond shape (**see figure 2**).

6. Stitch the other type of gimp braid over the raw edges of the diamond (**fig. 3**).

II. Finishing The Pillow

1. Stitch pillow front to back right sides together. Leave an opening for turning and turn right side out.

2. Butt the edges of the wide loopy braid to the finished edge of the pillow and zigzag to the outside of the pillow using the same color thread as the braid (**fig. 4**). Be sure to pull the back side of the opening out of the way when stitching the brad to the top (**fig. 5**). Take care in turning the corners to put a little extra fullness in the loopy braid. You could also miter the corners so that the braid will not cup under.

3. Stuff the pillow and sew up the opening. Sign and date your pillow on the back with a fine point permanent marking pen. ▨

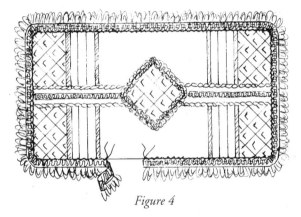

Figure 4

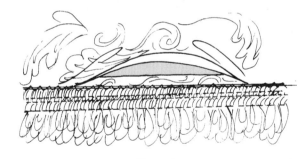

Figure 5

Making doll dresses is one of the most exciting hobbies in the U.S. I know heirloom sewers who meet with friends once a week just to sew for their dolls. For the gift of a lifetime, why don't you make a whole wardrobe for your child's or grandchild's favorite doll? For you who are porcelain doll makers, this section will be a little like heaven for you since we have so many classic and elegant dresses for your babies. We have used the techniques on each program and designed doll dresses using these concepts. I think you will find something to suit your fancy in the doll dress category in this section. There are several things you can do using the techniques, patterns and ideas from this section. Listed below are some ideas in making the greatest use of this portion of the television show and the book.

1. In this series of *Martha's Sewing Room*, we have featured 13 beautiful doll dresses. The style dress for this series is the "dropped waist" dress. The doll dress general style matches the little girl pattern which is also in this book. It would be fun to have matching little girl and doll dresses. The patterns for the doll dresses are included in this book; the directions for putting them together are found in this section. Some of your "how-to-French sewing" instructions are in the technique sections of this book.

2. Look for your size doll in the patterns. There are 13 different sizes of each variation on the pattern to fit 13 sizes of Seeley's composition bodies. To order Seeley's bodies, call 607-433-1240 or FAX 607-432-2042 or write Seeley's, 9 River St., Oneonta, NY 13820. On the following page are size and type doll information as it applies to the sizes of bodies that we have included patterns for. Naturally, these patterns will fit other bodies and commercial dolls also; we had to have some guidelines to go by and we felt the Seeley's bodies offered us an excellent industry standard to fit different types of dolls.

3. If you prefer to make your own body molds, Seeley's has molds to make your own in comparable sizes to these composition bodies. Of course, other companies have molds sizes similarly to these also.

4. Many doll artists have come to our School of Art Fashion here in Huntsville to learn how to dress their beautiful dolls which have no clothes. We have so many doll makers and dressers who subscribe to *Sew Beautiful* magazine and who buy our books with all of the antique fashions in them. Nearly all the fashions in all of our publications lend themselves perfectly to our dolls. With these basic patterns in this book, we think you can make almost any adaptation of any dropped waist fashion that you would choose. I think you will be surprised to find out how easy making these spectacular doll clothes really is. We show some general ideas on the doll dress on the television show; however, the show has these techniques used on other items in addition to the doll dress. I believe that what isn't completely explained on the television show you can learn quickly from the instructions in this book.

5. PLEASE create the most memorable gift that you can create for your little girls by making them a whole wardrobe to fit their favorite dolls. Now, porcelain dolls usually aren't meant to be played with. Beautiful plastic and cloth dolls are available for your little ones to really play with. My Mama's making me the wardrobe for my Toni doll was the best Christmas present that I ever received. I have had the good fortune of receiving many lovely gifts for Christmas presents; none can hold a candle to my handmade doll wardrobe that my Mama made when I was 8 years old. Some of the dresses in this section would take 4-8 hours to make. Some take much less time. Remember, you can make them as simple or as complicated as you want.

6. I know that some of you are involved with charities and their fund-raising. One of the best fund-raising ideas that has been used over and over is to make a wonderful wardrobe for a popular play with doll. You might enlist the aid of your smocking, quilting or sewing guild members to each make one dress. That way, something out of this world could be created and it wouldn't be too expensive for one person or take too much time. Sewing for charities has become a very popular way for women to do volunteer work. How exciting!

7. This doll dress section is not limited to just these size dolls or to dolls alone. Please look at each of these doll dresses and envision it as a child's dress. You have the basic child's dropped waist dress pattern included in this book also. You also have lots of collars for the child's version also. Take ideas from one doll dress and think about that technique on one of the collars of the dropped waist dress in this book. These ideas can be used on almost any pattern from any commercial pattern book also. I can just see lots of these techniques being used on a woman's blouse or collar. You would need to choose your favorite commercial pattern since we haven't included a woman's pattern in this book. Some quick suggestions if you use a child's pattern out of the commercial books. Sometimes the skirts aren't as full as we like them. Traditionally we use 45" in the front and 45" in the back to make our heirloom dresses very full. Another thing you might want to do is add a little length to the dresses in the pattern books if they aren't as long as we like them. Length can be added to the puffed sleeves if they look a little short. Adapting patterns is one of the most creative parts of heirloom sewing. Please look at any pattern as only a beginning guidepoint and let your imagination be your true guide.

8. We have loved designing these doll clothes for you to enjoy. The chart on the next page gives the fullness, length, etc. of the different sizes of dolls. This book is a real treasure of doll patterns which you can use for these sized dolls or any other size you have. Just make the adjustments for size. Actually, even if you have a favorite doll basic pattern, you probably can use the templates, sleeves, and skirts with very little adjustment. Don't forget that *Martha's Sewing Room* features one doll dress per show with living instructions on how to make the most intricate part of the construction. Please enjoy this section; please know that the instructions in this section also include new and different techniques. Even if you don't want to make doll dresses at this time, please read the section carefully. Ideas here will be wonderful for pillows, other clothes, quilt squares, and whatever else suits your fancy. ✺

Doll Dresses

The Seeley body types and sizes given in the charts below, French, Modern and German, are the most popular composition child bodies. These charts will be referred to in each set of doll dress directions to create the proper lengths and/or widths for the size of the doll being dressed. The doll bodies are also divided into small, medium and large bodies. After determining the doll body style and size being used, refer to the measurements on the charts for that specific body size to create any one of these beautiful dresses. The directions for each of the doll dresses are given in detail, listed by show number and dress name. The basic dress patterns can be found on pages 287-293.

FB - French Child Bodies

MB - Modern Child Bodies

GB - German Child Bodies

Small Bodies Include: FB12, FB14, GB11, GB13

Medium Bodies Include: MB140, MB160, GB15, GB16

Large Bodies Include: FB17, FB19, MB190, MB21.5, GB21

Skirt Measurements

These measurements are the finished skirt measurements (length and width) including seam allowances and ruffles (if any).
If a hem is desired instead of ruffle, add 1" to 2" to these lengths for a hem allowance.

FB12	5-1/2" x 37"	MB140	7-1/4" x 37"	GB11	6" x 37"
FB14	6-1/4" x 37"	MB160	8" x 37"	GB13	7-1/4" x 37"
FB17	8-1/4" x 43"	MB190	9-1/4" x 43"	GB15	7-1/4" x 37"
FB19	8-3/4" x 43"	MB21.5	11-1/4" x 43"	GB16	8-1/2" x 37"
				GB21	10-1/2 x 43"

Neck Band Measurements (unfinished)

FB12	6"	MB140	6-1/2"	GB11	5"
FB14	6-3/4"	MB160	7-1/2"	GB13	6-1/2"
FB17	7-1/2"	MB190	7-1/2"	GB15	6-3/4"
FB19	7-3/8"	MB 21.5	8-1/2"	GB16	6-3/4"
				GB21	8-1/2"

Sleeve Band Measurement (unfinished)

FB12	4"	MB140	4-1/2"	GB11	3-1/2"
FB14	4-1/2"	MB160	4-1/2"	GB13	4"
FB17	5-1/2"	MB190	5"	GB15	4-1/2"
FB19	5-1/2"	MB 21.5	5-1/2"	GB16	4-1/2"
				GB21	6-1/2"

Bodice Chart

(Length and width measurement for the front bodice created rectangle)

FB12	6" x 6"	MB140	8-1/2" x 7"	GB11	5-1/2" x 5"
FB14	7" x 6"	MB160	8-1/2" x 8"	GB13	6" x 6"
FB17	9" x 8-1/2"	MB190	10" x 8-1/2"	GB15	6-1/2" x 7"
FB19	9" x 8"	MB21.5	11" x 10"	GB16	7" x 7"
				GB21	10-1/2" x 9"

Scalloped Puffing Dress

I almost called this dress "ocean waves puffing dress" because the little strips of puffing curve at the center like waves on the shore. The ideas on this dress would be just as sweet on a child's dress as it is on a doll dress. The puffing is scalloped all the way around the dress and has lace insertion at the top and bottom of the puffing. Gathered lace finishes the bottom of this most elegant skirt. The front bodice has puffing; the back bodice has straight puffing. Scalloped lace insertion is found at the top and bottom of the dropped waistline puffing; gathered lace finishes this treatment at the bottom of the lace and puffing. This scalloped puffing on the bottom of the front and back bodice is actually stitched onto the straight dropped waist bodice piece. It just appears that the actual front bodice is scalloped when it is only the scalloped puffing treatment which is stitched onto the straight front bodice. This makes the stitching much easier than if the front bodice were actually curved. The neckline and sleeves have entredeux and gathered lace edging. The back closes with Velcro.

Scalloped Puffing Dress

Fabric Requirements

	Small Body	Medium Body	Large Body
Fabric	5/8 yd.	5/8 yd.	1 yd.
Lace Insertion (3/8")	5 yds.	5 yds.	7 yds.
Entredeux	1/2 yd.	1/2 yd.	1 yd.
Edging Lace (3/4")	4-1/2 yds.	5 yds.	6-1/2 yds.
Edging Lace (3/8")	1/2 yd.	1/2 yd.	1/2 yd.

Other Notions: Lightweight sewing thread, and Velcro™, snaps or tiny buttons for back closure.

All Seams 1/4" unless otherwise indicated.

Bodice and skirt template on centerfold pull out.

I. Bodice

1. Cut out the front bodice on a fold.

2. If selvage fabric is available cut the back bodices with the back edges on the selvage. If the selvage is not available, simply cut out the bodice backs and serge or overcast the back edges of each bodice piece.

3. Place the front bodice to the back bodice pieces, right sides together, at the shoulders. Stitch using a 1/4" seam. Overcast or serge the seam allowance (**fig. 1**).

II. Neck

1. Cut a strip of entredeux to the neck band measurement given in the chart for the specific doll body to be dressed.

2. Cut a piece of 3/8" edging lace two times this length and gather to fit the entredeux strip.

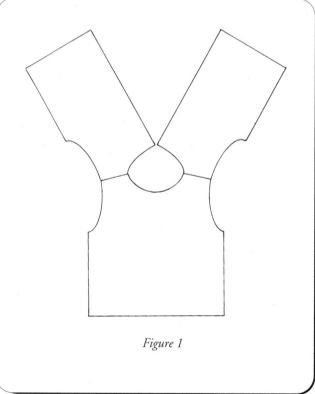

Figure 1

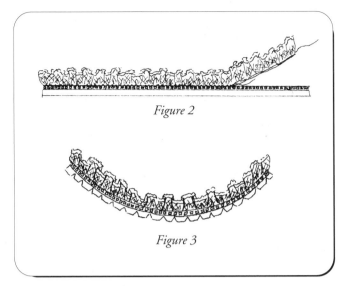

Figure 2

Figure 3

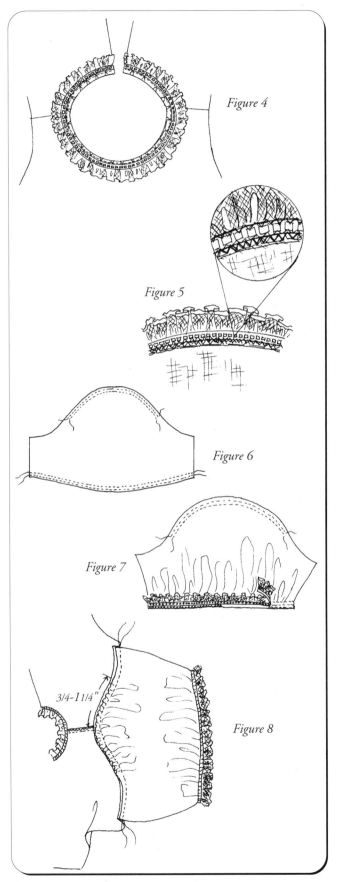

Figure 4

Figure 5

Figure 6

Figure 7

3/4-11/4"

Figure 8

3. Trim away one side of the entredeux and attach the gathered edging lace to the trimmed entredeux using the technique entredeux to gathered lace (**fig. 2**).

4. If the fabric edge remaining on the entredeux is not already 1/4", trim to 1/4". Clip this fabric so that it will curve along neck edge of the dress (**fig. 3**). Place this strip to the neck of the dress right sides together. Attach using the technique entredeux to fabric (**fig. 4**).

5. Using a tiny zigzag, tack the seam allowance to the dress. This stitching will keep the entredeux/gathered lace standing up at the neck (**fig. 5**).

III. Sleeves

1. Cut out two sleeves.

2. Place two rows of gathering stitches 1/8" and 1/4" in the top and bottom of the sleeve (**fig. 6**).

3. Cut two strips of entredeux to the measurement for the specific doll body given on the sleeve band chart. Cut two pieces of 3/4" edging lace twice the length of the entredeux.

4. Gather the edging lace to fit the entredeux. Stitch together using the technique entredeux to gathered lace.

5. Gather the bottom of the sleeve to fit the entredeux/edging lace band. Stitch the band to the sleeve, right sides together, using the technique entredeux to gathered fabric (**fig. 7**).

6. Gather the top of the sleeve to fit the arm opening allowing most of the gathers to fall 3/4" to 1-1/4" on either side of the shoulder seam. Place the sleeve to the arm opening, right sides together, stitch using a 1/4" seam. Overcast or serge the seam allowance (**fig. 8**).

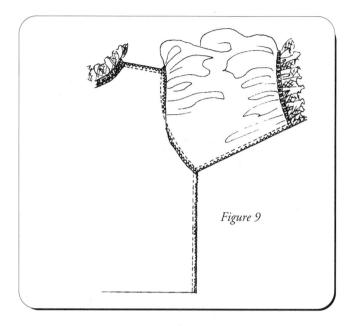

Figure 9

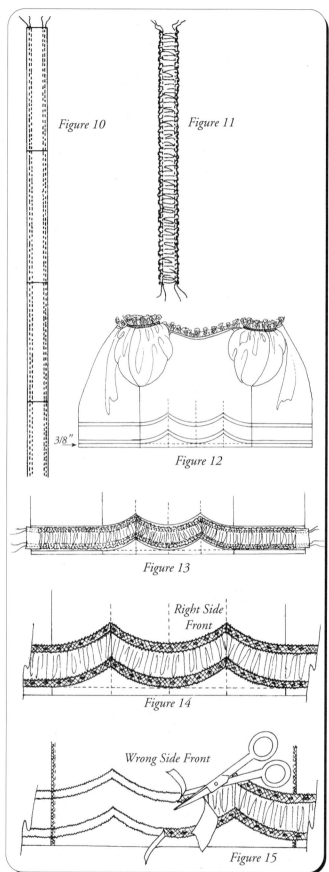

Figure 10   Figure 11

3/8"

Figure 12

Figure 13

Right Side
Front

Figure 14

Wrong Side Front

Figure 15

7. Place the sides of the bodice/sleeves right sides together. Stitch, using a 1/4" seam allowance. Overcast or serge the seam allowances (**fig. 9**).

IV. Decorating with Puffing

1. Cut 3 strips of fabric 1-1/2" long by 45" wide for medium and small dolls. Cut 4 strips 2" long by 45" wide for large dolls.

2. Attach strips using a 1/4" seam creating one long fabric strip. Trim seam to 1/8". Overcast using a zigzag or serge.

3. Run two gathering rows on each side of the fabric strip 1/4" and 3/8" (**fig. 10**) and gather to 1/2 the original size (**fig. 11**). Option: a gathering foot can by used to gather each side of the fabric.

4. Divide the front bodice into four equal parts as seen in figure 12. Trace the template across the front bodice with the lowest area of the scallop being placed 3/8" from the edge of the bodice. The center scallop should take up the two middle sections of the divided bodice. Half scallops should be placed on either side of the full scallop. The template should continue straight across the back 3/8" from the lower edge of the bodice (**fig. 12**).

5. Using the technique found under shaped puffing, shape the puffing along the template lines. Allow 3/4" at the center back edge to remain flat and ungathered. This will be the placket later (**fig. 13**).

6. Shape 3/8" lace insertion on top of the puffing following the template and using the directions under lace shaping. Press. Stitch along each side of the lace insertion using a small zigzag (**fig. 14**). Trim the fabric away under the shaped puffing and lace (**fig. 15**).

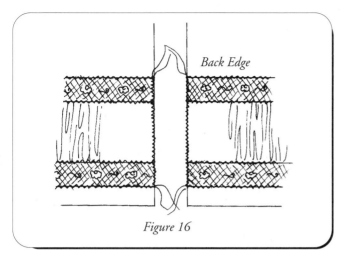

Back Edge

Figure 16

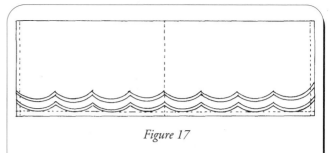

Figure 17

Figure 18

7. Use a small zigzag to overcast the raw edges of the lace and puffing along the back edges of the bodice (**fig. 16**).

V. Skirt

1. Refer to the length and width given in the skirt chart for the specific doll body to create the skirt piece.

2. Skirt template - Use scallops only, no curl, for the small dolls. Use entire template for medium and large dolls. Trace the skirt template with the lower edge of the template 3/4" from the edge of the skirt. Start the center of the scallop in the center of the skirt for small dolls (**fig. 17**). Start the curls on either side of the center for the medium and large dolls (**fig. 18**).

3. Shape puffing strip and lace insertion along the template lines of the skirt as described in section IV - steps 6 and 7. To finish the ends of the curls, stitch the inside heading of the lace first. Then, cut away the excess puffing strip from underneath the lace only on the end of the curl (**fig. 19**). Pin the lace back in place and stitch the outer heading of the lace. Cut away fabric from behind the lace insertion and puffing.

4. Gather lace edging and attach it to the bottom edge of the scalloped lace insertion. Use the technique "gathered lace to lace" (**fig. 20**).

5. Run two gathering rows at 1/4" and 1/8" in the top edge of the skirt piece starting and stopping 1/2" from the back edges.

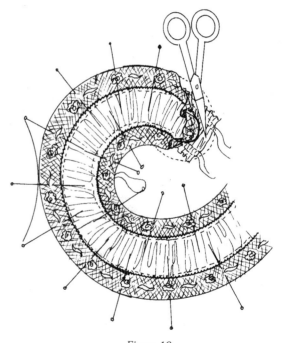

Figure 19

VI. Finishing the Dress

1. Creating the Skirt Placket

Note: The placket can be omitted if desired. The dress is much easier to get on and off if a placket is used.

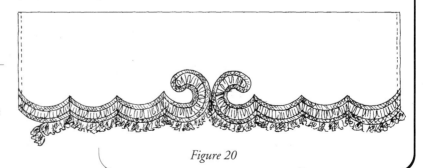

Figure 20

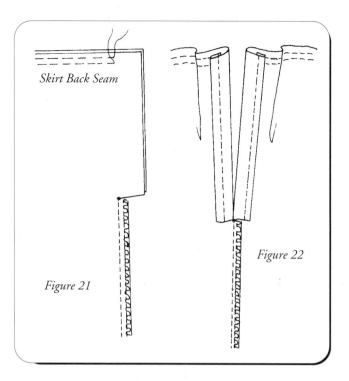

Skirt Back Seam

Figure 21

Figure 22

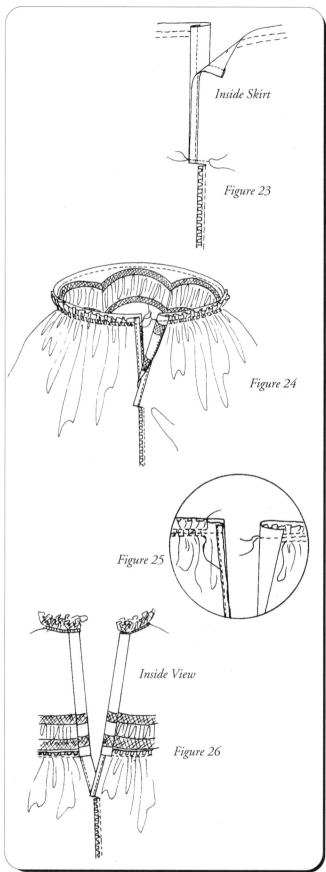

Inside Skirt

Figure 23

Figure 24

Figure 25

Inside View

Figure 26

a. Place the back edges of the skirt right sides together. Start stitching from the bottom of the skirt using 1/2" seam. Stop the seam 1-1/2" from the top on a small doll and 2-1/2" from the top on a medium or large doll. Clip across the seam allowance at the end of the stitching. Trim the seam allowance along the stitching line to 1/8". Overcast or serge (**fig. 21**).

b. Turn each side of the remaining upper seam allowance to the inside 1/8" and stitch in place (**fig. 22**). Place the seam allowances right sides together and stitch 3/8" across the skirt at the end of the opening. This stitching will be made from the inside of the skirt (**fig. 23**). Press to the left side of the skirt.

c. From the top of the skirt fold the right hand side of the opening 3/8" to the inside. Press in place.

2. Mark the center and quarter points of the skirt. Place the skirt to the bodice, right sides together matching the quarter points to the side seams and the center front to the center. Gather the top edge of the skirt to fit the bodice (**fig. 24**). Place the left side of the skirt opening 3/8" from the left edge of the bodice and wrap the bodice over the edge of the skirt. Place the right edge of the skirt opening even with the edge of the bodice (**fig. 25**). Stitch in place using a 1/4" seam. Overcast or serge. Pull the bodice up away from the skirt allowing the back placket to flip to the inside of the bodice (**fig. 26**).

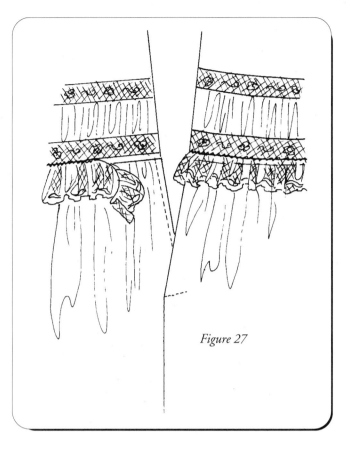

Figure 27

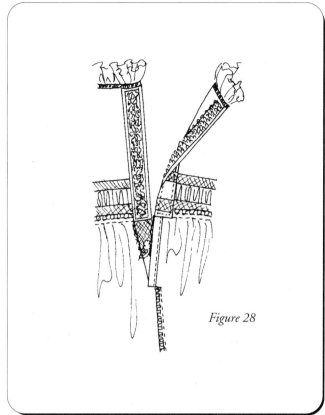

Figure 28

3. Fold the right side of the bodice/skirt to the inside 3/8".

4. Gather 3/4" edging lace to be placed on the bodice front under the lower lace scallops. Starting at the right back, fold the lace to the inside of the dress butting the lace against the lower lace scallops. Top stitch the edging lace in place using a small zigzag. Continue across the bodice ending at the left back. Fold the lace under 1/4" to end (**fig. 27**).

5. Buttonholes, snaps or Velcro™ should be placed along the back openings to hold the folds in place (**fig. 28**). ▨

Dupioni Silk With Organdy Hearts Dress

Ready to go to a party, a wedding, or a tea, any doll would adore having this pink dupioni silk drop waisted dress. Three interlocking lace hearts embellish the front of the collar; gathered lace edging travels all the way around the collar. The organdy elbow length sleeve has a diamond shaped inset with mitered lace at the bottom of the pink silk dupioni fabric. The bottom of the sleeve is gathered onto to entredeux with a gathered lace edging finish. Entredeux with silk ribbon run through it is found at the bottom of the bodice. Precious is the word to describe the gathered skirt. Organdy hearts are surrounded by lace insertion hearts which are linked with lace scallops on the bottom of the skirt. Gathered lace edging finishes the lowest part of the skirt. The back of the dress is closed with Velcro.

Dupioni Silk with Organdy Hearts Dress

Fabric Requirements

	Small Body	Medium Body	Large Body
Fabric - Silk	5/8 yd.	5/8 yd.	1 yd.
Fabric - Organdy	1/4 yd.	1/4 yd.	3/8 yd.
Lace Insertion (3/8")	5 yds.	5 yds.	1 yds.
Lace Insertion (5/8")	—	—	5 yds.
Entredeux	1 yd.	1 yd.	1-1/4 yds.
Edging Lace (3/8")	4 yd.	—	—
Edging Lace (3/4")	—	5 yds.	6 yds.
Silk Ribbon (7 mm)	3 yds.	3 yds.	3 yds.

Other Notions: Lightweight sewing thread, and Velcro™, snaps or tiny buttons for back closure.

All Seams 1/4" unless otherwise indicated.

I. Bodice

1. Cut out the front bodice on a fold.

2. If selvage fabric is available cut the back bodices with the back edges on the selvage. If the selvage is not available, simply cut out the bodice backs and serge or overcast the back edges of each bodice piece.

3. Place the front bodice to the back bodice pieces, right sides together, at the shoulders. Stitch using a 1/4" seam. Overcast or serge the seam allowance (**fig. 1**).

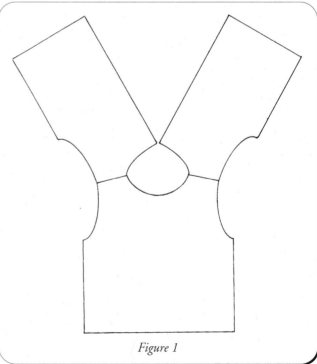

Figure 1

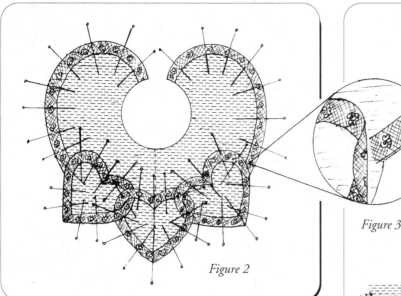

Figure 2

Figure 3

Figure 4

II. Collar

1. Cut one collar piece placing the center front of the pattern on the fold of the fabric. Using a fabric marker, trace off lace shaping lines. Shape the 3/8" insertion lace along the heart shape of the small and medium collar and the triple heart shapes of the large collar. Use the techniques for lace shaped hearts found in the lace shaping section. Then shape the lace along the outer edges and up the center backs of the collar (**fig. 2**). The lace insertion along the sides of the collar will be placed under the lace heart(s) (**fig. 3**). Collar template on page 305-307.

2. Zigzag lace in place along the inside of the insertion lace along the sides and along the top of the heart(s). Do not zigzag along the outer edge of the insertion or inside the heart(s). Starch and press. Trim the fabric from behind the lace. The fabric in the center of the heart will be cut away (**fig. 4**).

3. Place a strip of organdy in the center of the heart(s). Zigzag in place (**fig. 5**). Trim away the excess organdy from underneath, leaving only the centers of the hearts.

4. Cut a piece of edging lace two times the length around the outer edges of the collar. Gather and attach along the collar insertion using the technique lace to lace (**fig. 6**).

5. Place the wrong side of the collar to the right side of the dress. Pin in place.

6. Cut a bias strip 1" wide by the length of neck band measurement given in the neck band chart. Fold the bias strip in half and press. Place the cut edges of the strip to the neck of the collar/dress. Cut the ends of the strip off 3/8" from each side of the back bodice edges.

Figure 5

Figure 6

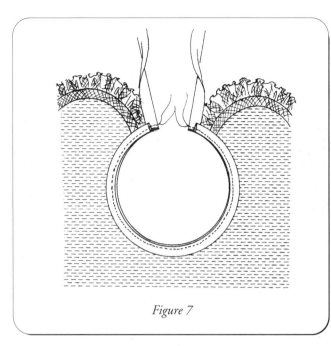

Figure 7

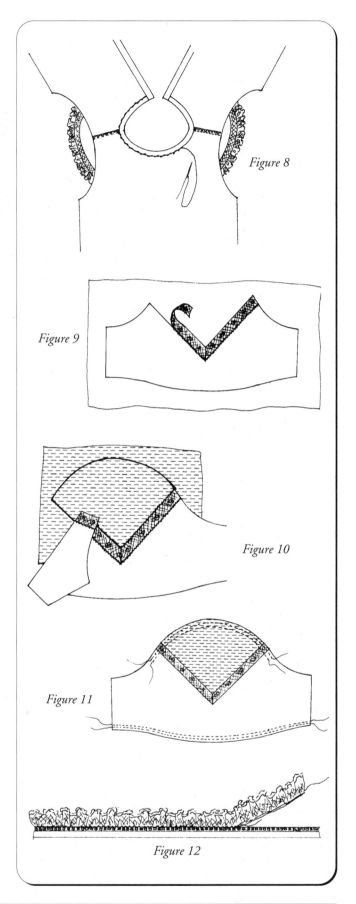

Figure 8

Figure 9

Figure 10

Figure 11

Figure 12

7. Flip the back bodice edges to the outside 3/8" under the folded bias strip. Stitch the bias strip to the neck edge using a 1/4" seam (**fig. 7**). Trim the seam allowance to 1/8". Flip the bias strip and the back bodice edges to the inside of the bodice. Hand stitch the bias strip in place finishing the neck edge (**fig. 8**).

III. Sleeves

1. Using a fabric marker and sleeve template, trace the "V" shape on the sleeve pattern. Trace the "V" shape and lower sleeve pattern on the organdy. Trace the "V" shape and the upper sleeve pattern on the other fabric. Repeat for both sleeves. Shape insertion lace on the lower sleeves, using the mitering techniques at the points of the "V". Zigzag along the lower edge of the lace (**fig. 9**). Trim the fabric from behind the insertion lace and along the pattern lines.

2. Place the upper sleeve fabric under the lower organdy/lace sleeve, lining up the lace "V" with the upper sleeve "V". Zigzag along the upper edge of the lace (**fig. 10**). Trim the fabric from behind the insertion lace and along the pattern lines. Stitch with a small zigzag along the fold of the miter. Repeat for other sleeve.

3. Place two rows of gathering stitches 1/8" and 1/4" in the top and bottom of the sleeve (**fig. 11**).

4. Cut two strips of entredeux to the measurement for the specific doll body given on the sleeve band chart. Cut two pieces of edging lace twice the length of the entredeux.

5. Gather the edging lace to fit the entredeux. Stitch together using the technique entredeux to gathered lace (**fig. 12**).

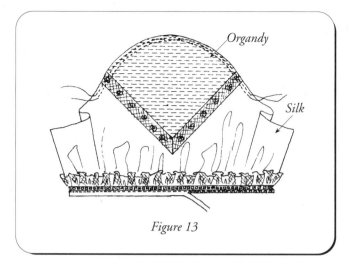

Organdy

Silk

Figure 13

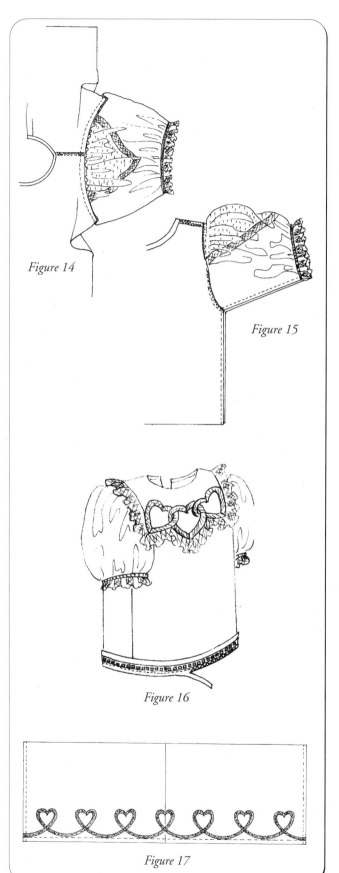

Figure 14

Figure 15

Figure 16

Figure 17

6. Gather the bottom of the sleeve to fit the entredeux/edging lace band. Stitch the band to the sleeve, right sides together, using the technique entredeux to gathered fabric (**fig. 13**).

7. Gather the top of the sleeve to fit the arm opening allowing most of the gathers to fall 3/4" to 1-1/4" on either side of the shoulder seam. Place the sleeve to the arm opening, right sides together, stitch using a 1/4" seam. Overcast or serge the seam allowance (**fig. 14**).

8. Place the sides of the bodice/sleeves right sides together. Stitch, using a 1/4" seam allowance. Overcast or serge the seam allowances (**fig. 15**).

9. Attach entredeux to the lower edge of the bodice using the technique entredeux to fabric (**fig. 16**).

IV. Skirt

1. Refer to the length and width given in the skirt chart for the specific doll body to create the skirt piece.

2. Using a fabric marker, trace the heart/scallops skirt template starting in the center of the skirt fabric. The lowest point of the scallop should be traced 3/8" from the edge of the skirt for small bodies and 3/4" from the edge of the skirt for large and medium bodies. Skirt template on centerfold pull out.

3. Shape lace along the skirt template lines following the directions under lace scallops and lace hearts (**fig. 17**).

4. Stitch along the upper edge of the lace insertion using a small, tight zigzag. Trim away the fabric from behind the lace. This will remove the fabric in the center of the hearts.

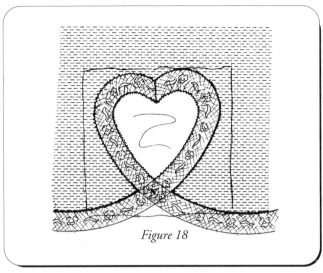

Figure 18

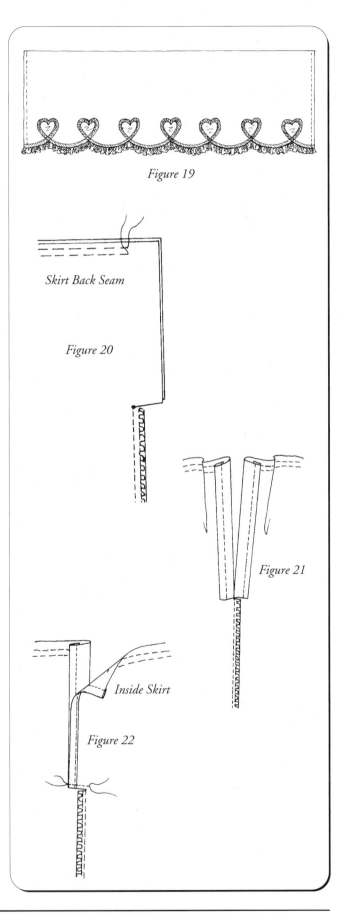

Figure 19

Skirt Back Seam

Figure 20

Figure 21

Inside Skirt

Figure 22

5. Place organdy fabric in the center of the hearts and stitch in place using a zigzag or decorative stitch. Trim away the excess organdy. Do not zigzag along the bottom edge of the hearts/scallops. Starch and press (**fig. 18**).

6. Cut a strip of edging lace twice the length of the skirt. Gather and attach to the insertion lace along the bottom of the skirt using the technique lace to lace (**fig. 19**).

7. Run two gathering rows at 1/4" and 1/8" in the top edge of the skirt piece starting and stopping 1/2" from the back edges.

V. Finishing the Dress

1. Creating the Skirt Placket

Note: The placket can be omitted if desired. The dress is much easier to get on and off if a placket is used.

a. Place the back edges of the skirt right sides together. Start stitching from the bottom of the skirt using 1/2" seam. Stop the seam 1-1/2" from the top on a small doll and 2-1/2" from the top on a medium or large doll. Clip across the seam allowance at the end of the stitching (**fig. 20**). Trim the seam allowance along the stitching line to 1/8". Overcast or serge.

b. Turn each side of the remaining upper seam allowance to the inside 1/8" and stitch in place (**fig. 21**). Place the seam allowances right sides together and stitch 3/8" across the skirt at the end of the opening. This stitching will be made from the inside of the skirt (**fig. 22**). Press to the left side of the skirt.

c. From the top of the skirt, fold the right hand side of the opening 3/8" to the inside. Press in place.

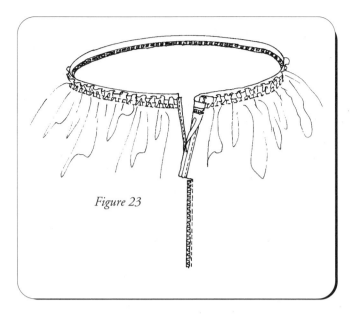

Figure 23

Figure 24

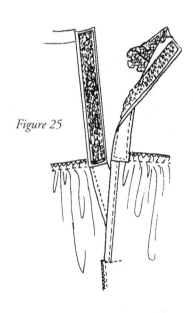

Figure 25

2. Mark the center and quarter points of the skirt. Place the skirt to the bodice entredeux, right sides together matching the quarter points to the side seams and the center front to the center. Gather the top edge of the skirt to fit the bodice entredeux (**fig. 23**). Place the left side of the skirt opening 3/8" from the left edge of the bodice and wrap the bodice over the edge of the skirt. Place the right edge of the skirt opening even with the edge of the bodice (**fig. 24**). Stitch in place with a 1/4" seam using the technique entredeux to gathered fabric. Overcast or serge. Pull the bodice up, away from the skirt allowing the back placket to flip to the inside of the bodice.

3. Fold the right side of the bodice/skirt to the inside 3/8".

4. Buttonholes, snaps or Velcro™ should be placed along the back openings to hold the folds in place (**fig. 25**).

5. Cut two pieces of 7mm silk ribbon 10" longer than the arm band measurement. Weave (over two bars and under two bars) through the arm entredeux beginning and ending at the center front of the sleeve. Weave remaining ribbon through the entredeux at the waist beginning and ending starting to the left of center. Tie the excess ribbons into bows. Trim the ends of the bows as desired and apply a fabric sealant to the ends of to keep the silk ribbon from fraying. ❈

Machine Crazy Patch Dress

This type of crazy patch is so much fun to do! A lot of people want lots of ways to use those fabulous decorative stitches on their sewing machines. Here's one way for you to really explore your sewing machine. This dress appears to be crazy patch, but it isn't. It's really "crazy stitched." Machine stitches are stitched on strips of fabric, cut into geometrical shapes and stitched to a flat piece of fabric. The edges of the shapes are covered with silk ribbon and feathered stitched in place. This technique is fabulous on garments as well as on home decorating items and gifts. This machine crazy patch is featured on the dropped waist bodice of the dress. Entredeux and gathered lace trims the puffed sleeve and the neckline. A perky little bow is on the waistline of the dress. The plain gathered skirt has two rows of narrow ecru French edging stitched flat along the hem.

Fabric Requirements

Fabric Scraps with Decorative Stitching

Lace Scraps

Embroidered Insertion Scraps

Crazy Patch Base Fabric - 1/4 yd. all sizes (Muslin, Batiste and Broadcloth)

	Small Body	Medium Body	Large Body
Dress Fabric	1/2 yd.	1/2 yd.	2/3 yd.
Entredeux	1 yd.	1 yd.	1 yd.
Edging Lace (1/2")	3 yds.	4 yds.	5 yd.
Silk Ribbon - 4mm	2 yds.	3 yds.	5 yds.

Other Notions: Lightweight sewing thread, decorative thread, and Velcro™, snaps or tiny buttons for back closure.

All Seams 1/4" unless otherwise indicated.

I. Bodice

1. Cut a rectangle of base fabric 1/2" longer and wider than the rectangle measurement given in the bodice chart for your specific doll body.

2. Trace the front bodice pattern on the base fabric rectangle (**fig. 1**).

3. Decorate 1-1/2" to 2" fabric strips with decorative stitches and decorative thread. Place pieces of decorated fabric, cut in geometric shapes on the base fabric. Fit the pieces together like a puzzle, butting the edges of the fabric together. Zigzag along the edges of each piece (**fig. 2**). Repeat this process until all the base fabric for the front bodice is covered.

Machine Crazy Patch Dress

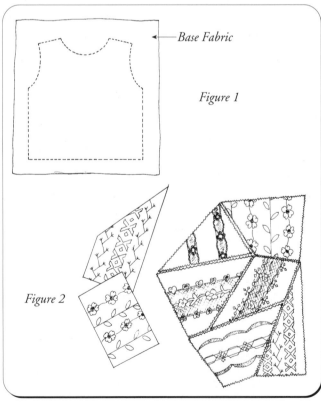

← Base Fabric

Figure 1

Figure 2

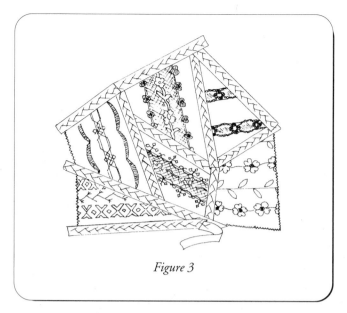

Figure 3

4. Place silk ribbon over the zigzag stitches. Silk ribbon is very easy to work with and can be folded (mitered) to turn a corner. Stitch the silk ribbon in place using a machine feather stitch, zigzag decorative stitch or straight stitch along each side of the ribbon. Make sure any raw ends of ribbon are placed under another piece of ribbon or will be stitched in a seam of the bodice (**fig. 3**).

5. Retrace the bodice front on the crazy patch created fabric (**fig. 4**). Straight stitch just inside the traced line.

6. Cut out the bodice front along the traced lines.

7. If selvage fabric is available, cut the back bodices with the back edges on the selvage. If the selvage is not available, simply cut out the bodice backs and serge or overcast the back edges of each bodice piece.

8. Place the front bodice to the back bodice pieces, right sides together, at the shoulders. Stitch using a 1/4" seam. Overcast or serge the seam allowance (**fig. 5**).

II. Neck

1. Cut a strip of entredeux to the neck band measurement given in the chart for the specific doll body to be dressed.

2. Cut a piece of 1/2" edging lace two times this length and gather to fit the entredeux strip.

3. Trim away one side of the entredeux and attach the gathered edging lace to the trimmed entredeux using the technique entredeux to gathered lace (**fig. 6**).

4. If the fabric edge remaining on the entredeux is not already 1/4", trim to 1/4". Clip this fabric so that it will curve along neck edge of the dress (**fig. 7**). Place this strip to the neck of the dress right sides together. Attach using the technique entredeux to fabric (**fig. 8**).

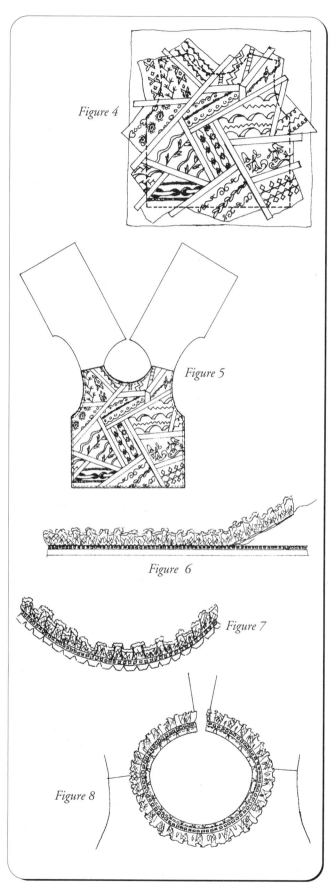

Figure 4

Figure 5

Figure 6

Figure 7

Figure 8

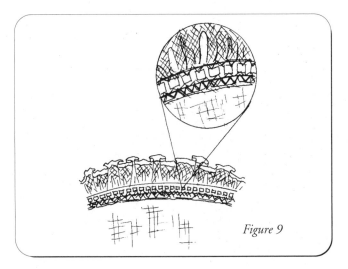

Figure 9

5. Using a tiny zigzag, tack the seam allowance to the dress. This stitching will keep the entredeux/gathered lace standing up at the neck (**fig. 9**).

III. Sleeves

1. Cut out two sleeves.

2. Place two rows of gathering stitches 1/8" and 1/4" in the top and bottom of the sleeve (**fig. 10**).

3. Cut two strips of entredeux to the measurement for the specific doll body given on the sleeve band chart. Cut two pieces of edging lace twice the length of the entredeux.

4. Gather the edging lace to fit the entredeux. Stitch together using the technique entredeux to gathered lace, see figure 6.

5. Gather the bottom of the sleeve to fit the entredeux/edging lace band. Stitch the band to the sleeve, right sides together, using the technique entredeux to gathered fabric (**fig. 11**).

6. Gather the top of the sleeve to fit the arm opening allowing most of the gathers to fall 3/4" to 1-1/4" on either side of the shoulder seam. Place the sleeve to the arm opening, right sides together, stitch using a 1/4" seam. Overcast or serge the seam allowance (**fig. 12**).

7. Place the sides of the bodice/sleeves right sides together. Stitch, using a 1/4" seam allowance. Overcast or serge the seam allowances (**fig. 13**).

IV. Skirt

1. Refer to the length and width given in the skirt chart for the specific doll body to create the skirt piece. This skirt has a hem. Add 1" to the length for a small doll, 1-1/4" to the length for a medium doll and 2" to the length for a large doll.

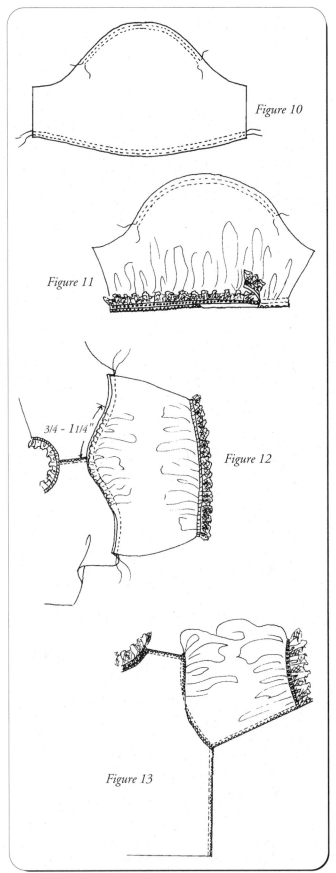

Figure 10

Figure 11

3/4 - 1 1/4"

Figure 12

Figure 13

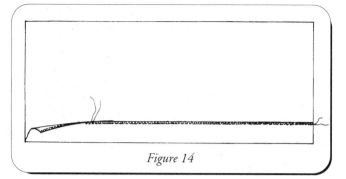

Figure 14

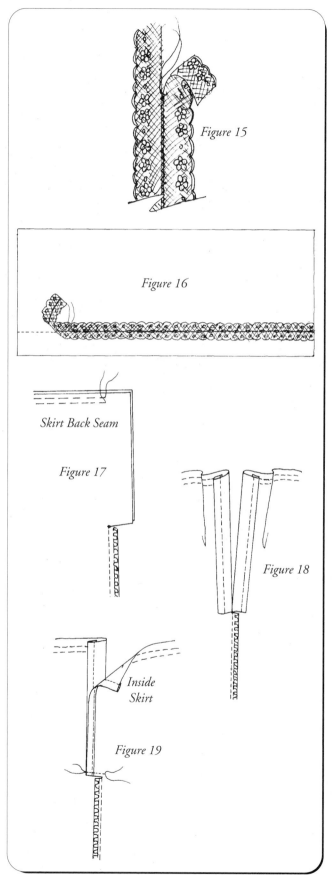

Figure 15

Figure 16

Skirt Back Seam

Figure 17

Figure 18

Inside Skirt

Figure 19

2. Cut a piece of fabric to this measurement. Overcast or serge one long edge and the two short edges of the skirt piece. Turn the serged edge of the skirt to the inside the amount given in step 1 above. Straight stitch in place (**fig. 14**). The edging lace trim attached in step 3 will hide this stitching.

3. Place two pieces of edging lace side by side, heading to heading. Zigzag in place using the technique lace to lace (**fig. 15**). Place this trim over the straight stitch of the hem and stitch in place using a zigzag or decorative stitch (**fig. 16**).

4. Run two gathering rows at 1/4" and 1/8" in the top edge of the skirt piece starting and stopping 1/2" from the back edges.

V. Finishing the Dress

1. Creating the Skirt Placket

   a. Place the back edges of the skirt right sides together. Make sure the lace trim on the skirt lines up at the seam. Start stitching from the bottom of the skirt using 1/2" seam. Stop the seam 1-1/2" from the top on a small doll and 2-1/2" from the top on a medium or large doll. Clip across the seam allowance at the end of the stitching. Trim the seam allowance along the stitching line to 1/8". Overcast or serge (**fig. 17**).

   b. Turn each side of the remaining upper seam allowance to the inside 1/8" and stitch in place (**fig. 18**). Place the seam allowances right sides together and stitch 3/8" across the skirt at the end of the opening. This stitching will be made from the inside of the skirt (**fig. 19**). Press to the left side of the skirt.

   c. From the top of the skirt, fold the right hand side of the opening 3/8" to the inside. Press in place.

2. Mark the center and quarter points of the skirt. Place the skirt to the bodice, right sides together matching the quarter points to the side seams and the center front to the center. Gather the top edge of the skirt to fit the bodice

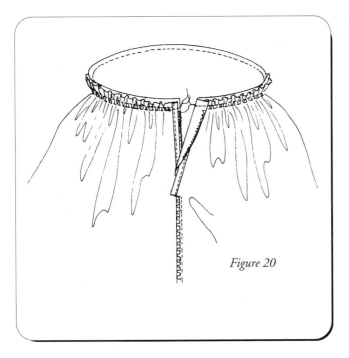

Figure 20

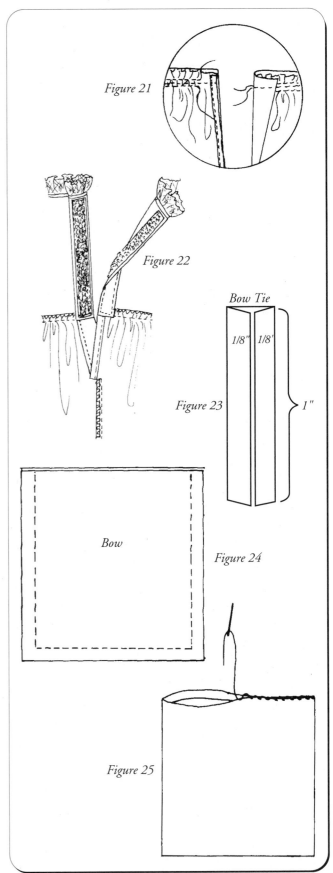

Figure 21

Figure 22

Bow Tie

1/8" 1/8'

Figure 23   1"

Bow

Figure 24

Figure 25

(**fig. 20**). Place the left side of the skirt opening 3/8" from the left edge of the bodice and wrap the bodice over the edge of the skirt. Place the right edge of the skirt opening even with the edge of the bodice (**fig. 21**). Stitch in place using a 1/4" seam. Overcast or serge. Pull the bodice up away from the skirt allowing the back placket to flip to the inside of the bodice, see figure 22.

3. Fold the right side of the bodice/skirt to the inside 3/8". Place buttonholes, snaps or Velcro™ along this fold to hold in place. Place closures along the left side of the back bodice (**fig. 22**).

4. Bow Tie: Cut a piece of fabric 1" long by 1/2" wide for small dolls, 3/4" wide for medium dolls and 1" wide for large dolls. Fold the 1" edges of the fabric to the inside 1/8" press (**fig. 23**). Set aside.

5. Bow - Cut two pieces of fabric to the following measurement: Small Dolls 1-3/4" by 1-3/4", Medium Dolls: 2-1/4" by 2-1/4", Large Dolls: 2-3/4" by 2-3/4".

Place the two squares right sides together and stitch along three sides using a 1/4" seam (**fig. 24**). Turn and fold the edges of the fourth side to the inside 1/4" and hand stitch in place (**fig. 25**). Gather the square in the center. Wrap with the bow tie created in step 4 above. Overlap the ends of the tie to the desired size. Trim excess if needed. Hand stitch the ends of the tie together to complete the bow.

6. Stitch the bow in place to the right of the dress center at the bodice/ skirt seam. ▩

Celtic Lace Dress

Celtic lace shaping is easy to do as long as you use narrow laces. The fabric is blue Swiss Nelona; the laces are bridal white French. Ever so pretty is this doll dress with its three Celtic loops on the bodice and its intricate design on the skirt. The neckline and sleeves are finished with entredeux and gathered lace edging; silk ribbon is run through the entredeux around both the sleeves and the neckline. Entredeux and gathered lace edging also finishes the bottom part of the skirt. Centered on the front skirt is the sweetest Celtic design which features eight loops joined in a most interesting manner. Velcro makes this dress a very easy one to take on and off your doll.

Fabric Requirements

	Small Body	Medium Body	Large Body
Fabric	1/2 yd.	1/2 yd.	1 yd.
Lace Insertion 3/8"	1-3/4 yds.	2 yds.	3 yds.
Entredeux	1-1/2 yds.	1-1/2 yds.	2 yds.
Edging Lace 3/4"	2-1/2 yds.	2-1/2 yds.	3 yds.
Edging Lace Neck - 3/8"	1/2 yd.	1/2 yd.	1/2 yd.
Silk Ribbon (2mm)	3 yds.	3 yds.	3 yds.

Other Notions: Lightweight sewing thread, and Velcro™, snaps or tiny buttons for back closure.

All Seams 1/4" unless otherwise indicated.

I. Bodice

1.   Cut out the bodice front on the fold of the fabric.

2.   If selvage fabric is available cut the back bodices with the back edges on the selvage. If the selvage is not available, simply cut out the bodice backs and serge or overcast the back edges of each bodice piece.

3.   Place the front bodice to the back bodice pieces, right sides together, at the shoulders. Stitch using a 1/4" seam. Overcast or serge the seam allowance (**fig. 1**).

4.   Trace the lace template on the bodice front allowing the highest point of the template to fall 1/2" from the cut edge of the neck. Bodice and skirt templates on page 308.

5.   Shape lace insertion along the template lines using the directions under Celtic lace shaping in this book (**fig. 2**).

Celtic Lace Dress

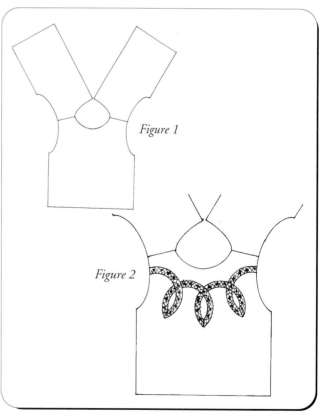

Figure 1

Figure 2

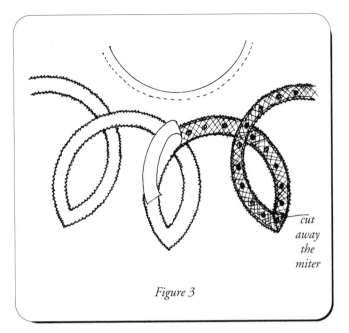

Figure 3

6. Zigzag along the inner and outer edges of the lace. Carefully trim the fabric from behind the lace insertion (**fig. 3**).

II. Neck

1. Cut a strip of entredeux to the neck band measurement given in the chart for the specific doll body to be dressed.

2. Cut a piece of edging lace two times this length and gather to fit the entredeux strip.

3. Trim away one side of the entredeux and attach the gathered edging lace to the trimmed entredeux using the technique entredeux to gathered lace (**fig. 4**).

4. If the fabric edge remaining on the entredeux is not 1/4", trim to 1/4". Clip this fabric (**fig. 5**) so that it will curve along the neck edge of the dress. Place this strip to the neck of the dress, right sides together. Attach using the technique entredeux to gathered fabric (**fig. 6**).

5. Using a tiny zigzag, tack the seam allowance to the dress. This stitching will keep the entredeux/gathered lace standing up at the neck (**fig. 7**).

III. Sleeves

1. Cut out two sleeves.

2. Place two rows of gathering stitches 1/8" and 1/4" in the top and bottom of the sleeve (**fig. 8**).

3. Cut two strips of entredeux to the measurement for the specific doll body given on the sleeve band chart. Cut two pieces of edging lace twice the length of the entredeux.

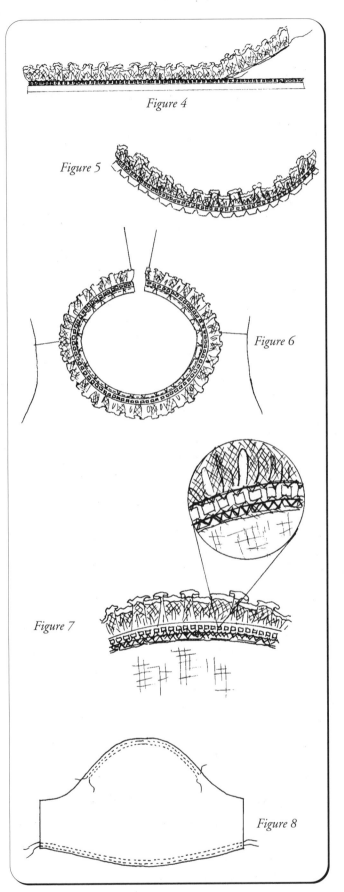

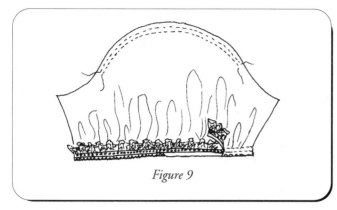

Figure 9

4. Gather the edging lace to fit the entredeux. Stitch together using the technique entredeux to gathered lace (**see fig. 4**).

5. Gather the bottom of the sleeve to fit the entredeux/edging lace band. Stitch the band to the sleeve, right sides together, using the technique entredeux to gathered fabric (**fig. 9**).

6. Gather the top of the sleeve to fit the arm opening allowing most of the gathers to fall 3/4" to 1-1/4" on either side of the shoulder seam. Place the sleeve to the arm opening, right sides together, stitch using a 1/4" seam. Overcast or serge the seam allowance (**fig. 10**).

7. Place the sides of the bodice/sleeves right sides together. Stitch, using a 1/4" seam allowance. Overcast or serge the seam allowances (**fig. 11**).

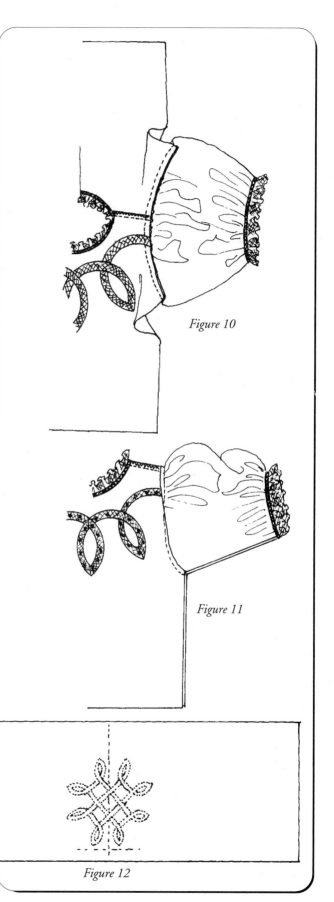

Figure 10

Figure 11

Figure 12

IV. Skirt

1. Refer to the length and width given in the skirt chart for the specific doll body to create the skirt piece. Cut a piece of fabric 1/2" shorter than to this measurement. The edging lace added later to the skirt bottom will give you the correct finished length

2. Using a fabric marker, trace the Celtic skirt template in the center of the skirt fabric 5/8" from edge of the fabric for medium and large dolls and 3/8" for small dolls (**fig. 12**).

3. Shape lace along the template lines following the directions under Celtic lace shaping (**see figure 3**).

4. Zigzag along the inner and outer edges of the insertion lace. Starch and press. Trim the fabric carefully from behind the lace.

5. Cut a piece of entredeux the width of the skirt. Trim one fabric edge of the entredeux completely away. Cut a piece of edging lace twice the length of the entredeux. Gather the lace and attach to the trimmed entredeux with a zigzag (**see figure 4**). Trim the other side of the entredeux to 1/4" if it is not already 1/4".

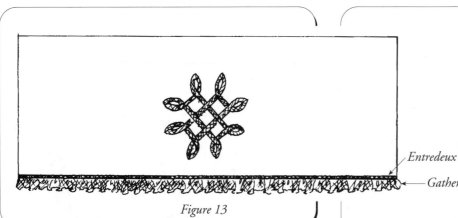

Figure 13

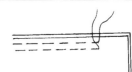

Skirt Back Seam

Figure 14

Entredeux

Gathered Lace

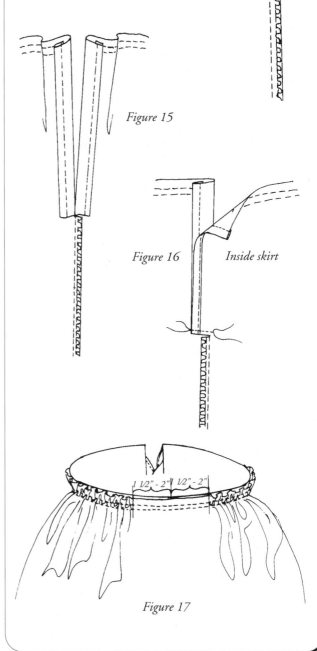

Figure 15

Figure 16   *Inside skirt*

Figure 17

6. Attach the entredeux/edging lace to the lower edge of the skirt using a 1/4" seam. Refer to the technique fabric to entredeux (**fig. 13**).

V. Finishing the Dress

1. Creating the Skirt Placket

    a. Place the back edges of the skirt right sides together, matching entredeux and edging lace. Start stitching from the bottom of the skirt using 1/2" seam. Stop the seam
        1-1/2" from the top on a small doll and 2-1/2" from the top on a medium or large doll. Clip across the seam allowance at the end of the stitching (**fig. 14**). Trim the seam allowance along the stitching line to 1/8". Overcast or serge.

    b. Turn each side of the remaining upper seam allowance to the inside 1/8" and stitch in place (**fig. 15**). Place the seam allowances right sides together and stitch 3/8" across the skirt at the end of the opening. This stitching will be made from the inside of the skirt (**fig. 16**). Press to the left side of the skirt.

    c. From the top of the skirt, fold the right side of the opening 3/8" to the inside. Press in place.

2. Mark the center and quarter points of the skirt. Place the skirt to the bodice, right sides together matching the quarter points to the side seams and the center front to the center. Gather the top edge of the skirt to fit the bodice leaving 1-1/2" to 2" ungathered on either side of the center front (**fig. 17**). Place the left side of the skirt opening 3/8"

from the left edge of the bodice and wrap the bodice over the edge of the skirt. Place the right edge of the skirt opening even with the edge of the bodice (**see fig. 18**). Stitch in place using a 1/4" seam. Overcast or serge. Pull the bodice away from the skirt allowing the back placket to flip to the inside of the bodice.

3. Fold the right side of the bodice/skirt to the inside 3/8". Place buttonholes, snaps or Velcro™ along this fold to hold in place. Place closures along the left side of the back bodice (**fig. 19**).

4. Cut two pieces of 2mm silk ribbon 10" longer than the arm band measurement. Thread (over two entredeux bars and under two bars) through the arm entredeux beginning and ending at the center front of the sleeve. Tie excess into bows. Trim the ends of the bows as desired and apply a fabric sealant to the ends of to keep the silk ribbon from fraying.

5. Cut one piece of 2 mm silk ribbon 10" longer than the neck band measurement. Thread (over two entredeux bars and under two bars) through the neck entredeux. Tie excess into a bow. Trim the ends of the bows as desired and apply a fabric sealant to the ends to keep the silk ribbon from fraying. ▧

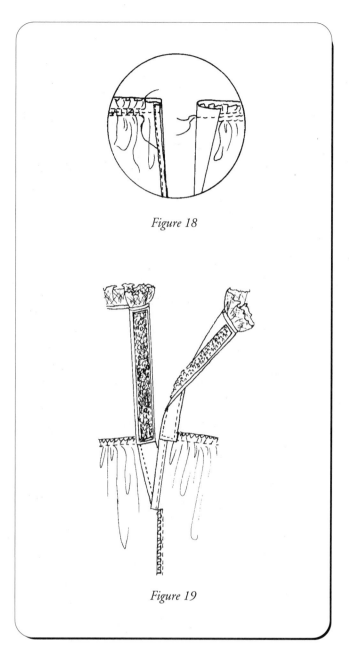

Figure 18

Figure 19

Lace Overlay Dress

If brides have lots of lace, why can't dolls? Sweet and very interesting is this doll dress with a created fabric made by zigzagging lots of rows of lace beading (without ribbon) and lace insertion together. The gathered lace edging used for the bodice trim is circled around one piece of lace insertion; this gives the effect of having a round yoke dress. The sleeves are of the same zigzagged beading and lace insertion. Entredeux and gathered lace trim finish the bottom of the puff sleeves and the neckline. Pink silk ribbon is run through all of the entredeux. A pink lining peeks through the laces. Three rows of gathered lace embellishes the skirt. The gathered lace is zigzagged to three rows of the lace skirt. This makes for a very pretty and interesting doll skirt. Velcro closes the back of the dress.

Fabric Requirements

	Small Body	Medium Body	Large Body
Fabric	1/2 yd.	1/2 yd.	2/3 yd.
Lace Insertion 5/8"	11-1/2 yds.	19 yds.	24-1/2 yds.
Lace Beading 5/8"	11 yds.	18-1/2 yds.	24 yds
Entredeux	1/2 yd.	1/2 yds.	2/3 yds.
Edging Lace 1-1/2"	—	—	13 yds.
Edging Lace 3/4"	—	11 yds.	1/2 yd.
Edging Lace 1/2"	10 yds.	1/2 yd.	—
Edging Lace 3/8"	1/2 yd.	—	—
Silk Ribbon (2 mm)	3 yds.	3 yds.	3 yds.

Lace Overlay Dress

Other Notions: Lightweight sewing thread, and Velcro™, snaps or tiny buttons for back closure.

All Seams 1/4" unless otherwise indicated.

I. Lace Overlay

1. Measure the length and width of the front bodice, back bodice and sleeve. Double the width measurement of each measurement since the front and sleeves are cut on the fold and the back has a right back and a left back. Create lace fabric to these measurements by attaching lace and beading pieces together using the technique "lace to lace." Starch and press the created lace fabric. Place the pattern pieces on top of the created lace fabric. Trace around each piece. Straight stitch 1/8" inside the traced lines. Cut out each pattern piece (**fig. 1**). Cut bodice front, bodice backs and 2 sleeves from this created lace fabric.

2. Cut out the lining bodice front on the fold of the fabric.

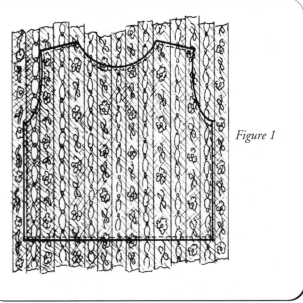

Figure 1

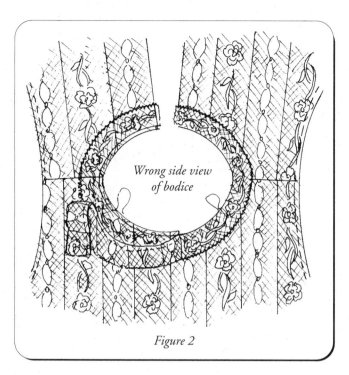

Wrong side view of bodice

Figure 2

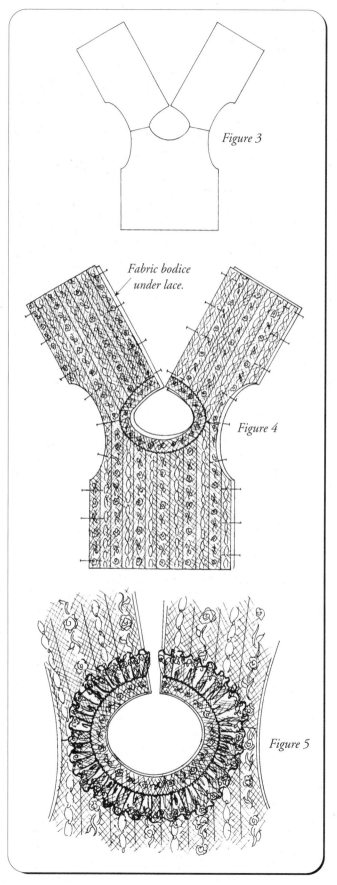

Figure 3

Fabric bodice under lace.

Figure 4

Figure 5

3. If selvage fabric is available cut the back bodices lining with the back edges on the selvage. If the selvage is not available, simply cut out the bodice backs and serge or overcast the back edges of each bodice piece.

4. Place the front lace overlay to the back lace overlays at the shoulders and stitch using a 1/4" seam. Overcast or serge the seam allowance.

5. Shape a piece of insertion lace 1/8" from the neck edge using the circular lace shaping techniques. Stitch the lower edge of the shaped lace in place using a small zigzag. Trim the lace from behind the shaped lace piece (**fig. 2**).

6. Place the fabric back bodice pieces to the fabric front bodice piece at the shoulders, right sides together. Overcast or serge the seam allowance (**fig. 3**).

7. Place the bodice lace overlay over the fabric bodice. All edges should meet except the neck edge. The lace overlay will fall 1/8" below the fabric neck edge. Pin the fabric layer and the lace layer together. Treat as one layer of fabric (**fig. 4**).

8. Gather a piece of edging lace along the lower edge of the shaped neckline insertion. Stitch in place using a small zigzag. This stitching will be through the edging lace, lace bodice and fabric bodice lining (**fig. 5**).

II. Neck

1. Cut a strip of entredeux to the neck band measurement given in the chart for the specific doll body to be dressed.

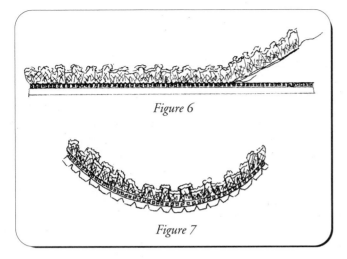

Figure 6

Figure 7

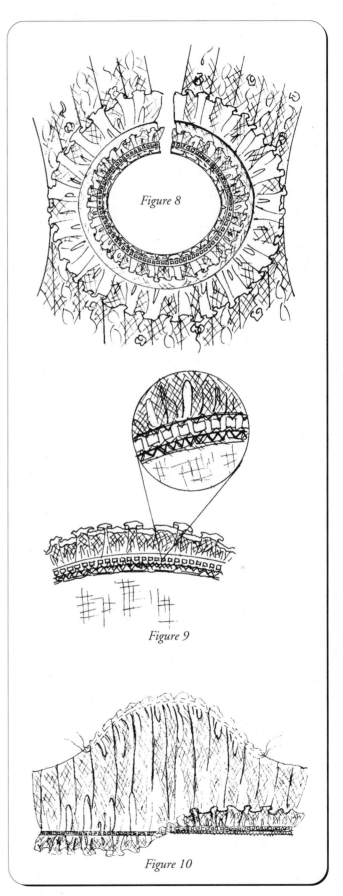

Figure 8

Figure 9

Figure 10

2. Cut a piece of edging lace two times this length and gather to fit the entredeux strip.

3. Trim away one side of the entredeux and attach the gathered edging lace to the trimmed entredeux using the technique entredeux to gathered lace (**fig. 6**).

4. If the fabric edge remaining on the entredeux is not 1/4", trim to 1/4". Clip this fabric so that it will curve along neck edge of the dress (**fig. 7**). Place this strip to the neck of the dress, right sides together. Attach using the technique entredeux to fabric. Make sure both layers of the bodice are caught in the seam (**fig. 8**).

5. Using a tiny zigzag, tack the seam allowance to the dress. This stitching will keep the entredeux/gathered lace standing up at the neck (**fig. 9**).

III. Sleeves

1. The lace sleeves will not have a fabric backing. Place two rows of gathering stitches 1/8" and 1/4" in the top and bottom of the sleeve.

2. Cut two strips of entredeux to the measurement for the specific doll body given on the sleeve band chart. Cut two pieces of edging lace twice the length of the entredeux.

3. Gather the edging lace to fit the entredeux. Stitch together using the technique entredeux to gathered lace (**see fig. 6**).

4. Gather the bottom of the sleeve to fit the entredeux/edging lace band. Stitch the band to the sleeve, right sides together, using the technique entredeux to gathered fabric (**fig. 10**).

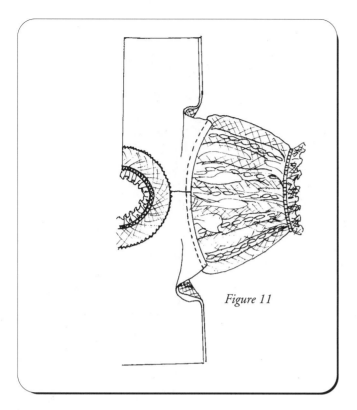

Figure 11

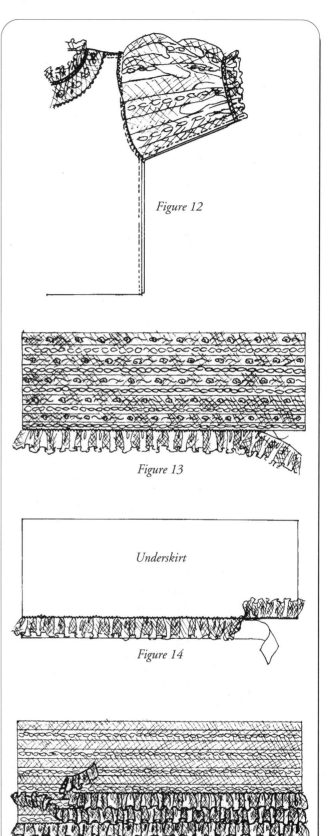

Figure 12

Figure 13

Underskirt

Figure 14

Figure 15

5. Gather the top of the sleeve to fit the arm opening allowing most of the gathers to fall 3/4" to 1-1/4" on either side of the shoulder seam. Place the sleeve to the arm opening, right sides together, stitch using a 1/4" seam. Overcast or serge the seam allowance (**fig. 11**).

6. Place the sides of the bodice/sleeves right sides together. Stitch, using a 1/4" seam allowance. Overcast or serge the seam allowances (**fig. 12**).

IV. Skirt

1. Refer to the length and width given in the skirt chart for the specific doll body to create the lace skirt and under skirt pieces. Create the lace skirt by attaching lace and beading together using a small zigzag. Attach gathered edging to the created lace fabric to achieve the correct measurement for the skirt (**fig. 13**).

2. Under skirt - Cut a piece of fabric to the skirt measurement. Gather edging lace and attach to this fabric by placing the edging on top of the skirt fabric. The edge of the lace should be even with the edge of the lace. Zigzag or hemstitch in place along the upper edge of the gathered edging. Trim the fabric from behind the lace (**fig. 14**).

3. Gather two pieces of lace edging to fit the lace skirt. Place on top of the lace skirt allowing the edge of the lace to overlap the lower edging by 1/8". Attach along the upper edge of the lace using a small zigzag. Attach the other gathered lace piece in the same manner (**fig. 15**).

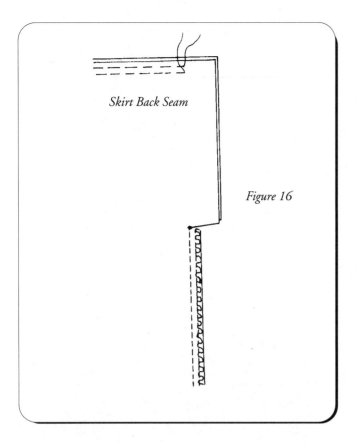

Skirt Back Seam

Figure 16

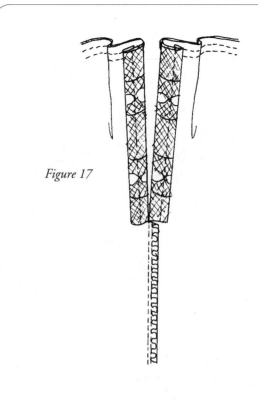

Figure 17

4. Place the lace skirt on top of the under skirt, right side of under skirt to wrong side of lace skirt. Pin together and treat as one layer of fabric. Run two gathering threads in the top of the skirt.

V. Finishing the Dress

1. Creating the Skirt Placket

   a. Place the back edges of the skirt right sides together, matching edging lace pieces. Start stitching from the bottom of the skirt using 1/2" seam. Stop the seam 1-1/2" from the top on a small doll and 2-1/2" from the top on a medium or large doll. Clip across the seam allowance at the end of the stitching (**fig. 16**). Trim the seam allowance along the stitching line to 1/8". Overcast or serge.

   b. Turn each side of the remaining upper seam allowance to the inside 1/8" and stitch in place (**fig. 17**). Place the seam allowances right sides together and stitch 3/8" across the skirt at the end of the opening. This stitching will be made from the inside of the skirt (**fig. 18**). Press to the left side of the skirt.

   c. From the top of the skirt, fold the right side of the opening 3/8" to the inside. Press in place

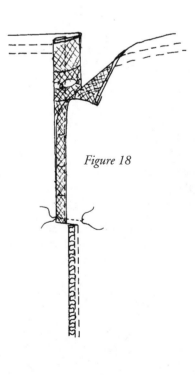

Figure 18

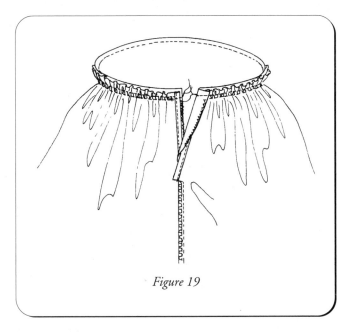

Figure 19

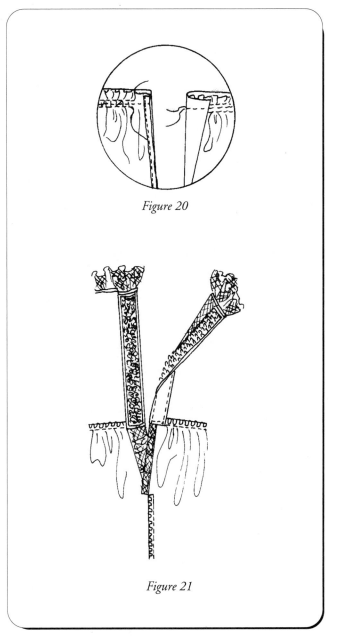

Figure 20

Figure 21

2. Mark the center and quarter points of the skirt. Place the skirt to the bodice, right sides together matching the quarter points to the side seams and the center front to the center. Gather the top edge of the skirt to fit the bodice (**fig. 19**). Place the left side of the skirt opening 3/8" from the left edge of the bodice and wrap the bodice over the edge of the skirt. Place the right edge of the skirt opening even with the edge of the bodice (**see fig. 20**). Stitch in place using a 1/4" seam. Overcast or serge. Pull the bodice away from the skirt allowing the back placket to flip to the inside of the bodice.

3. Fold the right side of the bodice/skirt to the inside 3/8". Place buttonholes, snaps or Velcro™ along this fold to hold in place. Place closures along the left side of the back bodice (**fig. 21**).

4. Cut two pieces of 2mm silk ribbon 10" longer than the arm band measurement. Thread (over two entredeux bars and under two bars) through the arm entredeux beginning and ending at the center front of the sleeve. Tie excess into bows. Trim the ends of the bows as desired and apply a fabric sealant to the ends of to keep the silk ribbon from fraying.

5. Cut the remaining ribbon in half. Start threading (over two entredeux bars and under two bars) each piece of ribbon at the center front through the neck entredeux. Tack the ends of the ribbons at each back opening. Tie excess ribbon into a bow at the center front. Trim the ends of the bows as desired and apply a fabric sealant to the ends to keep the silk ribbon from fraying. ▓

Watermelon Appliqué Dress

Summertime brings thoughts of swimming, family fun and of course watermelon. The appliqués of watermelon pieces on this precious green and white gingham seersucker doll dress have one piece in its entirety and one piece about half eaten. The skirt of this dress is "hemmed" with machine scallops in green thread. More green machine scallops trim the front treatment as well as pink scallops a pink ribbon strip down the front and more machine embellishment down the center of the ribbon. Bias bindings in the fashion fabric finish the neckline and sleeves. Velcro closes the back of this little cotton beauty.

Fabric Requirements

	Small Body	Medium Body	Large Body
Fabric	3/4 yd.	3/4 yd.	1 yd.
Silk Ribbon	2 yds.	2 yds.	2 yds.
Ribbon Sash (1/4")	1 yd.	1 yd.	1 yd.

Applique Fabric 1/8 yd. each color : Pink and green

Other Notions: Decorative thread to match applique fabric, white thread for applique, sewing thread, Wonder Under™ or other paper-backed bonding agent and Velcro™, snaps or tiny buttons for back closure.

All Seams 1/4" unless otherwise indicated.

I. Bodice

1   Trace the entire front bodice on the fabric.

2.   Apply paper backed bonding agent to the back of the pink applique fabric. Cut a strip of pink fabric with bonding agent the length of the bodice by 3/8" wide (small dolls), 1/2" wide (medium dolls) and 3/4" wide (large dolls).

3.   Center the pink strip along the center of the front bodice. Fuse the strip in place.

4.   Stitch along each side of the strip with a decorative stitch or a satin stitch using the directions for applique.

5.   Place a machine decorative stitch on each side of the pink strip (**fig. 1**).

6.   Cut out the bodice front.

7.   If selvage fabric is available cut the back bodices with the back edges on the selvage. If the selvage is not available, simply cut out the bodice backs and serge or overcast the back edges of each bodice piece.

Watermelon Appliqué Dress

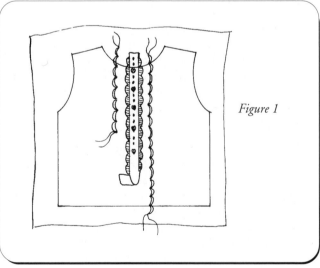

Figure 1

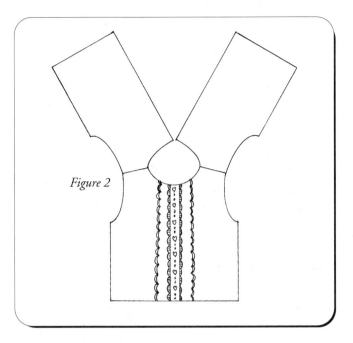

Figure 2

8. Place the front bodice to the back bodice pieces, right sides together, at the shoulders. Stitch using a 1/4" seam. Overcast or serge the seam allowance (**fig. 2**).

II. Neck

1. Trim off the edge of the neck 1/4". Fold the back edges of the back bodice to the inside 3/8". Press.

2. Measure around the neck with the back folds in place and add 1/2" to this measurement. Cut a bias strip 1" wide by this measurement. Fold each long side of the bias strip to the inside 1/4". Press in place (**fig 3**). Open out one side of the bias strip and stitch to the neck using a 1/4" seam (stitch in the fold) (fig. 4). The bias strip will extend 1/4" beyond the folded plackets of the back. Flip the bias up, away from the neck, fold the ends to the inside and pull the upper folded edge of the bias strip over the seam allowance (**fig. 5**). Press. Hand stitch or machine stitch in place.

III. Sleeves

1. Cut out two sleeves.

2. Place two rows of gathering stitches 1/8" and 1/4" in the top and bottom of the sleeve (**fig. 6**).

3. Cut two bias strips of fabric 1" wide by the measurement given on the sleeve band chart for your specific doll body.

4. Gather the bottom of the sleeve to fit the bias band. Stitch the band to the sleeve, right sides together, using a 1/4" seam. Fold the lower edge of the band to the inside 1/4". Place the folded edge just over the seam allowance on the

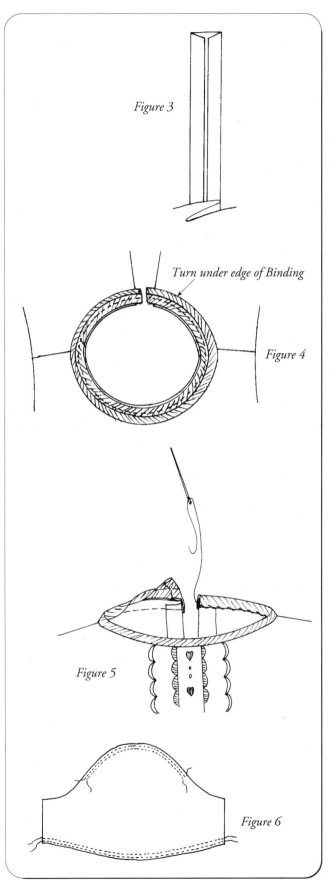

Figure 3

Turn under edge of Binding

Figure 4

Figure 5

Figure 6

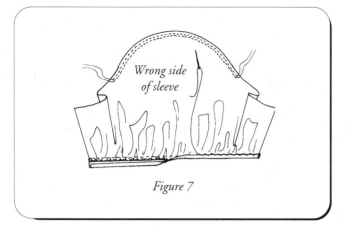

Wrong side of sleeve

Figure 7

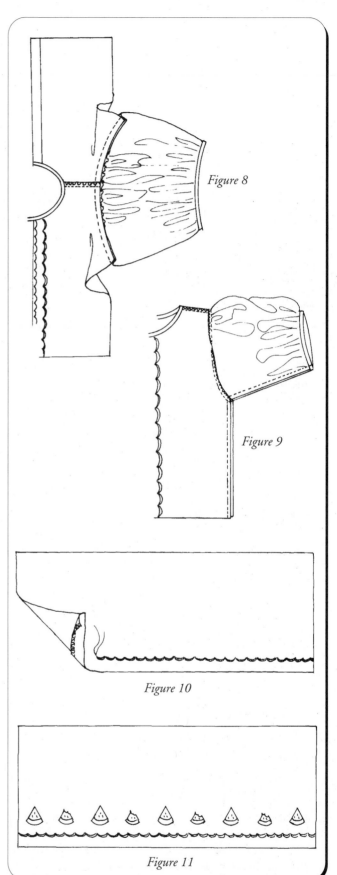

Figure 8

Figure 9

Figure 10

Figure 11

inside of the sleeve creating a 1/4" band. Hand stitch or machine stitch in place (**fig. 7**). This will finish the end of the sleeve.

5. Gather the top of the sleeve to fit the arm opening allowing most of the gathers to fall 3/4" to 1-1/4" on either side of the shoulder seam. Place the sleeve to the arm opening, right sides together, stitch using a 1/4" seam. Overcast or serge the seam allowance (**fig. 8**).

6. Place the sides of the bodice/sleeves right sides together. Stitch, using a 1/4" seam allowance. Overcast or serge the seam allowances (**fig. 9**).

IV. Skirt

1. Refer to the length and width given in the skirt chart to create the skirt piece for the specific doll body and add 1" to the length for small and medium dolls, and 2" to the length for a large doll.

2. Cut one piece of fabric to this measurement. Overcast or serge the long edge of skirt piece. Serge or overcast the back edges of the skirt piece.

3. Turn the hem of the skirt to the inside the following amounts: small doll and medium doll - 1", large doll 2". Use a decorative stitch such as a scallop to hold the hem in place (**fig. 10**). Watermelon templates on page 78.

4. Trace watermelon patterns onto the correct applique fabric color. This fabric should have paper-backed bonding agent applied. Place watermelons on the fabric 1/2" from the decorative stitch alternating between a whole slice and an eaten slice starting with a whole slice in the center of the skirt. The watermelons measure 3" apart from the center of one design to the center of the next design (**fig. 11**). The watermelons should be fused to the skirt in the following

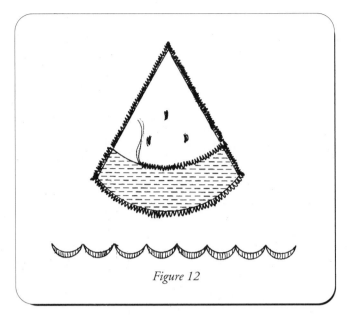

Figure 12

order: pink then green. Applique the pink part, the green part and then satin stitch with white to accent between the pink and green appliqued pieces (**fig. 12**).

5. Run two gathering rows at 1/4" and 1/8" in the top edge of the skirt piece starting and stopping 1/2" from the back edges.

V. Skirt

1. Creating the Skirt Placket

   a. Place the back edges of the skirt right sides together. Make sure the decorative stitching on the skirt lines up at the seam. Start stitching from the bottom of the skirt using 1/2" seam. Stop the seam 1-1/2" from the top on a small doll and 2-1/2" from the top on a medium or large doll. Clip across the seam allowance at the end of the stitching. Trim the seam allowance along the stitching line to 1/8". Overcast or serge (**fig. 13**).

   b. Turn each side of the remaining upper seam allowance to the inside 1/8" and stitch in place (**fig. 14**). Place the seam allowances right sides together and stitch 3/8" across the skirt at the end of the opening. This stitching will be made from the inside of the skirt (**fig. 15**). Press to the left side of the skirt.

   c. From the top of the skirt, fold the right hand side of the opening 3/8" to the inside. Press in place.

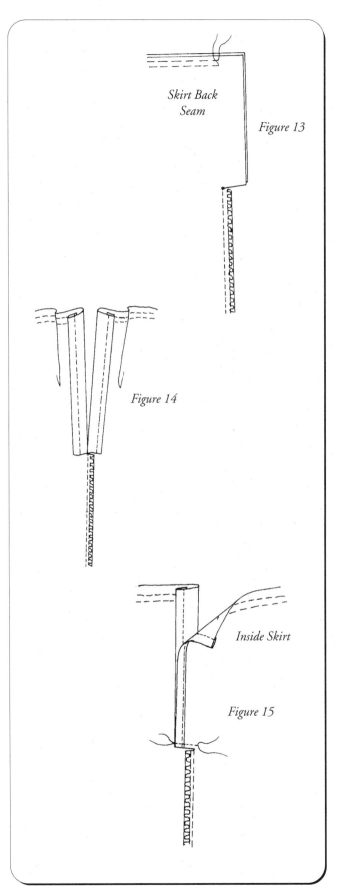

Skirt Back Seam

Figure 13

Figure 14

Inside Skirt

Figure 15

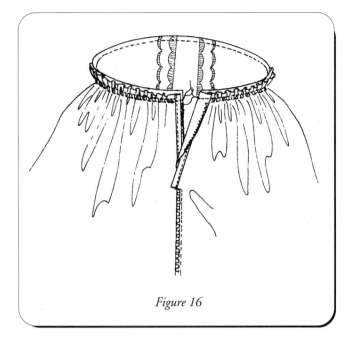

Figure 16

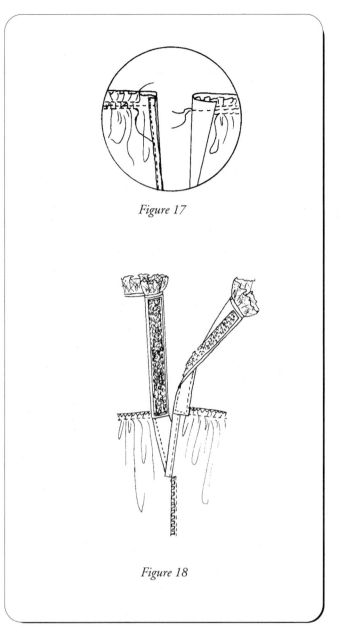

Figure 17

Figure 18

2. Mark the center and quarter points of the skirt. Place the skirt to the bodice, right sides together matching the quarter points to the side seams and the center front to the center. Gather the top edge of the skirt to fit the bodice (**fig. 16**). Place the left side of the skirt opening 3/8" from the left edge of the bodice and wrap the bodice over the edge of the skirt. Place the right edge of the skirt opening even with the edge of the bodice (**fig. 17**). Stitch in place using a 1/4" seam. Overcast or serge. Pull the bodice up away from the skirt allowing the back placket to flip to the inside of the bodice.

3. Fold the right side of the bodice/skirt to the inside 3/8". Place buttonholes, snaps or Velcro™ along this fold to hold in place. Place closures along the left side of the back bodice (**fig. 18**). 🞕

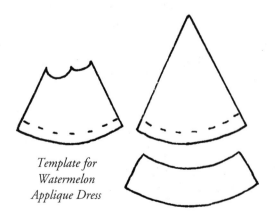

Template for Watermelon Applique Dress

Purple Tulip Shadow Appliqué Dress

Shadow appliqué is absolutely fascinating to me. It looks as if one had shadow embroidered for hours, yes days, and yet it is completely quick and easy. Purple, green and ecru combine to make this a happy dress for any doll that I know. The sleeves are very interesting with purple picot ribbon butted together with ecru French laces to form "striped sleeves." Gathered lace is gathered to the picot ribbon which is used as the cuff of the sleeve. The same picot purple ribbon is stitched on at the dropped waistline and a purple ribbon rosette plus streamer sits happily on the front waistline. The neckline is entredeux with gathered lace. Purple tulips, green leaves and green stems are found on the center front bodice and all around the ecru batiste skirt. Machine entredeux is stitched onto the bottom of the dress attaching the gathered ecru French lace edging while making beautiful stitches. Velcro closes the back of this dress.

Purple Tulip Shadow Appliqué Dress

Fabric Requirements

	Small Body	Medium Body	Large Body
Fabric	1/2 yd.	1/2 yd.	1 yd.
Lace Insertion 5/8"	1-3/4 yds.	2 yds.	3 yds.
Entredeux	1/2 yd.	1/2 yd.	1 yd.
Edging Lace 5/8"	2-1/2 yds.	2-1/2 yds.	3 yds.
Ribbon 1/4"	3 yds.	3 yds.	3 yds.

Shadow Applique Fabric Colors: 1/8 yd. each.

Other Notions: Lightweight sewing thread, and Velcro™, snaps or tiny buttons for back closure.

All Seams 1/4" unless otherwise indicated.

I. Bodice

1. Cut out the bodice front on the fold of the fabric.

2. If selvage fabric is available cut the back bodices with the back edges on the selvage. If the selvage is not available, simply cut out the bodice backs and serge or overcast the back edges of each bodice piece.

3. Place the front bodice to the back bodice pieces, right sides together, at the shoulders. Stitch using a 1/4" seam. Overcast or serge the seam allowance (**fig. 1**).

4. Trace the shadow applique template on the bodice front allowing the highest point of the template to fall 5/8" from the cut edge of the neck. Tulip templates on page 309.

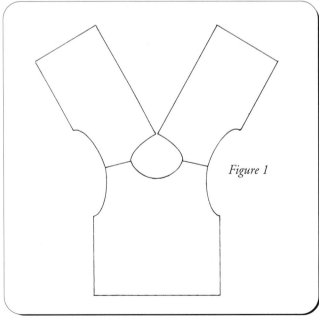

Figure 1

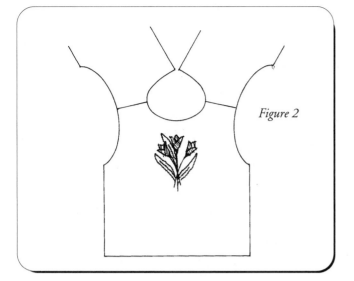

Figure 2

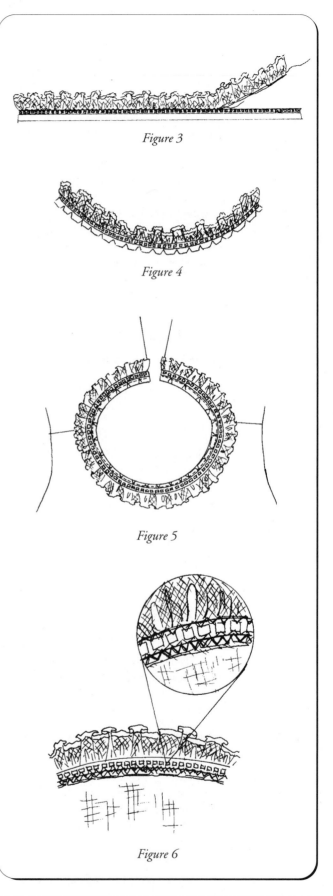

Figure 3

Figure 4

Figure 5

Figure 6

5. Refer to the shadow applique directions in this book for specific directions. Shadow applique the flowers in the following order: flowers and then leaves. Work detail line of the stems and leaves last (**fig. 2**).

II. Neck

1. Cut a strip of entredeux to the neck band measurement given in the chart for the specific doll body to be dressed.

2. Cut a piece of edging lace two times this length and gather to fit the entredeux strip.

3. Trim away one side of the entredeux and attach the gathered edging lace to the trimmed entredeux using the technique entredeux to gathered lace (**fig. 3**).

4. If the fabric edge remaining on the entredeux is not 1/4", trim to 1/4". Clip this fabric so that it will curve along neck edge of the dress (**fig. 4**). Place this strip to the neck of the dress/collar, right sides together. Attach using the technique entredeux to gathered fabric (**fig. 5**).

5. Using a tiny zigzag, tack the seam allowance to the dress. This stitching will keep the entredeux/gathered lace standing up at the neck (**fig. 6**).

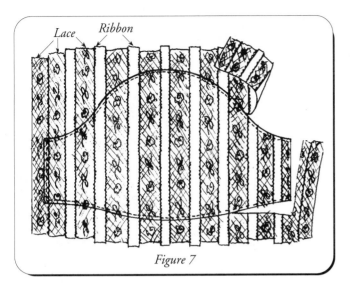

Lace Ribbon

Figure 7

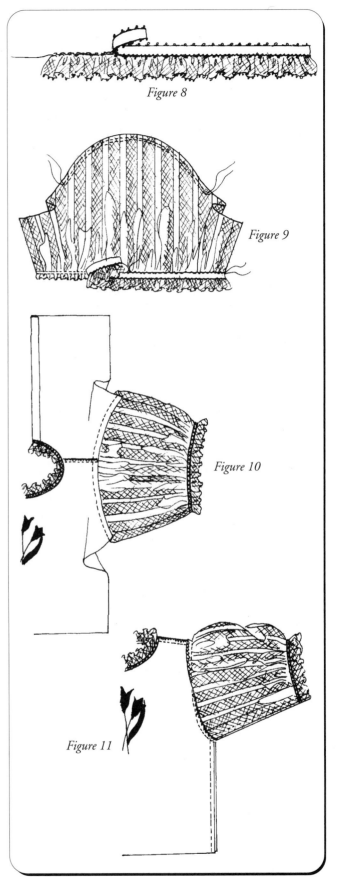

Figure 8

Figure 9

Figure 10

Figure 11

III. Sleeves

1. Measure full sleeve pattern. Create lace and ribbon fabric for the two sleeves by attaching the strips of lace and ribbon together with zigzag. When enough fabric has been created for two sleeves, trace the sleeve pattern on the fabric. Stitch just inside the traced lines. Cut out the sleeves along the pattern lines (**fig.** 7).

2. Place two rows of gathering stitches 1/8" and 1/4" in the top and bottom of the sleeve.

3. Cut two strips of ribbon to the measurement for the specific doll body given on the sleeve band chart. Cut two pieces of edging lace twice the length of the ribbon.

4. Gather the edging lace to fit the ribbon. Place the heading of the gathered lace edging slightly under the ribbon and zigzag in place (**fig.** 8).

5. Gather the bottom of the sleeve to fit the ribbon/edging lace band. Place the ribbon band on top of the gathered sleeve bottom. Stitch in place using a small zigzag. Trim away any excess lace under the band (**fig.** 9).

6. Gather the top of the sleeve to fit the arm opening allowing most of the gathers to fall 3/4" to 1-1/4" on either side of the shoulder seam. Place the sleeve to the arm opening, right sides together, stitch using a 1/4" seam. Overcast or serge the seam allowance (**fig.** 10).

7. Place the sides of the bodice/sleeves right sides together. Stitch, using a 1/4" seam allowance. Overcast or serge the seam allowances (**fig.** 11).

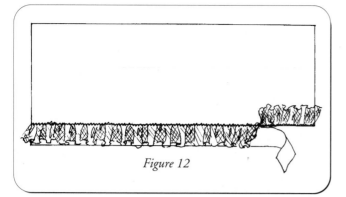

Figure 12

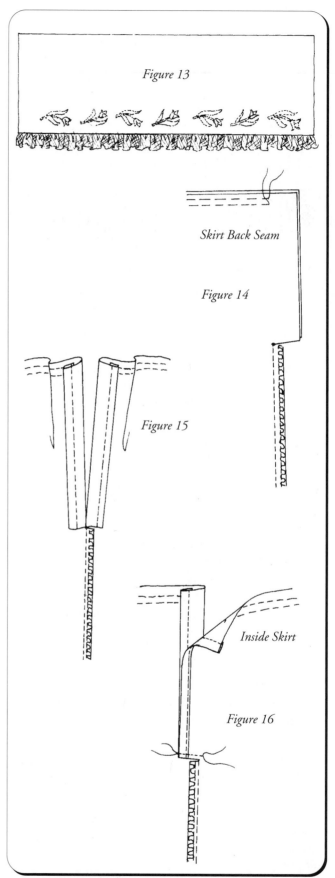

Figure 13

Skirt Back Seam

Figure 14

Figure 15

Inside Skirt

Figure 16

IV. Skirt

1. Refer to the length and width given in the skirt chart for the specific doll body to create the skirt piece. Cut a piece of fabric to this measurement for small and medium dolls. For large dolls cut the skirt to length given on the chart by 45" wide.

2. Gather edging lace to fit one long side of the skirt fabric. Place the edging on top of the fabric with the edge of the lace along the edge of the fabric. Stitch in place along the top of the lace with a small zigzag or wing needle hemstitch. Trim away the excess fabric from under the lace (**fig. 12**).

3. Using a fabric marker, trace the shadow applique design on the skirt. Start by tracing the center of the design in the center front of the skirt. Trace four flowers on either side of the center flower for small and medium dolls and five flowers on either side of the center flower for large dolls (**fig. 13**).

4. Shadow applique the flowers along the template lines as described above in I-step 5.

V. Finishing the Dress

1. Creating the Skirt Placket

   a. Place the back edges of the skirt right sides together, matching entredeux and edging lace. Start stitching from the bottom of the skirt using 1/2" seam. Stop the seam 1-1/2" from the top on a small doll and 2-1/2" from the top on a medium or large doll. Clip across the seam allowance at the end of the stitching (**fig. 14**). Trim the seam allowance along the stitching line to 1/8". Overcast or serge.

   b. Turn each side of the remaining upper seam allowance to the inside 1/8" and stitch in place (**fig. 15**). Place the seam allowances right sides together and stitch 3/8" across the skirt at the end of the opening. This stitching will be made from the inside of the skirt (**fig. 16**). Press to the left side of the skirt.

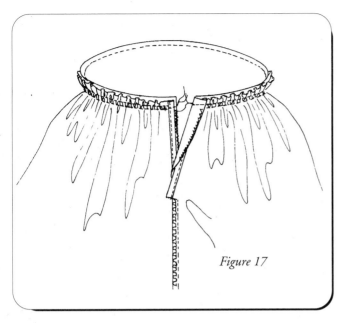

Figure 17

c. From the top of the skirt, fold the right side of the opening 3/8" to the inside. Press in place

2. Mark the center and quarter points of the skirt. Place the skirt to the bodice, right sides together matching the quarter points to the side seams and the center front to the center. Gather the top edge of the skirt to fit the bodice (**fig. 17**). Place the left side of the skirt opening 3/8" from the left edge of the bodice and wrap the bodice over the edge of the skirt. Place the right edge of the skirt opening even with the edge of the bodice (**fig. 18**). Stitch in place using a 1/4" seam. Overcast or serge. Pull the bodice away from the skirt allowing the back placket to flip to the inside of the bodice.

3. Place ribbon along the seam of the bodice and skirt. Top stitch in place using a straight stitch (**fig. 19**).

4. Fold the right side of the bodice/skirt to the inside 3/8". Place buttonholes, snaps or Velcro™ along this fold to hold in place. Place closures along the left side of the back bodice (**fig. 20**).

5. Ribbon rosette - Use a piece of ribbon 1 yd. long.

   Starting 4" or 5" from the end dot the ribbon every 1-1/2". With a hand sewing needle, doubled and knotted thread pick up the dots as shown in (**fig. 21**) creating loops

of ribbon. Stop about 4" or 5" from the end of the ribbon. Take several small stitches on the back of the rosette to hold all the loops in place. Stitch the rosette to the ribbon band to the left of center front. ▨

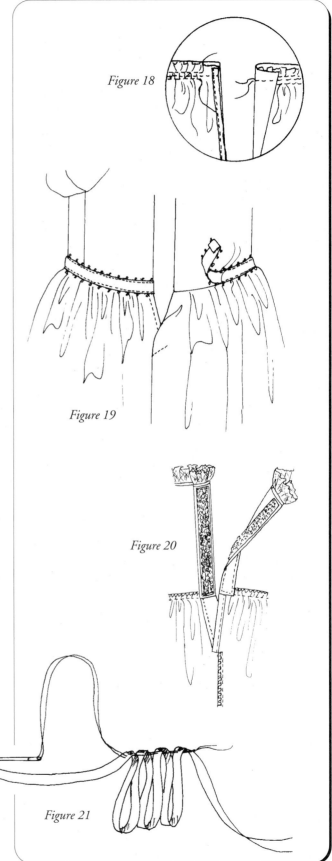

Figure 18

Figure 19

Figure 20

Figure 21

Madeira Appliqué Dress

A doll dressed in this navy linen and ecru Swiss Nelona masterpiece would be ready for a summer picnic or concert in a gazebo. The miniature collar of ecru Nelona has a Madeira appliqué border around it. The neckline is simply trimmed entredeux with navy silk ribbon run through the entredeux holes. The puffed sleeves have an entredeux and straight heavy lace trim. Entredeux attaches the bodice and the skirt of this dress; navy silk ribbon is run through this entredeux also. The gathered skirt has a Madeira design, some machine embroidered teardrops, and a Madeira appliquéd scalloped border. I have always loved Nelona and linen for children's or women's clothing, now doll clothing. Velcro closes the back of this beautiful creation made entirely on the machine.

Fabric Requirements

	Small Body	Medium Body	Large Body
Fabric	1/2 yd.	1/2 yd.	1-1/8 yd.
Applique Fabric	1/3 yd.	1/3 yd.	1/2 yd.
Entredeux	1 yds.	1 yds.	1-1/4 yds.
Tatted Edging	1/4 yd.	1/4 yd.	1/2 yd.
Silk Ribbon (2mm)	3 yds.	3 yds.	4 yds.

Other Notions: Lightweight sewing thread, thread to match applique fabric, water soluble marker, paper stabilizer (if dark applique fabric is used) and Velcro™, snaps or tiny buttons for back closure.

All Seams 1/4" unless otherwise indicated.

I. Bodice

1. Cut out the bodice front on the fold of the fabric.

2. If selvage fabric is available cut the back bodices with the back edges on the selvage. If the selvage is not available, simply cut out the bodice backs and serge or overcast the back edges of each bodice piece.

3. Place the front bodice to the back bodice pieces, right sides together, at the shoulders. Stitch using a 1/4" seam. Overcast or serge the seam allowance (**fig. 1**).

4. Press the back plackets to the inside of the bodice along the fold lines.

II. Collar

1. Trace the collar pattern and the Madeira template on a square of applique fabric. If the applique fabric is dark and the pattern can not be traced easily, layer the collar in the following manner to transfer the pattern and ready the

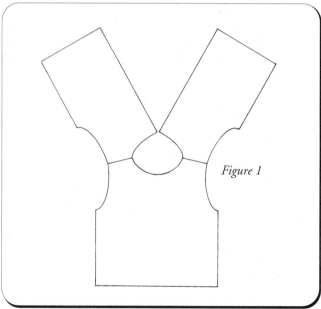

Figure 1

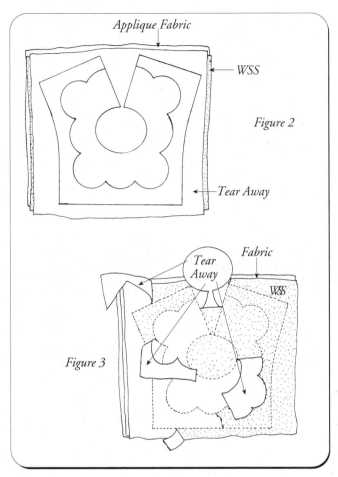

Applique Fabric

WSS

Figure 2

Tear Away

Tear Away

Fabric

WSS

Figure 3

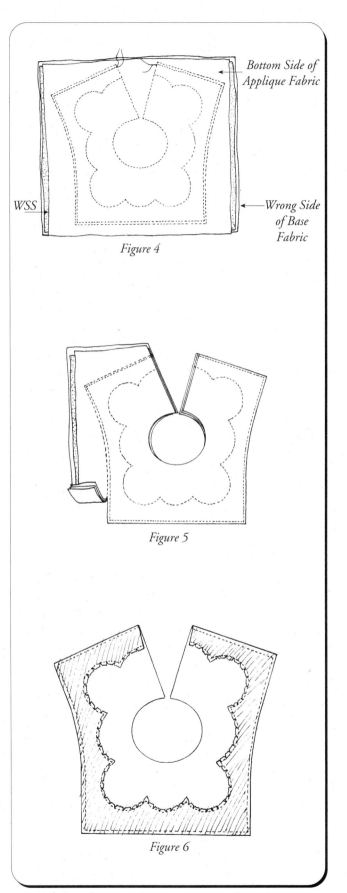

Bottom Side of Applique Fabric

WSS

Wrong Side of Base Fabric

Figure 4

Figure 5

Figure 6

applique fabric for application: applique fabric (right side up), water soluble stabilizer, and paper stabilizer with the traced pattern (**fig. 2**). Pin together. If the pattern can be traced on the applique fabric omit the paper stabilizer layer using just the water soluble stabilizer. The traced pattern should be seen through the water soluble stabilizer. Madeira collar templates on pages 300-304.

2. Stitch, with short straight stitches, around the outer edge, back edges and neck edge of the collar and the Madeira template lines.

3. Carefully tear away the paper stabilizer, if used. The Madeira fabric square and water soluble stabilizer will be left (**fig. 3**).

4. Place the collar fabric square and the applique fabric/WSS square together, with the wrong side of the collar fabric and the water soluble stabilizer side together. Pin in place.

5. With the applique fabric side up, stitch 1/4" inside the cutting line (stitching line sewn in step 2) (**fig. 4**).

6. Trim all layers along the outer stitching line, up the back and around the neck (**fig. 5**).

7. Trim applique fabric and WSS only, 1/8" away from the Madeira template stitching lines. Clip and/or notch the curves corners and points (**fig. 6**).

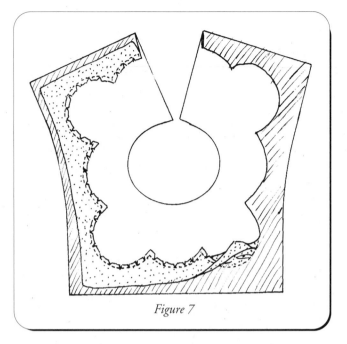

Figure 7

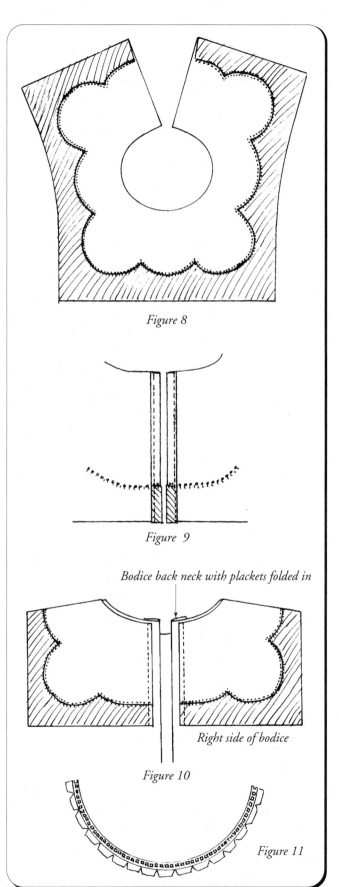

Figure 8

Figure 9

Bodice back neck with plackets folded in

Right side of bodice

Figure 10

Figure 11

8. Turn the applique border fabric to the right side of the collar fabric. The WSS will now be on the outside (**fig. 7**). Use a point turner to ensure sharp points. Pull or trim the WSS from the outer stitching and turn the WSS to the inside of the applique fabric. The WSS will now be between the applique fabric and the collar fabric (**see fig. 7**). The WSS will act as a facing for the applique border making the inside edges easy to turn under. Use a point turner to ensure sharp points. Press well.

9. Pin in place. Use a pinstitch or other desired stitch to attach the top edge of the applique fabric to the collar (**fig. 8**). We used a small pin stitch (blanket stitch) with a wing needle. See machine settings in the technique section of this book for details.

10. Fold the back edges of the collar to the inside 1/8" and 1/8" again. Stitch in place (**fig. 9**).

11. With the back folds folded to the inside of the bodice, place the collar on the bodice with the wrong side of the collar to the right side of the bodice. The finished edges of the collar should fall about 1/4" from the fold lines of the bodice (**fig. 10**).

II. Neck

1. Cut a strip of entredeux to the neck measurement plus 1/4".

2. Trim away one side of the entredeux.

3. If the fabric edge remaining on the entredeux is not 1/4", trim to 1/4". Clip this fabric so that it will curve along neck/collar edge of the dress (**fig. 11**). Place this strip to the

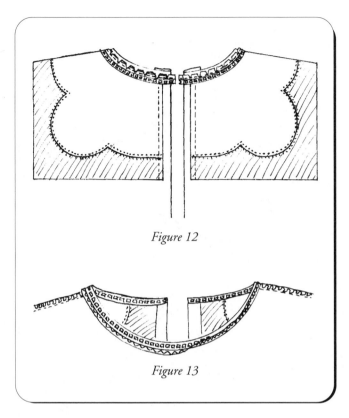

Figure 12

Figure 13

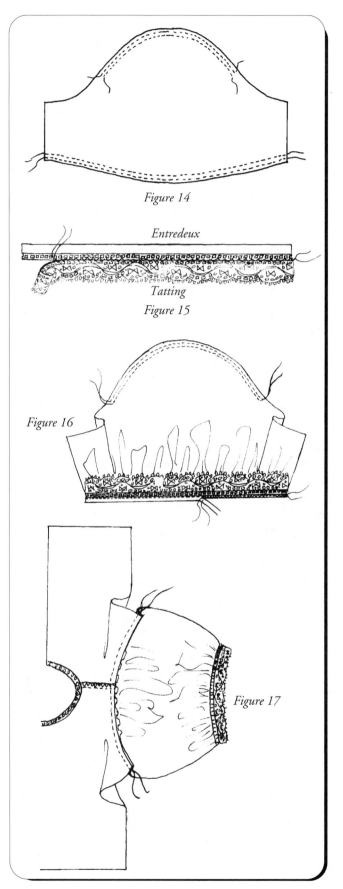

Figure 14

Entredeux

Tatting

Figure 15

Figure 16

Figure 17

neck of the dress/collar, right sides together. Attach using the technique entredeux to fabric (**fig. 12**). Trim the excess entredeux at the back opening even with the bodice.

5. Using a tiny zigzag, tack the seam allowance to the dress. This stitching will keep the entredeux standing up at the neck (**fig. 13**).

III. Sleeves

1. Cut out two sleeves.

2. Place two rows of gathering stitches 1/8" and 1/4" in the top and bottom of the sleeve (**fig. 14**).

3. Cut two strips of entredeux to the measurement for the specific doll body given on the sleeve band chart. Cut two pieces of tatted edging the length of the entredeux.

4. Attach the tatting to the entredeux using the technique entredeux to lace (**fig. 15**).

5. Gather the bottom of the sleeve to fit the entredeux/tatting band. Stitch the band to the sleeve, right sides together, using the technique entredeux to gathered fabric (**fig. 16**).

6. Gather the top of the sleeve to fit the arm opening allowing most of the gathers to fall 3/4" to 1-1/4" on either side of the shoulder seam. Place the sleeve to the arm opening, right sides together, stitch using a 1/4" seam. Overcast or serge the seam allowance (**fig. 17**).

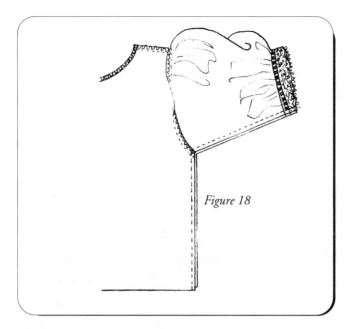

Figure 18

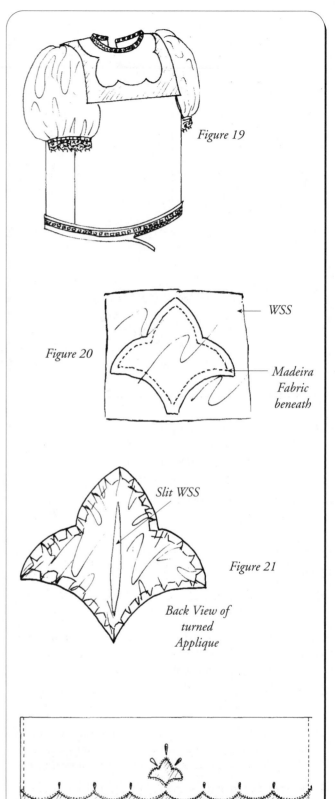

Figure 19

WSS

Figure 20

Madeira
Fabric
beneath

Slit WSS

Figure 21

Back View of
turned
Applique

Figure 22

7. Place the sides of the bodice/sleeves right sides together. Stitch, using a 1/4" seam allowance. Overcast or serge the seam allowances (**fig. 18**).

8. Attach a piece of entredeux along the waistline of the bodice using the technique entredeux to fabric (**fig. 19**).

IV. Skirt

1. Refer to the length and width given in the skirt chart for the specific doll body to create the skirt piece. Cut a piece of fabric 1/4" longer than to this measurement.

2. Attach the Madeira border using the same techniques used on the collar. Madeira skirt templates on page 309.

3. Center skirt design:

Cut out the design from the applique fabric. Place a piece of WSS on the right side of the design. Stitch the WSS to the design using a 1/4" seam allowance (**fig. 20**). Clip the curves and points. Cut a slit in the center of the WSS and turn the design through the slit (**fig. 21**). Use a point turner to ensure sharp points. Press. Place the design in the center front of the skirt. Pin in place. Stitch in place with a pinstitch or other decorative stitch (**fig. 22**).

V. Finishing the Dress

1. Creating the Skirt Placket

    a. Place the back edges of the skirt right sides together, matching borders. Start stitching from the bottom of the skirt using 1/2" seam. Stop the seam 1-1/2" from the top on a small doll and 2-1/2" from the top on a medium or large doll. Clip across the seam allowance

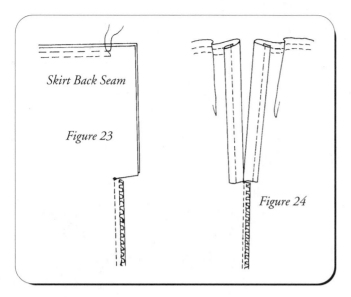

Skirt Back Seam

Figure 23

Figure 24

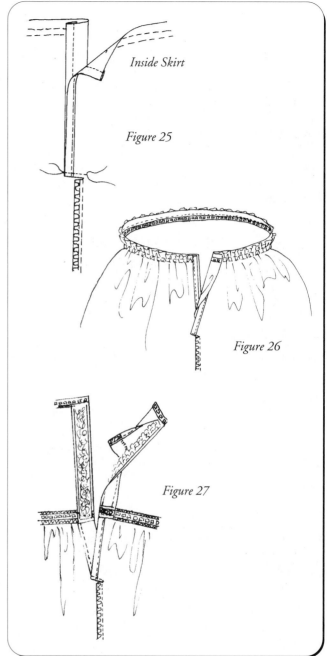

Inside Skirt

Figure 25

Figure 26

Figure 27

at the end of the stitching (**fig. 23**). Trim the seam allowance along the stitching line to 1/8". Overcast or serge.

b. Turn each side of the remaining upper seam allowance to the inside 1/8" and stitch in place (**fig. 24**). Place the seam allowances right sides together and stitch 3/8" across the skirt at the end of the opening. This stitching will be made from the inside of the skirt (**fig. 25**). Press to the left side of the skirt.

c. From the top of the skirt, fold the right side of the opening 3/8" to the inside. Press in place.

2. Mark the center and quarter points of the skirt. Place the skirt to the bodice entredeux, right sides together matching the quarter points to the side seams and the center front to the center. Gather the top edge of the skirt to fit the bodice (**fig. 26**). Place the left side of the skirt opening 3/8" from the left edge of the bodice and wrap the bodice over the edge of the skirt. Place the right edge of the skirt opening even with the edge of the bodice (**see fig. 26**). Stitch in place using a 1/4" seam and the technique entredeux to gathered fabric. Overcast or serge. Pull the bodice away from the skirt allowing the back placket to flip to the inside of the bodice.

3. Fold the right side of the bodice/skirt to the inside 3/8". Place buttonholes, snaps or Velcro™ along this fold to hold in place. Place closures along the left side of the back bodice (**fig. 27**).

4. Cut two pieces of 2mm silk ribbon 10" longer than the arm band measurement. Thread (over two entredeux bars and under two bars) through the arm entredeux beginning and ending at the center front of the sleeve. Tie excess into bows. Trim the ends of the bows as desired and apply a fabric sealant to the ends of to keep the silk ribbon from fraying.

5. Cut a piece of ribbon 10" longer than the neck measurement. Cut this ribbon in half. Start threading (over two entredeux bars and under two bars) each piece of ribbon at the center front through the neck entredeux. Tack the ends of the ribbons at each back opening. Tie excess ribbon into a bow at the center front. Trim the ends of the bows as desired and apply a fabric sealant to the ends to keep the silk ribbon from fraying.

6. Cut the remaining ribbon in half. Thread through the waist entredeux using the same technique described in step 5. The bow is tied to the left of the center front. ▨

Shark's Teeth Doll Dress

With the popularity of shark's teeth for women's and children's clothing, our doll thought she would love a dress also. Ecru Swiss Nelona is the base fabric with double shark's teeth trim down the front and single sharks teeth on the skirt. Swiss embroidered ecru trim is the bottom treatment of this beautiful skirt. Entredeux finishes the sleeves and neckline of the dress; green silk ribbon is run through the entredeux. Double entredeux edged Swiss beading trim has olive green silk ribbon run through it also. Velcro finishes the back of this little shark's teeth dress.

Fabric Requirements

	Small Body	Medium Body	Large Body
Dress Fabric	2/3 yd.	2/3 yd.	1 yd.
Entredeux	1/2 yd.	1/2 yd.	2/3 yd.
Entredeux/Beading	1/2 yd.	1/2 yd.	2/3 yd.
Edging Lace (1/2")	1 yd.	1 yd.	1-1/4 yds.
Embroidered Edging (2")	1 yd.	1 yd.	1-1/4 yds.
Silk Ribbon - 4mm	3 yds.	2 yds.	3-1/2 yds.

Other Notions: Lightweight sewing thread, decorative thread, and Velcro™, snaps or tiny buttons for back closure.

All Seams 1/4" unless otherwise indicated.

I. Bodice

1. Cut a rectangle of base fabric 1/2" longer and 5" wider than the rectangle measurement given in the bodice chart for your specific doll body. Shark's teeth template on page 310.

2. Shark's Teeth - Refer to shark's teeth directions in this book for general directions. Fold the rectangle in half and mark the fold. This is the center front. Measure and mark lines 1-1/8" on each side from the center front line (**fig. 1**). Fold, wrong sides together on these 1-1/8" lines and stitch 3/4" from the folds. Open the tuck and press the fold line of the tuck to the stitching line of the tuck creating a box pleat. Stitch down the center of the box pleats creating two 3/8" pleats side by side on each of the box pleats (**fig. 2**).

3. Place clips 3/4" apart along each of the four tucks. These clips should line up across the tucks. Clip from the fold to the stitching in the center of the box pleat (**fig. 3**).

Shark's Teeth

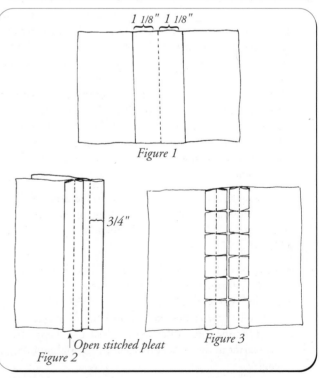

1 1/8" 1 1/8"

Figure 1

3/4"

↑ *Open stitched pleat*

Figure 2

Figure 3

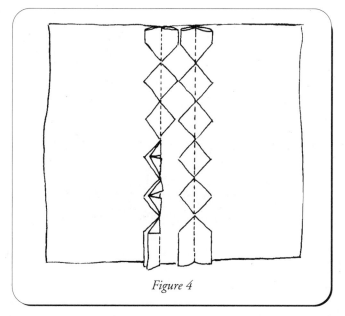

Figure 4

4. Fold each side of the clip to the back of the tuck creating a point (**fig. 4**). Glue stick can be used to hold the fold in place. When all folds are made, press.

5. Top stitch just inside the stitching line of the box pleat with a zigzag, pinstitch, blanket stitch or any other decorative stitch (**fig. 5**). This stitch should catch the ends or cut edges of the clips, tacking the folds in place. Repeat for all tucks.

6. Press. Cut out the bodice front centering the teeth in the center of the pattern (**fig. 6**).

7. If selvage fabric is available, cut the back bodices with the back edges on the selvage. If the selvage is not available, simply cut out the bodice backs and serge or overcast the back edges of each bodice piece.

8. Place the front bodice to the back bodice pieces, right sides together, at the shoulders. Stitch using a 1/4" seam. Overcast or serge the seam allowance (**fig. 7**).

II. Neck

1. Cut a strip of entredeux to the neck band measurement given in the chart for the specific doll body to be dressed.

2 Cut a piece of 1/2" edging lace two times this length and gather to fit the entredeux strip.

3. Trim away one side of the entredeux and attach the gathered edging lace to the trimmed entredeux using the technique entredeux to gathered lace (**fig. 8**).

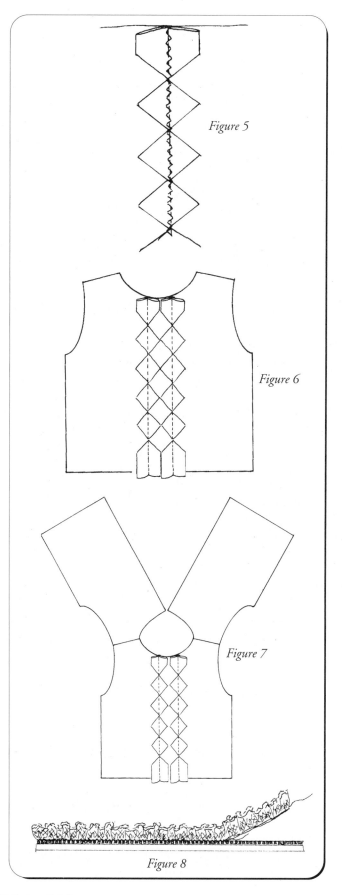

Figure 5

Figure 6

Figure 7

Figure 8

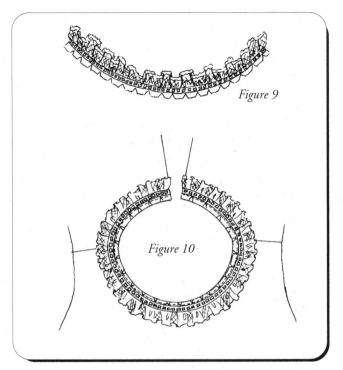

Figure 9

Figure 10

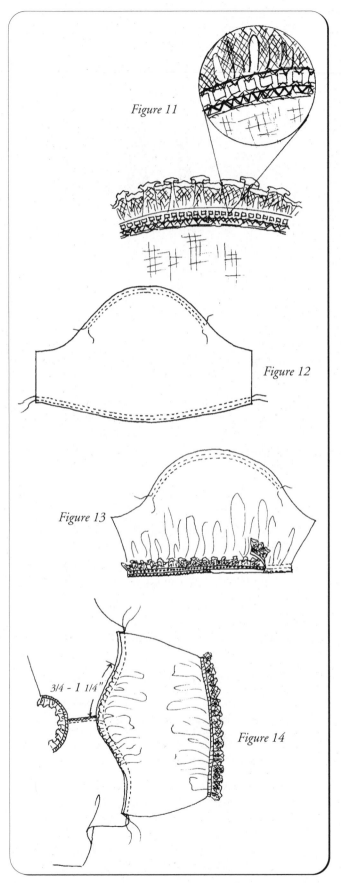

Figure 11

Figure 12

Figure 13

3/4 - 1 1/4"

Figure 14

4. If the fabric edge remaining on the entredeux is not already 1/4", trim to 1/4". Clip this fabric so that it will curve along neck edge of the dress (**fig. 9**). Place this strip to the neck of the dress right sides together. Attach using the technique entredeux to fabric (**fig. 10**).

5. Using a tiny zigzag, tack the seam allowance to the dress. This stitching will keep the entredeux/gathered lace standing up at the neck (**fig. 11**).

III. Sleeves

1. Cut out two sleeves.

2. Place two rows of gathering stitches 1/8" and 1/4" in the top and bottom of the sleeve (**fig. 12**).

3. Cut two strips of entredeux to the measurement for the specific doll body given on the sleeve band chart. Cut two pieces of edging lace twice the length of the entredeux.

4. Gather the edging lace to fit the entredeux. Stitch together using the technique entredeux to gathered lace see figure 9.

5. Gather the bottom of the sleeve to fit the entredeux/edging lace band. Stitch the band to the sleeve, right sides together, using the technique entredeux to gathered fabric (**fig. 13**).

6. Gather the top of the sleeve to fit the arm opening allowing most of the gathers to fall 3/4" to 1-1/4" on either side of the shoulder seam. Place the sleeve to the arm opening, right sides together, stitch using a 1/4" seam. Overcast or serge the seam allowance (**fig. 14**).

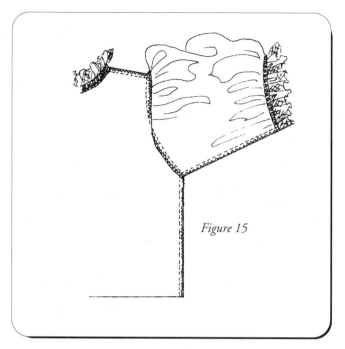

Figure 15

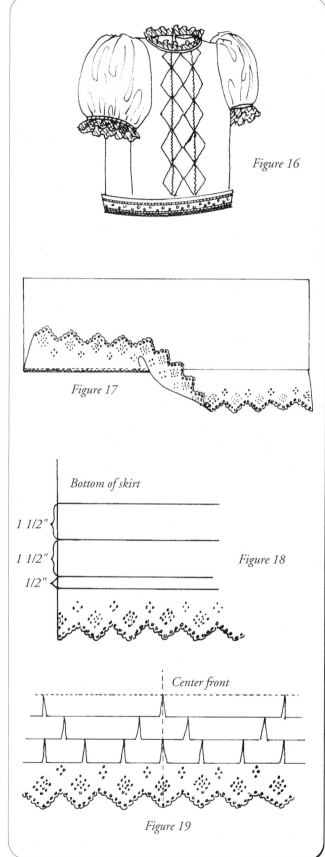

Figure 16

Figure 17

Figure 18

Bottom of skirt

1 1/2"

1 1/2"

1/2"

Center front

Figure 19

7. Place the sides of the bodice/sleeves right sides together. Stitch, using a 1/4" seam allowance. Overcast or serge the seam allowances (**fig. 15**).

8. Attach entredeux beading to the lower edge of the bodice using the technique entredeux to fabric (**fig. 16**).

IV. Skirt

1. Refer to the length and width given in the skirt chart for the specific doll body to create the skirt piece. Add 1-1/2" to the length of the skirt.

2. Cut a piece of fabric to this measurement. Stitch the embroidered edging to one long side of the skirt using a 1/4" seam (**fig. 17**). Overcast or serge the seam allowance. Press the seam toward the skirt. The skirt should measure the length stated in the chart plus 3 inches.

3. For the first tuck measure and mark 1/2" from the seam of the skirt and edging. Measure and mark 1-1/2" from the first line for the second tuck and 1-1/2" from the second line for the third tuck (**fig. 18**). Fold, wrong sides together, along the marked lines. Stitch 1/2" from each fold. Press the tucks toward the edging. Clip the bottom tuck starting in the center front, every 1 inch. Place the pyramid template (1/2" tucks) for shark's teeth in under the tucks to mark the remaining clips (**fig. 19**). (Refer to shark's teeth directions.)

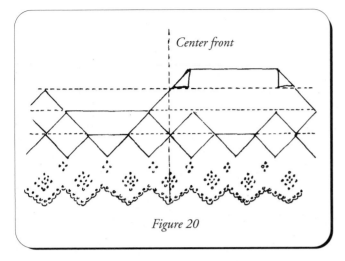

Center front

Figure 20

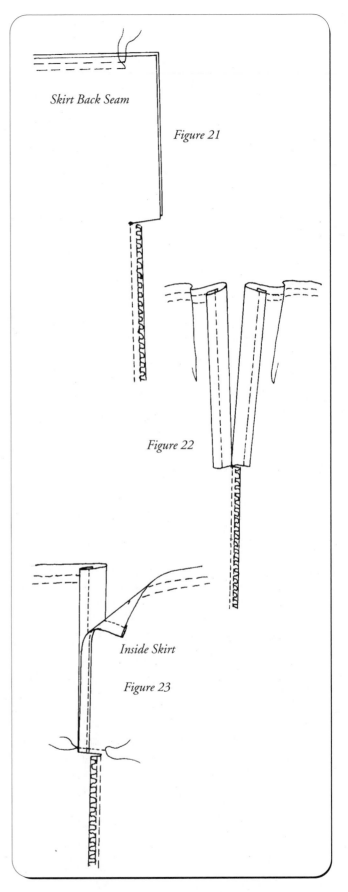

Skirt Back Seam

Figure 21

Figure 22

Inside Skirt

Figure 23

4. Follow the directions given for the bodice shark's teeth steps 4 and 5 to complete (**fig. 20**).

5. Run two gathering rows at 1/4" and 1/8" in the top edge of the skirt piece starting and stopping 1/2" from the back edges.

V. Finishing the Dress

1. Creating the Skirt Placket

    a. Place the back edges of the skirt right sides together. Make sure the gathered ribbon on the skirt lines up at the seam. Start stitching from the bottom of the skirt using 1/2" seam. Stop the seam 1-1/2" from the top on a small doll and 2-1/2" from the top on a medium or large doll. Clip across the seam allowance at the end of the stitching. Trim the seam allowance along the stitching line to 1/8". Overcast or serge (**fig. 21**).

    b. Turn each side of the remaining upper seam allowance to the inside 1/8" and stitch in place (**fig. 22**). Place the seam allowances right sides together and stitch 3/8" across the skirt at the end of the opening. This stitching will be made from the inside of the skirt (**fig. 23**). Press to the left side of the skirt.

    c. From the top of the skirt, fold the right hand side of the opening 3/8" to the inside. Press in place.

2. Mark the center and quarter points of the skirt. Place the skirt to the entredeux beading of the bodice, right sides together matching the quarter points to the side seams and the center front to the center. Gather the top edge of the

Figure 24

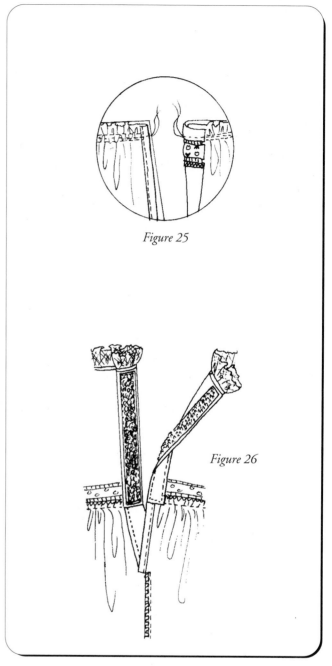

Figure 25

Figure 26

skirt to fit the entredeux beading (**fig. 24**). Place the left side of the skirt opening 3/8" from the left edge of the bodice and wrap the bodice over the edge of the skirt. Place the right edge of the skirt opening even with the edge of the bodice (**fig. 25**). Stitch in place using a 1/4" seam using the technique entredeux to gathered fabric. Overcast or serge. Pull the bodice up away from the skirt allowing the back placket to flip to the inside of the bodice.

3. Fold the right side of the bodice/skirt to the inside 3/8". Place buttonholes, snaps or Velcro™ along this fold to hold in place. Place closures along the left side of the back bodice (**fig. 26**).

4. Cut two pieces of 2mm silk ribbon 10" longer than the arm band measurement. Thread (over two entredeux bars and under two bars) through the arm entredeux beginning and ending at the center front of the sleeve. Tie excess into bows. Trim the ends of the bows as desired and apply a fabric sealant to the ends of to keep the silk ribbon from fraying.

5. Cut a piece of ribbon 10" longer than the neck measurement. Cut this ribbon in half. Start threading (over two entredeux bars and under two bars) each piece of ribbon at the center front through the neck entredeux. Tack the ends of the ribbons at each back opening. Tie excess ribbon into a bow at the center front. Trim the ends of the bows as desired and apply a fabric sealant to the ends to keep the silk ribbon from fraying.

6. Use the remaining ribbon to thread through the waist beading. ▩

Australian Windowpane Dress

Pink and peach used together have long fascinated my color sense. Loaded with sewing intricacies, this dress begins with a basic pink Nelona dropped waisted dress. The sleeves are of ecru organdy with peachy machine trim running horizontally around the sleeve. Entredeux and gathered lace trims both the neckline and the bottom of the sleeve. Gathered French edging makes almost a little collar at the neckline. A tied lace shaped bow is on the skirt center front; organdy peach butterflies flutter on either side of the lace bow; a double winged peachy organdy butterfly is at the bottom. All the butterflies use the Australian Windowpane Technique. Sweet scallops are formed by lace insertion and gathered lace is at the bottom of the scallops. A little machine embroidered butterfly perches at the top of each of the scallops all the way around to the back of the dress. The back of the dress closes with Velcro.

Australian Windowpane Dress

Fabric Requirements

	Small Body	Medium Body	Large Body
Dress Fabric	1/2 yd.	1/2 yd.	2/3 yd.
Organdy	1/4 yd.	1/4 yd.	1/4 yd.
Entredeux	1/2 yd.	1/2 yd.	2/3 yd.
Edging Lace (3/8")	3 yds.	3-1/4 yds.	5 yd.
Edging Lace (1-1/2")	1/2 yd.	2/3 yd.	1 yd.
Insertion Lace (3/8"	2 yds.	2 yds.	4 yds.

Other Notions: Lightweight sewing thread, decorative thread for Australian windowpane, and Velcro™, snaps or tiny buttons for back closure.

All Seams 1/4" unless otherwise indicated.

I. Bodice

1. Cut out the bodice front from the fold of the fabric.

2. If selvage fabric is available, cut the back bodices with the back edges on the selvage. If the selvage is not available, simply cut out the bodice backs and serge or overcast the back edges of each bodice piece.

3. Place the front bodice to the back bodice pieces, right sides together, at the shoulders. Stitch using a 1/4" seam. Overcast or serge the seam allowance (**fig. 1**).

II. Neck

1. Cut a strip of entredeux to the neck band measurement given in the chart for the specific doll body to be dressed.

2. Cut a piece of 3/8" edging lace two times this length and gather to fit the entredeux strip.

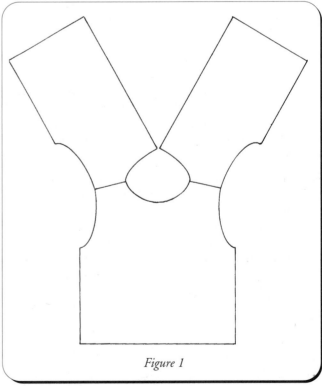

Figure 1

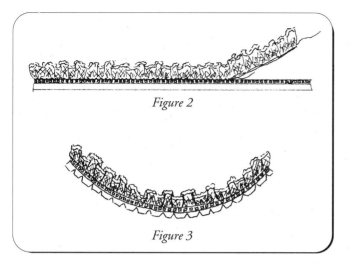

Figure 2

Figure 3

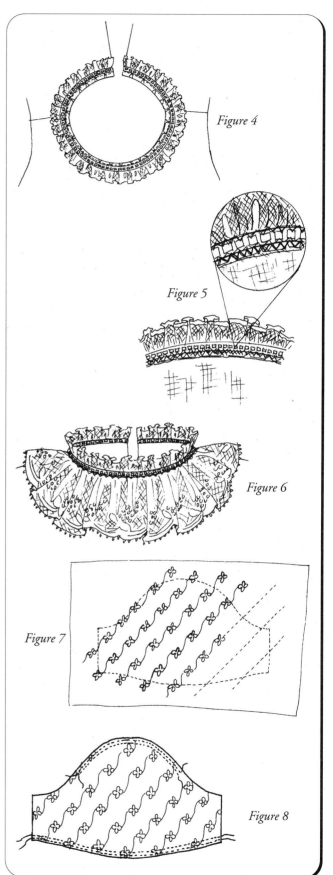

Figure 4

Figure 5

Figure 6

Figure 7

Figure 8

3. Trim away one side of the entredeux and attach the gathered edging lace to the trimmed entredeux using the technique entredeux to gathered lace (**fig. 2**).

4. If the fabric edge remaining on the entredeux is not already 1/4", trim to 1/4". Clip this fabric so that it will curve along neck edge of the dress (**fig. 3**). Place this strip to the neck of the dress right sides together. Attach using the technique entredeux to fabric (**fig. 4**).

5. Using a tiny zigzag, tack the seam allowance to the dress. This stitching will keep the entredeux/gathered lace standing up at the neck (**fig. 5**).

6. Gather the wide edging to fit the lower edge of the neck entredeux. Attach by butting the wide edging to the lower edge of the entredeux. Zigzag in place (**fig. 6**).

III. Sleeves

1. Trace the complete sleeve patterns on the organdy fabric. Draw diagonal lines about 1" apart. Stitch a decorative stitch along these lines to decorate the organdy (**fig. 7**). A butterfly motif stitch was used on the sample dress. Cut out two sleeves.

2. Place two rows of gathering stitches 1/8" and 1/4" in the top and bottom of the sleeve (**fig. 8**).

3. Cut two strips of entredeux to the measurement for the specific doll body given on the sleeve band chart. Cut two pieces of edging lace twice the length of the entredeux.

4. Gather the edging lace to fit the entredeux. Stitch together using the technique entredeux to gathered lace see figure 2.

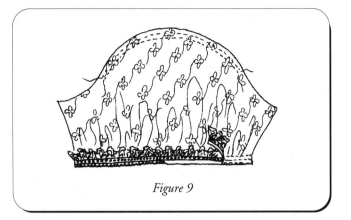

Figure 9

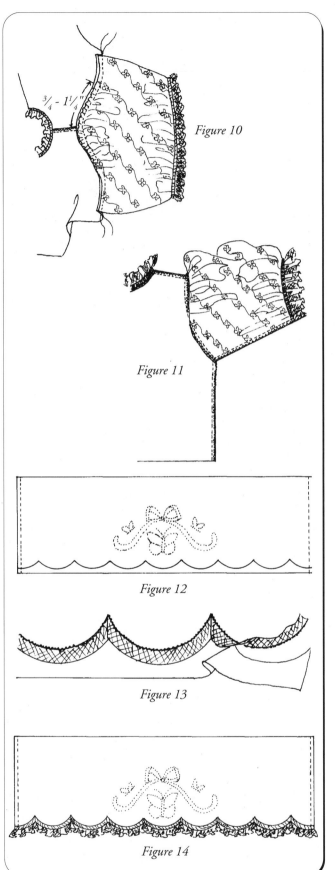

Figure 10

Figure 11

Figure 12

Figure 13

Figure 14

5. Gather the bottom of the sleeve to fit the entredeux/edging lace band. Stitch the band to the sleeve, right sides together, using the technique entredeux to gathered fabric (**fig. 9**).

6. Gather the top of the sleeve to fit the arm opening allowing most of the gathers to fall 3/4" to 1-1/4" on either side of the shoulder seam. Place the sleeve to the arm opening, right sides together, stitch using a 1/4" seam. Overcast or serge the seam allowance (**fig. 10**).

7. Place the sides of the bodice/sleeves right sides together. Stitch, using a 1/4" seam allowance. Overcast or serge the seam allowances (**fig. 11**).

IV. Skirt

1. Refer to the length and width given in the skirt chart for the specific doll body to create the skirt piece.

2. Cut a piece of fabric to this measurement. Trace the scallop template 3/8" from the bottom of the skirt. Trace butterflies and lace bow template for your doll body 1/2" above the scalloped lace (**fig. 12**). Templates on page 308.

3. Shape insertion lace along the top of the scalloped lace template line following the instructions under lace shaping/lace scallops. Stitch in place using a small zigzag along the upper edge of the lace. Trim the excess fabric behind the lace (**fig. 13**).

4. Gather lace edging for the skirt bottom. Stitch by butting the gathered edging to the lace insertion and zigzagging in place (**fig. 14**).

5. Work the butterflies using the instructions under the Australian Windowpane section of this book.

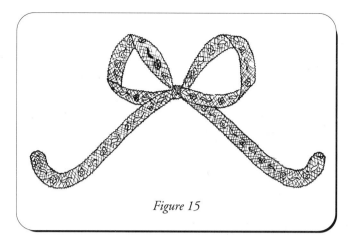

Figure 15

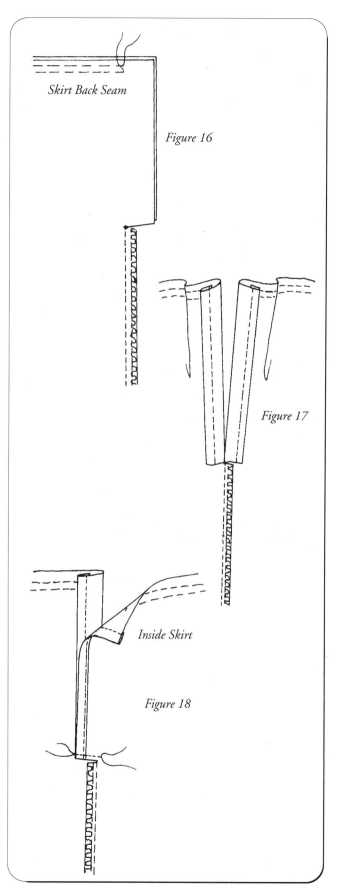

Skirt Back Seam

Figure 16

Figure 17

Inside Skirt

Figure 18

6. Shape the lace bow and stitch in place following this book's directions under lace shaping. Trim the fabric from behind (**fig. 15**).

7. Decorative machine stitching may be added above the lace scallop points, if desired.

8. Run two gathering rows at 1/4" and 1/8" in the top edge of the skirt piece starting and stopping 1/2" from the back edges.

───── V. Finishing the Dress ─────

1. Creating the Skirt Placket

   a. Place the back edges of the skirt right sides together. Make sure the lace scallop on the skirt lines up at the seam. Start stitching from the bottom of the skirt using 1/2" seam. Stop the seam 1-1/2" from the top on a small doll and 2-1/2" from the top on a medium or large doll. Clip across the seam allowance at the end of the stitching. Trim the seam allowance along the stitching line to 1/8". Overcast or serge (**fig. 16**).

   b. Turn each side of the remaining upper seam allowance to the inside 1/8" and stitch in place (**fig. 17**). Place the seam allowances right sides together and stitch 3/8" across the skirt at the end of the opening. This stitching will be made from the inside of the skirt (**fig. 18**). Press to the left side of the skirt.

   c. From the top of the skirt, fold the right hand side of the opening 3/8" to the inside. Press in place.

2. Mark the center and quarter points of the skirt. Place the skirt to the bodice, right sides together matching the quarter points to the side seams and the center front to the

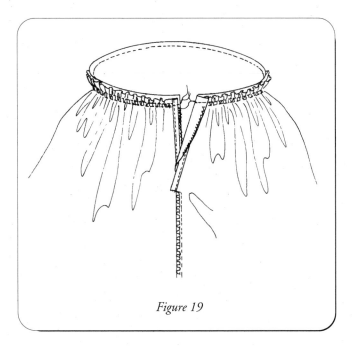

Figure 19

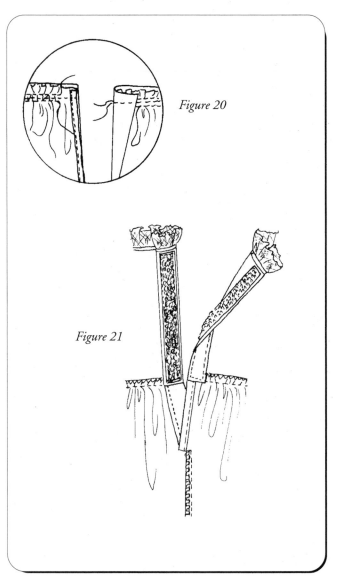

Figure 20

Figure 21

center. Gather the top edge of the skirt to fit the bodice (**fig. 19**). Place the left side of the skirt opening 3/8" from the left edge of the bodice and wrap the bodice over the edge of the skirt. Place the right edge of the skirt opening even with the edge of the bodice (**fig. 20**). Stitch in place using a 1/4" seam. Overcast or serge. Pull the bodice up away from the skirt allowing the back placket to flip to the inside of the bodice.

3.   Fold the right side of the bodice/skirt to the inside 3/8". Place buttonholes, snaps or Velcro™ along this fold to hold in place. Place closures along the left side of the back bodice (**fig. 21**). ▨

Smocked Dress with Tatted Trim

Yellow dotted Swiss fabric is perky and pretty in this dress which just breathes spring. Dotted Swiss fabric brings back childhood memories since I can remember several beautiful dresses of this fabric that my mother made for me. The round portrait collar has lavender embroidered flowers and a shadow work bow in the center. The little leaves and stems, of course, are green. The puffed sleeves are smocked with yellow and they feature ecru tatted trim as does the round collar. There is a tiny bits of white piping at the bottom of the bodice and yellow geometric smocking pulls in the gathers of this beautiful skirt. Velcro is used to close the back of the dress.

Smocked Dress with Tatted Trim

Fabric Requirements

	Small Body	Medium Body	Large Body
Fabric	1/2 yd.	1/2 yd.	3/4 yd.
Fabric - (for collar)	1/8 yd.	1/4 yd.	3/8 yd.
Tatting (3/8")	1 yd.	1-1/4 yd.	1-1/2 yds.

Other Notions: Lightweight sewing thread, baby piping, floss for smocking/embroidery and Velcro™, snaps or tiny buttons for back closure.

All Seams 1/4" unless otherwise indicated.

I. Bodice

1. Cut out the front bodice on a fold.

2. If selvage fabric is available cut the back bodices with the back edges on the selvage. If the selvage is not available, simply cut out the bodice backs and serge or overcast the back edges of each bodice piece.

3. Place the front bodice to the back bodice pieces, right sides together, at the shoulders. Stitch using a 1/4" seam. Overcast or serge the seam allowance (**fig. 1**).

II. Collar

1. Trace one full collar on fabric large enough to fit in an embroidery hoop. Trace and stitch embroidery design in the center of the collar front (**fig. 2**). Cut out the collar. Cut a second collar to use as the lining. Place the lining to the collar, right sides together. Template on page 102. Collar patterns on pages 294-295. Stitch in place along collar

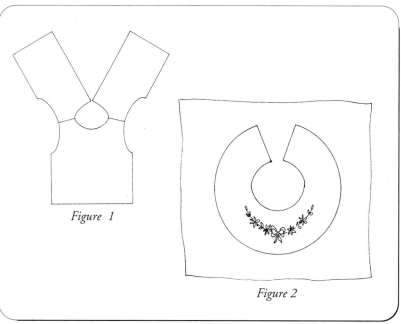

Figure 1

Figure 2

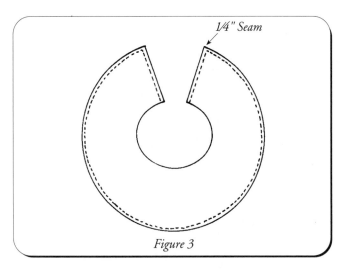

Figure 3

edge and up the collar back using a 1/4" seam (**fig. 3**). Clip and turn to the right side and press. Stitch tatting along the lower edge of the collar with a small zigzag (**fig. 4**).

2. Place the wrong side of the collar to the right side of the dress. Pin in place.

3. Cut a bias strip 1" wide by the length of neck band measurement given in the neck band chart. Fold the bias strip in half and press. Place the cut edges of the strip to the neck of the collar/dress. Cut the ends of the strip off 3/8" from each side of the back bodice edges.

4. Flip the back bodice edges to the outside 3/8" under the folded bias strip. Stitch along the neck edge and along the bias strip using a 1/4" seam (**fig. 5**). Trim the seam allowance to 1/8". Flip the bias strip and the back bodice edges to the inside of the bodice. Hand stitch the bias strip in place finishing the neck edge (**fig. 6**).

III. Sleeves

1. Add 1" to the bottom of the sleeve pattern. Cut out two sleeves.

2. Attach tatting lace to the bottom of each sleeve using the technique lace to fabric. Press tatting away from the sleeve. Re-zigzag on top of the seam allowance tacking it to the sleeve. This will keep the tatting from flipping up (**fig. 7**).

3. Pleat the sleeve with two rows of pleating 1" from the sleeve bottom. Smock, using the sleeve design, starting and stopping 1-1/8" from the side of the sleeve.

Embroidery Template for Smocked Doll Dress

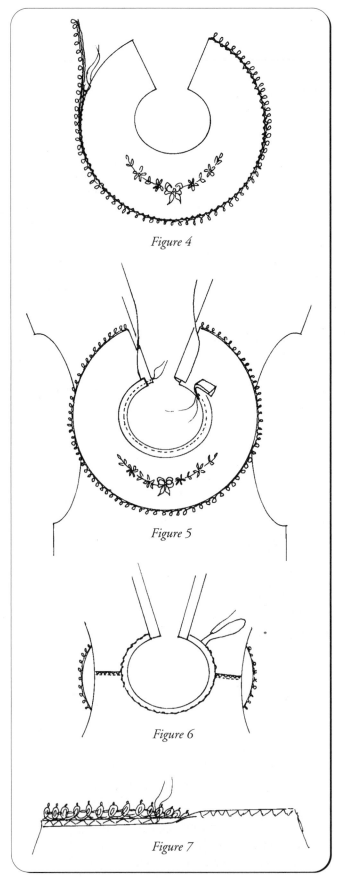

Figure 4

Figure 5

Figure 6

Figure 7

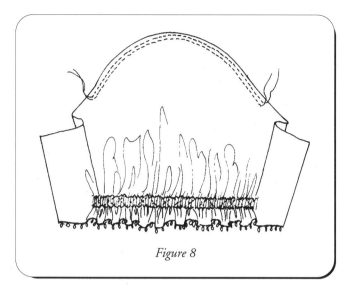

Figure 8

4. Place two rows of gathering stitches 1/8" and 1/4" in the top of the sleeve (**fig. 8**).

5. Gather the top of the sleeve to fit the arm opening allowing most of the gathers to fall 3/4" to 1-1/4" on either side of the shoulder seam. Place the sleeve to the arm opening, right sides together, stitch using a 1/4" seam. Overcast or serge the seam allowance (**fig. 9**).

6. Place the sides of the bodice/sleeves right sides together. Stitch, using a 1/4" seam allowance. Overcast or serge the seam allowances (**fig. 10**).

7. Attach piping along the lower edge of the bodice (**fig. 11**).

IV. Skirt

1. Refer to the length and width given in the skirt chart for the specific doll body to create the skirt piece. Add 1-1/4" to the length of the small doll skirt, 2-1/4" of the length of the medium doll skirt and 3-1/4" to the length of the large doll skirt.

2. Pleat the top edge of the skirt with 4 rows of pleating. Smock on the bottom three rows using the smocking design for the skirt. The first row of pleating will be used as a gathering row (**fig. 12**). Smocking design on page 293.

V. Finishing the Dress

1. Creating the Skirt Placket

Note: The placket can be omitted if desired. The dress is much easier to get on and off if a placket is used.

   a. Place the back edges of the skirt right sides together. Start stitching from the bottom of the skirt using 1/2" seam. Stop the seam 1-1/2" from the top on a small doll and 2-1/2" from the top on a medium or large

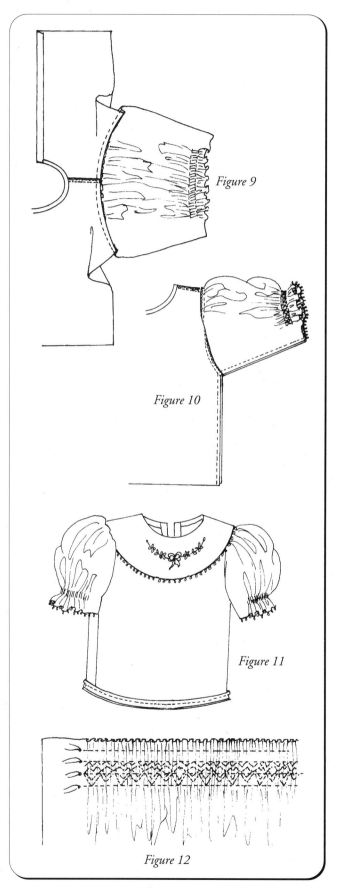

Figure 9

Figure 10

Figure 11

Figure 12

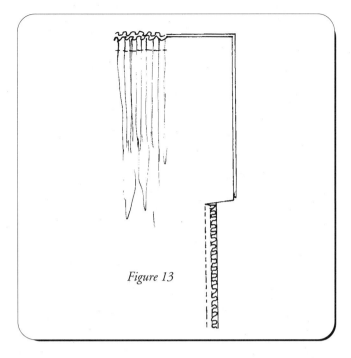

Figure 13

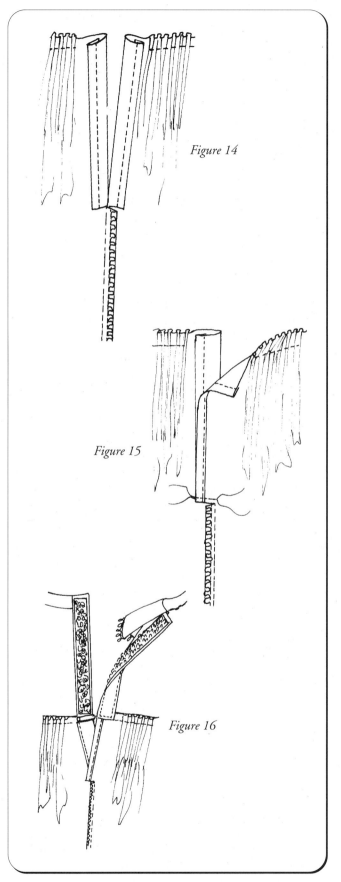

Figure 14

Figure 15

Figure 16

doll. Clip across the seam allowance at the end of the stitching (**fig. 13**). Trim the seam allowance along the stitching line to 1/8". Overcast or serge.

b. Turn each side of the remaining upper seam allowance to the inside 1/8" and stitch in place (**fig. 14**). Place the seam allowances right sides together and stitch 3/8" across the skirt at the end of the opening. This stitching will be made from the inside of the skirt (**fig. 15**). Press to the left side of the skirt.

c. From the top of the skirt fold the right hand side of the opening 3/8" to the inside. Press in place.

2. Mark the center and quarter points of the skirt. Place the skirt to the bodice entredeux, right sides together matching the quarter points to the side seams and the center front to the center. Gather the top edge of the skirt to fit the bodice entredeux. Place the left side of the skirt opening 3/8" from the left edge of the bodice and wrap the bodice over the edge of the skirt. Place the right edge of the skirt opening even with the edge of the bodice. Stitch in place so that the first row of smocking falls under the bodice piping. Overcast or serge. Pull the bodice up away from the skirt allowing the back placket to flip to the inside of the bodice.

3. Fold the right side of the bodice/skirt to the inside 3/8".

4. Hem the dress by folding the edge 1/4" to the inside and again 1" for the small dolls, again 2" for the medium dolls and again 3" for the large dolls.

5. Buttonholes, snaps or Velcro™ should be placed along the back openings to hold the folds in place (**fig. 16**). ❈

Diamond Lace Pintucks Dress

The women's version of this dress is featured in my book, *Heirloom Sewing For Women*; it is just as beautiful used for a woman or a child as it is for this beautiful doll. The dress has a medley of assorted sewing techniques. Using blue and white Swiss Nelona, the skirt features both colors of fabric. Two rows of lace diamonds are interspersed with mitered pintucks made with a double needle. Flat lace is stitched on the bottom and it is mitered at the diamond points. The collar has a deep V in the front with little inserts of blue batiste stitched with three rows of double needle pintucks. Tiny lace insertion and flat lace mitered at the corners finish the edge of the collar. The elbow length sleeves have a bias binding. A beautiful blue Swiss batiste sash is gathered and stitched to the dress at the side seams. Velcro closes the back of this dress.

Fabric Requirements

	Small Body	Medium Body	Large Body
Fabric	5/8 yd.	5/8 yd.	1 yd.
Fabric (second color)	1/4 yd.	1/4 yd.	3/8 yd.

Note: Lace requirements and templates in this pattern are for the following doll bodies: Small (as stated in chart), Medium (as stated in chart plus FB17, FB19 and MB190), Large (MB21.5 and GB21)

Lace Insertion A (3/8")	2-1/2 yds.	1/3 yd.	1 yd.
Lace Insertion B (3/8")	1 yd.	1 yd.	—
Lace Insertion C (5/8")	—	3-1/2 yds.	4 yds.
Lace Insertion D (5/8")	—	1 yd.	1-1/2 yd.
Lace Insertion E (3/4")	—	—	1-1/2 yds.
Edging Lace (5/8")	—	2 yds.	4 yds.
Edging Lace (3/8")	2-1/2 yds.	1 yd.	—
Silk Ribbon (7 mm)	1/3 yd.	1/3 yd.	1/3 yd.

Other Notions: Lightweight sewing thread, and Velcro™, snaps or tiny buttons for back closure.

All Seams 1/4" unless otherwise indicated.

I. Bodice

1. Cut out the front bodice on a fold.

2. If selvage fabric is available cut the back bodices with the back edges on the selvage. If the selvage is not available, simply cut out the bodice backs and serge or overcast the back edges of each bodice piece.

3. Place the front bodice to the back bodice pieces, right sides together, at the shoulders. Stitch using a 1/4" seam. Overcast or serge the seam allowance (**fig. 1**).

Diamond Lace Pintucks Dress

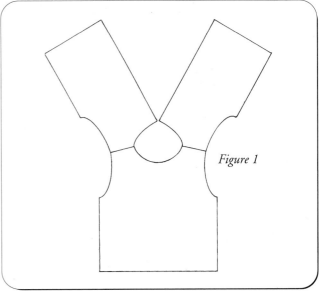

Figure 1

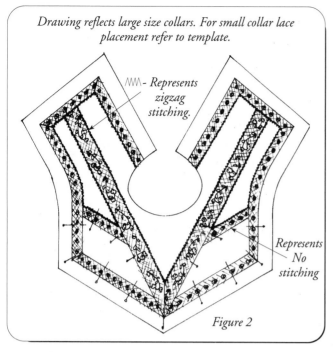

ᗯᗯ - *Represents zigzag stitching.*

Represents No stitching

Figure 2

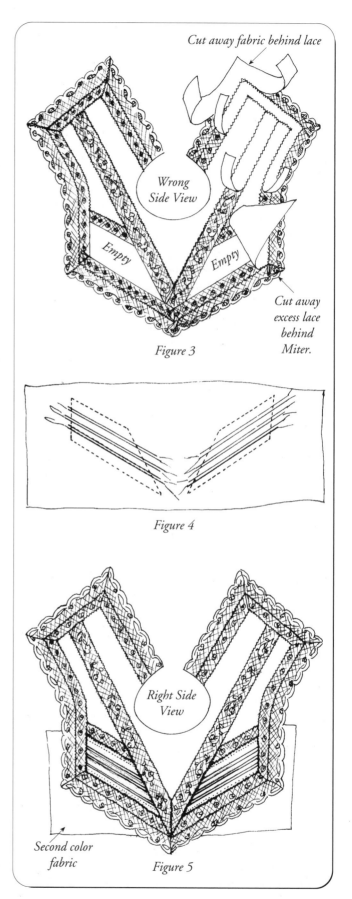

Cut away fabric behind lace

Wrong Side View

Empty

Empty

Cut away excess lace behind Miter.

Figure 3

Figure 4

Right Side View

Second color fabric

Figure 5

II. Collar

1. Cut one collar piece placing the center front of the pattern on the fold of the fabric. Using a fabric marker, trace off lace shaping lines. Refer to the collar template for the laces to be used. The number listed on the lace pieces of the template refers to the lace shaping order. Collar templates on pages 296-299.

2. Shape the insertion lace in the order stated using the techniques for lace shaping. After all lace insertion pieces are in place, zigzag all lace pieces in place but do not zigzag along the outer edge of the lace insertion pieces around the outside edge of the collar or the inside edge of the lace to be attached to the second color of fabric (**fig. 2**).

3. Shape the edging lace along the outer edge of the collar. Zigzag in place. Trim the fabric from behind the lace (**fig. 3**).

4. If pintucks are not used simply place the second color of fabric in the space and zigzag in place along the edge of the lace. If you are making pintucks, place the second color of fabric under the open space. Outline the space (rectangle) on the fabric using a fabric marker. Remove the fabric from the space and stitch two to three rows of pintucks in the middle of the rectangle (**fig. 4**). These pintucks should be parallel to the long sides of the rectangle. Place the pintucked rectangle back in the space. **Note:** The lines traced for the rectangle will not fit the rectangle exactly after the pintucks are placed in the fabric. Pin the fabric in place. Stitch along the inside edges of the lace using a small zigzag. Trim away the excess fabric under the lace (**fig. 5**).

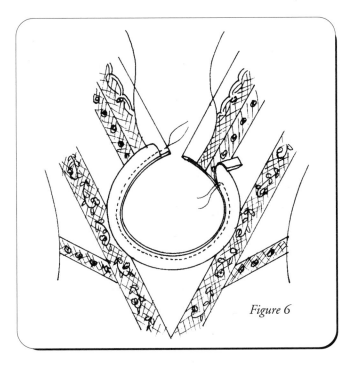

Figure 6

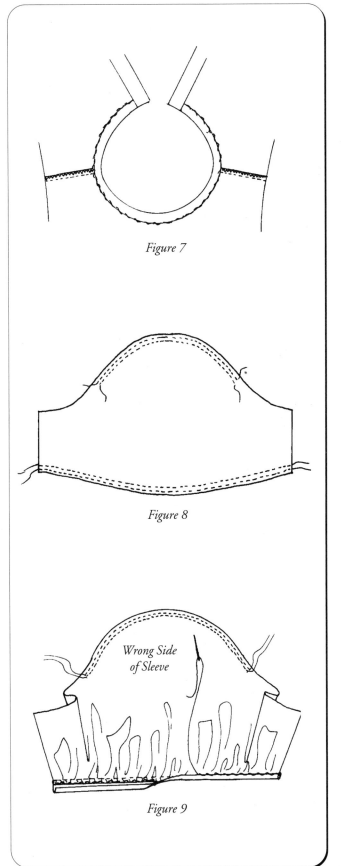

Figure 7

Figure 8

Figure 9

5. Place the wrong side of the collar to the right side of the dress. Pin in place.

6. Cut a bias strip 1" wide by the length of neck band measurement given in the neck band chart. Fold the bias strip in half and press. Place the cut edges of the strip to the neck of the collar/dress. Cut the ends of the strip off 3/8" from each side of the back bodice edges.

7. Flip the back bodice edges to the outside 3/8" under the folded bias strip. Stitch the bias strip to the neck edge using a 1/4" seam (**fig. 6**). Trim the seam allowance to 1/8". Flip the bias strip and the back bodice plackets to the inside of the bodice. Hand stitch the bias strip in place finishing the neck edge (**fig. 7**).

III. Sleeves

1. Cut out two sleeves.

2. Place two rows of gathering stitches 1/8" and 1/4" in the top and bottom of the sleeve (**fig. 8**).

3. Cut two bias strips of fabric 1" wide by the measurement given on the sleeve band chart for your specific doll body.

4. Gather the bottom of the sleeve to fit the bias band. Stitch the band to the sleeve, right sides together, using a 1/4" seam. Fold the lower edge of the band to the inside 1/4". Place the folded edge just over the seam allowance on the inside of the sleeve creating a 1/4" band. Hand stitch or machine stitch in place. This will finish the end of the sleeve (**fig. 9**).

5. Gather the top of the sleeve to fit the arm opening allowing most of the gathers to fall 3/4" to 1-1/4" on either side of the shoulder seam. Place the sleeve to the arm opening, right sides together, stitch using a 1/4" seam. Overcast or serge the seam allowance (**fig. 10**).

6. Place the sides of the bodice/sleeves right sides together. Stitch, using a 1/4" seam allowance. Overcast or serge the seam allowances (**fig. 11**).

IV. Skirt

1. Refer to the length and width given in the skirt chart for the specific doll body to create the skirt piece. Skirt templates on centerfold pull out.

2. Cut the skirt for the small dolls to the measurement given in the chart. Cut the medium and large skirt 3" shorter than the measurement on the chart. Using a fabric marker, trace the template starting in the center of the skirt fabric. The small doll template should be traced 3/8" from the edge. The medium and large doll templates have two sections; upper and lower. The upper section should be traced on the edge of the skirt fabric.

3. Refer to the directions for lace shaping and mitering laces in this book to complete the skirt. Follow lace directions below for your specific doll size:

   a. **Small doll** - Shape lace in the order stated. Starch and press lightly. Gently remove the #1 lace points and set aside. Zigzag along the upper edge of lace #2. Trim away excess fabric (**fig. 12**). Place second color of fabric below the shaped lace. Replace the lace points using the templates as a guide. Pin in place. Zigzag along the inside edges of lace rectangle created by the point. Trim away the excess fabric (**fig. 13**). Attach flat edging lace along the bottom of the skirt mitering at the

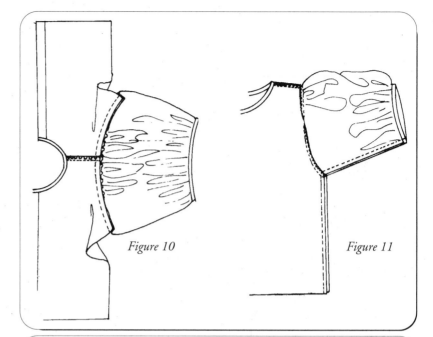

Figure 10

Figure 11

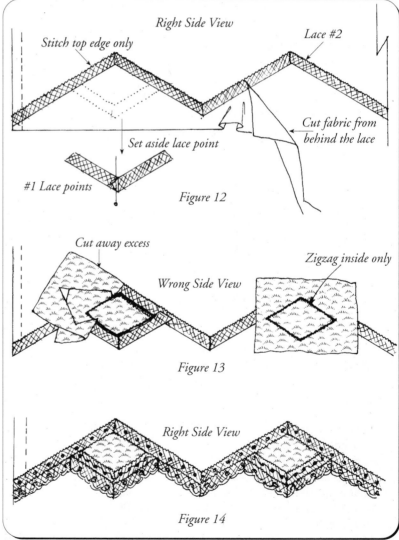

Right Side View

Stitch top edge only

Lace #2

Cut fabric from behind the lace

Set aside lace point

#1 Lace points

Figure 12

Cut away excess

Wrong Side View

Zigzag inside only

Figure 13

Right Side View

Figure 14

corners (**fig. 14**). Stitch laces at the miters and cut away the excess lace behind each miter.

b. **Medium dolls** (as stated on the chart plus FB17, FB19, and MB190) - Shape lace #1 along the upper skirt. Zigzag along the top edge only. Trim away the excess fabric under the skirt. Place a 6" strip of the colored fabric under the lace of the skirt. Pin in place. Zigzag along the lower edge of the lace attaching the colored fabric to the skirt (**fig. 15**). Trace the lower template along the colored fabric lining up the lace and upper template. Shape the lace insertion along the lines in the order stated. Zigzag along the upper edge of lace #3 and along the inside of the rectangle created by lace #2. Trim away the excess fabric (**fig. 16**). Attach flat edging lace along the lower edge of the skirt mitering at the corners. Stitch laces at the miters. Trim the excess lace behind each miter as in figure 14.

c. **Large dolls** -Shape the lace along the upper skirt. Zigzag along both sides of lace #1. Zigzag along the top edge only of lace #2 (**fig. 17**). Trim away the excess fabric under the lace. Place a 6" strip of the colored fabric under the lace of the skirt. Pin in place. Zigzag along the lower edge of the lace attaching the colored fabric to the skirt. Trace the lower template along the colored fabric lining up the lace and upper template. Shape the lace insertion along the lines in the order stated. Zigzag along the upper edge of lace #4 and along the inside of the rectangle created by lace #3. Trim away the excess fabric (**refer to directions under "b. medium dolls" and figure 16**). Attach flat edging lace along the lower edge of the skirt

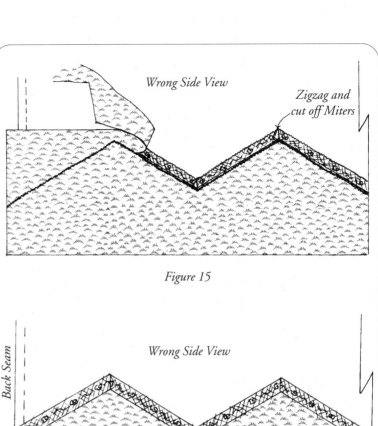

Figure 15

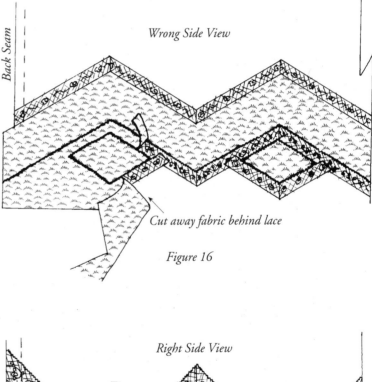

Figure 16

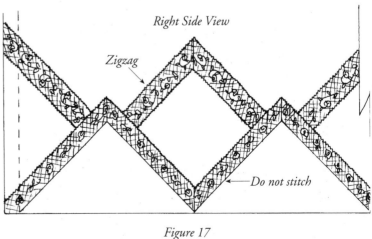

Figure 17

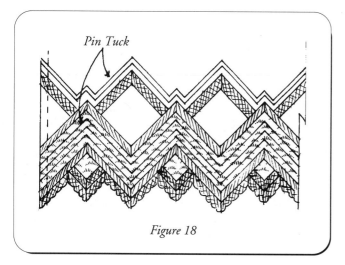

Pin Tuck

Figure 18

mitering at the corners. Stitch laces at the miters. Trim the excess lace behind each miter (**see figure 14**).

4. Pintucks (optional) - Stitch pintucks above the upper row of lace using the directions for shaped pintucks. Stitch pintucks on medium and large skirt in the colored fabric between the lace zigzags (**fig. 18**).

5. Run two gathering rows at 1/4" and 1/8" in the top edge of the skirt piece starting and stopping 1/2" from the back edges.

V. Finishing the Dress

1. Creating the Skirt Placket

Note: The placket can be omitted if desired. The dress is much easier to get on and off if a placket is used.

a. Place the back edges of the skirt right sides together. Start stitching from the bottom of the skirt using 1/2" seam. Stop the seam 1-1/2" from the top on a small doll and 2-1/2" from the top on a medium or large doll. Clip across the seam allowance at the end of the stitching (**fig. 19**). Trim the seam allowance along the stitching line to 1/8". Overcast or serge.

b. Turn each side of the remaining upper seam allowance to the inside 1/8" and stitch in place (**fig. 20**). Place the seam allowances right sides together and stitch 3/8" across the skirt at the end of the opening. This stitching will be made from the inside of the skirt (**fig. 21**). Press to the left side of the skirt.

c. From the top of the skirt fold the right hand side of the opening 3/8" to the inside. Press in place.

2. Mark the center and quarter points of the skirt. Place the skirt to the bodice entredeux, right sides together matching the quarter points to the side seams and the center front to the center. Gather the top edge of the skirt to fit the bodice

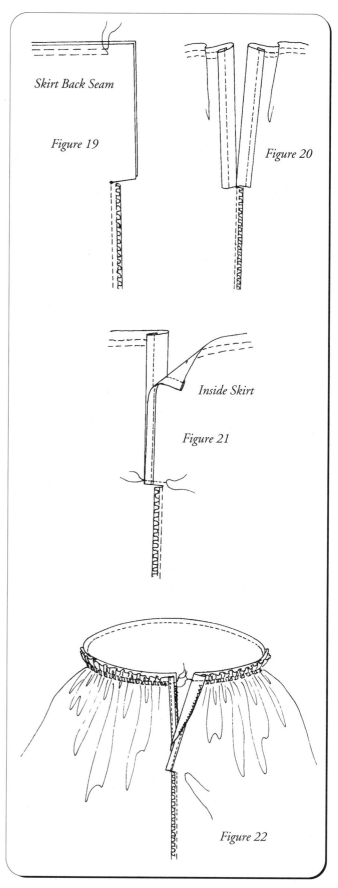

Skirt Back Seam

Figure 19

Figure 20

Inside Skirt

Figure 21

Figure 22

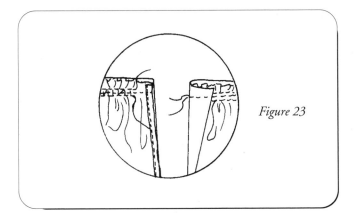

Figure 23

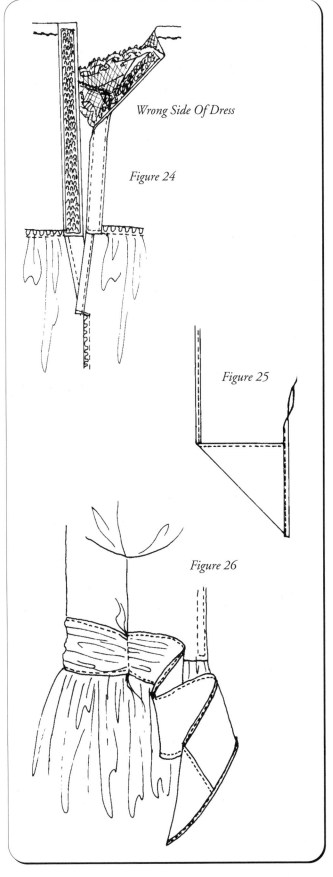

Wrong Side Of Dress

Figure 24

Figure 25

Figure 26

entredeux (**fig. 22**). Place the left side of the skirt opening 3/8" from the left edge of the bodice and wrap the bodice over the edge of the skirt. Place the right edge of the skirt opening even with the edge of the bodice (**fig. 23**). Stitch in place with a 1/4" seam using the technique "entredeux to gathered fabric. Overcast or serge. Pull the bodice up away from the skirt allowing the back placket to flip to the inside of the bodice.

3. Fold the right side of the bodice/skirt to the inside 3/8".

4. Buttonholes, snaps or Velcro™ should be placed along the back openings to hold the folds in place (**fig. 24**).

5. Cut silk ribbon in half. Tack the center of the ribbon to the center of the sleeve band by hand or machine . Tie the ribbon into bows. Trim the ends of the ribbon even. Apply a fabric sealant to the ends of to keep the silk ribbon from fraying.

6. Sash: Small dolls - cut a strip of fabric 2" wide by 30" long. Medium dolls - cut a fabric strip 2-1/2" wide by 36" long. Large dolls - cut a strip of fabric 3" wide by 44" long. Hem one long side of the tie by turning the edge to the inside 1/8" and 1/8" again. Fold the short edges to the unhemmed side and pin in place. Hem the other long side catching the short side in the hem (**fig. 25**). This creates a point at each end of the sash. Center on the dress. Gather to half the width and attach to the side seams using a straight stitch (**fig. 26**). ✹

Ribbon and Lace Party Dress

What an assortment of party fabrics and techniques all rolled into one beautiful doll dress! My thinking is that any little girl would also be enchanted with a dress made using these exact same fabrics, style and stitching. The bodice is green velveteen with a galloon of ecru French lace down the front. Ecru silk ribbon French knots follow the scalloped pattern of the lace; red, ecru and green silk ribbon lazy daisy flowers trim the center sections of lace. The neckline is trimmed with entredeux and gathered lace trim. The sleeves and tiers of the skirt are made of a green lamé fabric. The sleeves have entredeux beading and three rows of French edging stitched together to make a wide lace band. The tiers of the skirt have a tier of lamé, one row of ecru lace insertion, one row of polyester ribbon and one row of ecru French lace edging at the bottom. All three tiers are the same. Since the back closes with Velcro it is easy to change the doll's dress.

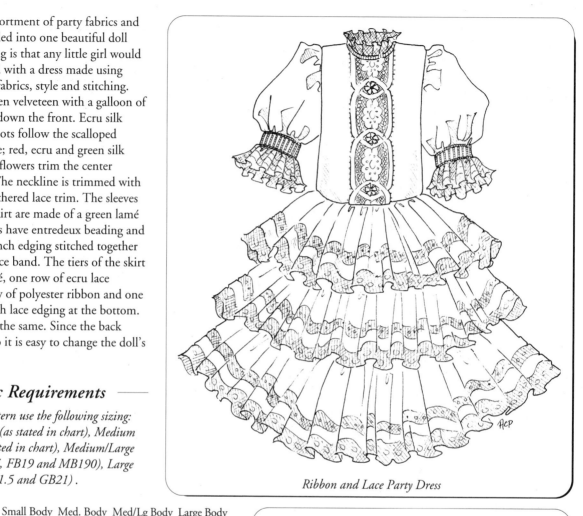

Ribbon and Lace Party Dress

Fabric Requirements

Note: For this pattern use the following sizing: Small Bodies (as stated in chart), Medium Bodies (as stated in chart), Medium/Large Bodies (FB17, FB19 and MB190), Large Bodies (MB21.5 and GB21).

	Small Body	Med. Body	Med/Lg Body	Large Body
Dress Fabric	1/2 yd.	3/4 yd.	1 yd.	1-1/4 yd.
Entredeux	1/4 yd.	1/4 yd.	1/4 yd.	1/4 yd.
Edging Lace (1/2")	3 yds.	4 yds.	5 yds.	6-1/2 yds.
Lace Insertion(1/2")	1-1/8 yds	2-1/8 yd.	2-1/2 yds.	3-3/4 yds.
Lace Gallooning	1/4 yd.	1/4 yd.	1/4 yd.	1/3 yd.
Entredeux/Beading	1/4 yd.	1/4 yd.	1/3 yd.	1/2 yd.

Other Notions: Lightweight sewing thread, silk ribbon for accent embroidery, decorative thread, and Velcro™, snaps or tiny buttons for back closure.

All Seams 1/4" unless otherwise indicated.

I. Bodice

1. Cut out the bodice front on the fold of the fabric. Center the strip of gallooning along the center front of the bodice. Stitch in place along the edges of the lace by hand or machine (**fig. 1**).

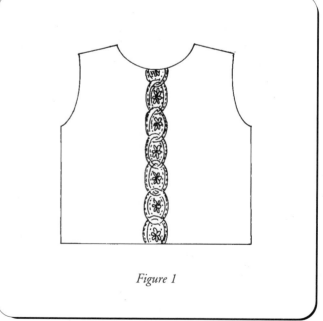

Figure 1

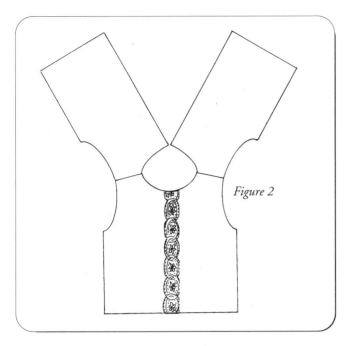

Figure 2

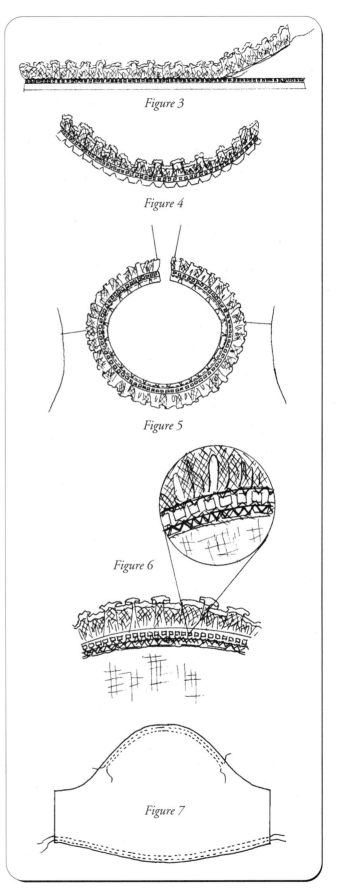

Figure 3

Figure 4

Figure 5

Figure 6

Figure 7

2. If selvage fabric is available, cut the back bodices with the back edges on the selvage. If the selvage is not available, simply cut out the bodice backs and serge or overcast the back edges of each bodice piece.

3. Place the front bodice to the back bodice pieces, right sides together, at the shoulders. Stitch using a 1/4" seam. Overcast or serge the seam allowance (**fig. 2**).

II. Neck

1. Cut a strip of entredeux to the neck band measurement given in the chart for the specific doll body to be dressed.

2. Cut a piece of edging lace two times this length and gather to fit the entredeux strip.

3. Trim away one side of the entredeux and attach the gathered edging lace to the trimmed entredeux using the technique entredeux to gathered lace (**fig. 3**).

4. If the fabric edge remaining on the entredeux is not already 1/4", trim to 1/4". Clip this fabric so that it will curve along neck edge of the dress (**fig. 4**). Place this strip to the neck of the dress right sides together. Attach using the technique entredeux to fabric (**fig. 5**).

5. Using a tiny zigzag, tack the seam allowance to the dress. This stitching will keep the entredeux and gathered lace standing up at the neck (**fig. 6**).

III. Sleeves

1. Cut out two sleeves.

2. Place two rows of gathering stitches 1/8" and 1/4" in the top and bottom of the sleeve (**fig. 7**).

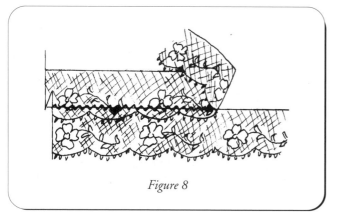

Figure 8

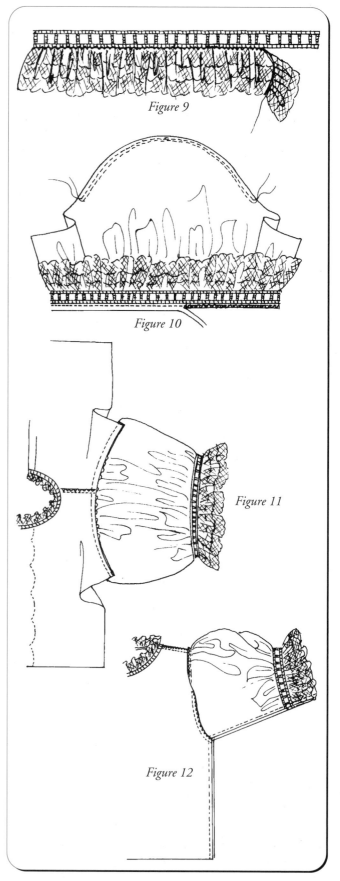

Figure 9

Figure 10

Figure 11

Figure 12

3. Cut two strips of entredeux/beading to the measurement for the specific doll body given on the sleeve band chart.

4. Cut two pieces of edging lace twice the length of the entredeux/beading for small dolls. Cut four pieces of edging lace twice the length of the entredeux/beading for medium and medium/large dolls. Cut six pieces of edging lace twice the length of the entredeux/beading for large dolls.

5. For the small dolls gather the edging lace to fit the entredeux/beading. For medium dolls attach two lace strips together, allowing the scallop of one lace to overlap the heading of the other lace. Zigzag in place (**fig. 8**). Repeat for other sleeve. Gather the upper lace piece to fit the entredeux/beading. Repeat in the same manner for large dolls with three rows of lace on each sleeve as in figure 8. Treat these three rows as one row. Gather the top piece of lace to fit the entredeux/beading.

6. Stitch the gathered lace to the entredeux/beading using the technique entredeux to gathered lace (**fig. 9**).

7. Gather the bottom of the sleeve to fit the entredeux/edging lace band. Stitch the band to the sleeve, right sides together, using the technique entredeux to gathered fabric (**fig. 10**).

8. Gather the top of the sleeve to fit the arm opening allowing most of the gathers to fall 3/4" to 1-1/4" on either side of the shoulder seam. Place the sleeve to the arm opening, right sides together, stitch using a 1/4" seam. Overcast or serge the seam allowance (**fig. 11**).

9. Place the sides of the bodice/sleeves right sides together. Stitch, using a 1/4" seam allowance. Overcast or serge the seam allowances (**fig. 12**).

IV. Skirt

1. Refer to the length and width given in the skirt chart for the specific doll body to create the skirt piece.

2. The small skirt will not be tiered. The medium and medium/large skirt will have two tiers. The large skirt will have three tiers.

   a. Small skirt - Cut a piece of lace insertion, ribbon, and edging lace to 37". Attach the lace pieces on either side of the ribbon with a zigzag (**fig.13**). Cut a piece of fabric 1-1/2" shorter in length than the chart measurement. Attach the band to the bottom of the fabric using the technique lace to fabric (**fig. 14**).

   b. Medium skirt and medium/large skirt - Cut two pieces of lace insertion, ribbon, and edging to 37" for medium dolls and 43" for medium/large dolls. Create two bands. Attaching one piece of lace insertion and one piece of edging on either side of one ribbon piece with a zigzag (**see figure 13**). Repeat for second band. Cut a piece of fabric 1-1/2" shorter in length than the chart measurement and a second piece 4-1/4" shorter than the chart measurement. Attach the bands to the bottoms of each piece of fabric using the technique lace to fabric (**see figure 14**). Place the smaller piece on top of the larger, right sides up. Baste in place along the top edge. Treat as one layer of fabric.

   c. Large skirt (MB21.5 and GB21) - Cut three pieces of lace insertion, ribbon, and edging to 43". Create three bands by attaching with a zigzag one piece of lace insertion and edging on either side of a ribbon piece (**see figure 13**). Repeat for second and third band. Cut a piece of fabric 1-1/2" shorter in length than the chart measurement, a second piece 4-1/4" shorter than the chart measurement and third piece 7-1/2" shorter than the length given on the chart. Attach the bands to the bottoms of each piece of fabric using the technique lace to fabric (**see figure 14**). Place the smaller piece on top of the medium piece and then both on top of the larger piece, right sides up. Baste in place along the top edge to hold in place. Treat as one layer of fabric (**fig. 15**).

4. Run two gathering rows at 1/4" and 1/8" in the top edge of the skirt piece starting and stopping 1/2" from the back edges.

V. Finishing the Dress

1. Creating the Skirt Placket

   a. Place the back edges of the skirt right sides together. Make sure the tears (laces and ribbon) are lined up at the seam. Start stitching from the bottom of the skirt using 1/2" seam. Stop the seam 1-1/2" from the top on a small doll and 2-1/2" from the top on a medium or large doll. Clip across the seam allowance at the end of the stitching. Trim the seam allowance along the stitching line to 1/8". Overcast or serge (**fig. 16**).

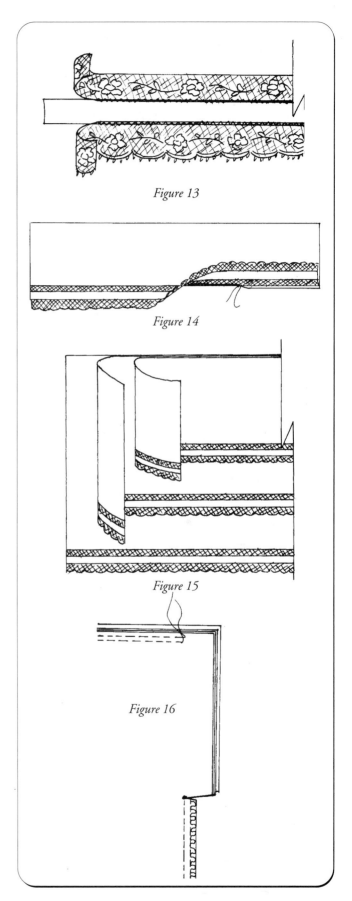

Figure 13

Figure 14

Figure 15

Figure 16

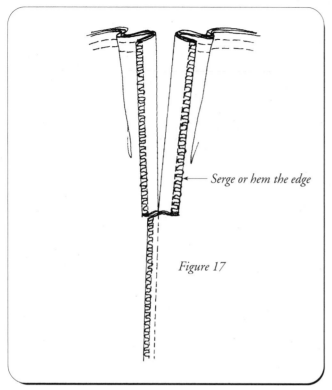

Serge or hem the edge

Figure 17

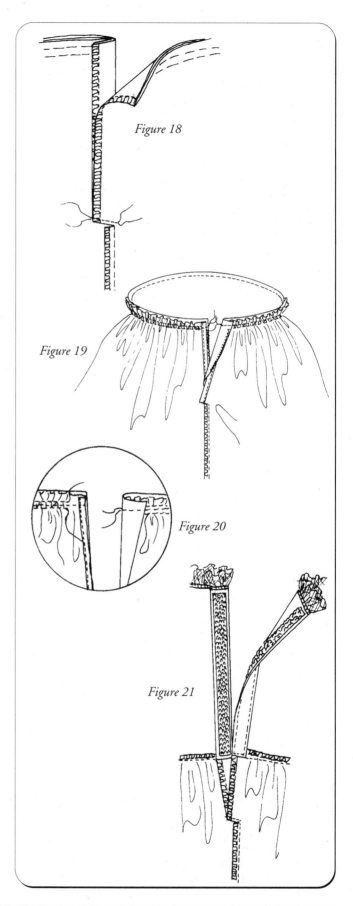

Figure 18

Figure 19

Figure 20

Figure 21

b. Turn all three layers on each side of the remaining upper seam allowance to the inside 1/8" and stitch in place. If you have a serger you may want to serge the raw edges instead of turning and stitching them. This will cut down on the bulk (**fig. 17**). Place the seam allowances right sides together and stitch 3/8" across the skirt at the end of the opening. This stitching will be made from the inside of the skirt (**fig. 18**). Press to the left side of the skirt.

c. From the top of the skirt, fold the right hand side of the opening 3/8" to the inside. Press in place.

2. Mark the center and quarter points of the skirt. Place the skirt to the bodice, right sides together matching the quarter points to the side seams and the center front skirt to the center front bodice. Gather the top edge of the skirt to fit the bodice (**fig. 19**). Place the left side of the skirt opening 3/8" from the left edge of the bodice and wrap the bodice over the edge of the skirt. Place the right edge of the skirt opening even with the edge of the bodice (**fig. 20**). Stitch in place using a 1/4" seam. Overcast or serge. Pull the bodice up away from the skirt allowing the back placket to flip to the inside of the bodice.

3. Fold the right side of the bodice/skirt to the inside 3/8". Place buttonholes, snaps or Velcro™ along this fold to hold in place. Place closures along the left side of the back bodice (**fig. 21**).

4. Embellish the lace gal.looning down the front of the dress with silk ribbon embroidery. ▨

Introduction To Crafts

One of my favorite activities is to walk through a craft store. I seem to be able to find them anywhere I travel. Recently, I visited a HUGE craft store in Gulf Shores, AL. I have never seen so many goodies under one roof as there. I am not much of a flower arranger; however, while in that store, I thought I could pattern my work in such a fashion that Architectural Digest would beckon me for a photo shoot. Since my art creations come mostly from a sewing machine, you can imagine my excitement in a craft store that has "soft" crafts in addition to the painting and gluing.

I have a true confession. Decorating a Christmas tree is one of my passions. One year during the decorating rush, Joe said, "Why don't you get someone to come help you get up the Christmas tree." That thought was not too much worse than if he had said that I should sell one of the children. I replied, "Joe, no one knows where I want the ornaments placed on the tree. How would anyone know how I want my lights on the tree?" Since none of my family except Joanna has ever offered to help with the tree, I knew that the "family activity" time of decorating the tree was not in my future plans. If the "family" wanted to decorate the tree, then, I wouldn't care how they put it up. It would be wonderful; however, no one other than the family would be allowed in my territory. I love decorating the Christmas tree.

I love crafts of all kinds. In this section, I think you will find treasures that are spectacular and very easy to make. We have jewelry, wall ornaments, a Battenburg decorated straw hat, a lace embellished bud vase, a cameo photo album, a Victorian tassel, and a porcelain jar with embroidery on the top to name a few of our crafts for this series.

For the baby in your family we have a "T"- bonnet, a crib sheet set, and a memorabilia hoop. Wedding type items include a flower hair wreath for the flower girl, a wedding garter for the bride and a lingerie bag to tuck away those special undies for the honeymoon. For yourself or for a gift for your special sewing friend, how about a crazy patch sewing basket or an antique sewing wreath for her den? Some of you mothers or grandmothers might be planning a spectacular birthday party for your little girl. Perhaps you will make the Victorian bear centerpiece to grace the middle of the party table.

In gift stores I have seen photo albums covered magnificently selling for as much as $100. I have seen them made for brides, little girls, little boys, living rooms, and men. You can have one for any of these occasions using out techniques found in the camel photo album instructions in this section. One of the places I love to use tassels is on my knobs on the furniture in my living room and dining room. I never realized how easy they are to make and how inexpensive. Try one using the instructions for the Victorian tassel. Everybody on your list can use a beautiful porcelain jar covered with any type of embroidery, especially shadow work. This gift would be great for anyone on your list.

Do you wonder each year what to make for teacher's gifts? Make the crocheted fan pin and I think you will please everybody since pins are back in style in a big way. I cannot imagine any woman's not loving the Victorian heart wall ornament hanging in her bedroom or dressing room. It can also be used as a pin cushion. One of the easiest crafts that we have ever featured is the lace covered bud vase. Talk about a quickie! Last but certainly not least is the Battenburg covered straw hat which can be made in a jiffy.

Let this craft section be an inspiration to you to use these and then create your own using these ideas as a starting point. We love to create fun and easy crafts for *Martha's Sewing Room* and we hope you enjoy them as much as we do! Get the glue gun and get started! ✺

Crocheted Fan Pin

Since I began traveling to Australia about six years ago, I have become fascinated with the idea of wearing broaches, as pins are called down under. The women there have the most imaginative pins available including teddy bears, dolls, antique ones, and other hand made ones. This little beauty starts with a purchased crocheted fan which has been stiffened. Silk flowers with pearls in the middle and porcelain buttons have then been glued on to give this pin a very Victorian look. A little ecru satin ribbon bow has been tied at the bottom of the fan. A pin for attaching the pin to one's clothing is glued on the back. This pin would be great as a favor for any type of party or for a gift for someone special. I think it would be very sweet to have one of these at a luncheon table for each woman present.

Crocheted Fan Pin

Materials Needed

* 1 purchased stiffened doily fan (found at craft supply stores or fabric stores)

* An assortment of buttons, pearls, or flowers

* Broach pin back (found at craft supply stores)

* Satin ribbon bow

* Hot glue gun and glue sticks

Directions

1. Arrange the buttons, pearls, flowers or whatever pretty baubles you choose, on the top of the doily fan and hot glue in place (**fig. 1**).

2. Hot glue the broach pin to the back (**fig. 2**).

3. Tie the satin ribbon bow to the bottom of the fan (**fig. 3**). ▩

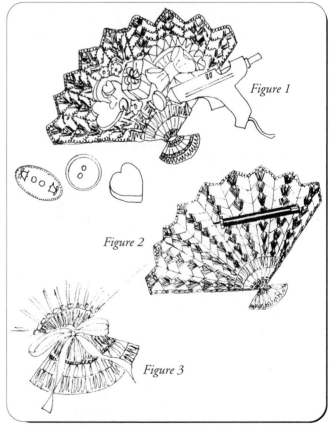

Figure 1

Figure 2

Figure 3

Victorian Heart Wall Ornament

Using the gorgeous English cotton netting lace, we gathered it around this puffed pink satin heart. The lace is mitered at the bottom of the heart. The pink satin heart is covered with the same English netting lace on the front and on the back. A lovely ribbon trim attached to wiring travels all the way around the heart on the front only. A beautiful piece of braid is used for the hanging portion of this heart and tiny silk flowers have been glued to both sides of this braid where it is attached and about half way up on the hanging portion of the braid. This would be a great gift for a bridal shower or for bridesmaids presents from the bride. This little heart decoration would be beautiful used as a pin cushion for the boudoir or a bedroom if you made it without the wall hanging braid part. In my dressing room, I am always needing a pin cushion to put the safety pins and straight pins that come out of my garments fresh from the laundry. Since I have a little bowl there for this purpose now, I think I will make one of these for myself in pink since our bedroom and bathroom are pink.

Victorian Heart Wall Ornament

Materials Needed

- ❀ 1/4 yd. base fabric (pink satin)
- ❀ 1 yd. of 3-1/4" lace edging
- ❀ 1/4 yd. of 8" to 12" wide lace
- ❀ 1/2 yd. decorative braid for hanging loop
- ❀ 5/8 yd. ribbon trim
- ❀ Hot glue gun and glue sticks
- ❀ Heart pattern on page 120

Directions

1. Cut 2 hearts out of the base fabric and 2 out of the wide lace. Arrange the heart on the lace so that the lace design lays evenly and balanced inside the heart (**fig. 1**).

2. Lay the lace hearts on the fabric hearts and baste stitch them together.

3. Run a gathering stitch in the wide lace edging tapering to the scalloped edge on the ends (**fig. 2**). Gather the edging and place around the heart beginning and ending at the

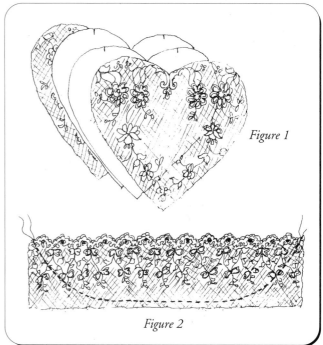

Figure 1

Figure 2

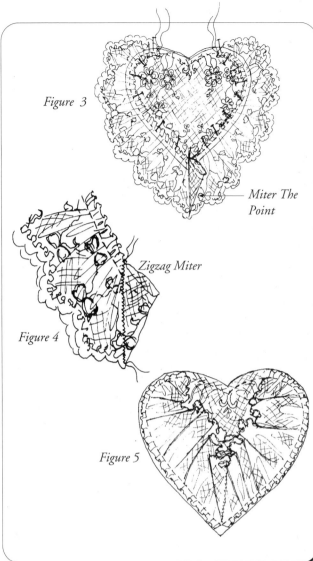

Figure 3

Miter The Point

Zigzag Miter

Figure 4

Figure 5

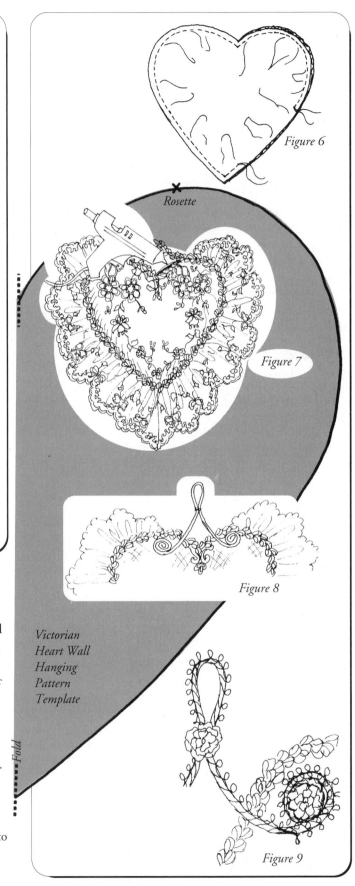

Figure 6

Rosette

Figure 7

Figure 8

*Victorian
Heart Wall
Hanging
Pattern
Template*

Fold

Figure 9

rosette marks (**fig. 3**). To miter the point, pinch in the excess lace at the point of the heart. Unpin and remove. Zigzag stitch tapering to the scalloped edge (**fig. 4**).

4. Pin the edging around the heart on top of the lace covered side with the scallops toward the center. Stitch the edging to the heart 1/4" around the edge (**fig. 5**).

5. Place the other side of the heart, lace side down, on top of the gathered edging and stitch 1/4" around the edge, leaving an opening on one side to turn the heart (**fig. 6**).

6. Turn, press, and stuff. Hand stitch the opening together.

7. Glue the ribbon trim around the edge of the heart (**fig. 7**). This trim is wired ribbon which looks like flowers.

8. Coil about 3" worth of the decorative braid on each end. Glue the coils on the rosette marks or where the lace edging ends. Tack the excess braid together in the center to create a loop (**fig. 8**). Glue a silk flower or pearls to the center of the coils and the loop (**fig. 9**). ❖

Crazy Patch Sewing Basket

Taking an inexpensive ($12.95) sewing basket from a local discount store, we transformed it into a designer's dream. Since it truly is elegant, it would be pretty enough to display permanently in your den or your bedroom. Crazy patch fabrics include velvet, satin, silk dupioni, water stained taffeta, silk printed ribbon and silk faille. Small patches were stitched together and every seam was trimmed with either decorative braid, decorative stitches from the sewing machine, fringe, or Swiss motifs. Wonderful buttons and charms were stitched onto the different squares. The gold charms include a swan, a hot air balloon, a French basket, a perky bow, a love bird in a heart, a key, a heart and gold daisy like flowers. The key and the hot air balloon have pink bows tied in the charm hole. Two porcelain buttons, a fan and a bow, are glued to the top also. The colors are blue, pink, yellow, brown, forest green, purple, mint green and dusty pink. Lots of gold braid and gold threads were used also in finishing the crazy patch seams. Pearls were glued all the way around the edge of the box where the crazy patch met the wooden box top. A perky multicolored ribbon with wiring in the edges is tied on one side of the handle. What a lovely gift for sewers or non-sewers alike!

Crazy Patch Sewing Basket

Materials Needed

- ❀ 1 Purchased sewing basket with a fabric covered lid.
- ❀ 1 Piece of muslin large enough to cover the lid with 1-1/2" excess on all sides
- ❀ Several scraps of fabric for patch work. (taffeta, drapery moiré, satin, and velveteen were used on sample shown in this book).
- ❀ Several charms, buttons, and various baubles for embellishing.
- ❀ Decorative braids, trims, sulky thread, metallic thread, silk ribbon, pearl trim etc. for embellishing (all are optional).
- ❀ Hot glue gun and glue sticks

Directions

1. Measure the fabric lid of the basket. Mark the shape of the lid on the muslin (allow over an inch excess on each side) (**fig. 1**).

2. Cut crazy patch fabric scraps into strips that will be easy to work with (3" to 6" wide). Begin in the center of the muslin with a 5 sided shaped scrap (**fig. 2**).

3. Lay the second strip on one of the 5 edges with right sides together and stitch a 1/8" to 1/4" seam (**fig. 3**). Fold the second strip back and press. Follow the directions for "Crazy Patch" found in this book for more detailed instructions.

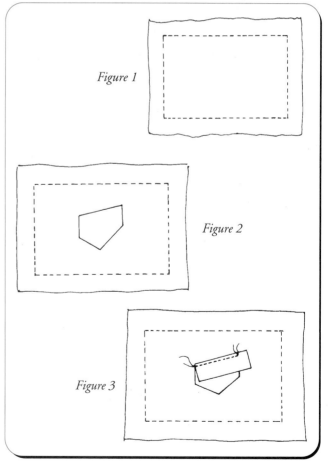

Figure 1

Figure 2

Figure 3

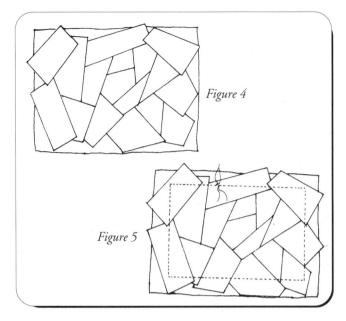

Figure 4

Figure 5

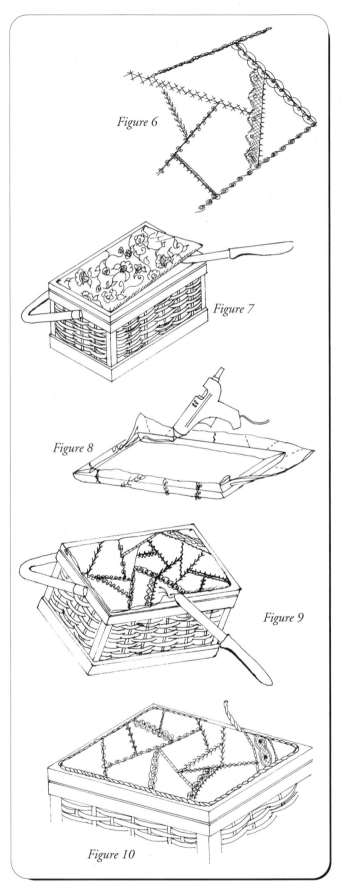

Figure 6

Figure 7

Figure 8

Figure 9

Figure 10

4. Continue stitching scraps working in a clockwise direction until the entire lid shape is covered with a little excess for tucking under (**fig. 4**).

5. Turn the muslin over and use the first line you drew as a guide. Baste stitch 1/4" out side the guide line. Make sure all of the patches lay flat while basting (**fig. 5**).

6. Embellish all of the seams with decorative braid, trims, decorative stitches with sulky thread, even silk ribbon embroidery (**fig. 6**). The feather stitch, blanket stitch, chain stitch, and Cretan stitch are just a few machine decorative stitches that work well over seams.

7. With a screw driver or a butter knife try to pry the fabric covered part of the lid away from the sewing basket lid. If you cannot pry it all the way off try to loosen it around the edges (**fig. 7**).

8. Cover the fabric lid with the crazy patch piece and fold the excess to the bottom side. Cut away excess muslin and patchwork (**fig. 8**). Hot glue the edges secure and glue the fabric lid back to the sewing basket lid. If the lid will not pry off, lay the patchwork over the fabric lid and trim the excess muslin so that you have enough left to tuck under. With a butter knife, tuck the edges underneath the fabric lid (between the fabric or soft lid and the hard sewing basket lid) (**fig. 9**). If tucking the fabric under does not work, then cut the crazy patch to fit exact and glue the raw edges, this will be covered later with braid.

9. Once you have covered the fabric lid, hot glue braid, upholstery rope, or a string of pearls around the edge (**fig. 10**).

10. Arrange charms, buttons, and baubles on top of the crazy patch and glue or tack in place. ❈

Battenburg Straw Hat

What a pretty hat to wear or to use for decorating your sun porch, bedroom or any other room in your house! Starting with a purchased straw hat, all you need to make this stunning beauty is a hot glue gun, Battenburg lace and your imagination. Talk about a quickie! The top trim of the hat is a doily with the fabric portion in the center cut away. Battenburg by the yard is used below that on the lower portion of the crown of the hat and more trim is used for the underside of the brim. A pretty piece of ribbon is used to tie a perky bow on the back of the hat. Isn't it exciting that hats are back in style? Do any of you remember the 1950's when a lady wouldn't be caught out at any dressed up occasion without her hat and white or ecru gloves?

Battenburg Straw Hat

Materials Needed

❀ 1 Purchased straw hat

❀ Enough Batternburg edging to go around the outside edge of the hat brim and around the crown.

❀ 1 Battenburg doily

❀ Fabric glue or craft glue

Directions

1. Glue Battenburg edging around the crown first (**fig. 1**).

2. The center of the doily was cut away on the sample so that the doily would lay flat on the crown (**fig. 2**) (this is optional). Dampen the doily and place on top of the crown. Dampening helps to shape the doily around the curves. Glue the doily on the crown around the edges of the battenburg (**fig. 3**).

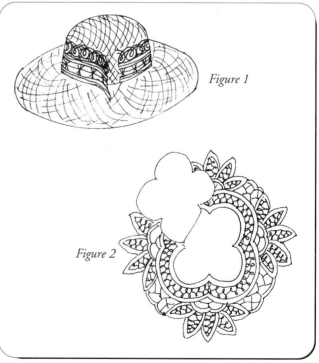

Figure 1

Figure 2

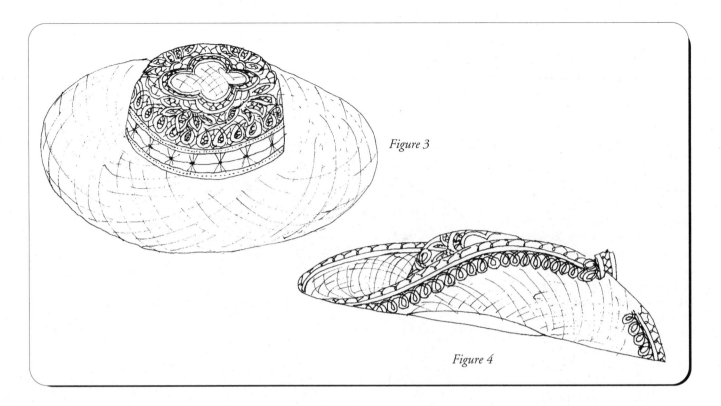

Figure 3

Figure 4

3. Lightly dampen the remaining edging and pin around the brim of the hat. The loopy part will lay on the bottom of the brim and the straight edge will lay on the top (**fig 4**). Using your fingers, press and tuck the loops so that they lay flat, some of the loops may fold under each other. Glue to the brim along the edges of the battenburg. Repeat on the top part on the brim and glue. Simply overlap the ends to finish.

4. Tie a ribbon bow around the crown or hot glue a tied bow on the back. ▨

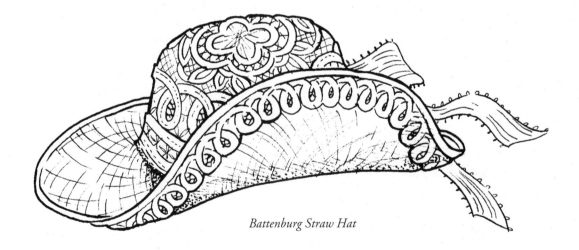

Battenburg Straw Hat

Flower Hair Wreath

Little girls look so pretty with flowers and bows in the hair. What prettier way could there be for a flower girl's hair to look than to have this magnificent wreath of flowers? I think it would be an especially nice gift for the little girls because when made of artificial flowers, it can then be worn with her Sunday school clothes until she is too old to wear it. This wreath has flowers and pearls woven around a wire for the circle part of the wreath; the back has more flowers, pearls and ribbons. We used two widths of ribbons for the streamers and one of them had wires so that it could be shaped. This wreath is very easy to make and inexpensive also. It makes the perfect keepsake for the special day since it is of silk flowers and will keep indefinitely. Please don't wait for a wedding to make this type of flower ornament for your little girls hair; it is perfect for Christmas, Easter, portrait time, or just plain Sunday school.

Materials Needed

❀ Florist or craft wire

❀ White florist tape (use green tape if you use colored flowers with green stems)

❀ Various silk flowers all white or assorted colors

❀ Wired pearl baubles

❀ Satin ribbon (wired or plain) the length desired for streamers and bows. You can use more ribbon for more streamers if desired.

❀ 5⁄8" Wired ribbon = 2 yds.

❀ 1⁄4" Unwired ribbon = 1yd.

Directions

1. Create a ring of wire the size desired. Wrap the wire ring with the white or green florist tape, stretching the tape as you wrap (**fig. 1**).

2. Place a flower sprig at the center back and wrap with florist tape (**fig. 2**). Place another sprig next to the first and wrap. Continue placing sprigs and pearl baubles one at a time wrapping with tape until the ring is covered (**fig. 3**). Leave a small space, about 1/2" wide in the back for placing the center back piece (**fig. 4**).

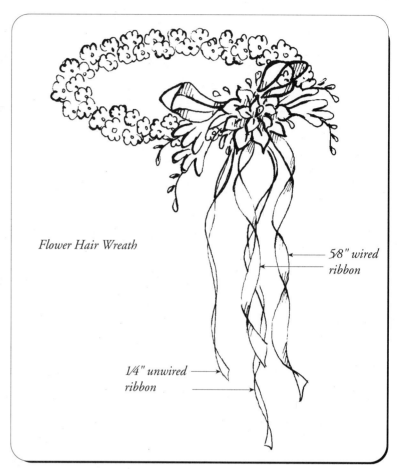

Flower Hair Wreath

5⁄8" wired ribbon

1⁄4" unwired ribbon

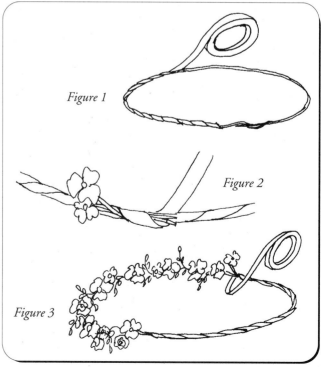

Figure 1

Figure 2

Figure 3

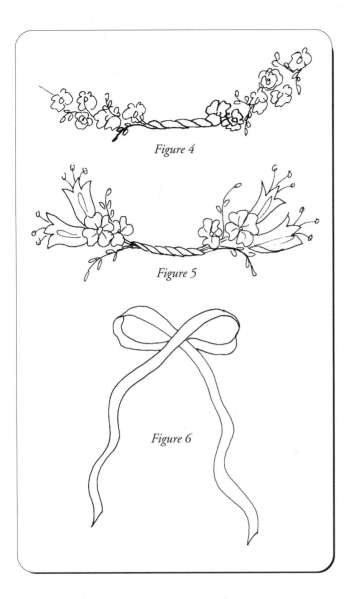

Figure 4

Figure 5

Figure 6

Figure 7

Figure 8

Figure's 8-10 show 6 streamers of 1/4" unwired ribbon. If you want 6, purchase 3 yds., 1/4" ribbon rather than 1yd.

Figure 9

Figure 10

3. Create a center back piece by wrapping flower sprigs and pearl baubles together (**fig. 5**).

4. Cut a long piece of wired ribbon to make a bow and curled streamers. Cut a couple of plain satin ribbon streamers (set one streamer aside). Loop the wired ribbon on both sides so that it crosses in the center (**fig. 6**). Lay the wire ribbon on top of the plain ribbon matching the centers. Place the center piece on top of the wire ribbon center (**fig. 7**). Place on center back of floral ring, hold in place with fingers (**fig. 8**).

5. Create a loop at the center of the extra streamer. Place on center back and wrap around pulling the tails up through the loop (**fig. 9**). To secure the bow and the streamers, place drops of hot glue on the back and secure to wreath. Hot glue a silk flower or a floral cluster at the center to cover the knot (**fig. 10**). ❊

Wedding Garter

This elegant wedding garter is beautiful and very easy to make. Using silk ribbon, ecru lace edging, and a little elastic, you have a keepsake for the bride. Two widths of ecru edging is stitched to two pieces of silk ribbon, one for the garter front and one for the back. A casing holds the elastic. Ecru French lace edging is gathered into a circle and two shades of narrow silk ribbon are used to tie a ribbon and the streamers to embellish the center of the lace rosette. What special gift to give to a bride months before her wedding; it would be nice to make one of these for your daughter or grand-daughter to keep in her hope chest or bottom drawer (as the English refer to hope chests). May I confess that I have the bottom drawer of my dresser in my bedroom filled with things for Joanna's future home. Some of them are as simple as dish drying towels which are souvenirs of my travels to Australia and New Zealand. Some are antique handkerchiefs which I just thought were pretty. Some are antique pieces of silver which I have been buying for years. I have her grandmother's jewelry kept there for her and some silver serving pieces to her sterling pattern which was her Grandmother Pullen's. As soon as I finish writing this book, I think I will tuck this little blue garter in the drawer for her to wear on her wedding day.

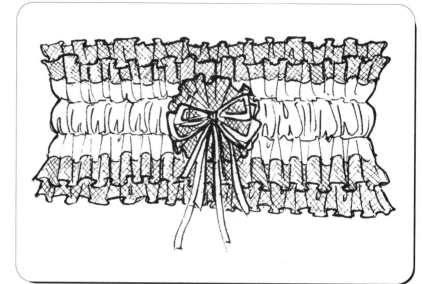

Materials Needed

* 1-1/2 yd - of 1-1/4" wide or (35mm) silk ribbon

* 3 to 4 - 12" pieces of (4mm and 2mm) silk ribbon in different shades

* 1-1/2 yds of 1/2" wide lace edging

* 1-5/8 yds of 3/4" wide lace edging

* 14" piece of 1/2" wide elastic

Directions

1. Cut the 1-1/2 yd piece of 35mm silk ribbon in half. Set one of the pieces aside. Cut the 1/2" lace edging in to two pieces. Stitch the 1/2" edging to both sides of one of the silk ribbon pieces by butting the lace edge against the ribbon edge and zigzag together as you would if you were stitching lace to lace (**fig. 1**).

2. Cut 4-1/2" off of the 3/4" lace edging then cut the remain-der in half. Stitch to both sides of the remaining piece of silk ribbon. Follow the same technique as above.

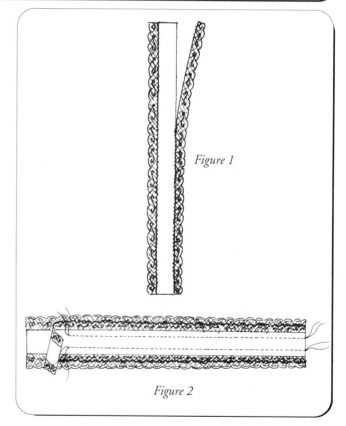

Figure 1

Figure 2

3. Place the strip with 1/2" edging directly on top of the strip with 3/4" edging, lining up the silk ribbon. Join the two strips with a straight stitch down both sides of the silk ribbon so that there is a 5/8" casing down the center of the ribbon (**fig. 2**).

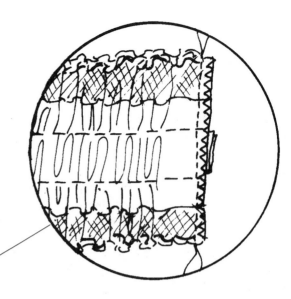

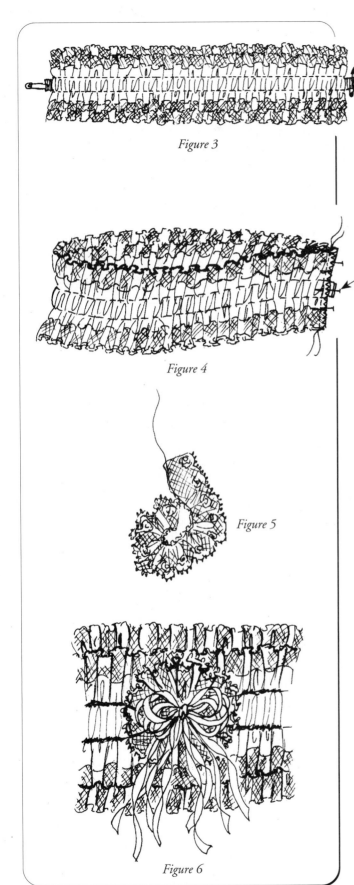

Figure 3

Figure 4

Figure 5

Figure 6

4. Insert the 1/2" elastic into the casing of the ribbon (**fig. 3**).

5. Join the two ends of the garter and stitch a seam and overcast, catching the laces and the elastic in the stitching (**fig. 4**).

6. Make a lace rosette with the 4-1/2" piece of 3/4" wide lace edging by gathering the edge and coiling it in a circle (**fig. 5**). Stitch to secure and tack to the front of the garter. Tie a bow using the 4 strips of 4mm and 2mm different colored ribbon. Tack the bow to the center of the lace rosette (**fig. 6**). ▨

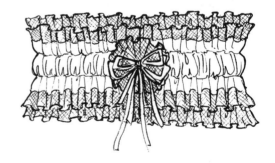

Veil with Crown Ruffle

This headpiece is fashioned with purchased flowers, pearls and white florist's wire. The nylon tulle veil is simple to make and so inexpensive, since the whole veil and headpiece could probably be made for less than $25! A piece of the tulle is simply folded over, puffed and stitched to the handmade round headpiece. To be so super simple to make, it is very beautiful on a bride's head. It seems to me that with veils this inexpensive and easy to make, there is no reason to pay $75 to $500 for a wedding veil.

Materials Needed

❀ 3 yds. netting

❀ Embellished circular wired headpiece

Note: The headpiece can be constructed from covered wire with flowers, filament pearl bobbles and pearls glued or taped in place with floral tape.

Directions

1. Embellish wired headpiece if not already decorated.

2. Fold down 7" of netting from one end of the veil.

3. Run a gathering thread 6" from the fold in the netting (**fig. 1**).

4. Gather by pulling the bobbin thread until the netting is gathered to 6" (**fig. 2**).

5. Center the netting along the inside, center back of the headpiece with the 6" poof above the headpiece. Hand stitch the netting to the headpiece along the gathering line (**fig. 3**). ❈

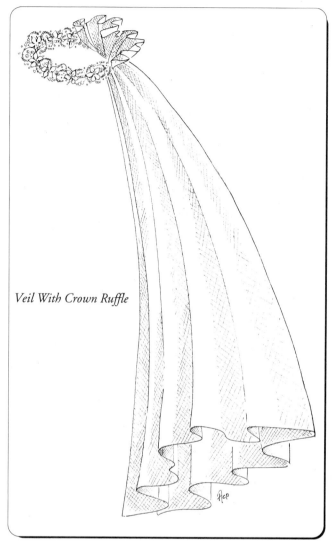

Veil With Crown Ruffle

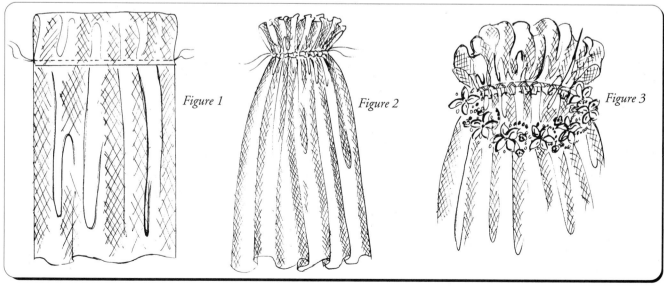

Figure 1 *Figure 2* *Figure 3*

Veil with Blusher

This VERY EASY TO MAKE veil has an interesting treatment around the outside edges of the veil which is made of inexpensive nylon tulle. A piece of 1/8" satin ribbon is stitched on with straight stitching to outline the veil. The round headpiece is purchased. After the ribbon is stitched to the veil portion, then the blusher amount was simply gathered in, tacked and stitched to the headpiece. The blusher can be worn over the face or back for the wedding. This total veil costs less than $40. If you made your round flowered headpiece, it would cost less than that!

Materials Needed

* 2-1/2 yds. netting
* 10 yds. of 1/8" polyester ribbon
* Embellished circular 1-1/2" wide headpiece

Note: The purchased headpiece can be decorated or undecorated. If an undecorated headpiece is purchased use a glue gun to cover with fabric and attach flowers, lace motifs and pearls.

Directions

1. Embellish headpiece if not already decorated.

2. Trim the corners of the netting to form an oval shape.

3. Stitch 1/8" ribbon along the edge of the netting using a straight stitch. This ribbon goes all the way around the veil.

4. Run a gathering thread about 28" from one end of the netting (**fig. 1**).

5. Gather by pulling the bobbin thread until the netting is gathered to 4-1/2" (**fig. 2**).

6. Center the netting along the inside, center back of the headpiece. Glue or stitch the netting to the headpiece along the gathering line (**fig. 3**). ▨

Veil with Blusher

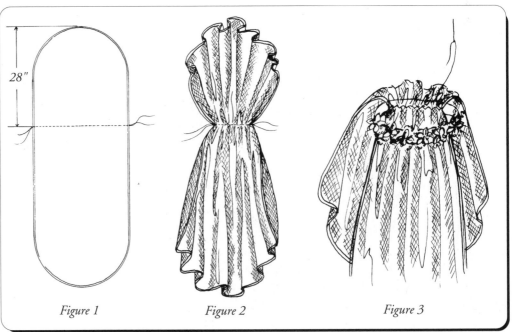

Figure 1 | *Figure 2* | *Figure 3*

28"

Antique Sewing Wreath

Shopping in any type of antique store is the only type of shopping that I love. It is amazing how many sewing relics one can find in an antique mall. Some of them are quite inexpensive such as old spools, tape measures, rusty scissors, etc. Collecting this type of sewing "stuff" is fun; however, one might wonder how to use this collection which many people would consider trash. I love this wreath of old sewing things and I think it would be perfect not only for the sewing room but also for the family room or kitchen. Start with a grapevine wreath purchased at any craft store and just begin to wrap and hot glue gun an old tape measure and an old zipper around the wreath. Other items to glue in are an old bobbin case, filled bobbin, button card, needle pack, hook and eye pack, old pincushion, old scissors, old glasses, and even an old patch intended for a quilt. Your imagination is the limit on choosing goodies to go in your antique sewing wreath.

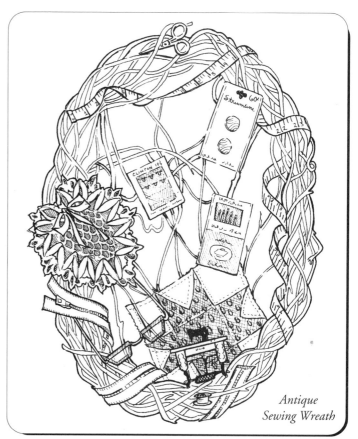

Antique Sewing Wreath

Materials Needed

* 1 Purchased grape vine, twig, or straw wreath (found in craft supply stores)
* Measuring tape and an assortment of sewing notions such as:
    * old sewing machine parts
    * bobbins
    * buttons
    * presser feet.
    * zippers
    * spools
    * needle packs
    * scissors
    * pin cushions
    * quilt scraps
    * thimbles etc.
* If you don't have antique notions make one with new sewing gadgets as a decoration or a gift idea.
* Hot glue gun and glue sticks

Directions

1. Begin by wrapping tape measurers and zippers and any lengthy materials around the wreath (**fig. 1**).

2. Arrange notions, scraps and various baubles on the wreath; when placed as desired, hot glue in place (**fig. 2**).

3. You may make a bow out of a tape measure to place on the top or bottom. ❈

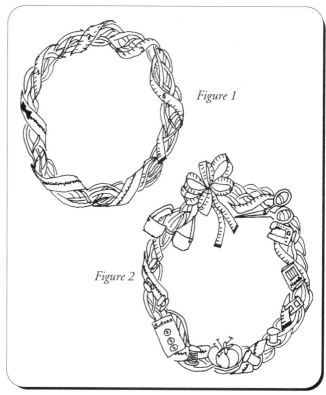

Figure 1

Figure 2

Victorian Bear Centerpiece

I almost called this "Bear On A Bench" because it is just that! Have you ever wanted a party centerpiece which would last for years and could be used as a decorative item in a child's room or a sun room? Expensive florist fresh flowers are just that—expensive. This cute centerpiece could be for a birthday party, an adult party, a luncheon, a dinner party, or a tea. The little purchased bear has a collar of gathered ecru French lace edging. Her hat has red and white polka dotted ribbon and a red ladybug perched on it. The little basket has plastic fruit and the seat of this bench is covered with striped summer fabric. The rocking chair bench sits on a round pizza board covered with moss and fake grass, glued on of course. The bench is wired through the pizza board to hold the rocking chair bench steady. Little butterflies are glued in several spots for interest. The arches over the bear consist of two stems of green leaves with yellow tiny rose like flowers about every six inches. This centerpiece can be made in a very short time with a hot glue gun and wire.

Bear
Centerpiece

Materials Needed

* ❋ 1- 12" round pizza or cake cardboard
* ❋ *1- Purchased twig rocker
* ❋ *1- Teddy bear 5" to 6" tall when sitting
* ❋ *1- doll size straw hat
* ❋ *1- bag of faux moss
* ❋ *1- Strand of green leaf or ivy garland long enough to fit around the rocking chair
* ❋ *1- Small doll size basket
* ❋ *3 to 4 small plastic veggies or fruit to fit in basket
* ❋ 12" piece of 1/8" ribbon for the hat
* ❋ *Tiny lady bugs and butterflies
* ❋ A remnant of fabric and a remnant of batting or fleece for bench seat
* ❋ 1- 10" to 12" remnant or lace edging for the bear's collar
* ❋ *Green florist tape and 2 florist sticks
* ❋ *Wire
* ❋ Hot glue gun and glue sticks

* Found at craft supply stores

Figure 1

Figure 2

Directions

1. Glue the moss to the round cardboard covering completely (**fig. 1**).

2. Place the rocker on the moss covered cardboard. Insert the wire into the cardboard wrapping it over the rocker blade and secure it on the bottom (**fig. 2**). Repeat on other side. You may also hot glue the rocker to the moss.

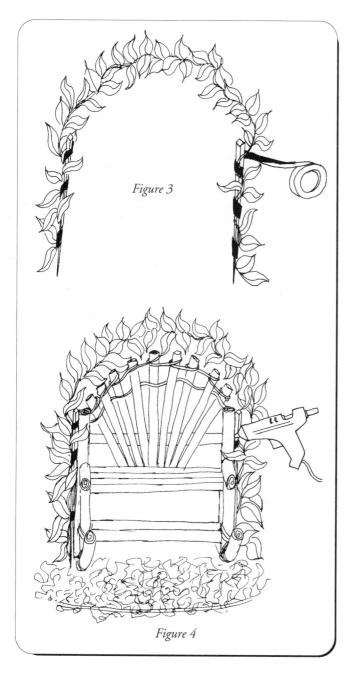

Figure 3

Figure 4

Figure 5

Figure 6

3. Beginning at the bottom of the rocker, wrap the garland over the left side, back , and right side of the rocker. Cut the garland to fit. Remove and place a wooden florist stick at each end and wrap with the green florist tape (**fig. 3**). Place on the rocker as before. Puncture the cardboard beside the rocker with the sticks and hot glue the sticks and garland to the sides of the rocker to secure (**fig. 4**).

4. Cut a piece of batting to fit the rocker seat. Fold the fabric remnant around the batting like you would wrap a gift and then glue to secure. You may also sew a seat cushion if you like. Place the cushion in rocker seat and glue (**fig. 5**).

5. Tie ribbon around straw hat and glue a lady bug to the top.

6. Glue the plastic veggies or fruit inside the small basket.

7. Gather the lace edging to fit around the bears neck and secure in back.

8. Glue the basket to the seat and the hat to the back to the rocker. Seat the bear on one side (**fig. 6**). You may leave the bear loose or you may glue him to the seat. Glue on bugs and butterflies if you wish. ▩

Lace Embellished Bud Vase

Some of you are probably asking, "Who in the world would know how to use a lace bud vase?" Well, I can answer that question. Have you ever wondered what to do with those relatively plain bud vases which you got years ago and you haven't used since? Here is the answer. Get scraps of laces, motifs, braid, netting, tatting or whatever and glue them to this plain little glass vase and take a sick friend a pretty fresh rose in a vase like this. Actually, she will have a little present long after the rose has died. This is the perfect project to use up those tiny scraps of lace that you really didn't want to throw away but which were not large enough to use for absolutely anything! Now you can use them. This vase is pretty in a living room, a bedroom, a sun porch, a little girl's room or a baby's room.

Materials Needed

❊ 1- Glass bud vase

❊ Several lace remnants and shiny cording

❊ Jewelry glue

Directions

1. Cut and arrange lace remnants on bud vase and glue. Overlap laces and motifs. Use cord to coil and wrap in unique designs. ❊

Lace Bud Vase

Lingerie Bag

This lingerie bag is absolutely gorgeous with burgundy water stained taffeta, burgundy heavy lace, ecru narrow lace trim, and a burgundy velvet covered button. The pearls around the outside edge of this bag are so delicate and I think everyone will wonder how you attached them! Ecru ribbons tie the two sides of the bag shut. Upon opening the bag, you will find two little pockets trimmed once again with the ecru narrow lace trim which almost looks like tatting. This bag would be nice for any small lingerie items for a trip or for just storing in your drawers. I have another suggestion for a bag like this. I have some treasures from Joe's mother's house which I don't keep on display such as a few pieces of jewelry and a few silver serving pieces. A lovely and special bag like this would be the perfect place to keep these treasures since I keep them in my dresser drawer. A bag like this would also be nice to keep antique handkerchiefs as well as antique silver. What a beautiful gift to make for family or friends!

Lingerie Bag

Materials Needed

* 1/2 - yd. of 45" fabric (moiré taffeta was used on sample)
* 12" x 15" piece of batting
* Lace trims (an embroidered lace collar was used on the sample)
* Lace edging (guipure lace edging was used on sample)
* 1-3/8 yd. ribbon
* 1- large button or a covered button (1-1/8" was used on sample)
* 2- 5" x 5" pieces of contrast colored taffeta to lay behind the lace (optional)
* 2- 5" x 5" pieces of double sided fusible web to fuse the lace to the contrast fabric.
* 50" of pearl trim, with or without a fabric edge. Piping or cord is also suitable.

Directions

1. Cut 2 pieces of taffeta 11" x 14" for the top and lining. Cut 2 pieces of taffeta 11" x 12" for the inside pockets.

2. Fold the top piece in half so that you have a 7" x 11" piece. Unfold and embellish the front half.

Embellishing The Front

1. Cut the large lace pieces to fit the front half of the bag. Experiment with the edgings and trims to arrange a desired design. For the sample, the large wine colored embroidered lace was fused to an ivory colored taffeta with double sided fusible web. The edges of the taffeta were peeled back slightly and cut in the shape of the lace so as not to show (**fig 1**). The embroidered lace and taffeta piece was then placed directly on top to the moiré taffeta front and stitched down along the edge with a small zigzag stitch (**fig 2**).

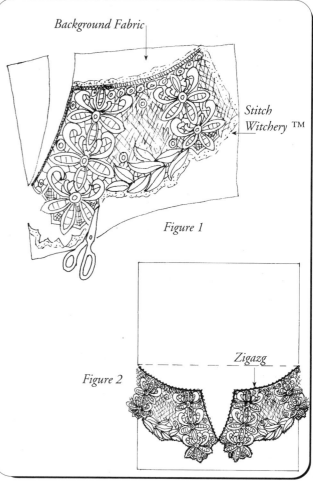

Background Fabric

Stitch Witchery ™

Figure 1

Figure 2

Zigazg

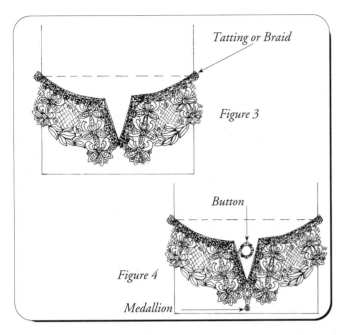

Tatting or Braid

Figure 3

Button

Figure 4

Medallion

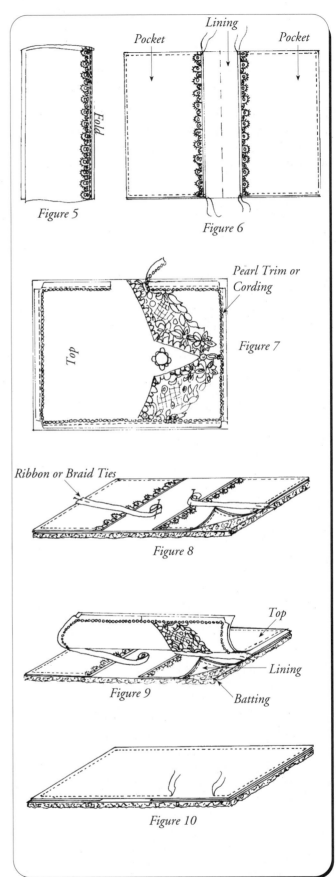

Lining

Pocket   Pocket

Fold

Figure 5   Figure 6

Pearl Trim or
Cording

Top

Figure 7

Ribbon or Braid Ties

Figure 8

Top

Lining

Figure 9   Batting

Figure 10

2. The guipure lace edging was then placed along the top edge of the embroidered lace and stitched to the front fabric (**fig. 3**).

3. A motif made from manipulating the guipure lace was glued to the center front and a velvet covered button was stitched to the center of the motif (**fig. 4**).

4. To complete the embellishment a medallion or lace motif was glued to the bottom center to cover the lace edging point (**see fig. 4**).

Constructing The Bag

1. Fold the 11" x 12" pocket pieces in half and embellish with edging on the fold, if desired (**fig. 5**).

2. Place the pocket halves, embellished side up, on the right side of the lining. Baste stitch around the pockets a scant 1/4" (the pockets will not meet in the center) (**fig. 6**).

3. Next, baste the pearl or cord trim around the edge of the lace embellished top on the right side (**fig. 7**).

4. To assemble, layer the batting on the bottom, then the lining with pockets and trim facing up, then take half of the ribbon and center it on one side, and center the other ribbon half on the other side to create the ties for the bag (**fig. 8**). You may want to coil and pin the ribbon to keep it out of the seams. Next, lay the embellished front piece face down on the lining (**fig. 9**). Pin all layers together.

5. With a zipper foot to guide along the cord or pearl trim, stitch using a generous 1/4" seam. Leave a 3" opening on the side of one of the pockets (**fig. 10**).

6. Clip corners and turn. Press.

7. Hand stitch the opening inside the pocket. The pocket will cover the stitching. ✤

Cameo Photo Album

This burgundy water stained taffeta photo album is absolutely wonderful. The burgundy taffeta covers the outside and the inside. Ecru heavy trim resembling tatting goes around the outside edge of the album. A Swiss motif of a mother and child is in the center; it is edged with this beautiful heavy ecru trim matching that on the outside of the book. This is so easy to make and I have seen beautiful albums like this selling for over $50 in book stores. I can see an album like this as a wonderful present for women and men. It would be especially fabulous if you filled it with pictures that you know the recipient would love. I read recently about a friend who took a camera and made candid shots of a wedding. Then she filled a photo album with these pictures and presented it to the bride and groom as a gift. Whether you make this album for yourself or for someone else, it is sure to be a treasure. If you make it for a man, just choose masculine fabrics and trims.

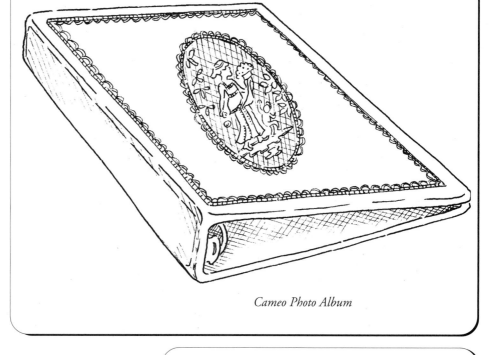

Cameo Photo Album

Materials Needed

* ❦ 1- Purchased photo album
* ❦ 1-3/8 yds. of fabric (covers a 10" x 11" album)
* ❦ Amount of fabric will vary according to the size of the album.

    Measure from front cover to back cover and the height of the album. Add an inch to all sides and double that figure to determine how much fabric it will take to cover the outside and the inside.

* ❦ Lace or crocheted motif for center.(available through Martha Pullen Company). A doily will also work well.

* ❦ Lace edging
* ❦ Poster board
* ❦ Hot glue gun and glue sticks
* ❦ Fabric glue

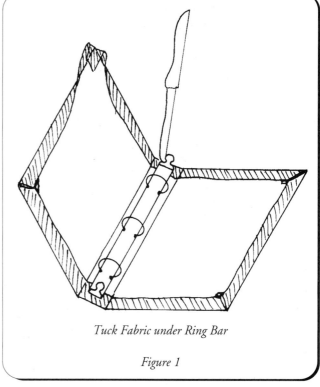

Tuck Fabric under Ring Bar

Figure 1

Directions

1. Remove pages and put aside. Lay the album out unfolded. Cut the fabric 1" larger all around than the album.

2. Lay the fabric on the outside and fold the edges over to the inside. Miter the corners and glue (**fig. 1**).

3. Stitch edging around motif if desired. With the fabric glue, glue the motif to the center of the album front. Glue edging around the edge, creating a decorative border (**fig. 2**).

4. Cut two pieces of poster board to fit inside the front and back cover. Cut them 1/4" smaller all around. The board will extend into the inside spine and under the ring bar. Crease the board where the album creases (**fig. 3**). Crease the boards before covering.

5. Cut two pieces of fabric to cover the poster board allow 1" extra on all sides except the side allowed for the spine. cover the two boards by folding the fabric over the edge and gluing (**fig. 4**).

6. Place the boards inside by gluing the spine end slightly underneath the metal hinge (**fig. 5**). Continue gluing around the edges covering the inside of the album. ❖

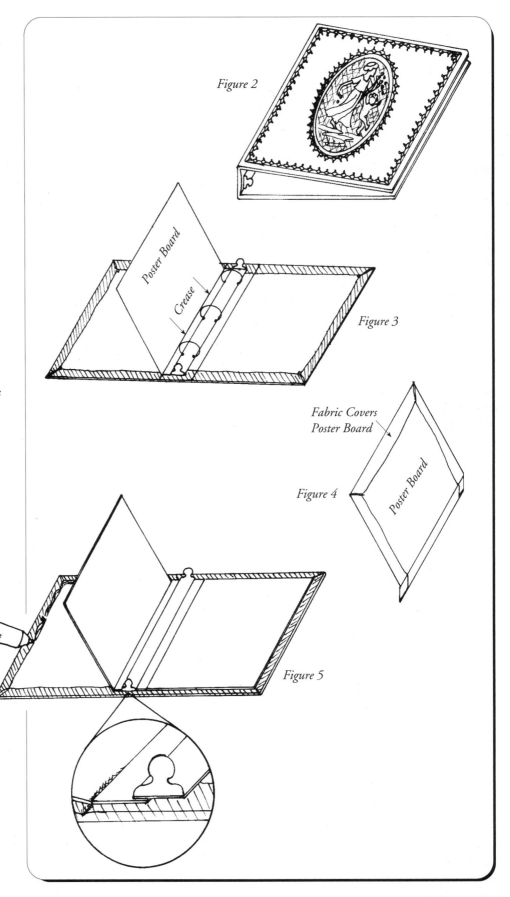

Figure 2

Poster Board

Crease

Figure 3

Fabric Covers
Poster Board

Poster Board

Figure 4

Figure 5

Baby "T" Bonnet

One of my very favorite bonnets for little girls is the T bonnet. The fact that is is super simple to make endears it more to many of us. This bonnet is made with Swiss embroidered handloom; however, with today's sewing machines making such gorgeous embroidery, you certainly might want to stitch your own insertion! Another fact which is nice about T bonnets is that they seem to fit for a long time. You can let it out as the child grows by tying the ribbons a little looser.

Materials Needed

❧ 20-3/4" of 1-1/2" to 1-3/4" wide embroidered insertion

❧ 1-1/4 - yd of 5/8" insertion lace

❧ 1-3/4 - yd of 3/4" lace edging

❧ 80 weight embroidery or very fine thread

❧ 1 - yd of 1/2" satin ribbon

❧ 1-1/3 - yd of 1/4" satin ribbon

❧ 2 - purchased ribbon rosettes or extra ribbon to make a rosette for the front corners. Bows or buttons may be substituted.

Directions

1. Cut the lace insertion in half. Using the technique "lace to fabric" found in the technique section of this book, stitch the lace insertion on both sides of the strip of embroidered insertion (**fig. 1**).

2. Cut 6-3/4" off of the embroidered/lace strip. Gather lace around three sides of the 6-3/4" strip, leaving one narrow end of the strip without gathered lace edging (**fig. 2**). This is the center back strip.

3. Gather lace edging to fit all around 4 edges of the 14" strip (**fig. 3**). This will be the strip for across the head.

4. Center the unfinished edge of the 6-3/4" piece under the 14" strip. This will create the "T". Allow the unfinished edge to extend 1/4" past the stitching where the lace insertion joins the embroidered insertion. Zigzag the back

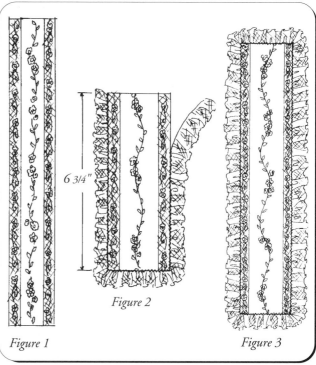

Baby "T" Bonnet

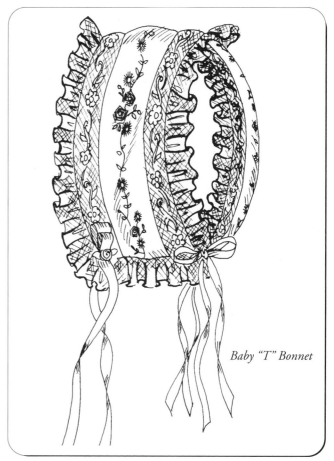

Figure 2

6 3/4"

Figure 1

Figure 3

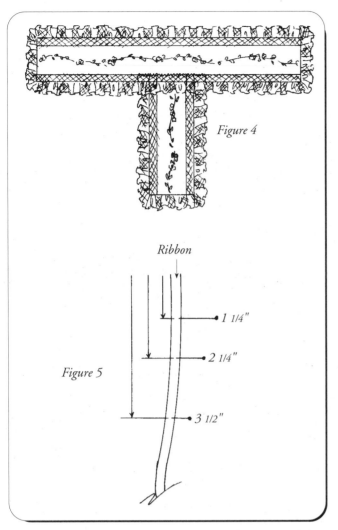

Figure 4

Ribbon

1 1/4"

2 1/4"

Figure 5

3 1/2"

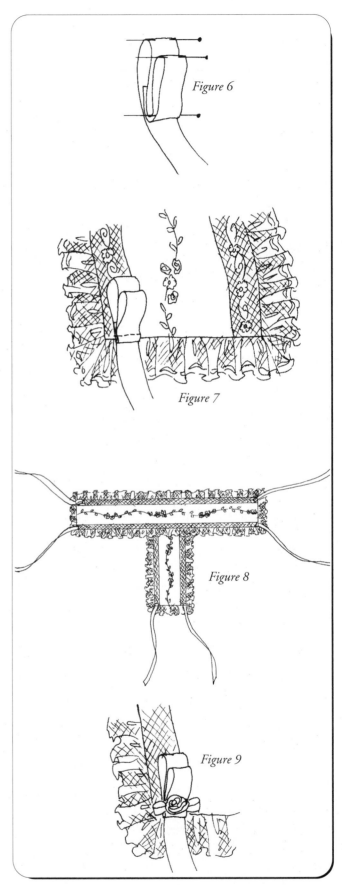

Figure 6

Figure 7

Figure 8

Figure 9

strip to the front strip on the zigzag stitch between the lace and embroidered insertion on the 14" strip (**fig. 4**). Turn over and cut off the excess edge of the center back strip close to the stitching line.

5. Cut the 1/2" satin ribbon in half. These are the ties for the 14" strip of the bonnet which will tie under the chin. To create ribbon folds, mark the ribbon from one end of each strip with straight pins as follows: 1-1/4", 2-1/4", and 3-1/2" (**fig. 5**). Fold the ribbon at the 1-1/4" mark. Fold the ribbon in the opposite direction at the 2-1/4" mark and again in the opposite direction at the 3-1/2" mark. Fold the 1/4" extension under the first fold (**fig. 6**). Stitch along the lower edge by hand or machine. Place along the front corner of the bonnet and stitch in place by hand or machine (**fig. 7**). Repeat for other side.

6. Cut the 1/4" satin ribbon into four, 12" pieces. Fold one end of the ribbon to the inside 1/4" and stitch to each remaining corner of the bonnet (**fig. 8**).

7. Tack a purchased or hand made ribbon rosette to the front corners on top of the front ribbon loops (**fig. 9**). You may even use a tiny bow or pretty button. ▧

Baby Crib Sheet Set

Using one purchased twin bed sheet we made two crib sheets, two baby pillowcases and two baby pillows. The top of the crib sheet and the end of the pillowcase are embellished with purchased Swiss trim. If you have a computerized sewing machine which does lovely decorative edging stitches such as a scallop, you can make your own "Swiss trim." The finishing touch to this crib sheet and pillowcase is the matching pillow which is the exact size to fit into the pillowcase.

Materials Needed

❊ 1- Twin size flat sheet (this will make 2 crib sheets, 2 pillow cases, and 2 pillows)

❊ 5-1/2 - yds of 3" to 3-1/2" wide Swiss edging (this accommodates 2 sheets and 2 pillow cases)

❊ 1- Bag poly fiber fill for pillow

❊ 3-1/2 yds of matching 1/2" wide twill tape, gross grain ribbon, or satin ribbon (this accommodates 2 sheets and 2 pillow cases).

Note: If the purchased sheet has twill tape at the casing you may use it for one sheet and one pillow case instead of ribbon.

Directions

As you will notice from the cutting diagram we have made full use of the finished edges of the twin sheet. Sheet (**a**) will have one hemmed edge and the wide casing of the sheet. Therefore, the right side and bottom is all that will need to be hemmed. Sheet (**b**) will have the bottom and right side hemmed and you will hem the left side. The extra length is to accommodate the wide 3" casing. Also, pillow case (**a**) will make use of the casing, and pillow case (**b**) has extra length to accommodate a 3" casing.

Crib Sheet (a)

1. Cut out. Take out the stitching across the top casing (if you find the right thread the whole row will easily unravel). Take out the stitching on the hemmed side far enough to clear the casing. Save the twill tape if your sheet has it. If you would like to narrow the width of the casing to 3", cut 2" off of the raw edge.

2. Press the casing edge under 1/2" and again 3". Cut 58" of the Swiss edging and hem both ends. Stitch a gathering thread and gather to fit across the sheet within 1" of each edge. This edge will be hemmed later. Place the raw edge of the Swiss edging 1/4" under the folded edge of the

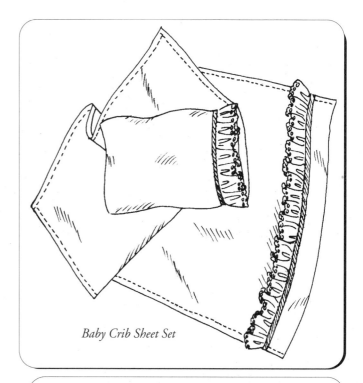

Baby Crib Sheet Set

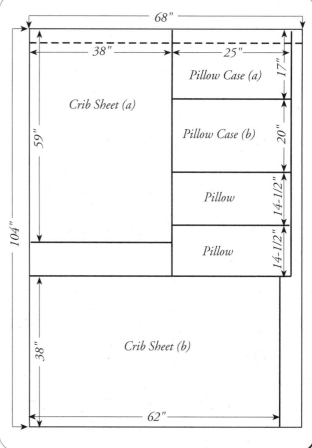

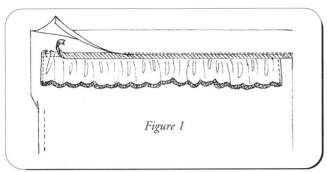

Figure 1

casing. Place the twill tape on top of the Swiss edging and under the folded edge of the casing. Stitch along the folded edge of the casing (**fig. 1**).

3. Finish the sides of the sheet by folding in 1/2" and 1/2" again. When you come to the Swiss edging, lift it and stitch underneath it, then tie off (**fig. 2**). Place the hem back under the presser foot and stitch the remaining hem on the casing with the edging down and out of the way (**fig. 3**).

Pillow Case (a)

1. Take out the stitching in the casing. Save the twill tape. Cut off 1" from the raw edge for a 3" casing.

2. Fold the raw edge under once 1/2". Press and hem. Fold under once more 7-1/4" and press. Fold the casing back up in the opposite direction creating a 1/2" deep tuck. Fold down in the opposite direction 3-1/4" (**fig. 4**). Press.

3. Cut 39" of the Swiss edging. Gather to fit the across the pillow case. Place the raw edge of the edging under the folded edge of the tuck. Place the twill tape of ribbon on top of the edging and under the folded edge of the tuck. Stitch along the edge of the tuck making sure to catch the hemmed edge of the casing on the back side (**fig. 5**).

4. Fold the pillow case in half and with right sides together, stitch a 1/2" seam along the side and bottom (**fig. 6**). Serge or finish the edge.

Crib Sheet (b)

1. Follow same instructions as for Crib Sheet (a) and omit step 1.

Pillow Case (b)

1. Follow the same directions as pillow case (a) and omit step 1.

Instructions For Pillow

1. Fold the fabric right sides together. Stitch the cut edges with a 1/2" seam and leave an opening to stuff.

2. Stuff with poly fiber fill and close. Insert into pillow case. ❖

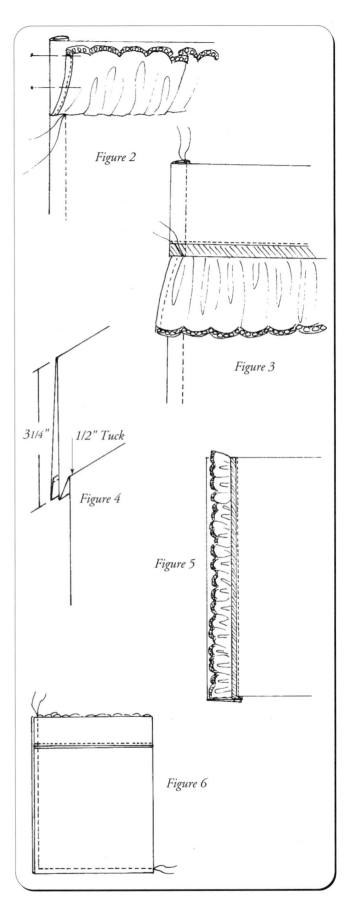

Figure 2

Figure 3

3 1/4"   1/2" Tuck

Figure 4

Figure 5

Figure 6

Baby Memorabilia Hoop

What a fun way to celebrate a new baby's arrival! Making this wonderful hoop for the new parent would be a treasure for now and for the baby's home when he/she is all grown up. This one has crocheted booties filled with cotton and potpourri, a rabbit dressed in a little sweet dress with beauty pins on the skirt, a necklace with a locket, a sterling baby rattle, dried roses, a hand made baby bonnet with a lock of hair glued onto it, a name bracelet, and a baby announcement. Of special interest in this hoop is a baby music box which has been covered with baby wrapping paper with a hole large enough for the winding stem of the music box to peek out. Satin ribbon ties this special musical baby present. and the song in the box is *Lullaby and Good Night*. A large embroidery hoop is covered with fabric and trimmed on the inside with satin ribbon—all glue gunned. Gathered French lace is glued around the outside rim and a large satin wired bow is tied to one side. Organdy is inside the hoop to hold all of the items.

Baby Memorabilia Hoop

Materials Needed

✿ 1- Quilting hoop 12" x 14" x 1" or 1/2"

✿ 1- Piece of organdy large enough to fit inside the hoop.

✿ Pink, blue or yellow bias fabric strip 1/2" wider than the hoop and long enough to wrap completely around the outside.

✿ Pink, blue, or yellow satin ribbon the same width as the hoop and long enough to fit around the inside.

✿ Lace edging the width desired, and twice the outside measurement of the hoop.

✿ 2-yds. of wired ribbon for bow.

✿ Fabric glue and hot glue and glue sticks.

✿ Memorabilia of your baby or if making a gift use an assortment of baby keepsakes

✿ Suggestions:Booties; potppourri; diaper pins; rattle; bonnet; announcement card; baby bracelet; a lock of hair; a small toy; a music box wrapped as a gift; and some dried flowers if you like.

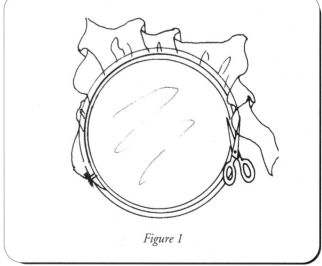

Figure 1

Directions

1. Insert organdy in the hoop as you would a quilt or embroidery. Pull taut and trim off excess (**fig. 1**).

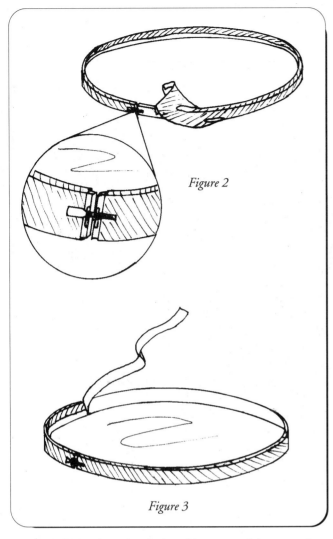

Figure 2

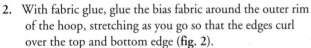

Figure 3

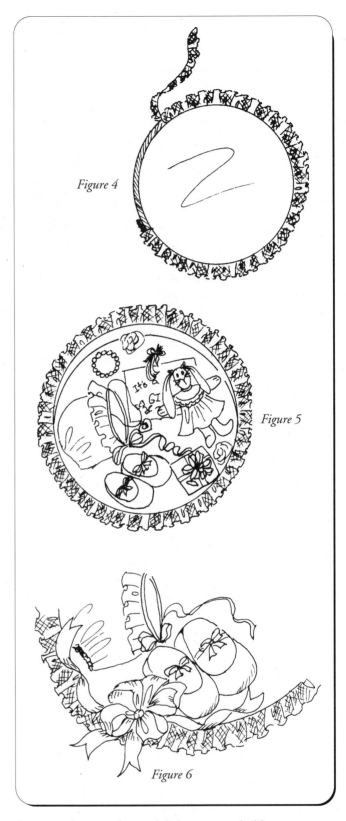

Figure 4

Figure 5

Figure 6

2. With fabric glue, glue the bias fabric around the outer rim of the hoop, stretching as you go so that the edges curl over the top and bottom edge (**fig. 2**).

3. Glue the satin ribbon to the inside rim, covering the raw edges of the bias tape (**fig. 3**).

4. Gather the lace edging and glue along the edge of the rim (**fig. 4**).

5. Arrange the keepsakes and hot glue or tack in place (**fig. 5**).

6. Make a 6 loop bow and tails out of the wide wire ribbon. Glue over the hoop screw or clamps (**fig. 6**).

Helpful Hints

1. Stuff the booties with foam to give them form. Glue dried rose petals to the foam at the opening.

2. Stuff the bonnet with batting of fiber fill to shape it.

3. To hold the rattle in place without a blob of glue, tack ribbons to the organdy with thread and tie the rattle on with bows.

4. Wrap the music box with baby paper and ribbon.

5. Scatter dried roses or flowers and glue. ▩

Victorian Tassel

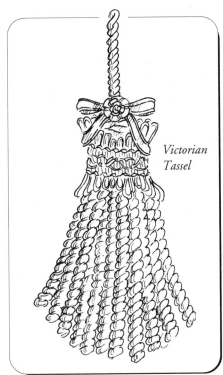

Victorian
Tassel

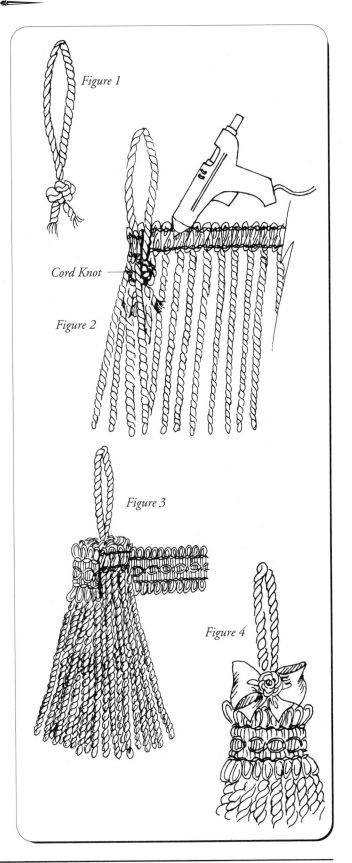

Figure 1

Cord Knot

Figure 2

Figure 3

Figure 4

This tassel would be so pretty in your living room, dining room, study, library, bedroom or den. Anywhere you have a pretty chest or draperies to tie back, this tassel would be lovely. Made with fringe in two shades of ecru, the fringe is wrapped around and around into a tassel shape. A piece of the fringe serves as the tie for the tassel and another piece of two inch fringe finishes the top and holds the wraps together. A tiny gold rosette with more ribbon trimmed with gold embellishes the top of the wraps. This tassel would be lovely for a gift for almost anyone on your list.

Materials Needed

- ❧ 6" of Braid
- ❧ 1/4 yd of heavy fringe or bullion fringe
- ❧ 12" cord to match fringe
- ❧ Hot glue gun and glue sticks
- ❧ Gold ribbon for rosette and bow

Directions

1. Fold cord in half, knot the end and glue the knot (**fig.1**).

2. Wrap fringe around the cord above the knot and glue as you go (**fig. 2**).

3. Wrap the top of the fringe with braid and glue (**fig. 3**).

4. Add wire ribbon or silk flowers and embellish as desired (**fig. 4**). ❧

Porcelain Jar With Embroidery

Using a pale blue porcelain jar from YLI, a pretty piece of pink, blue and green shadow work embroidery peeks from the padded top. Gathered ecru French lace dances all the way around this jar. This jar would be the perfect gift for any woman on your list. I can just see this jar in a lovely bedroom, dressing room, sun porch, or guest bathroom. I can see a little girl loving this jar to keep special pieces of jewelry and barrettes. Using a beautiful jar like this for a jewelry box would be nice too. These porcelain jar kits are easy to assemble and come in a beautiful gift box also.

Materials Needed

- ❊ 1 purchased porcelain jar kit*
- ❊ Enough fabric to fit into an embroidery hoop
- ❊ Beads or pearls
- ❊ Embroidery floss
- ❊ DMC Color #
- ❊ Pink #605
- ❊ Lt. Blue #800
- ❊ Green #911
- ❊ 1" wide lace edging twice the lid ring measurement

To order a porcelain jar kit or to receive a catalog, write or call toll free:

YLI Corporation
P.O. box 109
Provo, Utah 84601
1-800-854-1932

The porcelain jar kit provides basic instructions for assembling the decorative lid. These instructions are appropriate for flat paper designs such as a painted design or a photograph, however, they are not appropriate for fabric needlework. Follow the instructions below to apply fabric needlework to the decorative jar lid.

Directions

1. Complete the shadow embroidery design using the template provided and the shadow embroidery instructions in this book. Template on page 147.

2. Use the plastic or stiff paper circle from the lid provided in the porcelain jar kit to center the area of the design that will be exposed through the lid ring. Mark a circle 1/2" larger all around than the plastic circle (**fig. 1**). Cut the design out on this line.

3. With a needle and thread, straight stitch around the design 1/4" away from the raw edge (**fig. 2**).

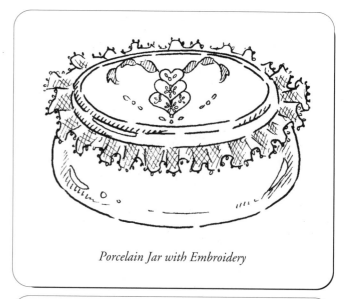

Porcelain Jar with Embroidery

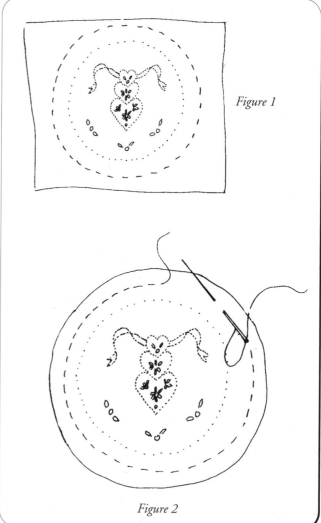

Figure 1

Figure 2

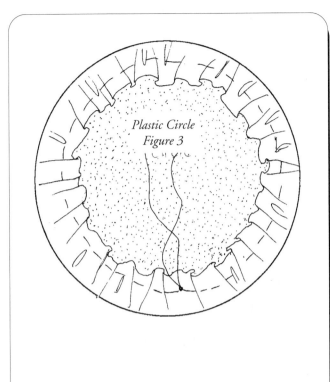

Plastic Circle
Figure 3

4. Place the silk ribbon design over the batting or foam and the plastic circle and pull the thread tightly to wrap the fabric around the circle and tie (**fig. 3**).

5. Place the lid frame ring over the embroidery, then snap the metal circle inside the frame.

6. Gather the lace and glue around the inside edge of the lid frame (**fig. 4**).

7. Glue the soft velvet-like bottom circle to the metal bottom (**fig. 5**). ▩

Shadow Embroidery Design Template For Jar

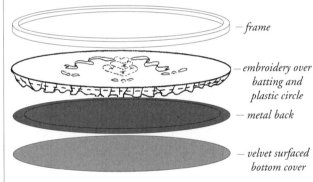

— frame

— embroidery over batting and plastic circle

— metal back

— velvet surfaced bottom cover

Figure 4

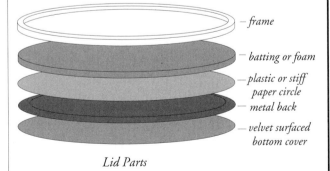

— frame

— batting or foam

— plastic or stiff paper circle

— metal back

— velvet surfaced bottom cover

Lid Parts

Figure 5

Introduction To Heirloom Quilt and Shadow Appliqué Quilt

Making heirloom quilts which are quick and easy has become a passion in our industry. We chose not one but two spectacular quilts for this television series. The shadow appliqué quilt could be called "Life's Celebration" quilt because it is designed to go from a baby's birth to his/her marriage. I called upon Angela Pullen to design the squares in this quilt and Louise Baird to interpret Angela's designs in the construction of the quilt. Putting these two talents together was pure genius, I think. We think you will love the quilt. The quilt is composed of twenty 13" squares with a 9 1/2" lace circle in the center of each square. Measuring 76" by 63" from ruffle to ruffle, the quilt could be made either smaller or larger, depending on your particular use of the quilt.

The names of the squares are "God Gave Us Joanna, Feb. 23, 1976, First Word, First Tooth, Baptism, First Party, First Haircut, First Birthday, First Step, First Recital, First Day of School, First Spend The Night, First Prom, First Date, Graduation, Engagement, and Wedding." The upper left and right and lower left and right squares are machine embroidered in little flowers. Louise used machine decorative stitches to do all of the writing, except for the "God Gave Us Joanna" square. That was done in appliqué stitch. She simply stitched along the lines of the alphabet given in this book with different decorative stitches. The dates of the events in each square (when known) were stitched in with the built in letters of the alphabet in the machine. Since this is a quilt for Joanna we left the engagement and wedding dates blank. I certainly plan for those dates to be a long time coming.

Louise used a combination of fabrics for the shadow appliqué. For the faces she used a pinkish peach tone of broadcloth; for the clothing, she used little tiny pastel quilting type prints; for the shoes, scissors, balloons, birthday cake, school house scene, and ballet costume, she used solid broadcloth colors. Using tiny quilting prints for shadow appliqué really gives an interesting look for this peek a boo technique. On shadow appliqué I really like to use lots of interesting fabrics for the underneath fabric; however, I like to match the fabric in the accent color with thread for the stitching on top. You will find the individual square designs along with the alphabet included in this book. Of course, we would love for you to make up your own squares based on your child's life.

The beautiful heirloom technique quilt (on page 149) which is the second quilt in this series, was designed by Kathy Brower and Margaret Taylor and constructed by Margaret. The squares in this masterpiece quilt have the following techniques in them: shark's teeth, heart appliqué, lacy pocket for a baby rattle, curved puffing, silk ribbon embroidery/Madeira border, interlocking hearts, Celtic lace shaping, Australian windowpane heart/shadow diamonds, circle lace on netting tea towel square, wedding bell lace shaping, heirloom crazy patch, and double hearts shadow appliqué. The quilt is sashed together and is made of Swiss Nelona in several colors. The blocks are alternately, pink, blue and ecru Nelona; six squares are pink, four are blue, and two are ecru. The sashing and border of the quilt is ecru Nelona. The laces are ecru and the silk ribbon embroidery is done in ecru, dusty pink, green and baby blue. The 1 1/4" wide ecru silk ribbon is twisted and tacked up and down the lengthwise sashing strips. Two large silk ribbon bows are tied in the middle of the quilt for embellishment. The corners of the quilt are leaf shaped. Once again, both of these quilts are easy to make and allow one to use many different techniques to create an heirloom to be treasured forever. ▨

General Directions for the Heirloom Technique Quilt

General Direction

1. The templates for each square are in the pattern sections of this book.

2. The directions for different techniques are in the technique sections of this book.

3. The general directions for putting this specific quilt together are found in this section of the book.

4. All seam allowances are 1/2".

5. Individual squares begin as 12 1/2" by 12 1/2" squares, except the Shark's Teeth Square which begins as a 12 1/2" by 20 1/2" piece of fabric.

6. For an added idea, any one of these quilt squares would make a beautiful pillow with a back and a ruffle added!

Materials Needed for the Heirloom Technique Quilt

- 3/4 yds. pink Nelona Swiss batiste or other fabric
- 3/4 yds. blue Nelona Swiss batiste or other fabric
- 4-1/2 yds. ecru Nelona Swiss batiste or other fabric for quilt back, sashing, border, and squares
- 6 yds. ecru broadcloth for lining
- 7 yds. 1 1/4" ecru YLI silk ribbon
- 1 pack each YLI silk
- 1 silver baby rattle
- 1 package of Mountain Mist quilt "light batting"
- 1 tea towel with embroidery
- 12 1/2" by 12 1/2" piece of netting
- 1/8 yd. organdy
- Lace scraps, buttons, and Swiss embroidery scraps for crazy patch square
- 1 3/4 yds. 5/8" ecru insertion lace
- 1 3/4 yds. 1/2" ecru insertion lace
- 1 1/4 yds. of ecru entredeux
- 3 yds. ecru 5/8" lace edging
- pink thread for Australian Windowpane heart

1. Lacy Pocket For A Baby Rattle Square

Having a fancy pocket in which to put a treasure seemed like a good idea for this pink Nelona quilt square. The ecru lace diamonds butt together to make a square. Entredeux travels around all three sides of both triangles to make a little opening which becomes a pocket. We used silk ribbon attached to the quilt to tie the sterling silver baby rattle onto the quilt. A fancy large silk ribbon bow was tied to make it even prettier and a little bit fussier. This would be just as pretty as a pillow for a baby gift.

Supplies:

- 1-3/4 yds. of lace insertion 5/8" wide
- 1-3/4 yds. of lace insertion 1/2 inch wide
- 1-1/4 yd. of entredeux
- 3 yds of 5/8" lace edging
- 1 yd. of 1-1/4" ecru silk ribbon
- A baby rattle or memento to place inside the pocket
- 1- 12-1/2" x 12-1/2" block of pink fabric

Directions:

1. Using a washout marker, trace a 6-1/4 inch square in the center of your block. Template on page 321.

2. After deciding which direction the lace insertion for the pocket will go, begin zigzagging the lace insertion pieces together to form the triangular template for each side of the square. Alternate the two widths of lace insertion. This project would be a great place to use all of those short pieces of lace insertion you have in your stash. The lace insertions do not have to match.

3. When you have 1/2 of the block completed, repeat the process for the other side. Place the completed piece of lace insertion on top of the pocket template leaving 1/2 inch between the two lace pieces. Using a washout marker, draw the pocket template on the lace pieces. Attach entredeux around all sides of the lace insertion triangles using the technique entredeux to lace.

4. Stitch the gathered lace edging along the outer edges of the whole triangular piece.

5. Place the lace triangles together to form a square; center this square on the fabric block; zigzag along the outside edges of the entredeux to attach to the quilt square. Do not stitch where the two inside sides meet. This will be a pocket.

6. It is now necessary to make the pocket opening smaller. This is done by stitching the pocket opening closed about 2" on each side. The opening is now about 3 inches.

7. The silk ribbon is tacked in the center of the pocket opening and the baby rattle is tied onto this ribbon. Tie a pretty bow with the ends of the silk ribbon. ✽

2. Silk Ribbon Embroidery/Madeira Appliqué Border Square

The base color of this square is ecru; the Madeira Appliqué border is baby blue Nelona stitched in ecru thread. The silk ribbon embroidery in the middle of the square features ecru silk ribbon for the bow and streamers, pale green for the leaves and stems, baby blue for the lazy daisy flowers and dusty peach for the rosebuds and one lazy daisy flower. The lazy daisy flowers have baby pearls stitched in the center.

Supplies:
- 1 - 12-1/2" x 12-1/2" block of ecru fabric for the background
- 1 - 12-1/2" x 12-1/2" block of blue fabric for border
- 1- 12-1/2" by 12-1/2" square of water soluble stabilizer (WSS)
- Washout marker
- Silk or Glass Head Pins
- 100 or 110 Wing Needle for Pinstitch
- Thread to match background fabric (ecru)
- YLI Silk Ribbons: Ecru (7mm) #156; Blue (4mm) #9; Green (2mm) #18; Lt. Green (2mm) #31; Dusty Peach (4mm) #76.

Directions:
1. Starch and press both blocks of fabric.

2. Refer to Madeira Appliqué Doll Dress for illustrations and specific stitching instructions. Using the washout marker, draw the Madeira appliqué template on the blue block. Place the WSS over his block. Straight stitch on the template lines. Cut 1/4" above this stitching line of fabric to remove the center. Clip curves and points. Turn the WSS to the other side, like a facing. Use a point turner along curves and points to ensure a sharp line. Press (no starch). Template on page 319 and 321.

3. Place border on ecru square. Pin in place. Starch and press. Stitch around along the inner edge of the border with a pinstitch or zigzag.

4. Trace the silk ribbon design in the center of the appliquéed block and stitch according to the silk ribbon instructions given in this program guide.

5. Soak the square to remove the WSS. ✽

3. Three Interlocking Hearts Square

This beautiful square has three ecru lace hearts on pink Nelona. They graduate in size from large to medium to small. Using the heart lace shaping directions in this book, you can make this type of interlocking hearts.

Supplies:
- 1 - 12-1/2" x 12-1/2" block of pink fabric
- 2 yds. of ecru 3/8" insertion
- Thread to match lace insertion
- Washout marker
- Silk or Glass Head Pins

Directions:
1. Using the template provided and a washout marker, trace the hearts on the block of fabric. Template on page 320.

2. Shape the lace according to the instructions given in the lace shaping section in this book. Do not cut the fabric from behind the lace.

3. Stitch in place using a zigzag stitch, entredeux stitch, or pinstitch. ✽

4. Celtic Circles Square

Since we introduced Celtic lace shaping in Sew Beautiful magazine, our heirloom sewers have just loved it. One of the "newest" ideas in lace shaping comes from the quilting industry. Of course, it isn't new at all! Buy those plastic quilting templates and use them for drawing your lace shaping designs. You can also use skinny puffing to shape in those shapes also. This Celtic square on blue Nelona with ecru lace has four interlocking circles. This is such a beautiful heirloom idea!

Supplies:
- 2 yds. of 3/8" ecru lace insertion
- 12-1/2" x 12-1/2" block of blue fabric

Directions:

1. Draw the template on the block of fabric. Template on page 318.

2. Follow the lace shaping techniques given in the Celtic Lace Shaping section of this book.

3. Stitch the lace insertion in place using a zigzag stitch, pinstitch, or entredeux stitch. ❋

5. Heart Appliqué Block

This ever popular appliqué technique is used on a blue Nelona square. Four larger hearts made of ecru broadcloth (a little heavier than Swiss batiste) are filled in with four smaller hearts of the same fabric. The appliqué thread is ecru to match the broadcloth hearts.

Supplies:

- ❊ Scraps of ecru fabric for the hearts
- ❊ Sulky 40 wt. rayon thread
- ❊ 1-12-1/2" x 12-1/2" block of blue Nelona fabric

Directions:

1. Follow the appliqué instructions given in the appliqué section of this book to attach the hearts. Template on page 319.

2. Using the template, stitch your hearts in place. ❋

6. Curved Puffing Square

This curved puffing square is simply a swirl of puffing placed from one side of the square to another. Actually, we didn't put in a template because you can swirl this puffing any way you want to including swirling it into a circle or oval or any shape. The puffing has shaped 5/8" lace on either side. You can use any width of lace you would like to encase the sides of the puffing.

Supplies:

- ❊ 1 yd. of 5/8" ecru lace insertion
- ❊ 1 strip of ecru fabric 2-1/4" wide by 45" long
- ❊ 12-1/2" x 12-1/2" block of pink fabric

Directions:

1. Run two rows of gathering thread along both sides of the 2-1/4" wide strip of fabric. You can also use the gathering foot on your sewing machine.

2. Using a washout marker, draw the shaped puffing design onto the quilt block.

3. Gather the strip of fabric and shape according to your chosen design. Pin in place using a fabric board.

4. Place the insertion lace on top of the puffing. The puffing strip has a 1/4" seam allowance for attaching the lace insertion.

5. Stitch the lace insertion on the insides to the puffing using a zigzag stitch.

6. Lift up the lace insertion and trim away the excess puffing.

7. Zig zag the other side of the lace insertion to the quilt square.

8. If desired, you can trim away the quilt fabric from behind the lace insertion but it isn't necessary and probably is a little stronger if you don't. ❋

7. Wedding Bell Lace Bow Square

This precious square has a lace shaped wedding bell, a tied bow and streamers for the top of the bell and gathered lace edging for the bell clapper. This little bell would be precious used on a ring bearer's pillow also. Another idea for using this precious wedding bell would be to make a memory pillow giving the wedding date, bride, groom, place, etc. I think this little bell is absolutely wonderful!

Supplies:

- ❊ Washout marker
- ❊ Silk or Glass Head Pins
- ❊ Thread to match lace
- ❊ 1-3/4 yards of 3/8" lace insertion
- ❊ 6" of lace edging
- ❊ 12-1/2" x 12-1/2" blue block of fabric

Directions:

1. Using the washout marker, trace the design on the square of fabric. Template on page 318.

2. Shape the lace bell following the instructions given under the lace shaping section of this book. Shape a piece of lace for the bottom of the bell .

3. The bow may be shaped using the flip-flop method or tied bow method. Place the bow at the top of the bell. Shape the bow streamers and slip them underneath the center of the tied bow.

4. Stitch in place using a zigzag stitch, entredeux stitch, or pinstitch.

5. The bell clapper is formed by gathering the lace insertion in a 1/2 circle and stitching in place. ❈

8. Australian Windowpane Heart/Shadow Diamonds Square

Australian windowpane is the technique for the larger heart in the center of this pink Nelona square. Pink thread is used for the appliqué stitching and also for putting the large monogram in the center of the heart. Four shadow diamonds are placed in each corner of the quilt square using the easy method of shadow diamonds.

Supplies:

❀ 1 8" block of white Swiss organdy

❀ 1 spool of thread to match the color of the quilt block

❀ 12-1/2" x 12-1/2" block of pink fabric

❀ Wing needle for wing needle entredeux stitch.

Directions:

1. Following the instructions given in the Australian Windowpane section of this book, place the heart in the center of the quilt square. Template on page 319.

2. The heart may have a single pattern decorative stitch or monogram placed in the center.

3. Using the directions given in the Shadow Diamonds section of this book. Place four organdy shadow diamonds around the square. ❈

9. Shark's Teeth Square

The shark's teeth technique has been so popular for children's clothing, women's clothing and items for the home. I have seen one ring bearer's pillow made using this technique. This square made on pink Nelona has four tucks facing one direction and four facing the other. The shark's teeth section in the center of each makes a pretty design. As with every other square on this quilt, this would make a lovely pillow for your bedroom.

Supplies:

❀ 1-12-1/2" x 20 1/2" block of pink fabric

❀ Washout marker

❀ Silk or Glass Head Pins

Directions:

1. Using a washout marker, trace the Sharks Teeth template on the block of fabric, making sure that it is traced in the center of the block. Template on page 312.

2. Fold on the fold lines and stitch using 1/2" tucks. This is also marked on the fold guide on the shark's teeth template. There will be a total of 8 tucks, 4 on each side of the center.

3. Equally divide the tucks and press toward the center of the block.

4. Trace the shark's teeth 1/2" template in the center of each set of 4 tucks.

5. Complete the shark's teeth by following the directions found in the shark's teeth technique section of this book. Refer to Shark's Teeth Pillow for illustrations. ❈

10. Shadow Appliqué Block

Supplies:

❀ 12-1/2" x 12-1/2" block of ecru Nelona

❀ 12-1/2" x 12-1/2" block of blue fabric

❀ Washout marker

Directions:

1. Trace the heart template design on the top of the ecru block. Template on page 320.

2. Place the block of blue fabric underneath the top block. Pin.

3. Follow the directions given in the Shadow Appliqué section of this book. Use a tiny zigzag and stitch around all template lines. Turn to the back, refer to the template, cut away all the unshaded areas, leaving blue fabric in the shaded areas. This forms the heart design. ❈

11. Heirloom Crazy Patch Square

Sometimes mothers used to save scraps of each dress she made to use in making a quilt later. This is such a wonderful idea. Using that same idea, save scraps of laces, fancy bands, buttons, and other trims, and make this beautiful crazy patch square for your heirloom quilt. This type of crazy patch would make a lovely collection of different shaped pillows for your precious one's bed. You might use these scraps to make a roll pillow, a heart pillow and a square one. Enjoy your crazy patch since it is the ultimate sewing recycling!

Supplies:

⚘ 12-1/2" x 12-1/2" block of fabric

⚘ Scraps of laces, Swiss trims, buttons—anything you like for crazy patch

Directions:

This is a great place to use any bits and pieces of lace insertion, Swiss trims, motifs, or pearl buttons that you might have. It is so easy to do. Simply lay the pieces on the block being careful that the raw edges will be under a finished edge or finished with a decorative stitch or zigzag stitch. Do all placement before beginning to stitch. Pin the pieces in place and stitch using a zigzag or decorative stitch. A word of caution regarding decorative stitches, is to make sure that the stitch chosen will cover the unfinished edges of the laces. You may use pearl buttons, decorative charms, silk ribbon bows, or any other decorative items desired. ▩

12. Circle Lace On Netting Tea Towel Square

Sometimes I have mismatched antique linens, new Chinese linens, handkerchiefs or napkins which are really beautiful and I really don't know what to do with just one of something. The lace shaping is a circle made around a Chinese tea towel with lovely appliqué and embroidery on it. You could use any scrap of anything you wanted treasured in the center of this type of quilt square. As a matter of fact, I think it would be beautiful to do a whole heirloom quilt using those special things put into circles, hearts, diamonds, or teardrops for the theme of the whole quilt.

Supplies:

⚘ 1 tea towel with a pretty design

⚘ 24" of 3/8" lace insertion

⚘ 1-12-1/2" x 12-1/2" block of netting

⚘ 1-12-1/2" x 12-1/2" block of fabric

Directions:

1. Draw a circle around the design on the tea towel. Be sure to center your design in the circle. Template on page 321.

2. Following the lace shaping instructions given in this book, stitch the lace insertion to the tea towel along the inside edge of the lace.

3. Trim the tea towel from behind the lace insertion.

4. Place the netting on the Nelona square and treat as one layer of fabric. Place the motif circle on top of the netting. Stitch in place through all layers along the outer edge of the lace circle. ▩

Constructing The Quilt

Supplies:

⚘ 4 yds. of fabric for quilt backing, border and sashing

⚘ 6 yds. broadcloth for quilt lining

⚘ 1 package of Mountain Mist, Quilt-Light Batting to fit the quilt

All Seams 1/2".

Directions:

Once the blocks are completed and the arrangement of the blocks decided upon, it is time to begin the process of sashing the blocks together.

1. For the quilt back, cut the 4 yards of fabric in half and stitch together forming a large fabric piece approximately 90" by 72". Press the seam to one side.

2. Cut the sashing and border strips from the sides of the piece (**fig.1**).

3. Cut 9, 12-1/2" strips from the 3" strip of sashing (**see fig. 1**). Sew a sashing strip to the bottom of block one.

4. Sew block two to the other side of the sashing strip (**fig. 2**).

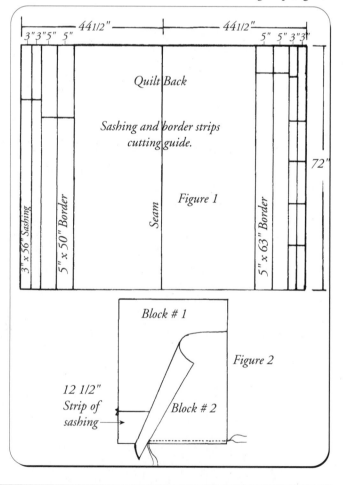

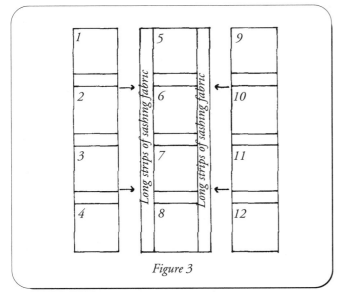

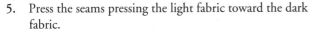

Figure 3

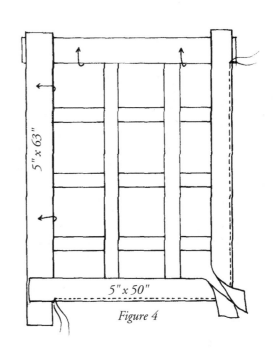

Figure 4

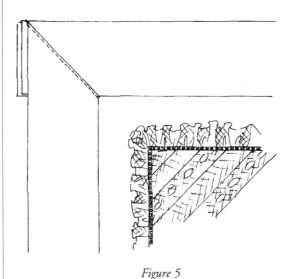

Figure 5

5. Press the seams pressing the light fabric toward the dark fabric.

6. Continue until you have a strip of 4 blocks. Repeat this process until you have 3 rows of 4 blocks.

7. Cut two 56" long strips from the remaining 3" wide sashing strips (**see fig. 1**).

8. Sew the long sashing fabric to each side of the center row. Place the outer rows on the outer edge of the long sashing strip and stitch in place (**fig. 3**).

9. Press the seams by pressing light fabric to dark.

10. Border - The border on this quilt is 4" wide finished and 5" wide unfinished.

11. Cut two strips of fabric 50 inches long from the 5" border strips (**see fig. 1**).

12. Cut two strips of fabric 63 inches long from the 5" border strip

13. Place the border pieces along the outside edge of the quilt top and stitch in place. When you come to the corners, do not stitch the border pieces together (**fig. 4**). Finish all 4 sides of the quilt in this manner.

14. Using the fold back miter technique, miter the four corners of the quilt border (**fig. 5**). Starch and press well. The corners may be stitched together using a regular seam or they may be stitched together by topstitching on the folded edge.

     **14. Lining- When selecting the fabric to make your lining, you may use a less expensive fabric such as Imperial batiste. Make sure that the fabric you choose does not alter the color of the quilt top in any way and remember that if you have trimmed the fabric from behind the laces, the lining will show through the lace insertions.

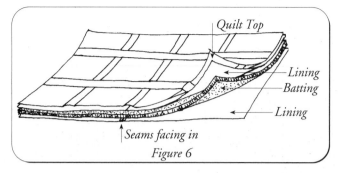

Quilt Top

Lining
Batting

Lining

Seams facing in

Figure 6

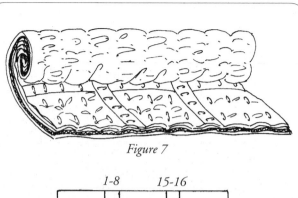

Figure 7

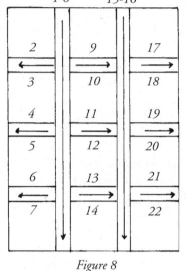

Figure 8

Follow this sequence to machine quilt the sashing. This will keep the top smooth.

15. Cut 4, two yard pieces of lining fabric. Place two pieces together, selvage to selvage, and stitch a seam. Repeat for the third and forth piece. This creates two lining pieces.

16. Layer: lining, batting, lining (seams facing the batting) and the quilt top facing up (**fig. 6**). Pin, (a lot), all layers in place (safety pins are great for this because they will not slip out). As you pin the pieces together, make sure that you remove all wrinkles and folds in the quilt top and batting sandwich. The more pins you use, the easier it will be to keep the pieces from slipping during quilting.

17. Roll the pinned quilt top and batting sandwich into a tube (**fig. 7**). When you start quilting, you will have to feed a great deal of bulk through the machine. Make sure that you do not pull or push the quilt top through the sewing machine because it will distort the stitches. This is where a walking foot or even feed foot comes in handy.

18. The quilt featured in this program guide was simply quilted using a straight stitch and stitching in the ditch along the sashing strips. When using a straight stitch, it will be necessary to lengthen your stitch to approximates 3. In order to determine what works best on your machine, use scraps of the fabric used for the quilt top, make a scrap batting sandwich, and test stitch your machine length.

19. Stitch along the outside edge of one of the long strips of sashing. Now stitch along the short sashing strips. (**refer to fig. 8**). Follow the directional arrows and stitching order of Figure 8.

20. Unroll the quilt and stitch the short sashing strips on the center row of blocks.

21. Repeat steps 19 and 20 for the last row of blocks (**fig. 8**).

22. Trim all layers even with the quilt top.

23. Place the right side of the quilt back to the right side of the quilt top. Pin in place. Trim even with quilt top. Place the corner template (found on the center pull out) along the corners of the quilt. Trace in all four corners. Stitch along the sides of the quilt and the traced lines of the template leaving a 12" opening for turning (**fig. 9**).

24. Carefully trim the seam allowance and clip the corners.

25. Turn the quilt and slip stitch the opening closed. ▧

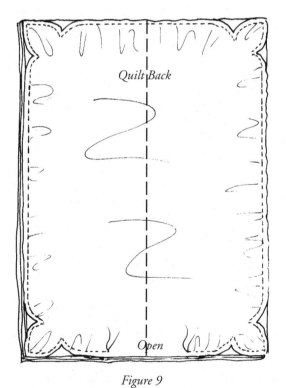

Quilt Back

Open

Figure 9

Shadow Appliqué Quilt

Shadow Appliqué Quilt

Supplies

- ❀ 1-1/2 yds. Swiss batiste
- ❀ 7 yds. Swiss broadcloth
- ❀ Extra loft batting (Single Bed - 72" by 90")
- ❀ 37 yds. of 1" :Insertion lace
- ❀ 20 yds. of 2-1/2" to 3" edging lace
- ❀ Machine embroidery thread, white and colors
- ❀ Various fabrics for shadow appliqué
- ❀ Open toe appliqué foot
- ❀ Water soluble marking pencils
- ❀ Water soluble stabilizer (Solvy, WSS)
- ❀ Size 70 and 80 needle
- ❀ Spray starch
- ❀ Soft tear away stabilizer
- ❀ Pocket or kindergarten scissors
- ❀ Appliqué scissors

All shadow applique quilt templates and letters are found in the pattern section of this book, page 322-327.

Directions

There are 15 event squares, four flower squares and one square with letters only.

1. Cut or tear the batiste into twenty 10" squares. These pieces will be used for the designs in the center of the circle.

2. Spray starch each of the batiste squares to give them body.

3. Find the center of the square by folding in half and then in half again. Mark center and quarter divisions.

4. Trace both lines of lace circle template on a piece of paper or tear away. Fold to find center and quarter points of the circle (**fig. 1**).

5. Event designs - Use the following directions on 15 squares for the event designs.

    a. On soft tear away stabilizer, mark a baseline and write (trace) the phrase on the baseline, spacing as needed. Fold this in half and mark the half way point. Trim close to the baseline and around the phrase. Snip in between each letter from the top to <u>(But not through)</u> the baseline (**fig. 2**).

    b. Mark a curved line 1-1/2 inches in from the inner line of the circle template. This is the line for the placement of the letters (**fig. 3**).

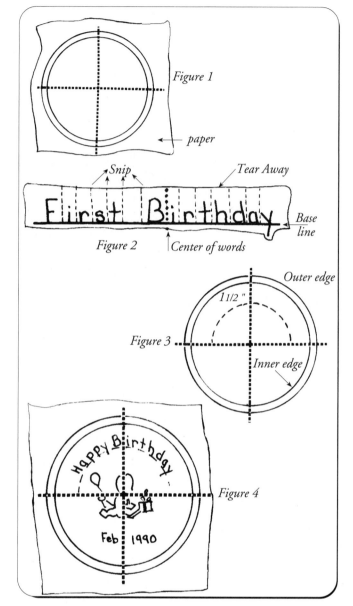

Figure 1 — paper

Figure 2 — Snip — Tear Away — Base line — Center of words

Figure 3 — Outer edge — 11/2 " — Inner edge

Figure 4

c. Match the center line of the circle with the center of the phrase. Match the baseline with the line drawn, curving the phrase. Trace the letters to the paper or Tear Away.

d. Trace design in desired position within the circle. A date can be added, if desired.

e. Place the fabric under the paper or tear away template and trace the design/lettering onto the batiste matching the centers of the fabric square and the circle design. Use a SHARP Dixon washout pencil or a quilting pencil that can be erased if necessary. Trace the outline of the circle onto the fabric also (**fig. 4**).

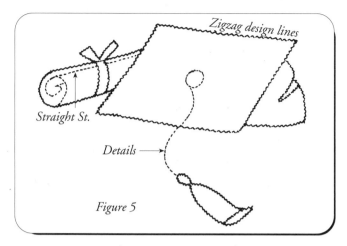

Zigzag design lines

Straight St.

Details →

Figure 5

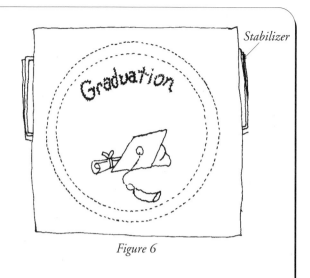

Stabilizer

Figure 6

f. *Shadow appliqué.* Place different fabrics between two layers of batiste to see what they will look like (some prints were used) on the sample. Prints with a white or light background and pastel colors worked the best. Match the top thread color to what shows through top layer. Use white thread in the bobbin. Stitch along the design lines using a narrow open zigzag (.5-1 mm width and .75 - 1.25 mm length)(**fig. 5**). Refer to the Shadow Applique directions in this book for specific instructions, page 265.

g Use a very short straight stitch for detailing (**see fig. 5**).

h. Use built in decorative stitches to stitch the letters. Place several layers of WSS under letters to prevent puckering. On a scrap of the same fabric that is stabilized try your decorative stitches. The width and length will need to be decreased, test to get correct proportions. When stitching on the letters, stitch slowly and watch how the stitch is formed. You should not pivot when the next move is a backward stitch. When turning curves or approaching a pivot, use the single pattern button if available (**fig. 6**).

6. Embroidery designs - 4 squares.

For the squares with the embroidery designs, position and trace in the center of the circle.

   a. Place the fabric in a hoop with several layers of WSS.

   b Use built-in stitches or a satin stitch zigzag changing the width to cover the flower or leaf design lines. The French knots are done with a narrow zigzag bar tack. The stems are a very narrow open zigzag (**fig. 7**).

7. Words only - 1 square.

   a. For the square with words only, position within the circle.

   b. Use a narrow satin stitch to cover all of the lines (**fig. 8**).

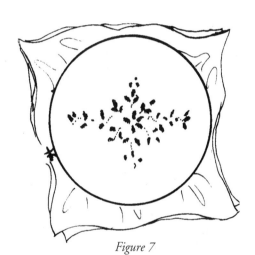

Figure 7

God Gave
Us
JOANNA
Feb. 23, 1976

Figure 8

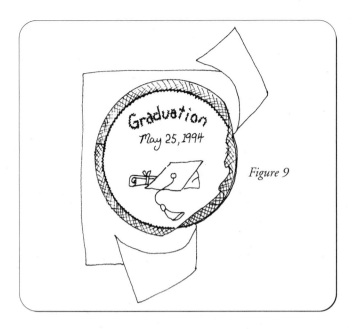

Figure 9

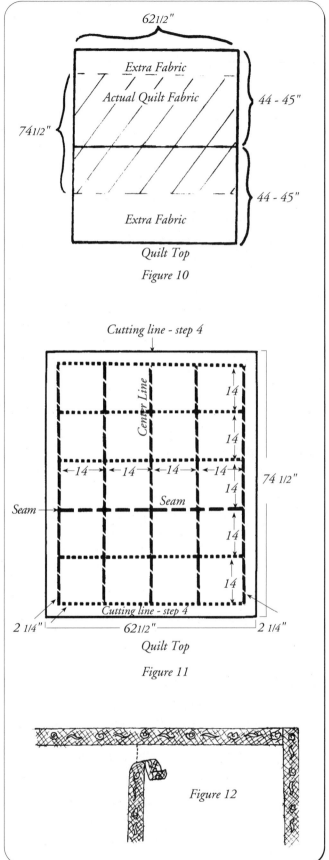

621/2"

Extra Fabric

Actual Quilt Fabric

44 - 45"

741/2"

44 - 45"

Extra Fabric

Quilt Top

Figure 10

Cutting line - step 4

Center Line

14

14

←14→ ←14→ ←14→ ←14→

14

74 1/2"

Seam

Seam

14

14

Cutting line - step 4

2 1/4"

621/2"

2 1/4"

Quilt Top

Figure 11

Figure 12

Construction of Quilt

1. Shape the insertion lace along the traced circle of each quilt square. Stitch along the inside edge of the lace circle only. Refer to the circle lace shaping directions in this book. Trim the excess fabric from under the lace close to the stitching. This will leave the lace circle and the inside design (**fig. 9**).

2. Cut or tear four pieces of broadcloth 62-1/2" long. Put two pieces aside for now.

3. Stitch two of the long edges together using a 1/4" seam. Press the seam open. The quilt will be cut to the correct size in step 4 (**fig.10**).

4. On the right side of the quilt top, measure three lines 14" apart above the seam and two lines 14" apart below the seam. These are the horizontal lace placement lines (**dotted lines on figure 11**). Add a line 2-1/4" from the last line on each end. This is the cutting line. The quilt top now measures 62-1/2" wide by 74-1/2" (**fig. 11**).

5. For vertical lace placement lines fold in half and mark this center line. Measure from this line and mark two line 14" apart on each side of this center line (**slashed line on fig. 11**).

6. Center lace insertion over the horizontal lines. Using a short narrow zigzag, stitch the lace to the fabric.

7. Repeat for vertical lace placement lines. At the ends of lace turn under about 1/4" before stitching (**fig. 12**).

Left: Diamond Lace Pintucks Doll Dress
Right: Celtic Lace Doll Dress ™

Left: Smocked Dress with Tatted Trim
Right: Watermelon Appliqué Doll Dress

Below Standing: Ribbon and Lace Party Doll Dress
Below Sitting: Purple Tulip Shadow Appliqué Dress

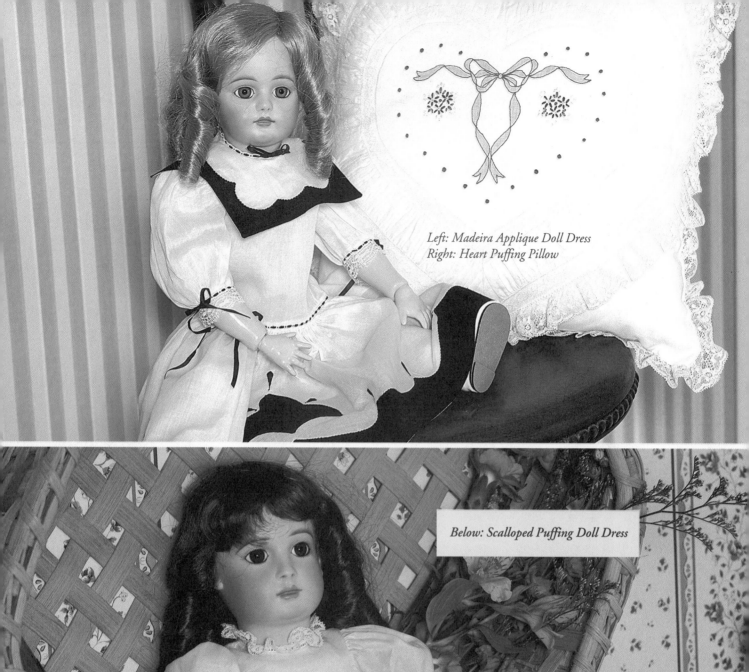

Left: Madeira Applique Doll Dress
Right: Heart Puffing Pillow

Below: Scalloped Puffing Doll Dress

Far Left: Crazy Patch Doll Dress
Middle Left: Dupioni Silk With Organdy Hearts Dress
Middle Right: Australian Windowpane Doll Dress
Far Right: Shark's Teeth Doll Dress

Lower Left: Baby Crib Sheet Set
Middle: T-Bonnet
Right: Lace Overlay Doll Dress

Insert Above: Battenburg Straw Hat
Below Far Left: Lace Embellished Bud Vase
Front Left: Crocheted Fan Pin
Right Back: Victorian Heart Wall Ornament
Right Front: Porcelain Jar With Embroidery

Left: Victorian Bear Centerpiece
Right: Flower Hair Wreath

Left: Veil With Blusher
Right: Veil With Crown Ruffle
Insert Below: Wedding Garter

Left: Lingerie Bag
Right: Cameo Photo Album

Below Left: Antique Sewing Wreath
Right: Crazy Patch Sewing Basket

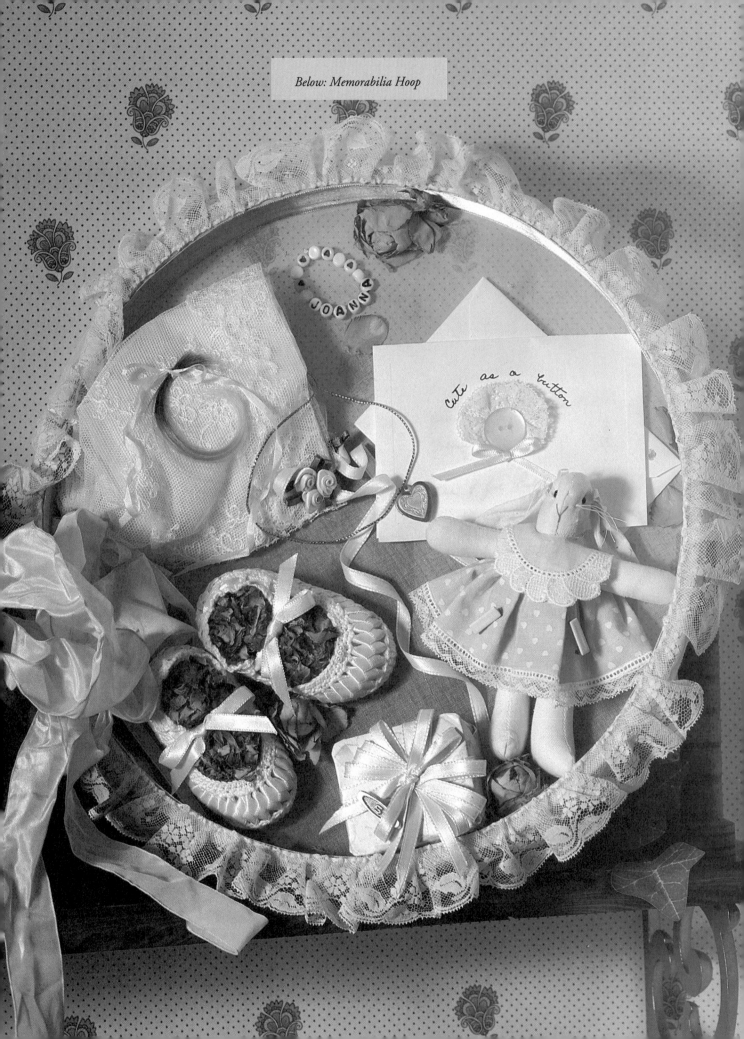

Cute as a button

Above Left: Victorian Tassel
Above Right: Diamond Braid Pillow

Below Left: Bi-Directional Shark's Teeth Pillow
Below Right: Pillow With Shark's Teeth

Above Left: Woven Basket Pillow
Above Right: Appliqued Rose Pillow

Below Left: Lace Shaped Baby Pillow
Below Middle: Lace Heart Demi-Pillow
Below Right: Celtic Boudoir Pillow

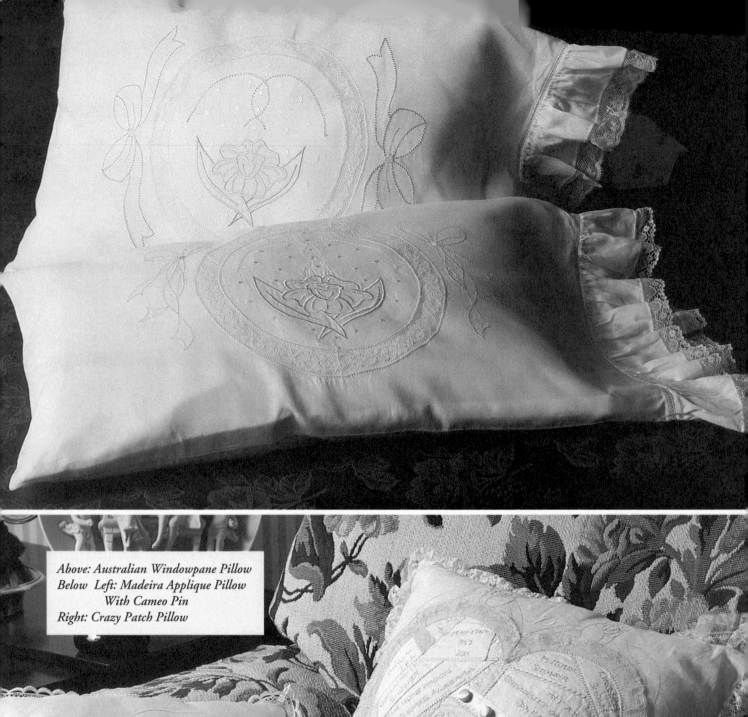

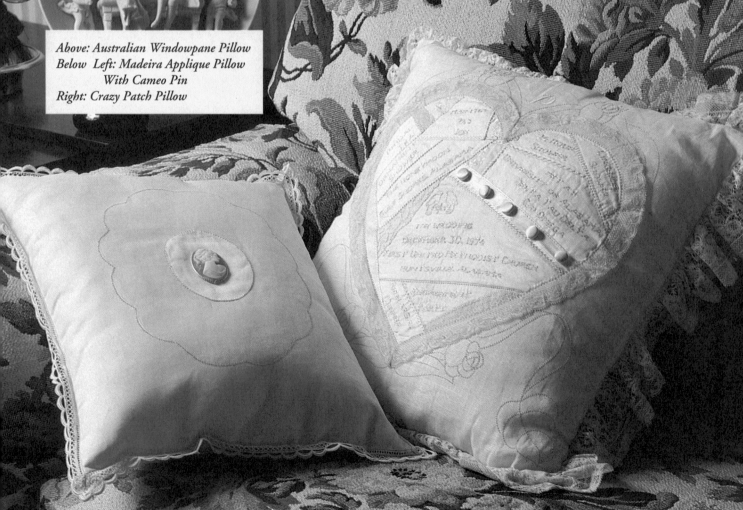

Above: Australian Windowpane Pillow
Below Left: Madeira Applique Pillow
With Cameo Pin
Right: Crazy Patch Pillow

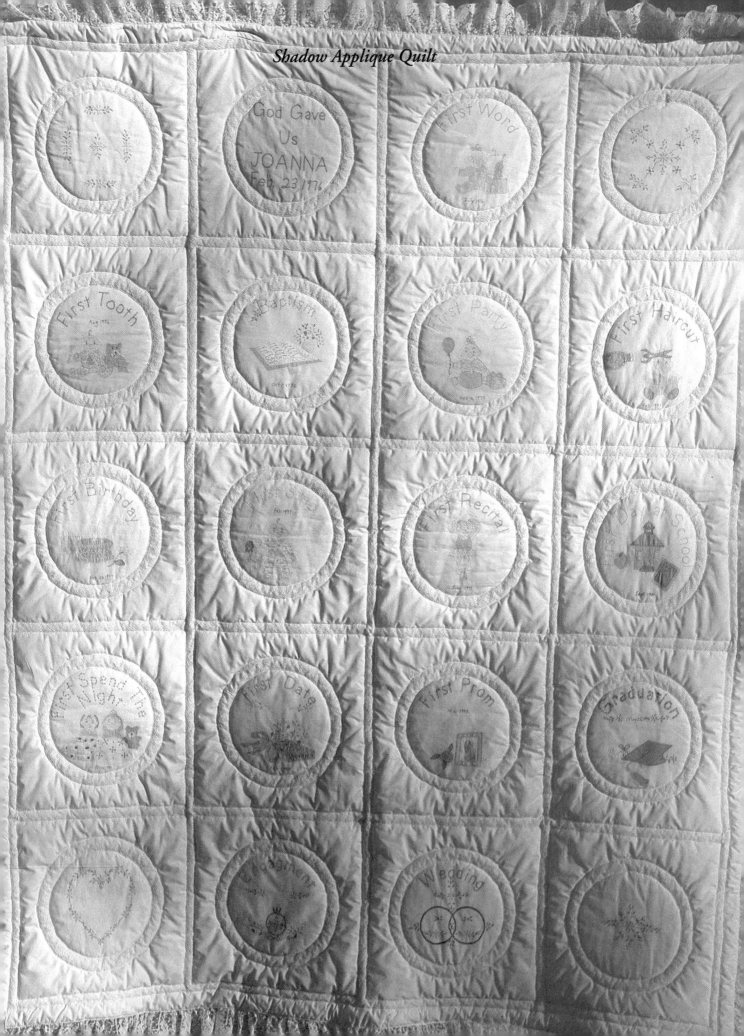

Shadow Applique Quilt

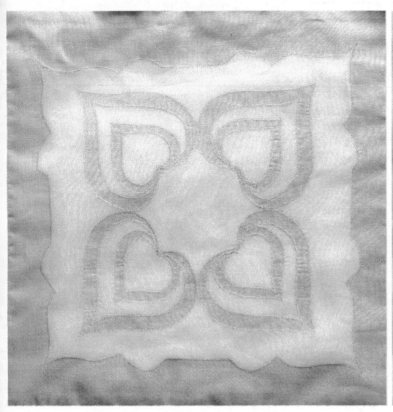

Shadow Applique Square from Heirloom Quilt

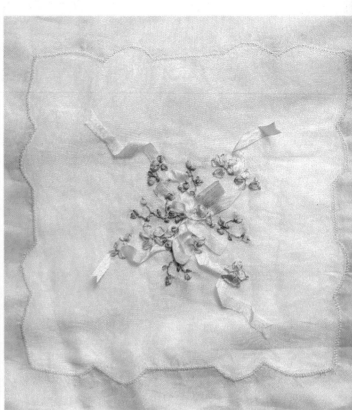

Silk Ribbon Madeira Applique Square from Heirloom Quilt

First Party Square from Shadow Applique Quilt

First Recital from Shadow Applique Quilt

Heirloom Quilt

Above Left: Applique Flowers Collar, Smiling Fish Shadow Applique Collar Dress and Madeira Applique Border Dress

Above Middle: Netting Australian Windowpane Dress and Crazy Patch Detachable Collar

Below Left: Triple Heart Dress, Layered Hearts With Pintucks Dress and Shark's Teeth Dress

Above Right: Shadow Diamond Dress and Ecru Celtic Lace Collar Dress

Below Right: Scallops and Loops of Puffing Dress and Flower Girl Portrait Collar Dress

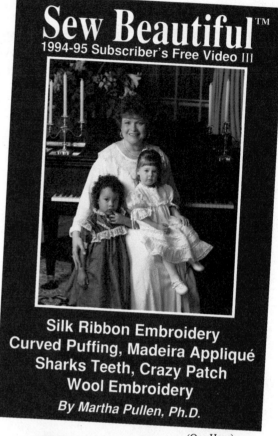

Dear Sewing Friend:

We at Clotilde, Inc., are proud to participate as a sponsor of Martha's Sewing Room on public television.

For over 24 years, Clotilde's fine products and reasonable prices have made sewing easier and more economical for millions of creative sewers in the United States and around the world. From extra-fine silk pins to gimp thread to the Perfect Pleater, our hard-to-find notions give your heirloom sewing the classic look.

If you're not already a Clotilde customer, we hope you will give us the opportunity to serve you by ordering from your Clotilde catalog. If you mention Martha's Program Guide when you order, we will be delighted to send you one of our famous Cloisonné sewing machine pins as a Free gift. Perhaps you've noticed your sewing friends wearing these lovely pins. Now you can start your own collection.

Happy Sewing,

Clotilde

11094 Sew Smart Way • PO Box 8031 • Stevens Point, WI 54481-8031 • 800-772-2891

BOOKS FROM MARTHA PULLEN COMPANY

THE JOY OF SMOCKING

Basic smocking and picture smocking instructions. Advanced smocking stitches. Patterns: Misty's Smocked Nightgown sized 6 months to 14 years & Donna's Smocked T-Bonnet. 13 smocking plates.

Soft Cover, 72 pages, 8 pages color photographs .... Retail: $14.00

SHADOW WORK, THE EASY WAY

Directions for shadow embroidery from the back and front. 50 designs.

Soft Cover, 64 pages, 10 pages color photographs .... Retail: $12.00

HEIRLOOM DOLL CLOTHES

Basic French sewing by machine instructions. Patterns fit 15" to 18" dolls. 25 doll patterns.

Soft Cover, 48 pages, 6 pages color photographs .... Retail: $12.00

BEARLY BEGINNING SMOCKING

Easy to follow beginning smocking directions. Comes with 7 complete patterns for bear clothes to fit Steiff bears and other bears sized 10-1/2" to 16-1/2". 6 smocking plate designs

Soft Cover, 60 pages, 10 pages color photographs .... Retail: $12.00

GRANDMOTHER'S HOPE CHEST

French Sewing by Machine

Beginning through advanced French sewing techniques. Illustrations of Martha's personal antique garment collection dating from the 1700s. Christening gowns adapted from antiques. Gift section. 30 pages of new embroidery designs and smocking designs. Free pattern supplement size 0 - 18 months. 30 patterns.

Hard Cover, 400 pages, 48 pages color photographs .... Retail: $39.95

HEIRLOOM SEWING FOR WOMEN

French Sewing by Machine

At last, and heirloom sewing book packed with designs women can really wear! Techniques covered: Beginning and advanced French sewing, Cutwork by machine, Shadow appliqué by machine, Shadow appliqué borders, Australian windowpane, Machine embroidery and Shadowwork by hand. Full size pattern, includes 5 women's blouse patterns.

Hard Cover, 400 pages, 48 pages color photographs .... Retail: $39.95

FRENCH HAND SEWING BY MACHINE, THE SECOND BOOK

Beginning techniques. Heirloom party dress sized 3 months to 10 years plus portrait collar patterns to fit each size. 92 French garments in full color.

Soft Cover, 52 pages, 16 pages color photographs .... Retail: $12.00

ANTIQUE CLOTHING

French Sewing by Machine

Shadow embroidery instructions. Beginning French sewing and beginning to advanced lace shaping techniques. Free pattern supplement - 4 patterns included. Adult Blouse (Ladies 4-24), Waisted Dress (Girls 4-14), and 2-Dropped Waist Dress (Girl 4-14).

Hard Cover, 352 pages, 48 pages color photographs .... Retail: $29.50

APPLIQUÉ, MARTHA'S FAVORITE

Easy to follow step-by-step instructions. Patterns included: Boy's One-Piece Jumper, sized 1-6; Girl's Jumper, sized 1-6; Apron, sized 1-6; and Infants Bib.

Soft Cover, 96 pages, 11 pages color photographs .... Retail: $14.00

MADAME ALEXANDER, 14" GIRL VICTORIAN DOLL PATTERNS

Beginning to advanced French sewing by machine techniques. 25 doll patterns included.

Soft Cover, 160 pages, 16 pages color photographs .... Retail: $14.00

Create Bouquets That Bloom For Generations.

The most beautiful arrangement of flowers fades in time, but a floral design of silk ribbon embroidery lasts for generations. Now your creativity can take bloom with this exciting new craft.

Ask your favorite craft store about YLI's complete line of silk ribbon and Esther's Silk Ribbon Embroidery, a clear, well-illustrated book of stitches, advice and how-to's.

Also look for other fine YLI products including Woolly ...ylon, our Rayon and Metallic specialty threads and ...ther's Silk Ribbon Needle Assortment.

Esther's
SILK RIBBON
By YLI

...LI Corporation, 482 North Freedom Blvd., Provo, Utah 84601. Call toll free (800) 854-1932

Fiskars underwriters for Martha's Sewing Room.

MARTHA'S SEWING ROOM
P.B.S. T.V. PROGRAM VIDEO SERIES 200

Filmed and produced by University of Alabama, Center For Public Television

$29.95
For Each Video
(postage paid)

Video 200-D contains 5 (26 min.) shows; Video 200-E contains 4 (26 min.) shows; Video 200-F contains 4 (26 min.) shows

Video 200-D

Show 1: Shaped Puffing; Curved and Circular Puffing Quilt Square; Scalloped Puffing Doll Dress; Crochet Fan Pin; Heart Puffing Pillow; Silk Ribbon Embroidery - Loop Stitch; Grandmother's Trunk Vintage Clothing.

Show 2: Advanced Lace Shapes; Curves and Angles Quilt Square; Silk with Organdy Hearts Doll Dress; Victorian Heart Wall Hanging; Lace Heart Demi Pillow; Wool Embroidery - Lazy Daisy and Chain Stitch; Grandmother's Trunk Vintage Clothing.

Show 3: Crazy Patch; "Mock Crazy Patch" Quilt Square; Crazy Patch/ Decorative Stitches Doll Dress; Crazy Patch Sewing Basket; Crazy Patch Baby Pillow; Silk Ribbon Embroidery - Cretan Stitch; Grandmother's Trunk Vintage Clothing.

Show 4: Celtic Lace Design; Celtic Design Ecru Lace Quilt Square; Celtic Design on Blue Batiste Doll Dress; Battenburg Straw Hat; Celtic Boudoir Pillow; Wool Embroidery - French Knot; Grandmother's Trunk Vintage Clothing.

Show 5: Wedding Show; Wedding Garter; Easy Wedding Veil; Sewing Bridal Motifs; Lace Overlay Doll Dress; Lace Wedding Bell Quilt Square; Flower Wreath Hair Ornament; Crazy Patch Wedding Pillow; Silk Ribbon Embroidery - Cascading; Grandmother's Trunk Vintage Clothing.

Video 200-E

Show 6: Machine Applique; Appliqued Hearts Quilt Square; Watermelon Appliqued Doll Dress; Antique Sewing Wreath; Appliqued Rose Pillow; Wool Embroidery - Herringbone; Grandmother's Trunk Vintage Clothing.

Show 7: Shadow Applique; Graduated Hearts Quilt Square; Purple Tulip Doll Dress; Shadow Applique Quilt; Victorian Bear Centerpiece; Woven Basket Pillow; Silk Ribbon Embroidery - Curved Whip Stitch; Grandmother's Trunk Vintage Clothing.

Show 8: Madeira Applique; Madeira Border with Silk Ribbon Quilt Square; Linen Madeira Applique Doll Dress; Lace Bud Vase; Peach Pillow with Cameo Pin; Wool Embroidery - Bullion Rose; Grandmother's Trunk Vintage Clothing.

Show 9: Shark's Teeth; Mirror Image Shark's Teeth; Shark's Teeth Doll Dress; Lingerie Bag; Bi-directional Shark's Teeth Pillow; Silk Ribbon Embroidery - Leaves; Grandmother's Trunk Vintage Clothing.

Video 200-F

Show 10: Australian Windowpane and Shadow Diamonds; Windowpane Hearts/Shadow Diamonds Quilt Square; Windowpane Butterflies and Lace Bows Doll Dress; Cameo Photo Album; Pink Flower Pillow; Wool Embroidery - Buttonhole Stitch; Grandmother's Trunk Vintage Clothing.

Show 11: Baby Show; Baby T-Bonnet; Baby Lace Pillow; Pillow/Crib Sheet Set; Smocked Doll Dress; Baby Memorabilia Hoop; Lace Pocket Quilt Square; Silk Ribbon Embroidery - Hand Twisted Rose; Grandmother's Trunk Vintage Clothing.

Show 12: Heirloom Sewing For Women; Lacy Pocket Square; Tea Towel Applique Quilt Square; Mitered Lace/Pintucks Doll Dress; Tassel; Diamond Braid Pillow; Wool Embroidery - Featherstitch; Grandmother's Trunk Vintage Clothing.

Show 13: Heirloom Sewing For Special Occasions; Shadow Embroidery; Party Lace/Ribbon Doll Dress; Shadow Embroidery Porcelain Jar; Heirloom Quilt Construction; Grandmother's Trunk Vintage Clothing.

• American VHS Format does not work on all foreign video systems.

Martha's SEWING ROOM

Video For T.V. Series 200

13 CRAFTS • 12 PILLOWS • 13 DOLL DRESSES
DROPPED WAIST DRESS PATTERN WITH COLLAR VARIATIONS (SIZE 4-14)
FRENCH SEWING BY MACHINE
BEGINNING THROUGH ADVANCED LACE SHAPING
SILK RIBBON EMBROIDERY • WOOL EMBROIDERY
SHADOW EMBROIDERY • CRAZY PATCH
HEIRLOOM SAMPLER QUILT • SHADOW APPLIQUE QUILT
SHADOW APPLIQUE • SHAPED PUFFING • CELTIC LACE SHAPING
MACHINE APPLIQUE • MADEIRA APPLIQUE BY MACHINE
SHARK'S TEETH • AUSTRALIAN WINDOW PANE
SHADOW DIAMONDS • WEDDING SHOW

by Martha Campbell Pullen, Ph.D.

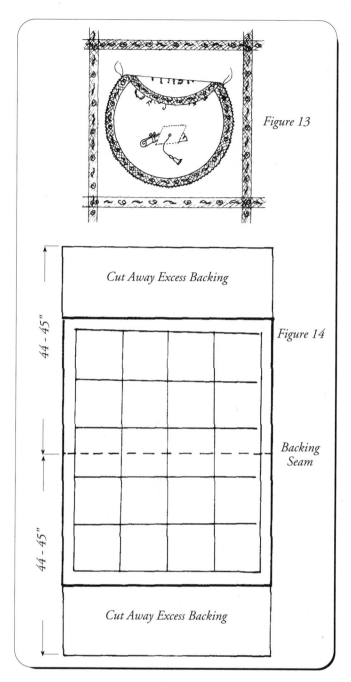

Figure 13

Cut Away Excess Backing

44 - 45"

Figure 14

Backing
Seam

44 - 45"

Cut Away Excess Backing

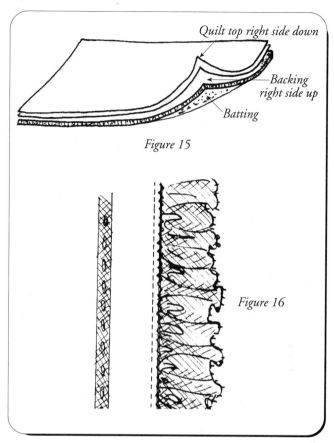

Quilt top right side down

Backing
right side up

Batting

Figure 15

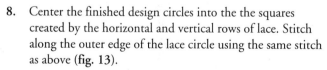

Figure 16

10. To form the quilt, layer on a large flat surface as follows (**fig. 15**):

> batting
> backing, right side up,
> quilt top, right side down.

11. Pin all layers together.

12. Stitch around the quilt. Leave 8-10" open.

13. Turn quilt to right side. Stitch opening closed.

14. Pin all layers together with safety pins. Use **plenty** of pins to prevent layers from shifting. Using a straight stitch, free motion or with the foot on, quilt as desired. This quilt is stitched on each side of the lace: lace circles, vertical lace lines and horizontal lace lines. ***Note:** Take care to prevent any pleats from forming on the back when quilting.

15. Top stitch 1/8" from the edges of the quilt to flatten the edge. Refer to the finished drawing of the quilt.

16. Gather the lace edging to fit the outer edge of the quilt. Overlap the ends of the lace. Stitch the gathered edging to the quilt edge with an open zigzag. Zigzag the lace overlap (**fig. 16**).

17. Wash to remove all of the markings and WSS.

18. Press if necessary. ▨

8. Center the finished design circles into the the squares created by the horizontal and vertical rows of lace. Stitch along the outer edge of the lace circle using the same stitch as above (**fig. 13**).

9. With the remaining two pieces of fabric, create the backing by stitching two pieces together, selvage to selvage, with a 1/2" seam. Press seams open. Place the quilt top on the backing piece centering the backing seam as shown on figure 14. Cut the excess backing away to match top front (**fig. 14**).

Introduction To Crazy Patch

Crazy patch quilting is fun, easy to do and delightfully Victorian. I guess the main reason for my including crazy patch quilting in this book is because it is one of the perfect ways to stitch memories. Sewing for the home with lots of wonderful family events recorded is a new twist for heirloom sewing. Since we have long made "love" clothes, now it is time to make the same sentimental items for the home. Crazy patch is almost like a scrapbook, if one wants to make it that way. It is the perfect way to make a one of a kind pillow for any room in the house. The materials are as varied as the items you can choose to make. Satin, velveteen, velvet, cotton, damask, silk, wool, ribbon, batiste, old linens, and corduroy are but a few. Please enjoy crazy patch and its embellishments. This is what I call "fun sewing." It is the perfect way to decorate every room in your home and record family memories at the same time.

Embellishing Crazy Patch

After having the fun of making crazy patch, embellishing it is a delight to stitch. This embellishment can be done by hand with silk ribbon embroidery or other embroidery and by machine with lots of threads. Perhaps you have been wondering where you will use all of those wonderful embroidery stitches on your sewing machine. Crazy patch brings the perfect canvas for truly enjoying the wonders of your computer machine. Have fun!

Use rayon or cotton machine embroidery thread in a machine embroidery needle through the sewing machine. Metallic threads are also perfect for crazy patch. Use fine cotton thread in the bobbin to match the underside of the crazy patch. Slightly loosen your needle tension. Straight stitch for attaching pieces in your crazy patch and use decorative stitches for embellishing seams. If you have a programmable memory, you may want to enter the embellishing stitches with the settings you like; then it will be easier to move from one stitch to another.

There are many types of stitching you can do to embellish crazy patch. Traditionally, there is embroidery of some sort on each seam. There can also be embroidery in the middle of any of the patches. Actually, since the sky is the limit on crazy patch embellishment, there are no rules for what type or for how much. Some people laugh and say, "There is no way you can put on too much crazy patch embellishment!" Using laces, buttons, motifs, scraps of "stuff" from your "stash," machine monograms, messages, dates of important events, old jewelry, ribbons, charms from the craft store, pearls, embroideries, beads, pieces of needlepoint, cross stitch, smocking—the list could go on and on! Imagination is the main key for embellishment of crazy patch.

Threads are as varied as your choice of stitches for sewing machine embellishment. Some people love rayon and cotton embroidery threads. Be sure to use a machine embroidery needle! You can use ribbon thread.

To embellish heirloom crazy patch, one might choose to use white or ecru threads for the embroidery. If using silk ribbon, heirloom pastel colors would probably be the best. Using ribbons, silk ribbon embroidery, machine embroidery, entredeux, laces, smocking, ribbon rosettes, antique buttons, entredeux, pearl buttons, tatting, elastic button loops and many other items, the look would be pastel and delicate. Pintucking also makes great crazy patch embellishment; pintuck the fabric before attaching it to your layers of crazy patch. Heirloom crazy patch would make a lovely bridal pillow, pillows for the bedroom, fabric for the front of a pinafore bib for a little girl's dress, valance for a bedroom curtain, tie backs for draperies, or Christmas stockings for your living room! The possibilities are unlimited! Here is the perfect place to use up all of the scraps of lace and bits from your "stash" that you didn't know how to use!

Heirloom crazy patch embellishment might be more delicate than bright Victorian crazy patch. If you are going to stitch dates, etc. on a square of your crazy patch, it seem to be easier if you do the stitching before you attach the piece of fabric into your item. In some of our stockings, we stitched the information with dates onto a silk organza fabric and then placed that over heavier fabric such as velveteen or heavy taffeta.

The more creativity you can muster up the better. Please use silk ribbon embroidery on crazy patch! Nothing is more beautiful! Then, layer other layers with everything wonderful on your sewing machine. Calling crazy patch, "kitchen sink" sewing might be appropriate. In other words, put everything but the kitchen sink into your garments or decorative item for your home. In this case, more is better and that is absolutely the most fun type of sewing.

Basic Crazy Patch

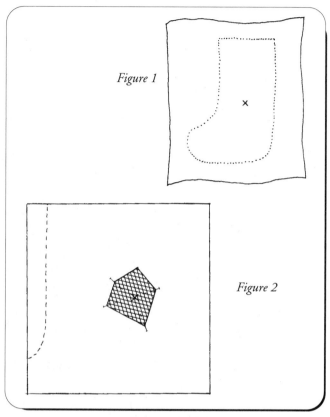

Figure 1

Figure 2

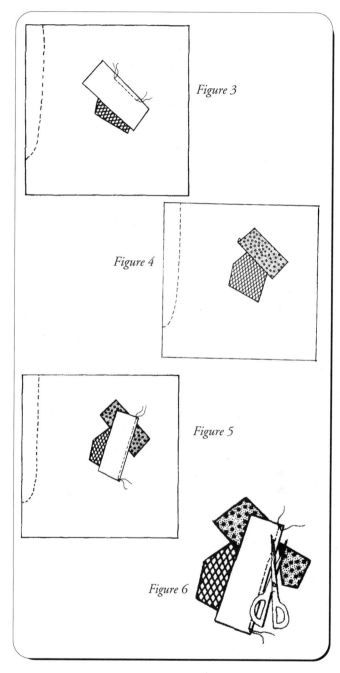

Figure 3

Figure 4

Figure 5

Figure 6

Directions

1. Cut a piece of base fabric larger than each pattern piece to be crazy patched. This base fabric can be any fabric since it will not show when the crazy patch is complete. We prefer to use unbleached muslin as the base fabric.

2. Outline the pattern piece on the base fabric. Find the center of the base fabric and mark with a fabric marker (**fig.** 1).

Optional: For a quilted look, batting may be placed under the base fabric. Pin the batting to the base fabric in several places to prevent the batting from slipping.

3. For the patchwork, start with a multi-sided fabric piece (patch "A") with at least five sides.

4. Pin patch "A" to the center of the base fabric (**fig 2**).

5. Place patch "B" to patch "A", right sides together. Line up one side of patch "B" with one side of patch "A". Patch "B" will overhang patch "A". Stitch using a 1/4" seam the length of the edge of patch "A" (**fig. 3**). This stitching will be made through the two patch pieces and the base fabric. The stitch length should be about a 3, which is a little longer than a normal stitch. Use a straight stitch.

6. Flip patch "B" to the right side and press (**fig. 4**).

7. Place one of the straight sides of patch "C" overlapping patches "A" and "B". The edge of patch "C" may extend beyond the length of the patches underneath. The patches underneath may extend above the straight edge of patch "C" (**fig. 5**).

8. Stitch along the straight edge of patch "C" the length of the under pieces. Trim away any excess of the "A" and "B" patches (**fig. 6**).

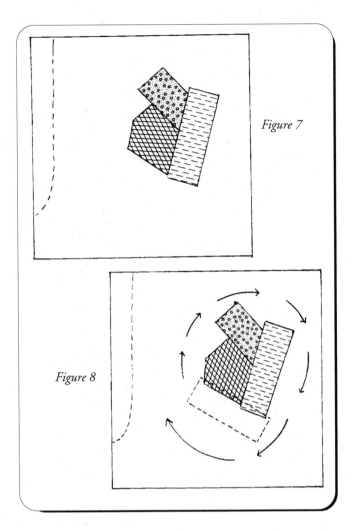

Figure 7

Figure 8

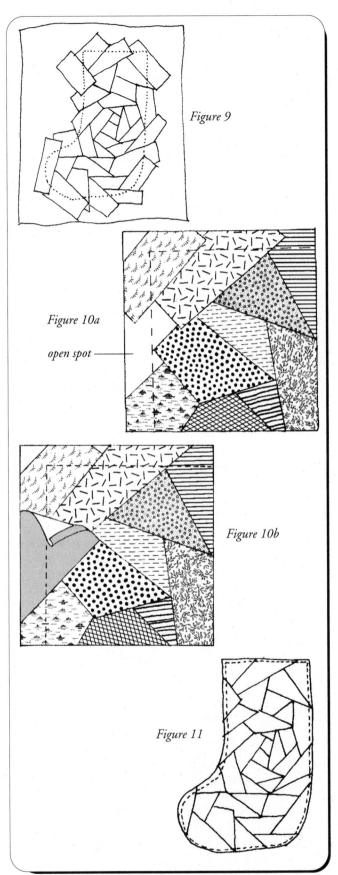

Figure 9

Figure 10a

open spot ——

Figure 10b

Figure 11

9. Flip patch "C" to the right side and press (**fig. 7**).

10. Continue working in a clockwise direction adding patches until the needed based fabric is covered (**fig. 8**). The patches should extend beyond the traced pattern lines. This will insure that the crazy patch design will fit the pattern piece (**fig. 9**).

Note: Eventually, when stitching crazy patch, an unusual angle will develop or you will come to an unfinished space. A piece of ribbon, lace or any trim can be hand or machine stitched in that space or a piece of fabric can be used to cover the space by turning the edge or edges of the fabric under and top stitching in the desired area. In other words, use anything and any technique to cover these unusual or hard-to-stitch spaces (**fig. 10a and 10b**).

11. Place the pattern piece on top of the crazy patch fabric. Trace around the pattern and stitch just inside the traced line. Cut out the pattern piece (**fig. 11**). ▨

Introduction To Silk Ribbon Embroidery

Contributed by YLI-Esther and Dan Randall

When Esther and Dan Randall purchased YLI Corporation in 1984 and transported the entire company in a U-Haul truck to Provo, Utah they had little thought where this decision would take them. But the two things they did know were that Dan was an experienced business executive and Esther loved fabrics and was an experienced, creative stitcher.

Because YLI's products included silk ribbon and silk thread, it didn't take Esther long to begin embroidering with silk. At first she used familiar iron-on patterns, but soon her creativeness took her artistic ability from her own flower garden to her embroidered needlework. She wrote in her book, Esther's Silk Ribbon Embroidery, "Before I begin a project I take an imaginary walk in a classic English flower garden, surrounded by an array of beautiful colors and hues. I pick an armful of flowers and mentally arrange them into a beautiful bouquet to adorn a favorite corner of my living room. This floral imagery is enhanced as I look at my basket of silk ribbons. Like the flowers in my imagined bouquet, my ribbons have all the delicate shades of color and are ready to portray in silk the exquisite shapes and colors of nature. No other stitching, I believe, can capture nature's floral beauty like silk ribbon embroidery."

Esther knew that silk ribbon embroidery was an ancient art and that through the ages it was found particularly in the Chinese, Japanese, European, and even early American cultures. Esther also knew she wanted to help bring this unique and exquisite needle art to those who love to do and those who love to view its beauty.

For many years Esther has made silk ribbon embroidery a focus of her creative needlework. She is well known for her artistic sewing, and particularly for her creative designs in silk ribbon embroidery. Her work has been featured in *McCall's Needlework*, *Sew Beautiful*, and *Creative Needle*. In addition, her needle work has been displayed at many trade shows. Esther has taught silk ribbon embroidery classes and seminars throughout the United States. Her book, *Esther's Silk Ribbon Embroidery*, has become well known internationally, and her designs and projects can be purchased as individual kits. Her great love of silk ribbon embroidery, her creative expertise, and her association with other needlework professionals have helped to associate her name with this international creative artwork.

As you begin to embellish your special projects with silk ribbon you will find that it is actually much easier than it looks and it takes far less time than floss embroidery to complete a design. The craft of silk embroidery is little more than mastering a few basic stitches and using those stitches in combinations with each other. With a change in color and ribbon width, a basic leaf becomes a rose or a tulip. A French knot is babies' breath in one design and a rose or a hyacinth in another design simply by a change in the ribbon or number of twists on the needle. As you fill in your design you will find that silk ribbon in very forgiving and mistakes are easily corrected. You will become familiar with what works best for you as you play with different needles, ribbons, and fabrics. We use YLI Silk Ribbons. They're Gorgeous!

Fabrics

Many fabrics are suitable for silk ribbon embroidery; of course, some are easier to work with than others. All of the natural fiber fabrics are beautiful and very suitable. Some are cotton, linen, cotton velveteen, silk taffeta, raw silk, silk dupioni, natural silk, batiste. The following synthetic fabrics are also useful; moire taffeta, tapestry, light-weight polyester taffeta, organdy, and satin. Experiment with several.

Needles

There are a variety of needles used for silk ribbon work, as you experiment you will find what works best with which fabric and stitches. Remember, the higher the size number the smaller the needle.

Chenille Needle - A large, sharp point needle with a long eye. Sizes range 18 to 24. Good for wide ribbon and tightly woven fabrics because it punctures a hole that will accommodate a wide ribbon.

Crewel Needle - This needle has a long eye and a sharp point. Sizes range 1 to 10, however, sizes 3 to 9 is all you will ever need.

Tapestry Needle - A large eyed needle with a blunt end. Prevents snagging, and is great for passing through other ribbon. Good for loosely woven fabrics. Size ranges 13 to 26, 18 to 26 being the most useful.

Straw Needle - This needle is a long, narrow needle which stays the same thickness from top to bottom, which means the needle does not get fatter at the eye. This aspect makes it a great needle for french and colonial knots.

Darner - A very large eyed, long needle used for wide ribbons and heavy thick threads. Sizes 14 to 18.

Beading needle - Used for assembling roses and gathering stitches and tacking. It is a thin, long needle with a small eye.

Threading

For best results, work with ribbon no longer than 10" at a time. The ribbon becomes frayed and hard to work with quickly, so if the ribbon is longer the 10" it will probably be wasted before it can be used.

To keep the needle threaded insert the needle into the tail of the ribbon after it has been threaded through the eye of the needle (**fig. 1**). **Then,** pull the tail back over the main ribbon so that it forms a loop (**fig. 2**). Next, pull the main ribbon until the loop is closed (**fig. 3**). (This passes easily through the fabric and keeps the ribbon from coming unthreaded. The stitch illustrations have not been drawn using this technique for the sake of clarity.)

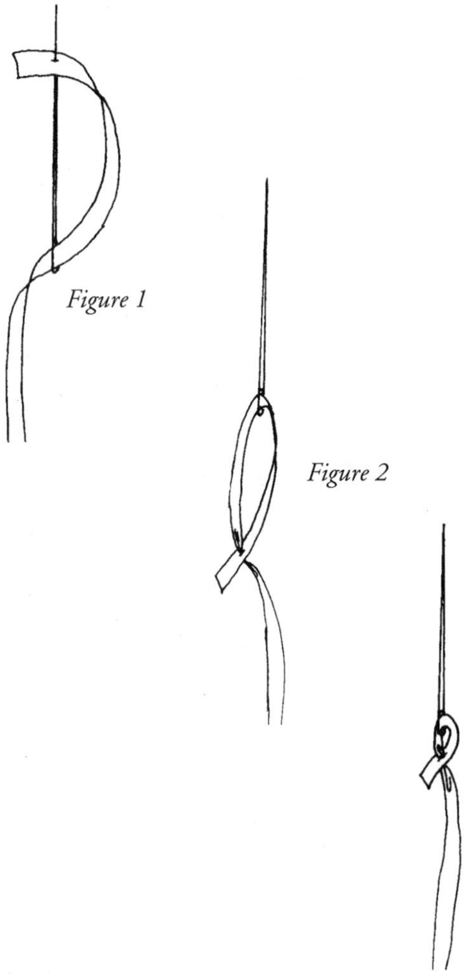

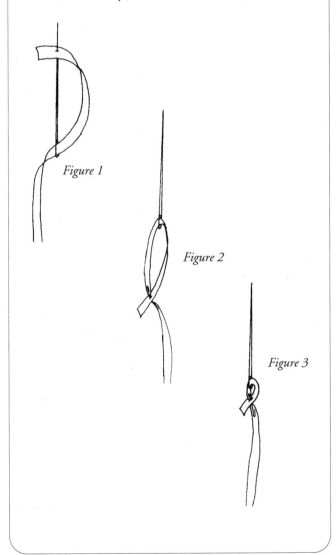

Figure 1

Figure 2

Figure 3

Tying Off

There are two ways to tie on and to tie off the ribbon. One way is to simply tie knots. Knots are best for small projects. The second way is to leave about 1/2" of extra ribbon underneath the fabric and when the needle is inserted back through to complete a stitch, insert the needle through the extra ribbon to secure it. When cutting the ribbon, leave an extra 1/2" and insert the needle through it when making another stitch. This method helps keep the back side free of so many knots, which can eventually get in the way when working a complicated design. ▧

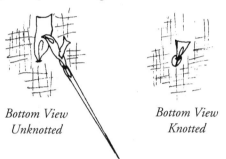

Bottom View
Unknotted

Bottom View
Knotted

Straight Stitch

This stitch is used for almost everything. By itself or in combination with other stitches it becomes leaves, flowers, stems, vines, rose buds, and more. Use any size ribbon. Narrow ribbons are good for vines and stems and tiny leaves, while wide ribbons are great for flower petals and big leaves.

Simply bring the needle up from under the fabric and insert it down into the fabric a short distance in front of where the needle came up. It is an in and out stitch. Remember to pull the ribbon loosely for nice full stitches. ▧

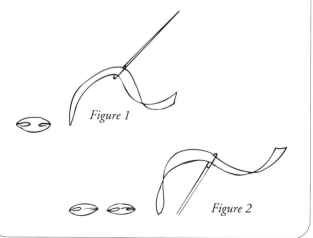

Figure 1

Figure 2

Japanese Ribbon Stitch

This stitch is simply a glorified straight stitch and may be used in as many variations. A rosebud is simply a Japanese ribbon stitch with straight stitches on both sides.

Use any size ribbon. Bring the needle up from under the fabric, loop it around and insert the needle down into the center of the ribbon a short distance in front of where the needle came up. Pull the ribbon so that the end curls in on itself loosely so that it does not disappear. ▧

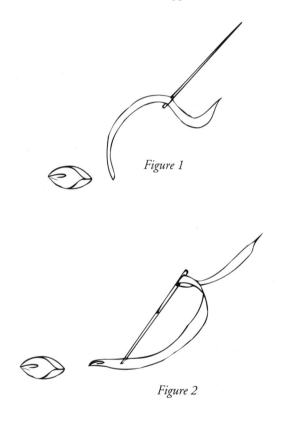

Figure 1

Figure 2

Left: Rosebud created by one Japanese Ribbon Stitch and two straight stitches

Whipped Running Stitch

This stitch is used for vines, stems, and stalks.

Use a 2mm or 4mm ribbon. You may also use embroidery floss.

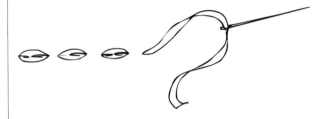

Figure 1

1 - Stitch a line of straight stitches along the design line (**fig. 1**). Refer to straight stitch instructions.

Figure 2

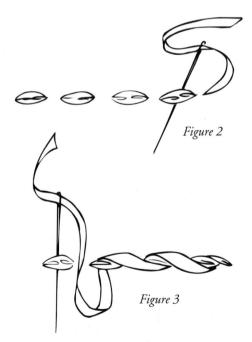

Figure 3

2 - Bring the needle up at the end of the line of straight stitching (**fig. 2**) and begin wrapping the ribbon under and around the straight stitches (**fig. 3**).

 Loop flower with French Knot

Loop Stitch

This stitch is to be made very loose while keeping the ribbon straight. It can be used for daisies and bows or anywhere a loop look is needed. Experiment with different ribbon widths to achieve a variety of styles and uses.

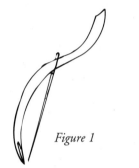

Straight Loop

Figure 1

Figure 2

Straight Stitch Method - Insert the needle up through the fabric and loop around away from you, inserting the needle just slightly beside where you came up (**fig. 1**). Pull the ribbon straight (without twists) and loosely adjust the loop to the desired size (**fig. 2**).

Japanese Loop

Figure 4

Figure 3

Japanese Stitch Method - Insert the needle up through the fabric and this time loop it towards you, inserting the needle through the center of the ribbon just beside where the needle came up (**fig. 3**). Again, pull loosely while keeping the ribbon straight.

Lazy Daisy Stitch

This stitch is used in a variety of silk ribbon flowers and leaves. It is one of the most popular basic stitches. This stitch is best with a 4mm or 2mm ribbon.

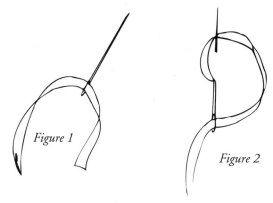

Figure 1

Figure 2

1 - Bring your needle up through the center point if you are stitching a flower, and up just next to a vine or flower for leaves. (**fig. 1**).

2 - Insert the needle down into the same hole in which you came up. In the same stitch come through about 1/8 inch to 3/8 inch above that point (**fig. 2**). Wrap the ribbon behind the needle and pull the ribbon through, keeping the ribbon from twisting (**fig. 3**).

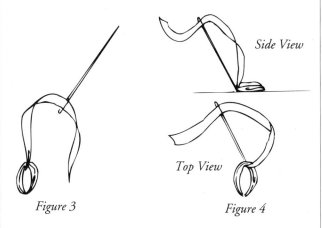

Side View

Top View

Figure 3

Figure 4

3 - Insert the needle straight down into the same hole or very close to the same hole that you came up (**fig. 4**). Notice in the side view of figure 4 that the needle goes down underneath the ribbon loop. The top view of figure 4 shows that the stitch is straight and will lock the ribbon loop in place. ▨

Pansy

A few pearls or a French knot in the center this flower will provide color, coverage and dimension. It is made by hand first and then tacked on to the fabric with a needle and thread. Four mm or wider ribbon works best.

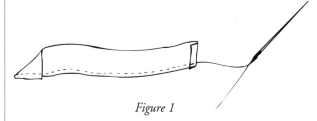

Figure 1

1 - Begin with a flat piece of ribbon 2-1/2 inches long. Fold one end at a right angle and stitch across the edge with a needle and thread. Fold the end. (**fig. 1**).

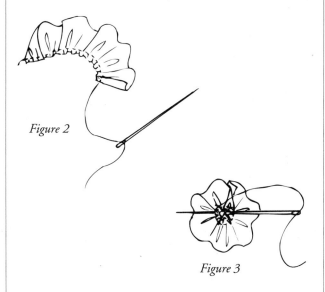

Figure 2

Figure 3

2 - Pull the thread tightly to gather the ribbon (**fig. 2**)

3 - Curl the ribbon around so that the ends overlap. Tack the center with a couple of stitches to secure it and tie a knot (**fig. 3**). Tack to the fabric with thread and cover the center with pearls or a French knot. ▨

Spider Web Rose

This rose is one of the prettiest and easiest of all the silk stitched roses. Use 13mm for large puffy roses, 7mm for medium roses, and 4mm for small roses. The spokes or "legs" on the spider will be shorter for 4mm ribbon than for 7mm ribbon. You will gain a good judgement of this after you have stitched a few roses and played with the different sizes.

Begin with a five legged "spider", or five spokes, stitched with either a single strand or a double strand of embroidery floss. For larger roses use a double strand. It may be helpful to mark a center with five evenly spaced dots around it using a washout pen or pencil as you are learning to make this rose.

Figure 1

Figure 2

1 - To stitch the spider, come up from the bottom of the fabric with your needle through dot "a" then down in the center dot "b" (**Fig. 1**). Come up through "c" then down in "b" (**fig. 2**). Continue around; up in "d" down in "b", up in "e" down in "b" etc... until the spider is complete and tie off underneath.

Figure 3

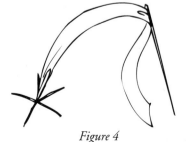

Figure 4

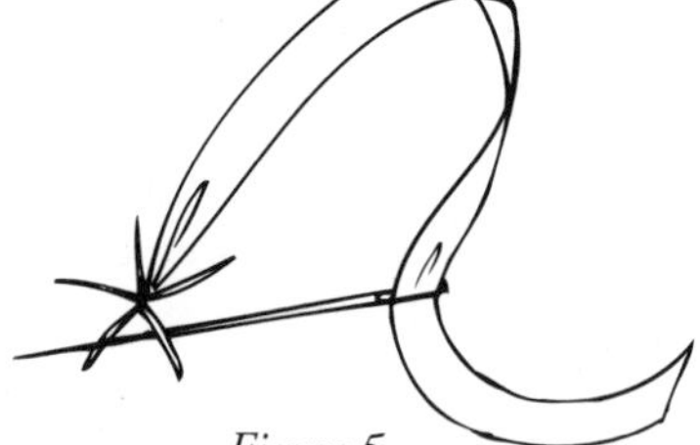

Figure 5

2 - Now, with your silk ribbon insert the needle up through the center "b" (fig. 4). Slide the needle under a spoke or "spider leg" and pull ribbon through loosely (**fig.** 5).

Figure 6

Figure 7

3 - Skipping **over** the next spoke go **under** the third spoke (**fig.** 6) and begin weaving in a circle over and under every other spoke (**fig.** 7).

4 - Continue weaving until the spokes are covered. Insert the needle underneath the last "petal" and pull through to the back.

You may stitch leaves first and then stitch the rose on top, or you may bring your needle up from underneath a "petal" and stitch leaves under the rose.

Hand Twisted Rose

This rose adds a wonderful dimensional appearance to any floral design and can be made in a variety of sizes.

Use a 7mm or wider ribbon to make this rose.

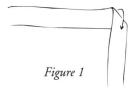

Figure 1

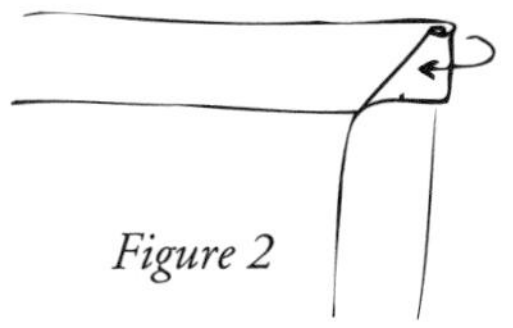

Figure 2

1- Beginning with a flat piece of ribbon about 15 inches long, fold down about three inches at a right angle (**fig. 1**). Fold again, this time fold the ribbon back on itself. This will create a triangle in the corner (**fig. 2**)

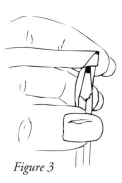

Figure 3

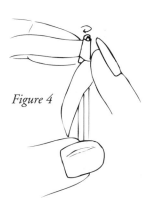

Figure 4

2 - Place a pointed object such as the sharp tip of a chalk pencil or light colored pencil up through the "triangle" (**fig. 3**) and begin twisting with about two twists (**fig. 4**).

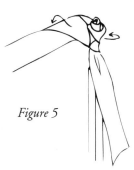

Figure 5

3 - Begin folding the ribbon back while twisting the pencil (**fig. 5**). Continue folding and twisting until you have about 5 to 7 full twists for a full rose and about 4 twist for a small rosette.

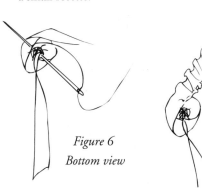

Figure 6
Bottom view

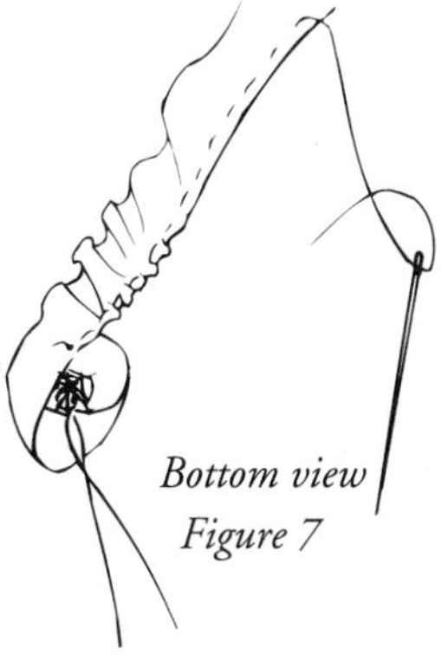

Bottom view
Figure 7

4 - Remove the rose from the pencil and hold between your thumb and finger. Tack the bottom securely with a needle and thread, leaving the tails dangling (**fig. 6**). At this point you may apply the rose to your project or you may make a full cabbage rose by gathering about 1-1/2 inch of the tail with a needle and thread (**fig. 7**).

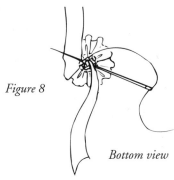

Figure 8

Bottom view

5 - Wind this around the bottom of the rose and tack with the needle and thread (**fig. 8**).

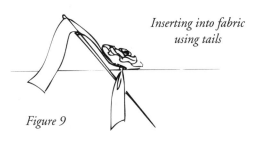

Inserting into fabric using tails

Figure 9

6 - To apply the rose to fabric, thread one of the dangling tails and insert into the fabric, pulling the ribbon to the back side. Thread the other tail and insert underneath the rose into the fabric to the back side and tie the tails together (**fig. 9**).

Hand Stitched Leaves

This leaf is perfect for large flowers where a lazy daisy, Japanese, or straight stitch is inadequate.

Use a 7mm or wider ribbon.

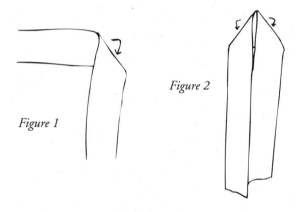

Figure 2

Figure 1

1 - Beginning with a flat ribbon about 6 inches long, fold down one side at a right angle and leave about a 3 inch tail (**fig. 1**). Fold the other side the same so that the two sides meet edge to edge (**fig. 2**).

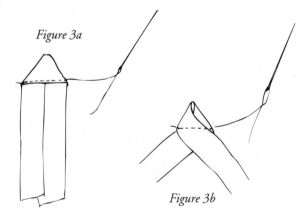

Figure 3a

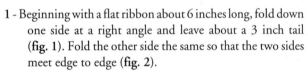

Figure 3b

2 - With a needle and thread, stitch across the flat edge of the ribbon. (**fig. 3a**) For a slightly different look using the same technique, simply wrap the ribbon across each other instead of meeting edge to edge and stitch across (**fig. 3b**).

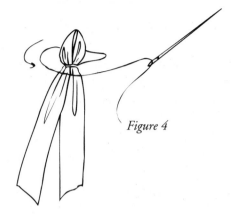

Figure 4

3 - Pull the thread to gather the leaf. Wrap the thread around the stitching a couple of times to secure the gathers and insert the needle through the ribbon and tie a knot (**fig. 4**).

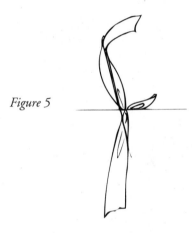

Figure 5

4 - To apply the leaf to fabric, thread one of the dangling tails and insert into the fabric, pulling the ribbon to the back side. Repeat for the other tail and tie the tails together underneath. (**fig. 5**). You may apply these before or after making a flower.

Curved Whip Stitch

This is a great stitch for snap dragons, ropes, buds, and blooms.

Use a 2mm for tiny blooms and 4mm for larger blooms.

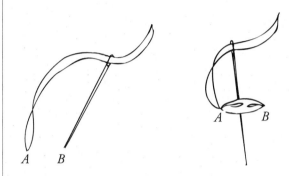

Figure 1   *Figure 2*

1 - Stitch a regular straight stitch (**fig. 1**) and bring the needle back up at point "A" (**fig. 2**).

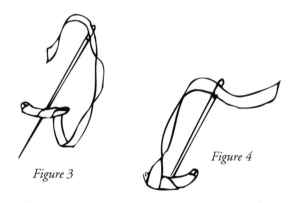

Figure 3   *Figure 4*

2 - Keeping the ribbon straight, firmly wrap it around the stitch 2 or 3 times from point "A" to "B" and then back to point "A" 2 or 3 wraps. Insert the needle under the stitch and just slightly to the side to secure the curve. Pull to the back side.

Cascading

This is a beautiful embellishment to add elegance and color when woven loosely through a floral design. It also secures and shapes the tails of a bow.

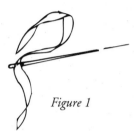

Figure 1

Bring the needle up through the fabric from underneath a bow or flower or from where ever your streamers will be attached (**fig. 1**). Next, take a small stitch in the fabric about 1 inch or more away from where you came up and twist the ribbon so that it rolls and loops (**fig. 2**). Pull the ribbon very loosely and let it lay naturally. ✛

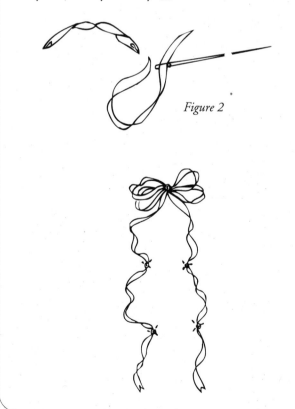

Figure 2

Feather Stitch

This is a great embellishing stitch for crazy patch and is also used for stems and vines.

Use a 2mm ribbon or floss.

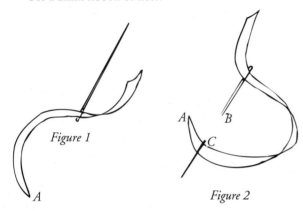

Figure 1

A

Figure 2

A   *B*

C

1 - Bring the needle up through the fabric in point "A" (**fig. 1**). Insert the needle down about 1/4 to 3/8 inch across from "A" into point "B". In the same stitch bring the needle back through about 1/4 to 3/8 inch down and center at point "C" (**fig. 2**). With the ribbon behind the needle, pull the ribbon through (**fig. 3**). This stitch is much like the lazy daisy only the needle does not insert into the same hole in which it came up. Notice that the stitch is simply a triangle.

Figure 3

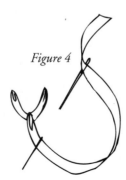

Figure 4

Figure 5

2 - Now you will begin working your triangle from right to left, or left to right. Point "C" will now become point "A" for your next stitch. Repeat the stitch as in 1 (**fig. 4**).

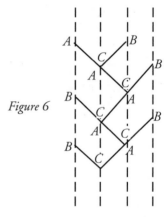

A   *B*

C

A   *C*

B   *B*

C   *A*

A   *C*

B   *B*

C   *A*

A   *C*

B

Figure 6

3 - This time repeat the stitch on the other side (**fig. 5**). The trick is that "A" and "B" will always be straight across from each other and that all of the "A" points, "B" point, and "C" points will line up vertically (**fig. 6**). ❖

French Knot

This is another great basic stitch. It is used in a variety of ways. I love it for tiny rosettes and hyacinths.

Use a 2mm or 4mm ribbon for this stitch.

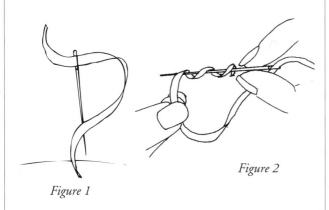

Figure 1

Figure 2

1 - Insert the needle up through the fabric (**fig. 1**)

2 - Hold the needle horizontally with one hand and wrap the ribbon around the needle with the other hand (**fig. 2**). One or two wraps create small knots; 3 to 4 wraps create medium knots; and 5 to 6 wraps create large knots, depending on the width of your ribbon.

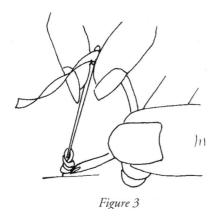

Figure 3

3 - While holding the tail of the ribbon so that it does not unwind off the needle, bring the needle up into a vertical position and insert into the fabric just slightly beside where the needle came up (**fig. 3**). Pull the ribbon through while still holding the tail with the other hand. ▨

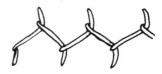

Cretan Stitch

The Cretan Stitch is a beautiful embellishment for crazy patch. This stitch is in the same family as the feather stitch. It takes a little practice at first, but if you have mastered the feather stitch it will be no problem. For beginners it helps to mark the points on your fabric to practice the stitch until you get the hang of it.

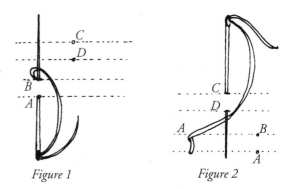

Figure 1

Figure 2

1 - To begin this line of stitching, bring the needle up through the fabric at point "B". Insert the needle through "A" and back up through "B" again in one stitch. Wrap the yarn or ribbon around behind the needle (**fig. 1**).

2 - Pull the ribbon through and insert the needle through point "C" and "D", keeping the needle over the yarn or ribbon (**fig. 2**).

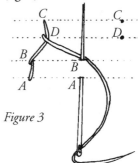

Figure 3

3 - Repeat step 2 going in the opposite direction, inserting the needle in point "A" and up through point "B" (**fig. 3**).

4 - Continue repeating the "A, B, C, D" sequence and you will begin to see the pattern. ▨

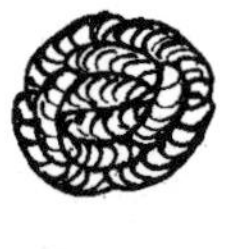

Bullion Rose

This ever popular rose embellishes the most elegant embroidery projects. It takes practice, but once the basic bullion stitch is mastered all the different bullion roses and flowers will be a cinch.

Use a 24 or 26 chenille needle.

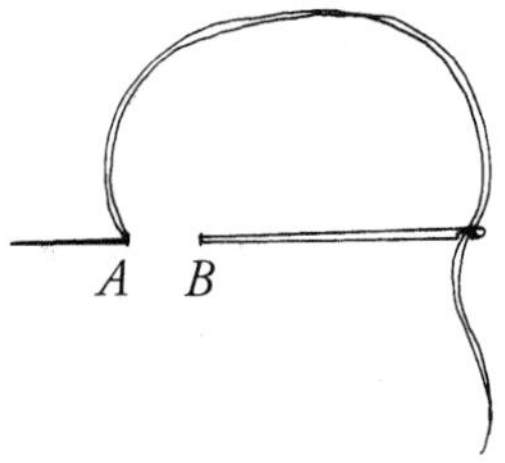

Figure 1

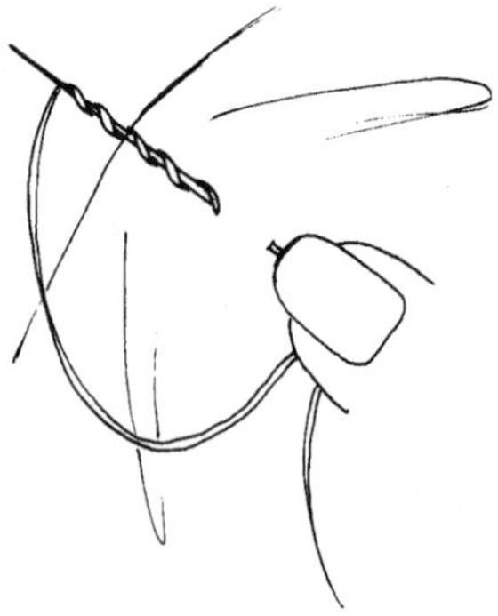
Figure 2

1 - Bring the needle up from under the fabric at point "A" and take a stitch down in "B" about 3/8" to 1/4" and come back up through "A" beside (not through) the yarn. <u>Do not pull the needle all the way through (**fig. 1**).</u>

2 - Now, hold the end of the needle down with your thumb. This will pop the point of the needle up away from the fabric. Wrap the floss or yarn coming from point "A" around the needle 5 to 6 times (**fig. 2**).

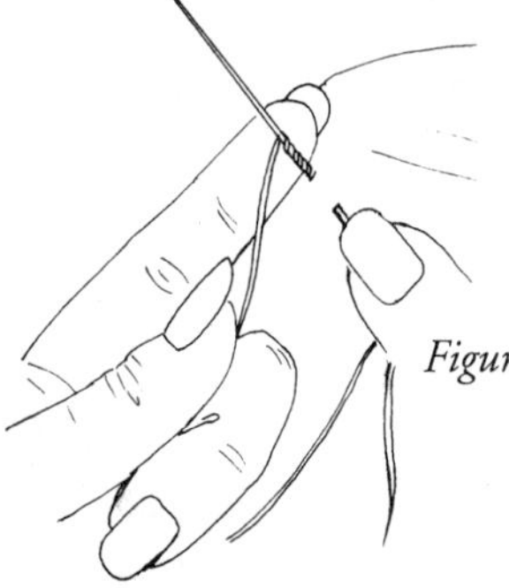
Figure 3

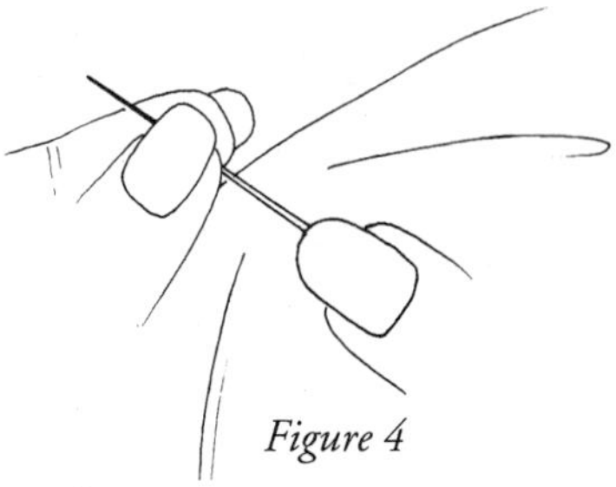
Figure 4

3 - With your finger, push the wraps of yarn to the bottom of the needle next to the fabric so that they are all lined up tight (**fig. 3**). With your other hand, place your finger under the fabric and your thumb on top of the bullion and gently pull the needle and yarn through the wraps (**fig. 4**).

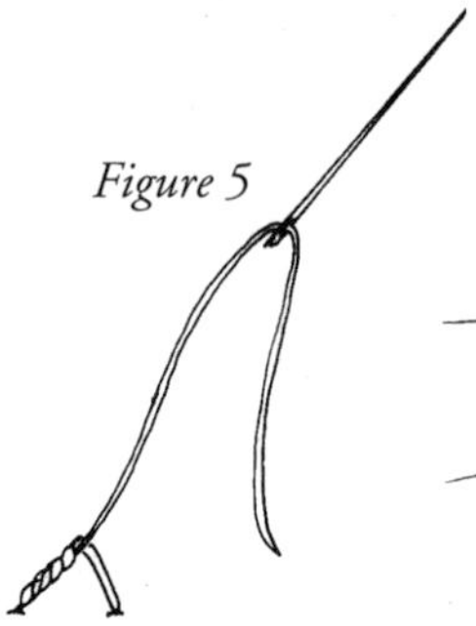
Figure 5

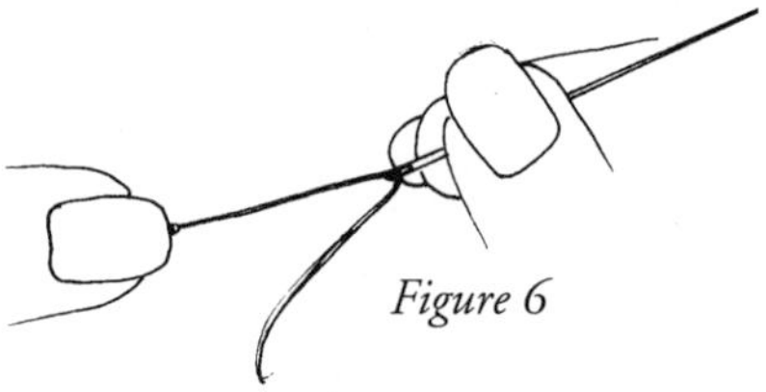
Figure 6

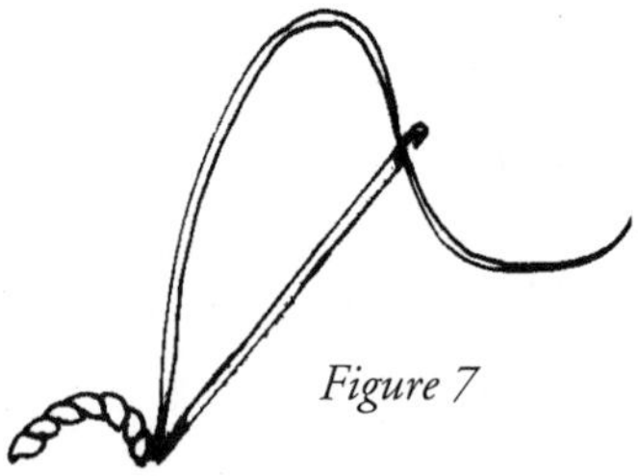
Figure 7

4 - You almost have a bullion, but first you most lay the coils over to the opposite side and take up the slack yarn (**fig. 5**). To do this, lay the bullion over and place you finger under the fabric and your thumb on top of the bullion and gently pull the yarn until the slack is out (**fig. 6**). Insert the needle into the fabric at the end of the bullion (**fig. 7**) and go on the next stitch, repeating the steps above.

Note: The distance from point "A" to point "B" will determine the length of your bullion, and the number of yarn wraps will determine the amount of curve. So, be sure you always have enough wraps to cover the distance.

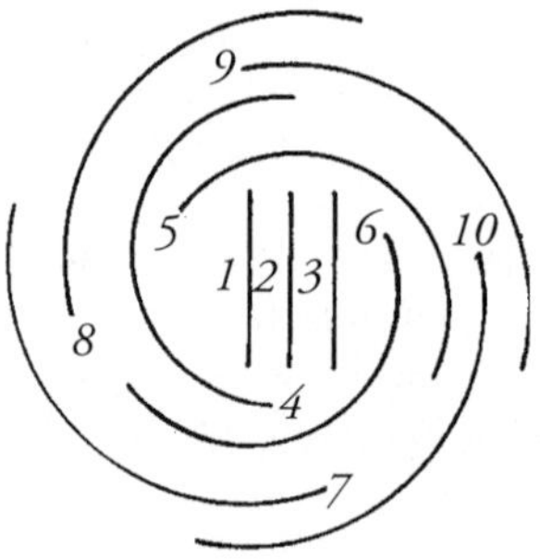

Bullion Rose Template

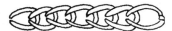

Chain Stitch

This is a glorified lazy daisy stitch and once again it goes great with crazy patch. It also makes a great outline stitch for stems and vines when done with one or two strands of floss.

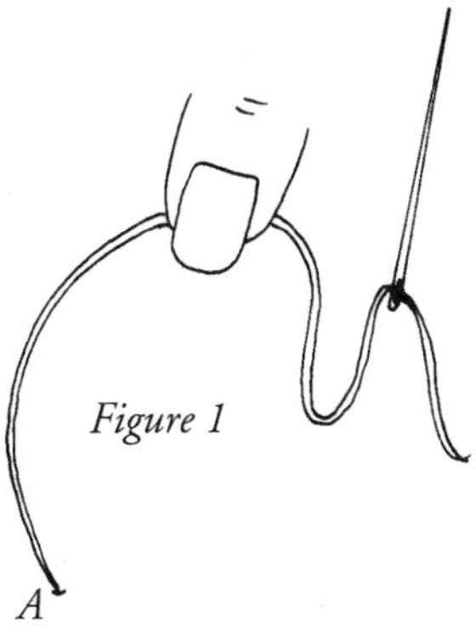

Figure 1

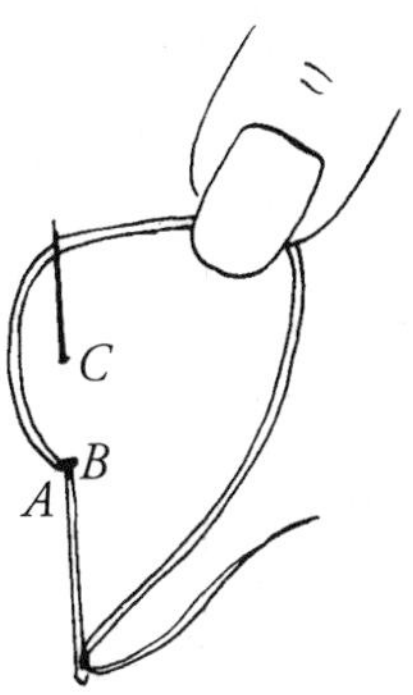

Figure 2

1 - Bring the needle up through the fabric at point "A". Swing the thread or ribbon around in a loop and hold the loop with your thumb (**fig. 1**).

2 - While holding the loop, insert the needle in point " B" and through point "C" in one stitch. Keep the needle and yarn or ribbon going over the loop (**fig. 2**).

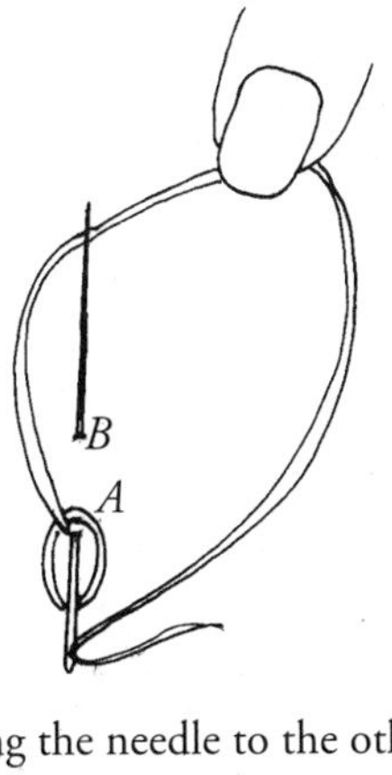

3 - Instead of inserting the needle to the other side like a lazy daisy, you will make another loop and insert the needle down, right beside point "C" were you last came up, this will become a new point "A". In the same stitch bring the needle through point "B" and pull (**fig. 3**). keep the needle over the loop.

4 - Continue looping and stitching in an "A, B" - "A, B" sequence. ▩

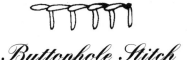

Buttonhole Stitch

This row of stitching is another great embellishment for crazy patch work. It is also a beautiful way to outline the edge of an appliqué shape. Free standing it makes a great fence when used on a embroidered picture. When stitch in a circle you have a Forget me Knot or a pansy.

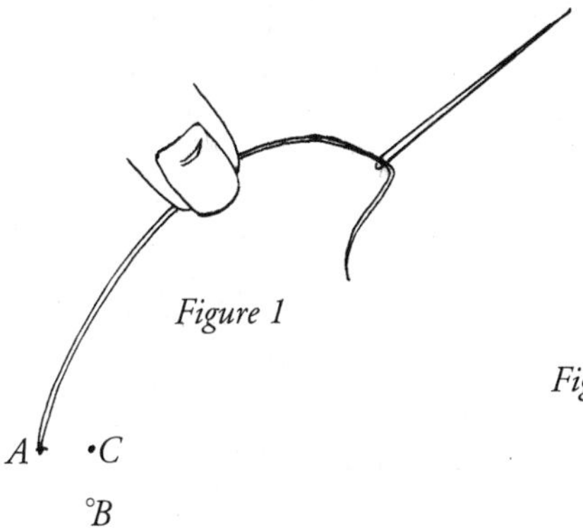

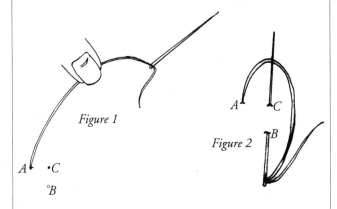

Figure 1

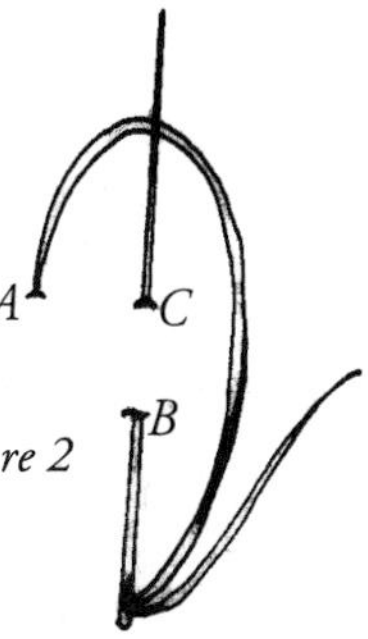

Figure 2

1 - Bring the needle up through the fabric at point "A". Pull the yarn above and to the right of point "A" and hold it in place with your thumb (**fig. 1**).

2 - Insert the needle in point "B" and up through point "C" in one stitch, keeping the ribbon under the needle. Pull through (**fig. 2**).

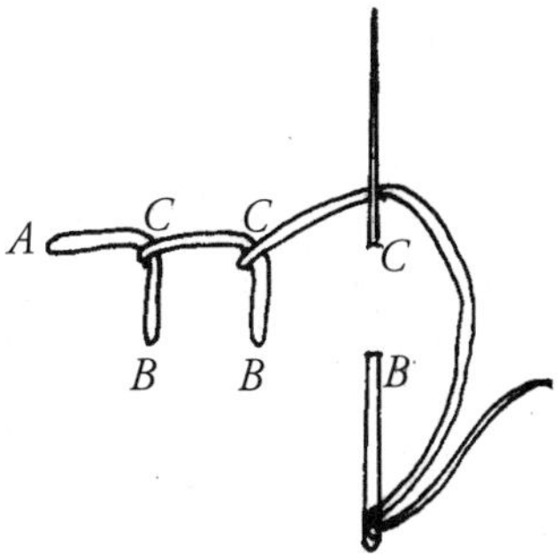

3 - Point "C" now becomes point "A" and you repeat the sequence. You may see the sequence as "A, B, C - B, C - B, C and on and on (**fig. 3**). Notice that the stitch looks like a series of upside down "L's". ▩

A C C C C C

B B B B B

Template for Buttonhole Stitch

Herringbone Stitch

This beautiful line of stitching is a great decorative stitch for crazy patch. It can be stitched in silk ribbon for a different effect. When doubled, this stitch becomes what Esther Randall calls a "victorian stacking stitch." If using silk ribbon, use a 2mm width for best results.

This stitch is basically an elongated row of cross stitches. It reminds me of looking down on a wood rail stacked fence. The kind you might see in the country leading up a driveway.

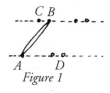

Figure 1

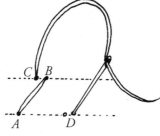

Figure 2

1 - Make a long straight stitch from point "A" to point "B" (**fig. 1**). To practice you may want to mark dots on your fabric and label each point until you get the hang of it.

2 - Bring the needle back up through the fabric at point "C" and make another long straight stitch to point "D" (**fig. 2**).

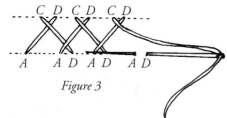

Figure 3

3 - Repeat step 1 and 2 and continue the "A, B, C, D" pattern (**fig. 3**). You will begin to notice the sequence of overlaps and that the current straight stitch overlaps the previous stitch. Also, notice that the crosses are high and low, not in the center. This is controlled by the distance you set between point "C" and "B" and point "A" and "D" when bringing you needle up through the fabric for the next stitch. ▨

Note: The Lazy Daisy Stitch, French Knot and Feather Stitch directions can be found in the silk ribbon section of this book.

 — Hand Rose or Spider Web Rose

 — Panzy w/3-beads or pearls

 — Hyacinth (all French Knots)

 — Straight Stitch Leaves or Petals

 — Loop Stitch Flowers

 — Lazy Daisy Leaves or Petals

 — French Knots

 — Hand Stitched Leaves

 — Stem Stitch w/floss or whipped running st. w/floss

 — Curved Whip Stitches

 — Long Curved Whip Stitches

 — French Knot Rosette w/straight st. leaves

 — Cascading

 — Japanese Ribbon St.

Introduction To The Dropped Waist Pattern In This Book

Since the beginning of Martha Pullen book publishing, we have loved including a multi-sized pattern which could be used many ways with the different techniques presented in the book. We have enjoyed knowing that our books are known for their beauty, their great ideas and their value for the dollar. With the price of single patterns being so high, most people enjoy knowing that they have patterns included in their technique books. Anyway, that has been our philosophy. For the 200 series program guide, we planned this adorable dropped waist pattern with collar variations for several reasons. First, it looks precious on any size little girl from very skinny to not so skinny! Second, it is very easy to make. Third, with collar variations, it can be used for school clothing, church clothing, wedding attendant's clothing or any other occasion. This dress is just as cute in calico or gingham as it is in Swiss batiste.

In this section we have used garments made by this pattern and shown on the television show. We made our dropped waist dresses using techniques shown on individual shows. In the pattern section we have given basic instructions for making a plain dropped waist dress. You will have to use the different techniques given in this book in

order to make this basic dropped waist dress into the variations shown in this section. Sometimes we call this method, "cut and paste." All the time, we call it "employing creativity" in using a pattern for many different dresses. The templates for the loops, for example, are included in this book. The collar patterns are square, double square, V, and round. The different lace treatments are to be placed on these different collars. Some of the skirts have fancy treatments also. They are described in this section with the pictures. Please let your creativity be your only guide in using this wonderful pattern with hundreds of variation possibilities. I remember my children saying when they were little, "Did you get it, Mom?" I think after you read this section, go over the pattern, work with the techniques, and let your creativity wheels begin to turn, that you will "get it." Hopefully you will have *Martha's Sewing Room* on Public Television in your area; that makes it all especially fun and easy! If you don't have *Martha's Sewing Room*, then you can order the tapes from Martha Pullen Company. Please enjoy this pattern as much as we have enjoyed creating it for you. ✳

Scallops and Loops of Puffing Dress

Ecru Swiss Nelona and ecru laces make this a dream dress. The round collar pattern is the beginning of this scalloped puffing portrait collar. Using the techniques for curving laces and mitering at the points, we added machine gathered puffing in the same manner. Entredeux is at the bottom of this scalloped collar section with French insertion at the top and bottom and ecru narrow puffing in the middle. The curved collar template is found in the pattern section of this book. The sleeves have entredeux/beading/entredeux at the bottom of the sleeve. The gathered lace edging is actually a piece of insertion butted together and zigzagged to a piece of French edging; this double lace is then gathered and butted to the trimmed edge of the bottom piece of the entredeux. I simply cannot imagine a more beautiful skirt on any dress. Machine gathered puffing is shaped into the loops; French insertion is on the outside and inside of this shaped puffing. Pintucked strips are inserted in-between the loops and purchased entredeux is found on the bottom of the dress. Once again, for the wide gathered edging on the bottom of the dress, one piece of French insertion has been butted to a piece of edging; the double piece has been gathered and stitched to the trimmed and curved entredeux. The scalloped templates for the bottom of this dress are found in the pattern section of this book. Don't be afraid of curved laces and curved puffing! It is really very easy to do with a lace shaping board, glass head pins, and your iron! The whole dress is unlined and the back closes with buttons and buttonholes. ▩

Show 1
Scallops and Loops
of Puffing Dress

Show 2
Layered Hearts With Pintucks Dress

Layered Hearts With Pintucks Dress

Using the dropped waist pattern in this book. we creatively placed heart shapes around the skirt of this pale robin's egg blue Swiss Nelona dress trimmed with bridal white French laces. The collar also has two of these interlocking hearts on it. Each heart is filled with double needle pintucks made by machine, of course. The square collar has two hearts with pintucks centered on it; flat lace edging is mitered around the square collar. Entredeux, beading, entredeux, and gathered lace edging finish the puffed sleeves.

Making these intertwined hearts with pintucks behind each heart isn't hard; however, it is a little tricky. The hearts are placed one above the other at 1 1/2 inch intervals. In other words, the hearts are on two levels on the skirt. Making the lace shaped hearts, isn't hard at all. Lace shape them and put one side on top of or underneath the next heart. Using a lace shaping board, shape all of the hearts on the whole skirt. Pin, press, remove from the board one section at a time until hearts are all the way across the skirt with one being 1 1/2" higher or lower than the next one. Here is the trick to easy placement of the pin tucked strips which need to go behind each heart.

After having shaped all of the hearts, stitch the top sections of all the hearts to the whole dress. DO NOT STITCH ANY OF THE OVERLAPPING HEART SECTIONS AT ALL. LEAVE THEM UNSTITCHED. Then, stitch the bottom sections of all the hearts to the whole dress. **Do not stitch any of the insides of the lace hearts or any of the overlapping sections of the hearts**. Now you can cut away all of the robin's egg blue Nelona fabric sections of the skirt from behind the heart sections.

Make a section of double needle pintucks long enough and wide enough to go behind the whole skirt section. Place one section at a time behind the center of one heart. Stitch the inside of the heart to a pintucked section. Trim away. Put another pintucked section behind the next heart and once again, stitch the inside of the pintucked section. Trim away the excess. Finish stitching any of the "humps" of the hearts which overlap the inside sections with the same stitching used to attach the hearts to the dress. You can either use a tiny zigzag or any of the wing needle/entredeux or pinstitch combinations to attach the hearts and the pintucked sections behind the hearts. ▩

Crazy Patch Detachable Collar Dress

Using the robin's egg blue dress from Show 10, this square crazy patch collar fits over the garment to make another adorable look. The crazy patch collar has Swiss embroidered handlooms, pink, robin's egg blue, peach, lavender, and blue fabrics, and machine stitches on ecru fabrics. The trims are buttons, silk ribbon embroidery, machine embroidery, and decorative stitching to join the pieces of crazy patch. Below the crazy patch embellishment fabric is a beautiful strip of very wide Swiss beading which carries 1 1/2 inch ribbon. Entredeux is on both sides of this beading. A strip of ecru French insertion is below this beading and gathered lace edging finishes the bottom of the collar. The crazy patch portion of the collar is completely lined. Crazy patch is very elegant when made of heirloom fabrics. It is also fabulous made of the more traditional fabrics and jewel colors. I can see this crazy patch collar made in velvets, taffetas, satins, and ribbons in jewel colors used on a velveteen or silk dupioni dress! What a spectacular holiday dress this would be! ▨

*Show 3
Crazy Patch
Detachable Collar
Dress*

*Show 3
Crazy Patch
Pinafore Bib
Dress*

Crazy Patch Pinafore Bib Dress

Although this white Swiss batiste Nelona and organdy dress does not use the pattern found in this book, I wanted to include it for your enjoyment. Margaret Boyles' book has the pattern for the basic dress and the pinafore bib. There is a skirt and an underskirt. Using antique yellowish/brownish lace this dress is a masterpiece of machine stitching. We used one very creative idea concerning antique laces. It is nearly impossible to find antique edging lace; insertions are much more readily available. Claudia Newton dreamed up this idea for making edging out of 1/2 inch insertion. For the bottom lace of this dress, she zigzagged three rows of insertion together; then, using a wide pointed scallop from today's new sewing machine stitches and the same color thread as the lace, she stitched wide scallops across the bottom row of insertion making it look like edging with a wide scallop. It is absolutely gorgeous! She used the same technique around the organdy ruffle on the pinafore bib by stitching only one row of the antique insertion on the edge of the organdy; then, she used the same wide scallop in the yellowish color thread, making the ruffle look as if it had edging stitched on the edge rather than the insertion which was all we had. This dress uses machine stitches to embellish the skirt of the dress, the narrow organdy portion of the fancy band, the organdy ruffle around the bib, and the sleeves. The same scallop used on the insertion is stitched on the Peter Pan collar; the collar has a machine/wing needle entredeux stitched above the scallop and a pretty and delicate row of machine embroidery at the top of that. The collar is a double collar of organdy.

The crazy patch pinafore bib is made of all types of ecru, brownish, yellowish, antique laces and lots of machine stitching. Satin ribbons, plain and printed, in shades of ecru are found in-between these laces. Some of the patchwork pieces have a variety of machine decorative stitches on them made with ecru thread on ecru fabric. In making heirloom crazy patch, please let your imagination be your guide. Heirloom sewing is truly the medium for using every gorgeous stitch on your sewing machine. Crazy patch is on the front and back of this fabulous bib; it is completely lined and is closed in the back with buttons and buttonholes. ▨

Ecru Celtic Lace Collar Dress

Using the gorgeous Swiss batiste, Nelona, this ecru on ecru beauty is simple to make and ever so elegant. The unlined square collar has Celtic lace shaping on the center and it is stitched down with wing needle entredeux. Purchased entredeux goes around the square collar and 1 1/2 inch wide ecru French edging which is gathered nice and full is butted against the trimmed entredeux and zigzagged on. The bottom of the sleeve is finished with purchased entredeux and the same 1 1/2 inch lace edging gathered to the bottom. A five inch hem finishes the skirt; a ribbon sash is tied in a bow in the back of the dress. The dress is closed with buttons and buttonholes. The pattern for the Celtic lace shaping is in the pattern section of this book. ▨

Show 4
Ecru Celtic
Lace Collar
Dress

Show 5
Flower Girl Portrait
Collar Dress

Flower Girl Portrait Collar Dress

One of the most wonderful times for heirloom sewing is in stitching wedding clothing from the wedding dress to the mother's dresses, to the attendant's clothing, or to the flower girl and ring bearer's clothing. This pink Swiss Nelona batiste flower girl dress is special in many ways. For the collar, use the round collar pattern included in the pattern section of this book. The round puffing portrait collar is easy to make and ever so elegant. A fabric band forms the top; entredeux, ecru French insertion, machine puffing, ecru French insertion, another strip of ecru French insertion, entredeux and gathered English netting edging form this collar. The English cotton netting lace is among the prettiest in the world and it certainly makes this dress special. A gathered row is also used as the bottom ruffle of the dress. The fancy band of this dress has entredeux, ecru French insertion, machine gathered puffing, ecru French insertion, entredeux and gathered English netting. This dress is super simple to make and ever so elegant to wear.

This round portrait collar could be made detachable and used on other garments if you so desire. This particular pink collar would be beautiful on an ecru dress or on burgundy velveteen for colder weather. I must hasten to add here that the round portrait collar is just as elegant used on bridesmaid's blouses as it is on flower girl dresses. One of the most beautiful weddings that I ever attended had ecru round portrait collar blouses and water stained dusty rose skirts for the grown women attendants. One of the real advantages for this type of garment for the women is that they really can wear this blouse for the rest of their lives as opposed to most purchased dresses that I can't imagine ever wearing again.

As with all of these heirloom dresses for children, please have your child's picture made in them. It is not necessary to use an expensive photographer to have perfectly lovely pictures made. Please find a photographer whom you can afford and take your precious one for lots of pictures. When Joanna was little my friend Judy DeRosier and I used to look in the paper for the drug stores with traveling photographers who would take a picture for $1. Needless to say, we always purchased more than the $1 picture; however, we got lots of pictures for very little money. John and Suzanne have a family picture made every Christmas at one of the nation's largest discount chains. The pictures are beautiful and needless to say, the family is beautiful also! ▨

Appliquéd Flowers Collar Dress

The dress is a basic version of the dropped waist dress made in a lovely pima cotton in forest green and white miniature gingham. The detachable Appliquéd collar has a green border on the bottom of both the front and back of the square collar with little flowers Appliquéd on the collar. They look as if they were growing out of the green grass. The fabric is a textured Swiss white on white fabric which has vertical lines woven in the fabric. The little flowers are cut out of several different baby calico patterns; the leaves and stems are green. The stems are green satin stitch and the leaves are cut out of fabric and then Appliquéd on. The centers of all the flowers have a yellow satin stitch machine embroidered touch. The back of the collar is exactly like the front. A facing is made to hold the collar in place when it is worn with the jewel neckline dress. The neckline of the dress is finished with a bias binding and the back is closed with buttons and buttonholes. The Appliquéd flowers patterns are found in the pattern section of this book and we used the square collar pattern, also in this book. ▨

Show 6
Appliquéd Flowers
Collar Dress

Smiling Fish Shadow Appliqué Collar Dress

Using the same precious green and white pima gingham cotton dress, this collar offers a way for the dress to look very different. The principle here is two looks for one dress. That is part of the beauty of detachable collars; they make one basic dress into two wonderful outfits. This collar is so sweet with the green undersea stems forming the perfect backdrop for the happy fish who are swimming along. These fish actually have smiles on their faces and have several colors of calico used under the white collar for a very "salt water fish" look. A consideration for creativity when using the shadow appliqué technique is the variety of fabrics which can be used for special effects. The white batiste top fabric softens the look of the printed fabric and makes it look very much like a real fish would look. A rule of thumb for shadow appliqué is to use brighter colors than you would ordinarily, so they will show through with reasonable intensity. The surface embroidery work such as the eyes and the smiles on the fish were done from the top using decorative stitches on the machine. Shadow appliqué is such an easy technique and can be used for any type of "embroidery" from tiny delicate flowers to smiling fish to borders to anything! If you have a little pin stitch or Madeira appliqué stitch on your sewing machine, you can use this. If you only have a plain zigzag, then that will be perfectly O.K. also. This variation uses the square collar pattern found in this book; the smiling fish patterns are in the pattern section of this book also. The dress closes in the back with buttons and buttonholes. ▨

Show 7
Smiling Fish
Shadow
Appliqué
Collar Dress

Madeira Appliqué Border Dress

This beautiful dress has a Madeira appliqué scalloped border around the collar and around the skirt. The border is of robin's egg blue Swiss Nelona and the dress is white. There is a beautiful silk ribbon embroidery flower design on both sides of the front of the collar; there is an initial Swiss motif stitched on in the middle of the collar with silk ribbon intertwined in the holes of the Swiss embroidery. The colors of the silk ribbon are lavender, robin's egg blue, peach and yellow; ecru silk ribbon was used on the Swiss motif. To attach the border to the dress we used a machine Madeira appliqué stitch and a wing needle. If your machine does not have this type of stitch, simply use a tight zigzag. You might even try a tight zigzag with a wing needle. The Madeira border pattern for the collar and the skirt are found in the pattern section of this book.

This Madeira appliqué border technique is absolutely beautiful not only on children's clothing but also on adult clothing. Try this technique on a round or square collar blouse for yourself, on a table cloth, on a placemat, or on a pillow for your home. It can be very elaborate and used in conjunction with shadow work embroidery or silk ribbon embroidery or it can be very plain. Using the techniques for Madeira appliqué borders by machine found in this book, I think you will find it easy to enough to become one of your favorite new things to do. ▓

*Show 8
Madeira
Appliqué Border
Dress*

Shark's Teeth Dress

Shark's teeth are used creatively on this dress in three different places-the collar, the cuffs and the skirt. Pale blue Nelona Swiss batiste is the gorgeous fabric used for this dropped waist dress. The double square collars are lined; the top one has a fancy band of three rows of shark's teeth in the middle and one row on the bottom. Swiss ecru embroidered insertion with double entredeux edges is used on both sides of the three tiered layer of shark's teeth; the single row of shark's teeth is on the bottom of the top collar. The sleeves are trimmed with the same double edged entredeux Swiss insertion with a row of single shark's teeth on the bottom of the sleeve. The skirt has the same treatment of Swiss insertion, three rows of shark's teeth, Swiss insertion, and one row of shark's teeth as the collar. The tucks are wider than on the collar and the sleeves showing the great versatility of shark's teeth.

Since the first time shark's teeth appeared in *Sew Beautiful* magazine, people all over the world have loved it. Some of the comments I have heard are, "At last, this is a technique that my teen aged daughter says she will really wear." "Shark's teeth is tailored enough for my taste." "This is truly something different in the heirloom sewing industry." Whatever your comment, please try this easy technique. Remember it is not hard, just a little time consuming. We have seen gorgeous shark's teeth on Christening gowns, women's clothing, little girl dresses, pillows, calico garments, and even doll clothing. Let your imagination be your guide in your creativity in using shark's teeth! ▓

*Show 9
Shark's Teeth Dress*

Netting Australian Windowpane Dress

What an exciting idea for getting two for one! This robin's egg blue Nelona dress has an unlined detachable collar with the Australian Windowpane technique done in netting in the center of the graceful point of the V-collar. The design is a three sectioned tulip type flower and is found in the pattern section. Gathered ecru French edging is serged to the outside of the collar and the neckline is finished with a bias strip. The dress can be worn without the collar since the neckline of the dress is finished with a bias strip with gathered French ecru lace edging at the top. The sleeves have elastic to gather in the fullness and flat French edging is stitched to the bottom of the sleeve. The skirt has an underlining of the robin's egg blue Swiss Nelona which has flat ecru French edging serged to the bottom of the underlining. The bottom of the skirt is very pretty with its three 1/2 inch tucks perching at the top of four strips of insertion followed by a 3/4 inch piece of edging stitched on flat. Covered buttons and buttonholes close the back of this pretty dress. ▓

*Show 10
Netting
Australian
Windowpane
Dress*

Shadow Diamonds Dress

This is one of those "to die for" dresses, I think. How could a dress be any sweeter with batiste, ecru French laces, shadow diamonds and silk ribbon embroidery? The lined bodice is made of pale blue Swiss Nelona. Three white Swiss organdy shadow diamonds are placed vertically down the front of this bodice; an organdy shadow diamond panel travels around the fancy band. The shadow diamond template is found in the pattern section of this book. Ecru French beading is at the top and bottom of the shadow diamond fancy band; entredeux joins the beading and the panel at both the top and bottom of the panel. Gathered ecru French edging finishes the bottom of the dress. The sleeves are finished with entredeux, beading and gathered French edging. The neckline has entredeux/gathered lace for the finish. The skirt has an underskirt of blue Nelona with flat French edging at the bottom. The underlining skirt is about 1 1/2 inches shorter than the dress skirt. All of the shadow diamonds have a five petal lazy daisy silk ribbon flower in medium/dusty blue with a yellow silk ribbon French knot in the center. All of the shadow diamonds are stitched onto the organdy with a wing needle/ machine entredeux stitch. ▓

*Show 10
Shadow
Diamonds
Dress*

Dropped Waist Dress Directions

Dress Fabric Requirements
(not including a collar)

	Dress with a Hem, Puffing, or Shark's Teeth	Dress with Lace Edging or a Fancy Band
Size 4	2 yds.	1-1/2 yds.
Size 5	2-1/4 yds.	1-3/4 yds.
Size 6	2-1/2 yds.	2 yds.
Size 7	2-1/2 yds.	2 yds.
Size 8	2-2/3 yds.	2-1/4 yds.
Size 10	2-3/4 yds.	2-1/4 yds.
Size 12	3 yds.	2-1/3 yds.

Collar Fabric Requirements

	Size 4-6	Size 7-12
Long Square Collar	2/3 yd.	2/3 yd.
V Collar	1/2 yd.	2/3 yd.
Square Collar	1/2 yd.	1/2 yd.
Inner Square Collar	1/2 yd.	1/2 yd.
Double Square Collar	1 yd.	1 yd.
Round Portrait Collar	1/2 yd.	2/3 yd.
Shaped Collar	1/2 yd.	2/3 yd.

**Lined Collar - double the fabric requirment for the collar.

Sach

Sash   2-1/2 yds. Ribbon

Lace and Trims Requirement

Refer to specific directons under each dress title.

All pattern pieces are found on the pattern pull-out.

All seams 1/2", trimmed to 1/4" and overcast using a zigzag or serger. French seams can be used.

I. Cutting and General Sewing Directions:

1. Cut out bodice front on the fold.

2. Cut out two bodice backs from the selvage. Mark the placket fold lines along the backs.

3. Cut out two sleeves.

4. The skirt will be cut out later. The skirt measurement will depend on the skirt design. Specific directions for each skirt are given under each dress title.

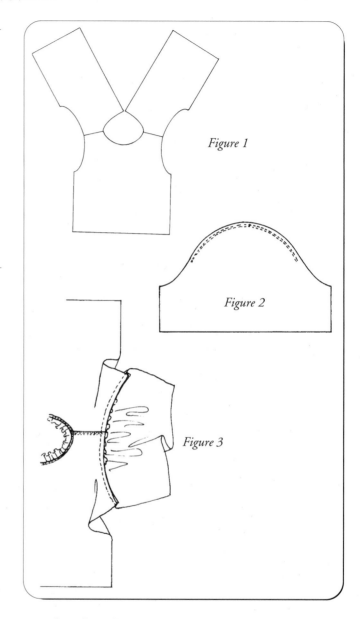

Figure 1

Figure 2

Figure 3

5. The collar will also be cut later. The directions for the specific collars are given under each dress title.

6. Place the shoulders of the dress, right sides together and stitch (**fig. 1**).

7. Finish the collar using specific collar directions under each dress title.

8. Finish the neck of the dress either with a collar or no collar (refer to Neck Finishes).

9. Run two gathering rows in the top of each sleeve 1/4" and 1/2" (**fig. 2**). Repeat for the sleeve bottom unless elastic is used. Gather the sleeve top to fit the arm opening of the dress. Stitch in place using a 1/2" seam (**fig. 3**).

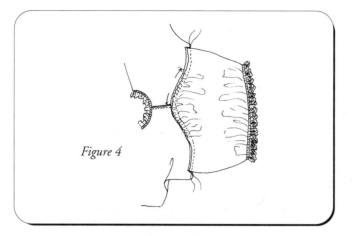

Figure 4

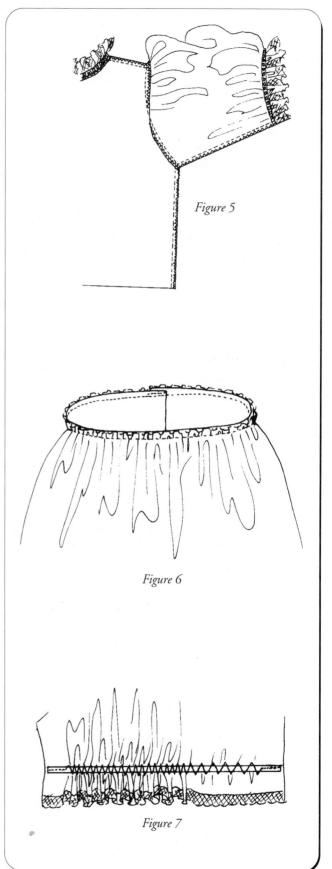

Figure 5

Figure 6

Figure 7

10. Finish the ends of the sleeve with lace and elastic or entredeux, beading and gathered lace (refer to Sleeve Finishes) (**fig. 4**).

11. Place the sides of the bodice right sides together and stitch using a 1/2" seam. Trim to 1/4". Overcast using a zigzag or serger (**fig. 5**).

12. Press the back facings to the inside of the dress. Overlap the back bodices so that the center backs line up. Pin in place.

13. Skirt - Refer to specific skirt directions under each dress title.

    Sew in one side seam of the skirt. Decorate the skirt bottom, if desired. Sew second side seam. Run gathering rows in the top of the skirt 1/4" and 1/2". Gather the skirt to fit the bodice, matching the side seams to side seams, center front and back of skirt to center front and back of bodice. Pin in place. Stitch using a 1/2" seam (**fig. 6**).

14. Add buttonholes and buttons to close the back. A ribbon sash can be added at the dropped waist line if desired.

II. Sleeve Finishes

*Sleeve Binding Measurement:** Size 4=9-3/4", 5=10-1/2", 6=10-3/8", 7=10-1/2", 8=10-3/4", 10=11", 12=11-1/4".

*These are the cutting measurements. All finished sleeve measurements will be smaller.

A. Elastic

Supplies: 2/3 yd. 1/8" elastic, 1-1/4 yd. edging lace.

Mark a line for elastic placement on the wrong side of the sleeve, 1" from the sleeve bottom. Attach flat edging lace to the ends of the sleeves using the technique lace to fabric. Cut a piece of elastic to the arm measurement plus 1" or to the measurement given above for the binding. Lay the elastic along the drawn line. Straight stitch along the middle of the elastic 5/8". Zigzag **over** the elastic, pulling the elastic to the edge of the sleeve. Stop the zigzag 5/8" from the edge; continue to the edge with a straight stitch (**fig. 7**).

Figure 8

B. Entredeux and Gathered Edging

Supplies: 2/3 yd. entredeux and 1-1/3 yd. edging lace

Cut two strips of entredeux to the measurement given for the sleeve binding. Cut away one side of the fabric from the entredeux. Cut two pieces of edging lace twice the length of the entredeux. Gather the lace to fit the entredeux. Zigzag together using the technique gathered lace to entredeux (**fig. 8**). Gather the bottom of the sleeve to fit this strip. Attach the strip to the sleeve bottom using the technique entredeux to gathered fabric (**fig. 9**).

C. Entredeux/Beading/Entredeux/Gathered Lace.

Supplies: 1-1/4 yds. entredeux, 2/3 yd. beading, 2-1/2 yds. ribbon to fit beading and 1-1/4 yds. edging lace.

Cut four pieces of entredeux and two beading pieces to the measurement given for the sleeve binding. Attach entredeux to each side of the beading using the technique lace to entredeux. Cut away one side of the fabric from the entredeux/beading strip. Cut two pieces of edging lace twice the length of the strip. Gather the lace to fit the entredeux (**fig. 10**). Zigzag together using the technique gathered lace to entredeux. Gather the bottom of the sleeve to fit this strip. Attach the strip to the sleeve bottom using the technique entredeux to gathered fabric (**fig.11**).

D. Binding

Supplies: Fabric only (no extra supplies required).

Cut a bias strip 2-1/4" wide to the measurement given for the sleeve binding. Fold the strip in half and press. Gather the bottom of the sleeve to fit the strip. Stitch the strip in place, raw edge to raw edge, using a 1/2" seam (**fig. 12**). Trim seam allowance to 1/4". Stitch the side seam of the bodice/sleeves in place. With the seam allowance of the binding pressed toward the binding. Fold the binding to the inside of the sleeve enclosing the seam allowance. Hem the binding to the inside of the sleeve (**fig. 13**).

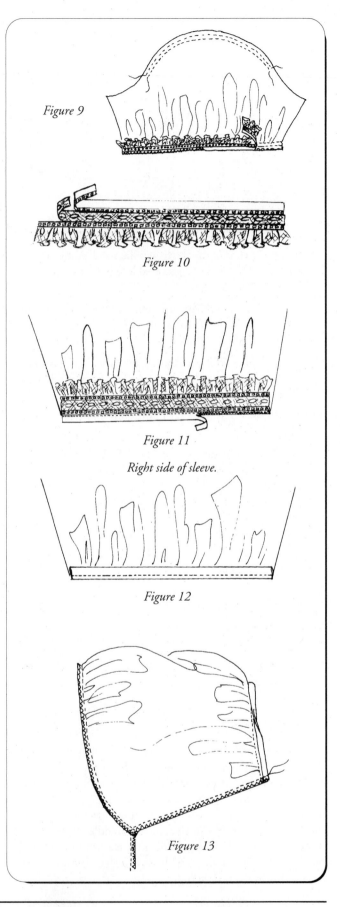

Figure 9

Figure 10

Figure 11

Right side of sleeve.

Figure 12

Figure 13

III. Neck Finishes

These dresses are made with attached collars or finished necks so that detachable collars can be used.

A. Bias Facing Only (Use with a detachable collar)

Supplies: No extra supplies required.

1. Measure the length around the neck of the dress with the back plackets folded to the inside of the dress. Cut a bias strip 1-1/2" wide by the length around the neck minus 1".

2. Fold the bias facing strip in half and press.

3. With the back plackets folded to the outside of the dress, place the raw edges of the strip to the right side of the dress at the neck edge. The strip will be on top of the facings.

4. Stitch along the neck edge using a 1/2" seam. Trim the seam to 1/8" and clip the curves (**fig. 14**).

5. Flip the back facings and the bias facing to the inside of the collar and stitch bias facing in place by hand or machine (**fig. 15**).

6. If desired, place the collar on a dress using a hook and eye on each side of the collar back to close the collar.

B. Bias Facing Used To Attach A Collar

Supplies: No extra supplies required.

1. Measure the length around the neck of the dress with the back plackets folded to the inside of the dress. Cut a bias strip 1-1/2" wide by the length around the neck minus 1".

2. Fold the bias facing strip in half and press.

3. Place the collar on the dress with the wrong side of the collar to the right side of the dress. The back edges of the collar should fall on the center back lines of the dress.

4. Fold the back plackets over the collar to the outside of the dress. Place the raw edges of the strip to the neck edge on the right side of the collar. The strip will be on top of the facings.

5. Stitch along the neck edge using a 1/2" seam, stitching through the strip, collar, facings and dress. Trim the seam to 1/8" and clip the curves (**fig. 16**).

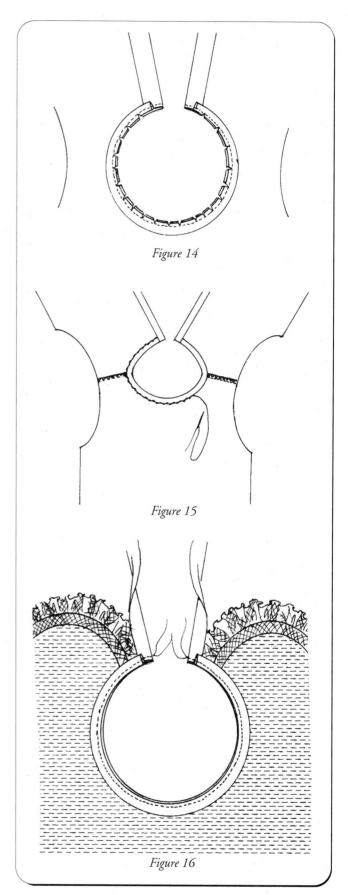

Figure 14

Figure 15

Figure 16

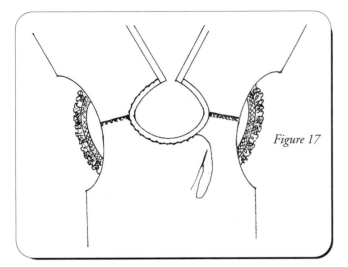

Figure 17

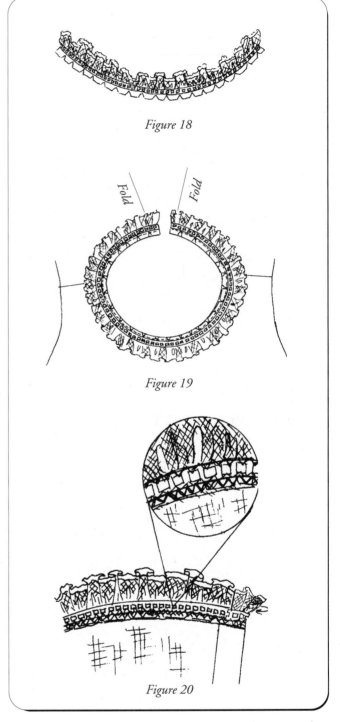

Figure 18

Figure 19

Figure 20

6. Flip the back facings and the bias facing to the inside of the dress. Stitch the bias facing to the dress by hand or machine (**fig. 17**).

C. Entredeux and Edging Lace (Used with a detachable collar or without a collar.)

Supplies: 5/8 yd. entredeux and 1-1/4 yds. edging lace

1. Measure the length around the neck of the dress with the plackets folded to the inside. Cut a strip of entredeux to this length plus 1".

2. Cut one side of the fabric completely away from the entredeux. Cut a piece of edging to twice the length of the entredeux. Gather the edging to fit the entredeux. Stitch the entredeux to the gathered edging using the technique entredeux to gathered lace (**see figure 8**).

3. Cut clips along the remaining fabric side of the entredeux (**fig. 18**). Place the clipped edge to the right side of the neck. 1/2" tabs will extend past the folded back edges of the bodice.

4. With a 1/2" seam, stitch the entredeux/gathered lace in place using the technique entredeux to fabric (**fig. 19**).

5. Flip the entredeux/gathered lace away from the dress. Fold the entredeux/lace tabs to the inside of the dress.

6. Stitch this seam allowance to the dress using a small zigzag. This makes the lace stand up at the neck and tacks the entredeux/lace tabs in place (**fig. 20**).

D. Entredeux and Edging Lace To Attach A Collar

Supplies: 5/8 yd. entredeux and 1-1/4 yd. edging lace

1. Fold the plackets to the inside of the dress. Place the collar on the dress with the finished back edges of the collar to the center back lines of the bodice. Pin in place.

2. Follow section C, steps 1-6 above to finish the neck and attach the collar.

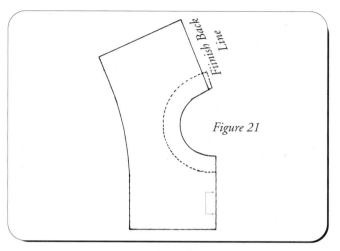

Figure 21

IV. Detachable Collar - Finishing The Neck

A. Facing

1. Cut a facing for the collar by tracing the neck edge and the finished back edge line on a piece of tissue paper. Measure 2-1/2" from the neck edge and mark. Add 1/4" to the finished back line and mark to add a seam allowance to the back of the collar. This is the pattern for the facing (**fig. 21**). Cut one facing from the fold of the fabric.

2. Finish the back edges of the facing by turning 1/4" to the wrong side and stitch in place or serge along the original finished back line removing the 1/4" allowance. Finish the outer edge of the facing, 1/4" and stitch in place or serge the edge.

3. Place the facing to the neck edge of the collar, right sides together and stitch in place using a 1/2" seam (**fig. 22**). Trim the seam to 1/8". Clip the curves.

4. Turn the facing to the inside of the collar. Lift the collar and stitch the seam allowance to the facing (**fig. 23**).

5. Place the collar on the dress by tucking the facing to the inside of the dress. The dress neck should be finished with a bias facing (refer to Neck Finishes - Bias Facing Only). Snaps can be placed on the shoulder of the dress at the neck and to the under side of the collar to hold the collar in place.

B. Bias Facing

1. Measure around the collar neck edge. Cut a bias strip 1-1/2" wide by the length around the neck plus 1".

2. Fold the bias strip in half and press. Place the raw edges of the strip to the right side of the collar. 1/2" tabs should extend along the back edges of the collar. Stitch in place using a 1/2" seam. Trim the seam allowance to 1/8". Clip the curves.

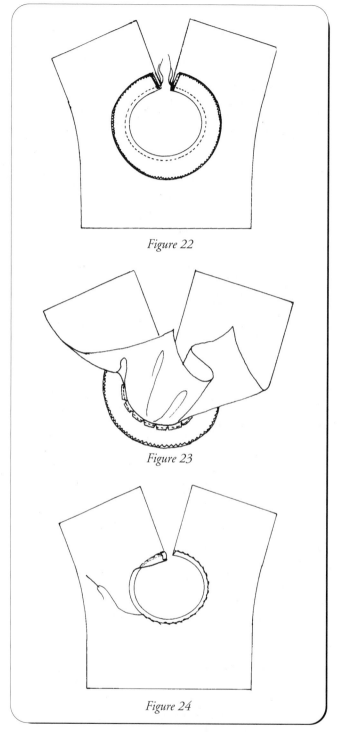

Figure 22

Figure 23

Figure 24

3. Flip the strip away from the the collar and fold the tabs to the inside. Fold the strip to the inside of the collar. Stitch in place by hand or machine (**fig. 24**). Close collar with a hook and eye.

C. Entredeux and Edging Lace

Follow the directions under section C, steps 1-6 above. ▧

Before You Begin This Section

In this section you will see rrreferences such as IIIB or IIC. These are used to refer you back to previous section "Dropped Wasit Dress Directions." The sections are for sleeve, neck and collar specific finishes.

Show 1 - Scallops and Loops of Puffing

Collar Supplies

❁ Fabric: 1/2 yd.(4-6), 2/3 yd.(7-12)

❁ 3 yds. of 5/8" insertion lace

❁ 4 yds. of 1" edging lace

❁ 2 yds. entredeux

Hem Supplies

❁ **Note:** Skirt pieces are cut 37" wide instead of 45" wide.

❁ 6 yds. of 5/8" insertion lace

❁ 4 yds. of 1-1/2" edging lace

❁ 3 yds. entredeux

Sleeves Supplies

❁ 1-1/4 yds. entredeux

❁ 2/3 yd. beading

❁ 2-1/2 yds. ribbon to fit beading

❁ 1-1/4 yds. of 1" edging lace

A. Collar Directions

1. Trace the round collar and scallop template found on the pattern pull-out onto a square of fabric.

2. Cut puffing strips 2" by 45". This dress used 8 strips for the hem and the collar. The number of strips will vary according to the fullness of the puffing. All the strips can be stitched together and then gathered or gathered in smaller pieces and then stitched together. Create puffing by stitching with a gathering foot 1/2" from each side of the strip or by running gathering row 1/4" and 1/2" from each edge and gathering by hand.

3. Place the puffing along the template lines. Shape lace above and below the puffing, mitering at the points. (Refer to shaped puffing and lace shaping directions.) Zigzag along the inside and outside edges of the top lace piece. Zigzag along the upper edge of the lower lace piece. Trim fabric away behind the puffing and lace scallops.

4. Attach entredeux along the lower piece of the lace using the technique entredeux to lace. Attach entredeux along the back edges of the collar using the technique entredeux to fabric.

5. Cut the edging twice the length around the collar and up the back. Gather to fit the entredeux. Attach using the technique gathered lace to entredeux.

6. Attach the collar to the dress using a bias facing (III-B)

B. Hem Directions

1. Skirt pieces are cut 37" wide instead of 45". Cut two skirts to the following lengths: 4=12", 5=14-1/2", 6=16-1/2", 7=18", 8=20", 10=21-1/2", 12=24". Stitch one side seam in place. Trace the loop template along front of the skirt 1-1/2" from the edge of the skirt, complete the scallop design along the back.

2. Follow directions above for puffing lace placement (step 2-4). Where the lace and puffing overlap at the loops stitch along the top piece. The underneath pieces will be cut away with the fabric.

3. Cut edging lace twice the length around the skirt. Gather to fit the entredeux along the skirt bottom. Attach using the technique entredeux to gathered lace.

4. Stitch along the second side seam. Trim and overcast with a zigzag. Attach to bodice as described in the general directions.

C. Sleeve Directions

Use the sleeve directions from section II-C. ▦

Show 2 - Layered Hearts With Pintucks

Collar Supplies

❁ Fabric: 2/3 yd.

❁ 1-1/4 yds. of 5/8" insertion lace

❁ 3-1/2 yds. of 1-1/4" edging lace

Hem Supplies

❁ 10 yds. of 5/8" insertion lace

Sleeves Supplies

✿ 1-1/4 yds. entredeux

✿ 2/3 yd. beading

✿ 2-1/2 yds. ribbon to fit beading

✿ 2-1/2 yds. insertion lace

✿ 1-1/4 yds. edging lace

A. Collar Directions

1. Cut one long square collar. Trace the layered hearts in the center of the collar front. Shape the hearts using the technique for lace shaping. Using the template on the pull out section of this book. Interlock the lace of the hearts before stitching.

2. Stitch in place along the outer edge of the design. Trim the fabric from behind the lace. The center fabric will be removed.

3. Pintuck a piece of fabric to fit behind the hearts. Pin the tucked fabric in place and stitch along the inside edge of the hearts. Cut away the excess tucked fabric behind the lace. Refer to the technique section in this book for lace shaped hearts.

4. Place edging on top of the collar edge, mitering the corners. The edge of the lace should fall along the edge of the fabric. Stitch the lace in place using a zigzag or hemstitch.

5. The back edges of the collar should fall along the center back lines of the bodice. Attach the collar to the dress using a bias facing (III-B).

B. Hem Directions

1. Cut two skirts to the following lengths: 4=17", 5=19-1/2", 6=21-1/2", 7=23", 8=25", 10=26-1/2", 12=29". Stitch one side seam in place. Fold a 5" hem to the inside of the skirt. Do not stitch. Trace the layered heart skirt template starting at the side seam with the upper heart centered on the seam and the point 2-1/2" from the fold (hemline) of the skirt. Complete the template along the skirt bottom ending with a half upper heart on one end and a half upper heart on the other end. Measure 1/2" from the half hearts and cut off any excess skirt. Stitch the side seam in place, lining up the heart template to complete the heart. The finished skirt width measures 80".

2. Pin the hem in place. Shape lace along the interlocking hearts template lines using the technique for lace shaping. Stitch along the outer edge of the hearts using a zigzag or hemstitch. This will hem the dress. Cut the fabric from behind the hearts. Create a strip of pintucks 8" by the

width around the skirt. Pin in place behind the hearts and stitch along the inside edge of the lace. Trim away the excess pintucked fabric.

3. Attach to bodice as described in the general directions.

C. Sleeve Directions

Use the sleeve directions from section II-C. Two pieces of insertion have been zigzagged to the edging lace to create a wide lace ruffle piece. This piece is them treated as one wide piece.

Show 3 - Crazy Patch Detachable Collar

This collar is worn with the Netting Australian Window-pane Dress in our photographs and illustrations. It can be worn with any dress variation suitable to a detachable collar.

Collar Supplies:

✿ Fabric scraps, buttons, silk ribbon and other trims for crazy patch

✿ 1/2 yd. Base Fabric Muslin or Broadcloth

✿ 1 yd. Wide Swiss Beading

✿ 1 yd. Ribbon to fit beading

✿ 1 yd. of 5/8" Lace Insertion

✿ 2 yds. of 1" Edging Lace

Collar Directions

1. Trace off one complete square collar using the pattern from the pattern pull-out to work crazy patch. Cut out a second collar for the lining.

2. Starch and press traced collar piece. Work crazy patch to cover the drawn collar front and back. Refer to crazy patch directions in this book to complete design.

3. Cut around collar outline. Place the collar and the lining, right sides together. Stitch around the outer edges using a 1/2" seam allowance (not the neck edge). Turn the collar through the neck opening.

4. Cut Swiss beading pieces and lace insertion pieces 1/2" larger than the lower front and back edges of the collar. Attach lace insertion pieces to the beading pieces using the technique lace to entredeux. Cut edging lace pieces twice the measurement of the beading/lace strip. Gather the lace to fit the insertion. Attach to the edging to the insertion using the technique lace to lace.

5. Center the strips along the lower edges of the collar by butting the beading strip to the collar edge and zigzag in place. Turn the unfinished edges of the beading/lace strip to the under side of the collar. Stitch in place.

6. The neck of this collar is finished using IV-B. ✻

Show 4 - Ecru Celtic Lace Collar Dress

Collar Supplies

❀ 1 yd. fabric

❀ 1-1/2 yds. of 3/8" insertion lace

❀ 4 yds. of 1" edging lace

❀ 3 yds. entredeux

Sleeve Supplies

❀ 2/3 yds. entredeux

❀ 1-1/4 yds. of 1" edging lace

A. Collar Directions

1. Cut two square collars. Place the collars together and treat as one layer of fabric.

2. Trace Celtic design in the center of the collar front. Shape the lace into the Celtic design. Refer to Celtic lace shaping found in the lace shaping sections of this book.

3. Attach entredeux around the outer and back edges of the collar using the technique entredeux to fabric.

4. Cut the edging twice the length around the collar and up the back. Gather to fit the entredeux. Attach using the technique gathered lace to entredeux.

6. Attach the collar to the dress using a bias facing (III-B).

B. Hem Directions

1. Cut two skirts to the following lengths: 4=16", 5=18-1/2", 6=20-1/2", 7=22", 8=24", 10=25-1/2", 12=29". Stitch the two side seams in place.

2. Attach to bodice as described in the general directions.

3. Hem to the correct length. A 4" hem has been allowed in the measurment.

C. Sleeve Directions

Use the sleeve directions from section II-C. Omit the beading and one piece of entredeux. Attach the gathered edging to the entredeux. Attach the entredeux to the gathered sleeve. ✻

Show 5 - Flower Girl Portrait Collar Dress

Collar Supplies

❀ Fabric: 1/2 yd. (4-6), 2/3 yd. (7-12)

❀ 4 yds. of 5/8" insertion lace

❀ 4 yds. of 3" edging lace

❀ 4 yds. entredeux

Hem Supplies

Note: Skirt pieces are cut 37" wide instead of 45" wide.

❀ 5 yds. of 5/8" insertion lace

❀ 5 yds. of 3" edging lace

❀ 5 yds. entredeux

Sleeve Supplies

❀ 1-1/4 yds. entredeux

❀ 2/3 yd. beading

❀ 2-1/2 yds. ribbon to fit beading

❀ 1-1/4 yds. of 3" edging lace

A. Collar Directions

1. Trace two round collars from the pattern pull-out onto a square of tissue paper. Add 1/2" to the finished back edges of the pattern. Measure along one of the pattern pieces 2-1/2" from the neck edge. Cut along this line. This is the pattern for the yoke of the collar. Cut one yoke from the fabric. Place entredeux around the bottom of the collar yoke by cutting one side of the entredeux fabric completely away and clipping the other side of the entredeux so that the entredeux will curve. Attach using the technique entredeux to fabric. Press seam allowance to yoke and entredeux away from yoke.

2. Place the collar on the second tissue pattern. Place on lace shaping board. Shape insertion lace along the entredeux. Starch and press.

3. Cut puffing strips 2-1/2" by 45". This dress used 8 strips for the hem and the collar. The number of strips will vary according to the fullness of the puffing. All the strips can be stitched together and then gathered or gathered in smaller pieces and then stitched together. Create puffing by stitching with a gathering foot 1/2" from each side of the strip or by running gathering row 1/4" and 1/2" from each edge and gathering by hand.

4. Shape the puffing so that the seam allowance of the puffing fits under the insertion lace. Pin in place. Shape two rows of insertion lace along the lower edge of the puffing. Starch and press. Remove from the board and pin pieces to the tissue only. Zigzag all pieces together. Trim away the seam allowance of the puffing. (Refer to shaped puffing and lace shaping directions.)

5. Trim both fabric sides of a piece of entredeux and attach to the lower lace edge of the collar. Gather edging to fit the entredeux and zigzag in place. (Refer to shaped puffing and lace shaping directions.)

6. Turn the back edges of the collar to the inside 1/4" and 1/4" again and stitch in place.

7. Attach the collar to the dress using a bias facing (III-B).

B. Hem Directions

1. Skirts pieces are cut 37" wide instead of 45". Cut two skirts to the following lengths: 4=7", 5=9-1/2", 6=11-1/2", 7=13", 8=15", 10=16-1/2", 12=18". Stitch one side seam in place.

2. Create puffing strip as described for the collar. Create a French sewn band of entredeux, insertion lace, puffing, insertion lace, entredeux and gathered edging to the width of the skirt bottom. Attach the band to the skirt using the technique entredeux to fabric.

3. Stitch along the second side seam. Attach to bodice as described in the general directions.

C. Sleeve Directions

Use the sleeve directions from section II-C. ❂

Show 6 - Appliqued Flowers Detachable Collar and Dress

Collar Supplies

❀ Fabric scraps for applique

❀ 1 yd. Fabric (collar and lining)

Collar Directions

1. Cut out two square collars (one lining and one collar) using the pattern from the pattern pull-out.

2. Appliqued flowers stems need to start 1-1/4" from the lower edge of the collar. This allows for the border of green grass.

3. Applique flowers and leaves. Stems are a satin stitch zigzag. Flowers centers are satin stitch dots. Refer to applique directions in this book for futher instructions.

4. Cut a strip of green fabric 1-1/2" to fit the lower edge of the collar. Attach the strip to the lower edge of the collar at the bottom of the flowers using a 1/4" seam.

5. Place the collar and the lining, right sides together. Stitch around the outer edges using a 1/2" seam allowance (not the neck edge). Turn the collar through the neck opening.

6. The neck of this collar is finished using IV-A. Construct the dress using the general directions. The neck of the dress is finished with a bias facing, III-A.

Sleeve Directions

Sleeve direction from II - D.

Hem Directions

1. Cut two skirts to the following lengths: 4=16", 5=18-1/2", 6=20-1/2", 7=22", 8=24", 10=25-1/2", 12=29".

2. Stitch the two side seams in place. Attach to bodice as described in the general directions.

3. Hem to the correct length. A 4" hem has been allowed in the measurment. ❂

Show 7 - Smiling Fish Detachable Collar Dress

Collar Supplies

❀ Fabric scraps for shadow applique

❀ 1/2 yd. broadcloth collar lining

❀ 1/2 yd. Nelona or see-through fabric for shadow applique collar

Collar Directions

1. Trace one square collar on see-through fabric. Trace shadow applique designs on the collar. Follow the directions for shadow applique in this book for specific directions. Cut out collar. Cut out square collar lining from the broadcloth.

2. Place the collar and the lining, right sides together. Stitch around the outer edges using a 1/2" seam allowance (not the neck edge). Turn the collar through the neck opening.

3. The neck of this collar is finished using IV-A.

4. Construct the dress using the general directions. The neck of the dress is finished with a bias facing, III-A.

Sleeve Directions

Sleeve direction from II- D.

Hem Directions

1. Cut two skirts to the following lengths: 4=16", 5=18-1/2", 6=20-1/2", 7=22", 8=24", 10=25-1/2", 12=29".

2. Stitch the two side seams in place. Attach to bodice as described in the general directions.

3. Hem to the correct length. A 4" hem has been allowed in the measurement. ✖

Show 8 - Madeira Applique Border Dress

Collar Supplies

❁ 1/2 yd. collar fabric

❁ 1/2 yd. border fabric

❁ 1/2 yd. Water Soluable Stablizer (WSS)

Hem Supplies

❁ 1/3 yd. border fabric

❁ 1/2 yd. WSS

Collar Directions

1. Follow the directions for the Maderia Applique Doll Dress. The Madeira directions for this collar and the doll collar are the same. 1/2" seams are used on the seams of the collar. The back edges of the collar are finished turning the back edges to the inside 1/4" and 1/4" again. Stitch in place.

2. The collar is attached to the dress using the directions for Neck Finishes III-B.

Sleeve Directions

This dress has no sleeves. Stitch side seams in place. The arm openings are finished with bias facings. Cut bias strips 1-1/2" wide by the length around the opening. Follow III-A, step 2-5. Where the bias facing overlaps fold the top bias to the inside 1/4" and enclose the beginning of the bottom bias. Press to the inside of the dress and stitch in place by hand or machine.

Skirt Directions

1. Cut two border strips 5" wide by 38". Stitch one short side together to form a long strip. This strip will be a little longer than required. Starting at the seam trace the border design along the right side of the top edge of the strip. This design has a 12" repeat. The finished border on this dress is 72". Stitch the border into a circle so that the template design is continuous. Cut off excess.

2. Place a strip of water soluable stablizer 3" wide on the right side of the border strip at the drawn template. Edge of WSS to edge of fabric. Overlap the WSS when necessary to complete the entire border.

3. Stitch the WSS to the border along the template lines. Trim 1/4" above the stitching line. Clip the curves and turn the WSS to the wrong side of the border, much like a facing. Use a point turner to give crisp edges.

4. Measure the border from seam to seam. Cut two skirt pieces to this width plus 1" by the following lengths: 4=11-1/2", 5=14", 6=16", 7=17-1/2", 8=19-1/2", 10=21", 12=24-1/2". Stitch the two side seams in place. It is very inportant that the width of the border and the width of the skirt are the same. Place the straight edge of the border to the bottom of the skirt, right side of border to wrong side of skirt. Stitch in place using a 1/4" seam.

5. Flip the border to the right side. Starch and press. Pin the border in place and stitch along the top edge using a pinstitch or zigzag.

6. Attach to bodice as described in the general directions. ✖

Show 9 - Shark's Teeth Dress

Collar Supplies

❁ 1 yd. Swiss embroidery with entredeux

❁ 1 yd. fabric

Sleeve Supplies

❁ 2/3 yd. Swiss embroidery with entredeux

Skirt Supplies

❁ 5 yds. Swiss embroidery with entredeux

Collar Directions

Shark's Teeth Inner Collar

Template on page 310.

1. Cut out two Inner Double Collars and two Square Collars using the patterns on the pull-out pattern sheet. One collar piece will be for the lining and the other for the collar.

2. Measure across the front of the inner collar. Cut a fabric strip to this width by 4-1/4" long. Use the tucking guide found in the back of this book for 3/8" tucks. Make the tucks. Mark for shark's teeth using the template for 3/8" tucks. Create the teeth using the directions under shark's teeth in this book.

3. Attach entredeux-embroidery strip on each side of the shark's teeth strip using the technique entredeux to fabric. The trim should hit along the stitching line of the first tuck and just below the points of the lower teeth.

4. Create a second strip of teeth, cutting the fabric the width of the collar front by 2-1/2" long. Mark the fabric using the first tuck on the 3/8" tucking guide. Make the tucks. Mark for the teeth across the entire tuck using the lower teeth on the template for 3/8" shark's teeth. Create teeth as above.

5. Stitch this strip to the lower edge of the embroidery along the stitching line of the first tuck. Stitch as above.

6. Measure the length of the completed strip from the entredeux at the top, to the points of the teeth at the bottom plus 3/4", subtract 1/2" to get the "cut away" measurement. Cut away this measurement length from one of the inner collar front pieces to prepare it for the shark's teeth strip. Stitch the sharks's teeth strip to the prepared collar using a 1/2" seam.

7. Place the inner shark's teeth collar and the inner lining, right sides together and stitch around the edges 1/2" (not the neck edge). Trim the seams to 1/8". Clip the curves and turn to the right side through the neck opening. Press. Set aside.

Square Collar

Place the square collar and the square collar lining right sides together and stitch, clip and turn as above.

Completing the Collar

1. Place the shark's teeth collar on top of the square collar. Pin together and treat as one collar.

2. Attach to the dress using a bias facing.

Sleeves Directions

1. Cut two strips of entredux/embroidery and two strips of fabric to the following width 4=9-3/4", 5=10-1/2", 6=10-3/8", 7=10-1/2", 8=10-3/4", 10=11", 12=11-1/4" by 2-1/2". Create tucks as described in step 4 and 5 above.

2. Gather the lower sleeve to fit the band. Stitch the side seams of the bodice/sleeves using a 1/2" seam, trim to 1/4" and overcast.

3. Hem the sleeve with the fold of the hem just below the points of the teeth.

Hem Directions

1. Cut two fabric strips the 45" wide by 8" long. Stitch the strips together creating one long strip. Use the tucking guide found the the back of this book for 3/4" tucks. Make the tucks. Mark for shark's teeth using the template for 3/4" tucks. Create the teeth using the directions under Shark's Teeth in this book.

2. Attach entredeux-embroidery strip on each side of the shark's teeth strip using the technique entredeux to fabric. The trim could hit along the stitching line of the first tuck and just below the points of the lower teeth.

3. Create a second strip of teeth cutting the fabric the width above by 8" long. Mark the fabric using the first tuck on the 3/4" tucking guide. Make the tucks. Mark for the teeth across the entire tuck using the lower teeth template for 3/4" shark's teeth. Create teeth as above.

5. Stitch the upper edge of the strip to the lower edge of the embroidery along the stitching line of the first tuck. Stitch as above.

6. Fold the fabric below the teeth to the inside of the strip about 1/2" below the points of the teeth. Press. This is the hem line.

7. Measure the length of the strip from the entredeux at the top, to the hemline at the bottom, subtract 1/2" to get the "cut away" measurement. Subtract this measurement from the skirt measurements: 4=12", 5=14-1/2", 6=16-1/2", 7=18", 8=20", 10=21-1/2", 12=24".

8. Cut two skirt pieces to the length found above by 45". Stitch in one side seam. Stitch the shark's teeth strip in place using a 1/2" seam.

9. Fold the edge of the hem under so that it meets a stitching line in one of the tucks. Stitch in place by hand.

10. The skirt is complete, attach to the bodice.

Show 10 - Netting Australian Windowpane Dress

The dress has a bias facing at the neck embellished with gathered edging lace. The sleeves have edging lace and are gathered to fit with elastic. Tucks and lace are found at the hem of the skirt.

Collar Supplies

- Fabric: 1/2 yd. (4-6), 2/3 yd. (7-12)
- 6" square of netting
- 4 yds. of 1" edging lace

Hem Supplies

- 10 yds. of 5/8" insertion lace
- 2-1/2 yds. of 3/4" edging

Follow the general directions for dress construction.

Specific Instructions

Collar Directions

1. Trace the V collar from the pull-out pattern sheet. Cut the collar from the fold of the fabric. Trace the windowpane flower in the middle of the collar front.

2. Stitch the Australian Windowpane design using netting for the flower. Refer to the technique section for Australian Windowpane instructions.

3. Gather the edging lace to fit the outer edge of the collar. Place the lace to the collar, right sides together and zigzag in place using the technique lace to fabric.

4. This collar is detachable finished with a bias facing. Refer to IV- B.

Hem Directions - Skirt With Tucks And Lace

1. Cut 4 strips of lace insertion lace 90" long. Zigzag together using the technique lace to lace. Cut one piece of lace edging 90" long and attach to the lace strip in the same manner.

2. Cut two skirt pieces 45" by the following length: 4=12", 5=14-1/2", 6=16-1/2", 7=18", 8=20", 10=21-1/2", 12=24".

3. Stitch one side seam in the skirt and attach the lace band to the skirt bottom using the technique lace to fabric. Stitch the second side seam in place.

4. Mark the fold lines for the three tucks measuring the first line from the seam 7/8", 1-1/2" from this line and again 1-1/2". Fold the fabric wrong sides together along the fold lines and stitch 1/2" away from the fold. Press the tucks toward the lace.

5. When the skirt is complete, attach to the bodice. ❈

— *Show #10 - Shadow Diamonds Dress* —

Other Fabrics

❈ 1/3 yd. organdy (all shadow diamonds)

❈ Silk ribbon

Sleeves Supplies

❈ 2/3 yds. entredeux

❈ 2/3 yd. beading

❈ 2-1/2 yds. ribbon to fit beading

❈ 1-1/4 yds. of 1" edging lace

Hem Supplies

❈ 5 yds. entredeux

❈ 5 yds. beading

❈ 5 yds. of 1" edging lace

Bodice Directions

1. Trace shadow diamond template along the center front of the bodice. Refer to the shadow diamonds in the technique section of this book for specific directions.

2. Cut the diamond as described in the directions. Fold the slips to the wrong side of the bodice.

3. Place the organdy to the back side of the bodice. Stitch around the diamond, stitching the organdy to the folded edges of the diamond shape.

4. Trim the organdy and the extra bodice fabric from the stitching.

5. Add silk ribbon flower of lazy daisy stitches and a French knot in the center.

Sleeve Directions

Refer to sleeve directions III-C. Omit the entredeux between the beading and the gathered edging lace.

Hem Directions

1. Cut two strips of fabric and two strips of organdy 4" by 45. Stitch the fabric together to form one long piece of fabric. Stitch the organdy together to form one long piece of fabric.

2. Trace shadow diamonds along the fabric. Complete the shadow diamonds using the directions for the bodice.

3. Attach entredeux above and below the shadow diamond strip using the technique entredeux to fabric. Attach beading to the entredeux. Attach gathered edging to the lower beading. Attach the upper beading to the skirt.

4. Stitch the second side seam of the skirt in place. Attach the skirt to the bodice.

5. Work silk ribbon flowers in the shadow diamonds of the skirt. ❈

Pink Triple Heart Dress
Pictured in the color section of the book.

Collar Supplies

❀ 2 yds. of 5/8" insertion lace

❀ 4 yds. of 1" edging lace

❀ 2 yds. entredeux

Hem Supplies

❀ 5 yds. of 1" edging lace

❀ 2-1/2 yds. entredeux

Sleeves Supplies

❀ 2/3 yds. entredeux

❀ 2/3 yd. beading

❀ 2-1/2 yds. ribbon to fit beading

❀ 1-1/4 yds. of 1" edging lace

A. Collar Directions

Follow the directions for Celtic Lace Dress above using the shaped collar pattern and the triple lace hearts template.

B. Hem Directions

1. Skirts pieces are cut 37" wide instead of 45". Cut two skirts to the following lengths: 4=11", 5=13-1/2", 6=15-1/2", 7=17", 8=19", 10=20-1/2", 12=23". Stitch one side seam in place.

2. Attach entreduex to the skirt bottom using the technique entredeux to fabric.

3. Cut edging lace twice the length around the skirt. Gather to fit the entredeux along the skirt bottom. Attach using the technique entredeux to gathered lace.

4. Stitch along the second side seam. Trim and overcast with a zigzag. Attach to bodice as described in the general directions.

C. Sleeve Directions

Use the sleeve directions from section II-C. Omit the entredeux between the gathered lace and the entredeux. simply attach the gathered lace directly to the beading using the technique lace to lace. ❈

Beginning French Sewing Techniques

Lace Straight Edge To Lace Straight Edge

Use this technique when applying: lace insertion to lace insertion; lace insertion to lace beading; lace insertion or lace beading to non-gathered straight edge of lace edging; and Swiss embroidered trims to entredeux edgings.

1 Spray starch and press each piece.

2 Place the two pieces, side by side, butting them together, but not overlapping. It is not important to match patterns in the lace (**fig. 1**).

3. Begin 1/4 inch or 3/8 inch from the ends of the pieces to be joined. This keeps the ends from digging into the sewing machine (**fig. 2**).

4 Zigzag the two edges together. Zigzag again if spaces are missed.

5 Stitch just widely enough to catch the two headings of the pieces of lace (or embroidery). Laces vary greatly in the widths of the headings. The stitch widths will vary according to the lace heading placement and your preference.

6 Stitch the length as tightly or as loosely as you wish. You don't want a satin-stitch; however, you don't want the dress to fall apart either. Work with your trims and your sewing machine to determine the length and width you want. Suggested stitch width and length:

Width=2 to 3 — I prefer 2-1/2
Length=1 to 1/12 — I prefer 1

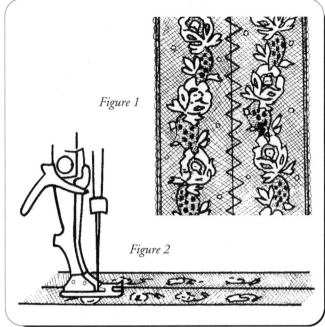

Figure 1

Figure 2

Lace Flat Edge To Fabric

Use this technique when applying lace edging to ruffle or skirt; embroidered insertion to straight edge of lace; lace edging to sleeve edge, as on smocked sleeve or bottom of sleeve with elastic casing; and Swiss edging (with scallops trimmed) to a flat surface to fabric edge, as on ruffles, sleeves, or collars.

Martha's Magic

1. Spray starch and press both the lace and the fabric.

2. Place right sides to right sides.

3. **NOTE:** Leave 1/8 inch to 1/4 inch of fabric edge before placing the lace to be joined (**fig. l**).

4. Zigzag with a satin stitch, going into the heading of the lace and all the way off the fabric edge (**fig. 2**).

5. Suggested stitch length:

Width=3-1/2 to 4
Length=l/2 or as short as possible

Figure 1

Leave 1/8 inch to 1/4 inch of the fabric edge before placing the lace to be joined.

Figure 2

Zigzag with a satin stich going into the heading of the lace and all the way off the fabric edge.

W=31/2 to 4
L=1/2

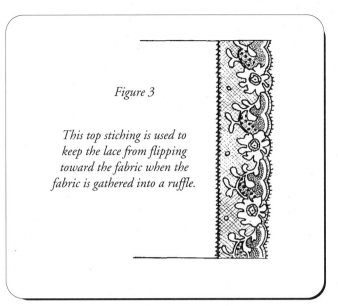

Figure 3

This top stiching is used to keep the lace from flipping toward the fabric when the fabric is gathered into a ruffle.

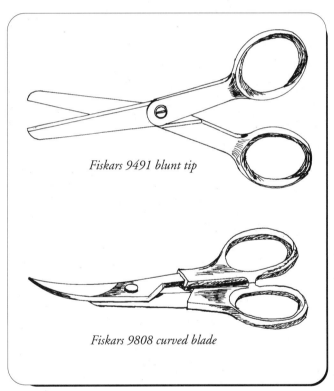

Fiskars 9491 blunt tip

Fiskars 9808 curved blade

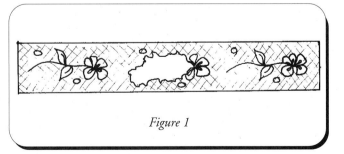

Figure 1

NOTE: l/8 inch to l/4 inch of the fabric is exposed before the lace flat edge is put into place. The fabric edge will completely fold into the stitch when you are finished.

6   Why shouldn't you just place the edge of the lace and the edges of the fabric together and zigzag? They will come apart. There is not enough strength in the edge of the fabric without the extra l/8 inch or l/4 inch folded into the zigzag.

7.   Press the lace and fabric open. A common question is, "Which way do I press this roll?" Press the seam however it wants to lie. Naturally, it will fold toward the lace.

Top Stitching Lace

1.   Work from the right side, after the lace has been pressed open.

2.   Zigzag on top of the little roll which is on the back of the garment. Your width should be very narrow — just wide enough to go from one side of the roll to the other side. It should not be too short. You want it to be as invisible as possible (**fig. 3**).

3.   This zigzag holds the lace down and gives added strength to the seam. Its main purpose, however, is to hold the lace down.

4.   Stitch width and length:
    Width=1/2 to l-l/2, Length=l to 2

Cutting Fabric From Behind Lace That Has Been Shaped and Zigzagged

I absolutely love two pairs of Fiskars Scissors for the tricky job of cutting fabric from behind lace that has been shaped and stitched on. The first is Fiskars 9491, blunt tip 5" scissors. They look much like kindergarten scissors because of the blunt tips; however, they are very sharp. They cut fabric away from behind laces with ease. By the way, both of the scissors mentioned in this section are made for either right handed or left handed people.

The second pair that I really love for this task are the Fiskars 9808 curved blade craft scissors. The curved blades are very easy to use when working in tricky, small areas of lace shaping. Fiskars are crafted of permanent stainless steel and are precision ground and hardened for a sharp, long lasting edge.

Reparing Lace Holes Which You Didn't Mean To Cut!

Trimming fabric away from behind stitched-down lace can be difficult. It is not uncommon to slip, thus cutting a hole in your lace work. How do you repair this lace with the least visible repair? It is really quite simple.

1.   Look at the pattern in the lace where you have cut the hole. Is it in a flower, in a dot series, or in the netting part of the lace (**fig. 1**)?

2. After you identify the pattern where the hole was cut, cut another piece of lace 1/4 inch longer than each side of the hole in the lace.

3. On the bottom side of the lace in the garment, place the lace patch (**fig. 2**).

4. Match the design of the patch with the design of the lace around the hole where it was cut.

5. Zigzag around the cut edges of the lace hole, trying to catch the edges of the hole in your zigzag (**fig 3**).

6. Now, you have a patched and zigzagged pattern.

7. Trim away the leftover ends underneath the lace you have just patched (**fig. 3**).

8. And don't worry about a piece of patched lace. My grandmother used to say, "Don't worry about that. You'll never notice it on a galloping horse."

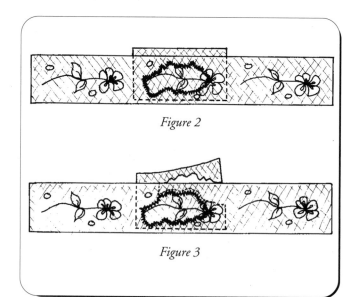

Figure 2

Figure 3

Piecing Lace Not Long Enough For Your Needs

From my sewing experience, sometimes you will need a longer piece of lace than you have. Perhaps you cut the lace incorrectly or bought less than you needed and had to go back for more. Whatever the reason, if you need to make a lace strip longer, it is easy to do.

1. Match your pattern with two strips that will be joined later (**figs. 1 and 3**).

2. Is your pattern a definite flower? Is it a definite diamond or some other pattern that is relatively large?

3. If you have a definite design in the pattern, you can join pieces by zigzagging around that design and then down through the heading of the lace (**fig. 2**).

4. If your pattern is tiny, you can zigzag at an angle joining the two pieces (**fig. 2**). Trim away excess laces close to the zigzagged seam (**fig. 4**).

5. Forget that you have patched laces and complete the dress. If you discover that the lace is too short before you begin stitching, you can plan to place the pieced section in an inconspicuous place.

6. If you were already into making the garment when you discovered the short lace, simply join the laces and continue stitching as if nothing had happened.

If Your Fancy Band Is Too Short

Not to worry; cut down the width of your skirt. Always make your skirt adapt to your lace shapes, not the lace shapes to your skirt.

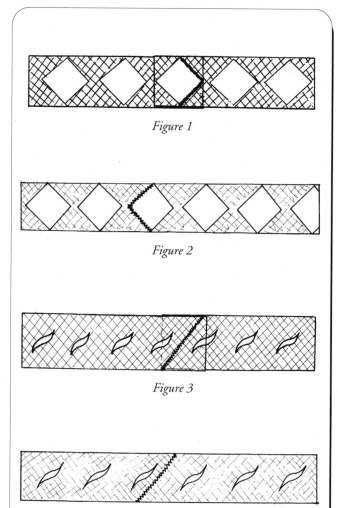

Figure 1

Figure 2

Figure 3

Figure 4

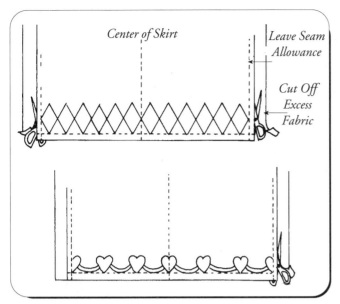

Center of Skirt

Leave Seam Allowance

Cut Off Excess Fabric

Making Diamonds, Hearts, Tear-Drops, Or Circles Fit Skirt Bottom

How do you make sure that you engineer your diamonds, hearts, teardrops, or circles to exactly fit the width skirt that you are planning? The good news is that you don't. Make your shapes any size that you want. Stitch them onto your skirt, front and back, and cut away the excess skirt width. Or, you can stitch up one side seam, and zigzag your shapes onto the skirt, and cut away the excess on the other side before you make your other side seam.

Ribbon To Lace Insertion

This is tricky! Lace has give and ribbon doesn't. After much practice, I have decided that for long bands of lace to ribbon, as in a skirt, it is better to place the lace on top of the ribbon and straight-stitch (Length 2 to 2-1/2). For short strips of lace to ribbon, it is perfectly OK to butt together and zigzag.

Directions for Straight-Stitch Attachment (fig. 1):

1. Press and starch your ribbon and lace.

2. Place the heading of the insertion just over the heading of the ribbon and straight-stitch (Length=2 to 2-1/2).

Directions for Zigzag-Stitch Attachment (fig. 2):

1. Press and starch your ribbon and lace.

2. Place the two side by side and zigzag (Width=1- 1/2 to 2-1/2, Length 1-2).

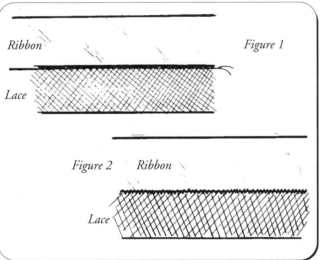

Ribbon

Figure 1

Lace

Figure 2   Ribbon

Lace

Flat Lace To Entredeux

1. Trim one batiste side of the entredeux.

2. Spray starch and press entredeux and lace.

3. Lay trimmed edge of entredeux beside the flat side of the lace. These should be right sides up. Butt them together; they should not overlap. In other words, zigzag, side by side, right sides up.

4. Zigzag them together, trying to make one stitch of the machine go into one hole of the entredeux and over, just catching the heading of the lace (**figs. 1 and 2**).

5. Suggested Width=2-1/2 to 3-1/2, Length=2-1/2

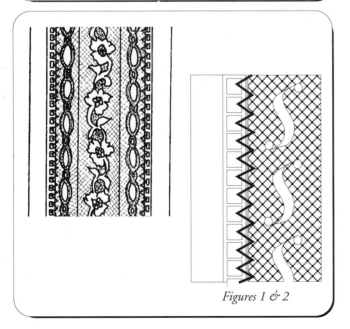

Figures 1 & 2

Entredeux To Flat Fabric
Method I - Stitch-In-The-Ditch

1. Do not trim entredeux.

2. Spray starch and press fabric and entredeux.

3. Place together batiste edge of untrimmed entredeux and edge of the fabric. (This is similar to the sewing of any two seams of a dress. Place the edges and sew the seam.)

4. Sew in straight, short stitches along the right hand side of the entredeux (the side of the entredeux that is next to the body of the sewing machine.) This is called "stitch-in-the-ditch" because it is just that — you stitch in the ditch of the entredeux (Length= 2-1/2) (**fig. l**).

5. Trim the seam, leaving about a 1/8-inch seam allowance (**fig. 2**).

6. Zigzag a tight stitch (not a satin) to go over the stitch-in-the-ditch and all the way off the edge of the fabric edge. This zigzag will completely encase the fabric left on the entredeux and the straight stitch you just made (Width=2-1/2 to 3, Length=1) (**fig. 3**).

7. Press the zigzagged seam toward the fabric. All of the holes of the entredeux should be showing perfectly.

8. This top stitching is not necessary if you are using entredeux to flat fabric; however, you may choose to make this stitching. When you make the top stitch, zigzag on top of the fabric. As close as possible, zigzag into one hole of the entredeux and into the fabric. Barely catch the fabric in this top zigzag stitch. Adjust your machine length and width to fit each situation (**fig. 4**).

9. My machine width and length:

    Width=l-1/2 to 2

    Length=2

10. You can choose to do top stitching from the back of the fabric. If you work from the back, you can hold the seam down and see a little better. On entredeux to flat fabric, the choice of top stitching from the top or from the bottom is yours.

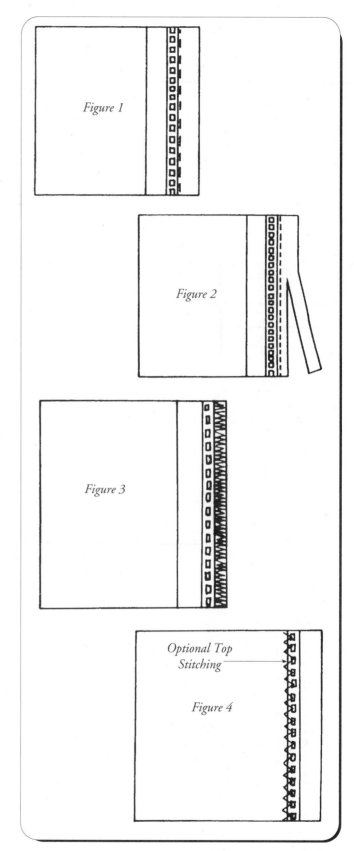

Figure 1

Figure 2

Figure 3

Optional Top Stitching

Figure 4

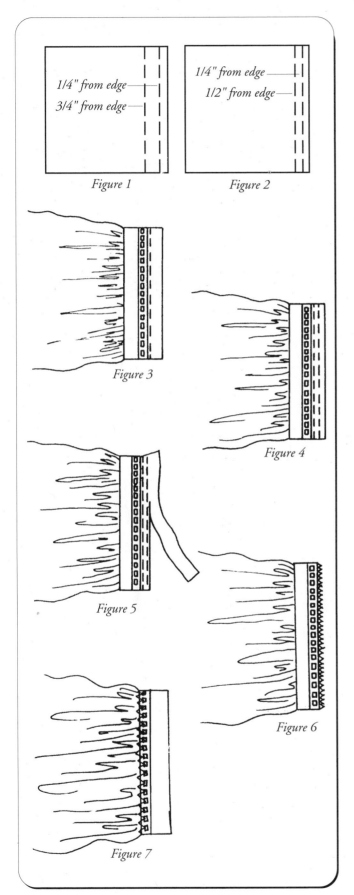

Figure 1

Figure 2

Figure 3

Figure 4

Figure 5

Figure 6

Figure 7

Entredeux To Gathered Fabric
Method I

1. Press, don't spray starch the fabric.

2. Do not cut off the edges of the entredeux.

3. Run two rows of long gathering stitches on the fabric (Length=4). There are two methods for running these gathering stitches.

   a. Sew the first gathering row 1/4 inch from the edge of the fabric. Sew the second gathering row 3/4 inch from the edge of the fabric (**fig.1**).

   b. Sew the first gathering row 1/4 inch from the edge of the fabric. Sew the second gathering row 1/4 inch below the first row. This is the more traditional method of running two gathering rows (**fig. 2**).

4. Gather by hand to adjust the gathers to fit the entredeux.

5. Lay right side of the entredeux to right side of the gathered fabric. This reminds me of the days when we put waistbands on very full gathered skirts. This is basic dressmaking.

   a. If you gathered with the first method (1/4-inch and 3/4-inch gathering rows), place the ditch of the entredeux below the first gathering line. The ditch of the entredeux would be about 3/8 inch from unfinished edge.

   b. If you used the second method (1/4-inch and 1/2-inch gathering rows), place the entredeux on or a little below the second gathering row.

6. Stitch in the ditch of the entredeux, using a short straight stitch. This stitch is on the right side of the entredeux. This side is closest to the body of the sewing machine (Length=2) (**fig. 3**).

7. Move over just a little and straight stitch the second time. This holds down the gathers under the entredeux (**fig. 4**).

8. Trim away both layers as close to the straight stitch as you can trim (**fig. 5**).

9. Zigzag to finish the process. This zigzag is not a satin stitch but close to a satin stitch. This zigzag stitch encloses the stitch-in-the-ditch seam, the second seam and goes off the side to catch the raw edges (Width=3 Length=3/4 to 1) (**fig. 6**).

10. Press the satin stitched roll toward the fabric.

11. Top stitch on the wrong side of the fabric. Zigzag into one hole of the entredeux and off into the zigzagged seam. This should be as narrow a seam a possible (Width=1-1/2 to 2-1/2, Length=2) (**fig. 7**).

12. This last can be zigzagged from the top also. It is easier to zigzag it from the bottom if it is "entredeux to gathered fabric" because of the bulk of the zigzagged seam. When zigzagging entredeux to flat edge (as given in the section just preceding this one) it seems easier to zigzag the final from the top.

1. Follow 1 through 6 of Method 1 (**fig. 1**).

2. Trim to within 1/8 inch of the stitch-in-the-ditch (**fig. 2**).

3. Zigzag, going into one hole of the entredeux and all the way off of the edge of the fabric. This will roll the fabric/ entredeux border right into the entredeux (Width=3 to 4, Length=1-1/2) (**fig. 3**).

Serger Fever

Oh what a wonderful tool the serger is for French sewing by machine! I cannot say enough about how this machine has simplified the "Entredeux To Flat Fabric" technique and the "Entredeux To Gathered Fabric" technique. First of all, the serger does three things at once. It stitches in the ditch, zigzags, and trims. Secondly, the serger goes twice as fast as your conventional sewing machine. Probably you can eliminate two sewings and do that one twice as fast. Kathy McMakin has written a how-to book, "French Sewing By Serger." It gives complete instructions and settings on how to do these wonderful French sewing techniques by serger. It is available from Martha Pullen Company.

Another way to use the serger is for French seams. I always did hate those little things. Now, I serge my French seams. I serge in my sleeves! I serge the sleeves in my smocked bishops; you will not believe the improvement in getting bishops through the pleater!

Holidays And Vacations

It's not uncommon to find a hole in the seam of laces, or between the laces and fabrics that have been joined. This occurs when both pieces of lace do not get sewn together in the zigzag or the laces do not get caught in the lace-to-fabric, zigzagged seam. This is not a mistake. I refer to this as a holiday or vacation. Sometimes we take long vacations (long holes) and sometimes we are only gone for a few hours (very tiny holes). These vacations and holidays are easily fixed by simply starting above the hole and zigzagging over the hole, being careful to catch both sides of lace or fabric to repair the opening. No back-stitching is necessary. Clip the excess threads and no one will ever know about your vacation. ▨

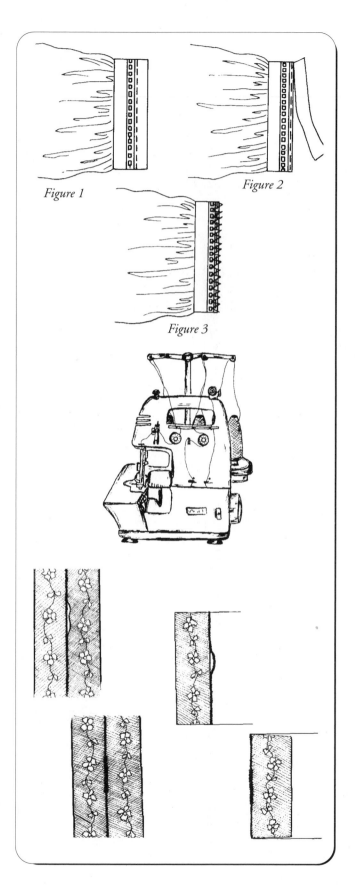

Figure 1

Figure 2

Figure 3

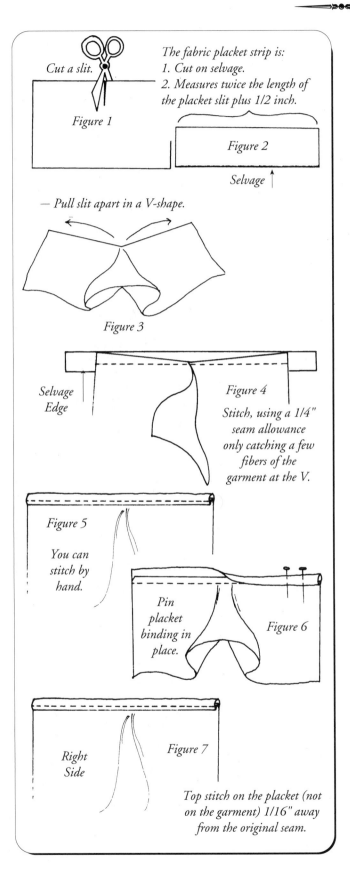

Cut a slit.

Figure 1

The fabric placket strip is:
1. Cut on selvage.
2. Measures twice the length of the placket slit plus 1/2 inch.

Figure 2

Selvage ↑

— Pull slit apart in a V-shape.

Figure 3

Selvage
Edge

Figure 4

Stitch, using a 1/4"
seam allowance
only catching a few
fibers of the
garment at the V.

Figure 5

You can
stitch by
hand.

Pin
placket
binding in
place.

Figure 6

Right
Side

Figure 7

Top stitch on the placket (not
on the garment) 1/16" away
from the original seam.

Continuous Lap Placket

1. Cut a slit in the garment piece the length needed for the placket (**fig. 1**). Cut a placket strip from the fabric along the selvage 3/4 inch wide and 1/2 inch longer than twice the length of the slit (**fig. 2**). Make the placket, using the following directions

2. Pull the slit apart in a V-shape (**fig. 3**).

3. Place the placket to the slit, right sides together. The slit is on the top and the placket is on the bottom. Note that the raw edge of the placket meets the V in the slit.

4. Stitch, using a l/4-inch seam allowance only catching a few fibers at the point. The placket strip will be straight. The skirt will form a V (**fig. 4**).

5. Press the seam toward the selvage edge of the placket strip. Fold the selvage edge to the inside (**fig. 5**). Whip by hand (**fig. 6**) or finish by machine, using the following directions.

6. Pin placket in place. From the right side of the fabric, top stitch ON THE PLACKET l/16 inch away from the original seam (**fig. 7**).

7. Pulling the placket to the inside of the garment, fold the placket in half, allowing the top edges of the garment to meet (**fig. 8**). Sew a dart, starting l/2 inch up from the outside bottom edge of the placket to the seam (**fig. 9**).

8. Turn back the side of the placket that will be on top when overlapped (**fig. 10**). ▧

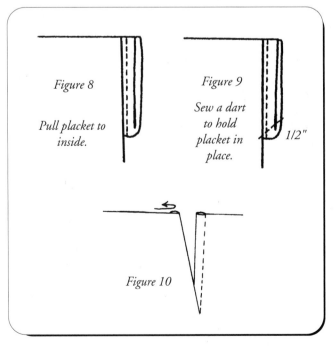

Figure 8

Pull placket to
inside.

Figure 9

Sew a dart
to hold
placket in
place.

1/2"

Figure 10

Gathering French Lace

Gathering French Lace

While Applying To Trimmed Entredeux Edge

NOTE: You must have a little extra lace when using this method. It may use more than the pattern requires. This method is easy and time saving. It can be used when attaching gathered lace around a collar that has entredeux at the bottom before the gathered lace. It is especially good when attaching gathered lace around a portrait collar. It is a great way to attach the gathered lace to an entredeux-trimmed neck edge. Actually, you can use this technique anytime you attach gathered lace to trimmed entredeux. It results in fairly even gathers, and saves you from having to pin, distribute, and straighten-out twisted lace.

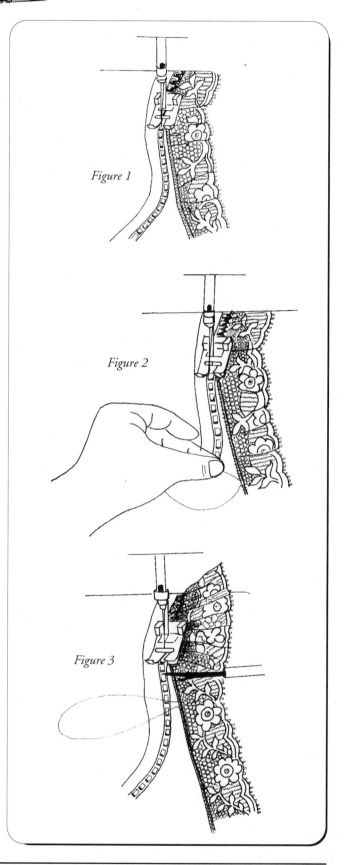

Figure 1

Figure 2

Figure 3

1. Trim off the outside edge of the entredeux, after the other edge has been attached to the garment.

2. Press both the entredeux and the lace.

3. Side by side, right sides up, begin to zigzag with lace still straight (**fig. 1**).

4. About 6 inches out on the lace, pull one of the gathering threads. I find that using a little pick of some kind is effective. The same little pick that is used to pull a lace gathering thread, can also be used to push the gathers into the sewing machine. A pin will suffice if necessary (**fig. 2**).

5. In order to get the gathers to move in the right direction (toward the foot of the sewing machine), you will need to pull on the side of the thread loop closest to the sewing machine. If you pull on the other side, the gathers will not go toward the sewing machine. Pull the thread, and push the gathers toward the sewing machine (**fig. 2**).

6. Lift your pressure foot, and push a few gathers under it. Zigzag a few stitches (Width=3-1/2, Length=2). You may notice that the width is a little wider than usual for zigzagging lace to entredeux. I have found that with gathered lace, it is necessary to make the width wider in order to catch all of the heading of the gathered lace. As always, you should adjust the width and length, according to the width of your entredeux and your lace heading. They vary so much it is hard to give one exact width and length. Lift your pressure foot again, and push a few more gathers under it. Continue, until all of your gathers on that one section have been stitched in (**fig. 3**).

7. Go out another 6 inches on your lace, and repeat the process. Continue, until all of the lace is gathered and stitched to the trimmed entredeux.

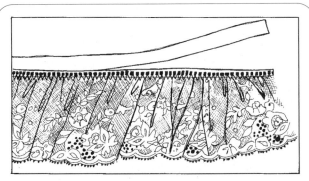

Figure 1

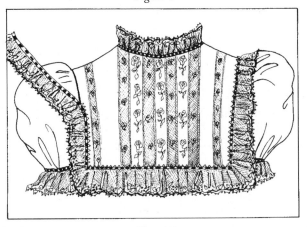

Figure 2

Making An Entredeux And Lace String

The method "Gathering French Lace A Little At A Time, While Applying It To Trimmed Entredeux Edge" is the perfect way to make an entredeux/gathered lace trim for the yoke of a French dress. This is the easy way to trim your yoke with entredeux and gathered lace. The hard way would be to apply your entredeux in the seams of the yokes and the sleeves.

1. Follow the techniques found in the technique "Gathering French Lace By Machine, While Applying It To Trimmed Entredeux Edge."

2. Make the entredeux and lace string as long as you need it to be to travel around the entire yoke (front and back) and over the shoulders of the dress. After making this long strip of entredeux and gathered lace, simply trim the other side of the entredeux (**fig. 1**). Pin into place, around the yoke edges, and zigzag the entredeux and lace string right onto the finished dress (**fig. 2**).

Finishing The Neckline

With Entredeux/Gathered Lace

So many times, French dresses have an entredeux/ gathered-lace neckline finish. Here is the technique I use.

1. Check the seam allowance on the neckline of your pattern. This is important.

2. Check the seam allowance on your entredeux. It is usually 1/2 inch; however, this is not always the case. Measure the seam allowance of your entredeux.

3. If the seam allowance at the neck of the pattern and the seam allowance of your entredeux do not match, trim the seam allowance of the entredeux to match the seam allowance of the neckline of your garment.

4. Using the techniques "Entredeux to Flat Fabric," attach the entredeux to the neckline of the garment.

5. Stitch in the ditch (**fig. 1**). Trim, leaving a 1/8-inch to 1/4-inch seam allowance (**fig. 2**).

6. Zigzag the seam allowance to finish (**fig. 3**).

7. Trim the remaining clipped seam allowance. Press the seam toward the body of the dress.

8. Gather the lace edging. Butt it to the trimmed entredeux and zigzag (**fig. 4**). ▩

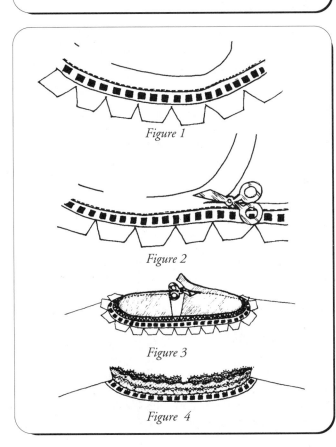

Figure 1

Figure 2

Figure 3

Figure 4

Making Entredeux (Or Hemstitching) On Today's Computer Sewing Machines

About eight years ago I was conned into purchasing a 1905 hemstitching machine for $1500. I was told that it had a perfect stitch and that stitch (about 2 inches) was demonstrated to me by the traveling salesman. I was very happy to finally have one of those wonderful machines. Guess how long that wonderful machine lasted before it broke down? I stitched about 10 inches more which looked great; at that point, the stitching was awful. I called several repairmen. It never made a decent hemstitch again.

The good news to follow this sad story is that today's new computer machines do an excellent job of making hemstitching and they work! I am going to give our favorite settings for our favorite sewing machines. Before you buy a new sewing machine, if you love heirloom sewing, please go try out each of these machines and see if you love these stitches as much as we do.

Using A Stabilizer With Wing Needle Hemstitching Or Pinstitching

Before you do any hemstitching or any decorative work with a wing needle which involves lots of stitching on these wonderful machines, first let me tell you that **you do have to have a stabilizer**! You can use stitch-n-tear, computer paper, tissue paper (not quite strong enough but o.k. in certain situations), wax paper, physician's examining table paper, typing paper, adding machine paper or almost any other type of paper. When you are doing heavy stitching such as a feather stitch, I recommend that type of paper which physicians spread out over their examining tables. You can get a roll of it at any medical supply place. If you use stitch-n-tear or adding machine paper in feather stitch type stitches, it is difficult to pull away all of the little pieces which remain when you take the paper from the back of the garment. This physician's paper seems to tear away pretty easily.

I do not like the thin, plastic looking, wash away stabilizers for heavy stitching with a wing needle because it doesn't have enough body. There is another type of wash away stabilizer which is absolutely wonderful. It is the paint on, liquid kind. In this country it is called Perfect Sew. You simply paint it on with a paint brush; let it dry, and stitch. You don't have to use any other stabilizer underneath it. It washes out after you have finished your stitching. It is available in this country from Pati Palmer, Palmer/Pletsch Publishing, Perfect Sew, P.O. Box 12046, Portland, OR 97212. 1-800-728-3784.

Make your own wash away stabilizer by using some water in a container and by dropping this wash away plastic looking sheet of stabilizer into the container. Some of the brand names are Solvy and Aqua Solve. Stir with a wooden spoon; keep adding the plastic looking wash away stabilizer sheets until it becomes the consistency of egg whites. Then, paint it on or brush it on with a sponge. Let it dry and then stitch. Both of the liquid, wash out stabilizers make batiste-type fabrics about as stiff as organdy which is wonderful for stitching. After stitching, simply wash the stabilizer away.

Preparing Fabric Before Beginning Hemstitching or Pinstitching

Stiffen fabric with spray starch before lace shaping or decorative stitching with the hemstitches and wing needles. Use a hair dryer to dry the lace before you iron it if you have spray starched it too much. Also, if you wet your fabrics and laces too much with spray starch, place a piece of tissue paper on top of your work, and dry iron it dry. Hemstitching works best on natural fibers such as linen, cotton, cotton batiste, silk or cotton organdy. I don't advise hemstitching a fabric with a high polyester content. Polyester has a memory. If you punch a hole in polyester, it remembers the original positioning of the fibers, and the hole wants to close up.

Threads To Use For Pinstitching Or Hemstitiching

Use all cotton thread, 50, 60, 70, 80 weight. If you have a thread breaking problem, you can also use a high quality polyester thread or a cotton covered polyester thread, like the Coats and Clark for machine lingerie and embroidery. Personally, I like to press needle down on all of the entredeux and pin stitch settings.

Pinstitching Or Point de Paris Stitch With A Sewing Machine

The pin stitch is another lovely "entredeux look" on my favorite machines. It is a little more delicate. Pin stitch looks similar to a ladder with **one of the long sides of the ladder missing**. Imagine the steps being fingers which reach over into the actual lace piece to grab the lace. The side of the ladder, the long side, will be stitched on the fabric right along side of the outside of the heading of the lace. The fingers reach into the lace to grab it. You need to look on all of the pinstitch settings given below and realize that you have to use reverse image on one of the sides of lace so that the fingers will grab into the lace while the straight side goes on the outside of the lace heading.

Pfaff 7550

Pin Stitch

-100 wing needle, A - 2 Foot, Needle Down
-Stitch 112, tension 3, twin needle button, 4.0
width, 3.0 length

Entredeux

-100 wing needle, A - 2 Foot, Needle Down

	width	length
Stitch #132	3.5	5.0
Stitch #113	4.0	2.0
Stitch #114	3.5	2.5
Stitch #115	3.5	3.0

Bernina

Pinstitch

- 100 wing needle
- 1230 stitch #26, SW - 2.5, SL - 2
- 1530 menu H, pattern #10, SW - 2.5, SL - 2
- 1630 menu G, Pattern #10, SW - 2.5, SL - 2

Entredeux (Baby Daisy)

- 100 wing needle
- 1230 stitch #27, SW - 3, SL - 2.5
- 1530 menu G1, pattern #6, SW - 3, SL - 2.5
- 1630 menu D1, pattern #6, SW - 3, SL - 2.5

Entredeux

- 100 wing needle
- 1230 stitch #18, long stitch, SW - 3, SL - 1.5
- 1530 menu H, pattern #2, long stitch, SW - 3, SL
  - 1.5
- 1630 menu G, pattern #5, SW - 3.5, SL - 3

Viking #1, 1100, 1090, #1 Plus

Pinstitch

- 100 wing needle
-Stitch D6, width 2.5-3; length 2.5-3

Entredeux

- 100 wing needle
-Stitch D7 (width and length are already set in)

Elna 9000 and DIVA

Pinstitch

- 100 wing needle
-Stitch #120 (length and width are already set in)

Entredeux

- 100 wing needle
-Stitch #121 (length and width are already set)

Attaching Shaped Lace

To The Garment With Machine Entredeux Or Pinstitching And A Wing Needle

Probably my favorite place to use the machine entredeux/ wing needle hemstitching is to attach shaped laces to a garment. Simply shape your laces in the desired shapes such as hearts, diamonds, ovals, loops, circles, or bows, and stitch the stitch. In addition to stitching this gorgeous decorative stitch, it also attaches the shaped lace to the garment (**fig. 1**). Always use stabilizer when using this type of heavy hemstitching.

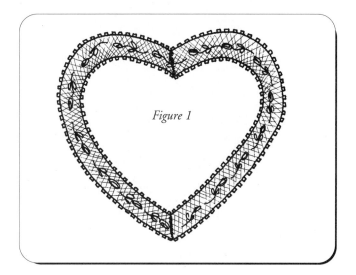

Figure 1

Attaching Two Pieces Of Lace With Machine Entredeux

There is nothing prettier than a garment which has entredeux in between each layer of fabric and lace. That would take a million years to stitch with purchased entredeux, not to mention the cost. Here is how you can use your hemstitch/ machine entredeux stitch and wing needle and make your laces look as if they had been joined with entredeux.

1. Butt two pieces of lace insertion together. Since entredeux/ hemstitching with a wing needle on your machine needs fabric underneath the stitching to hold the stitches perfectly, you need to put a narrow strip of batiste or other fabric underneath the place where these two laces will be joined.

2. Put a strip of stabilizer underneath the butted laces and the fabric strip.

3. Stitch using a wing needle and your hemstitching stitch. If your machine has an edge joining or edge stitching foot this is a great time to use it. It's little blade guides in between the two pieces of butted lace and makes it easy to

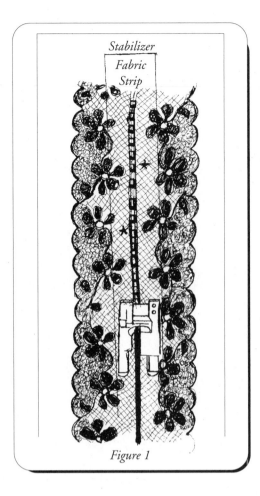

Stabilizer

Fabric
Strip

Figure 1

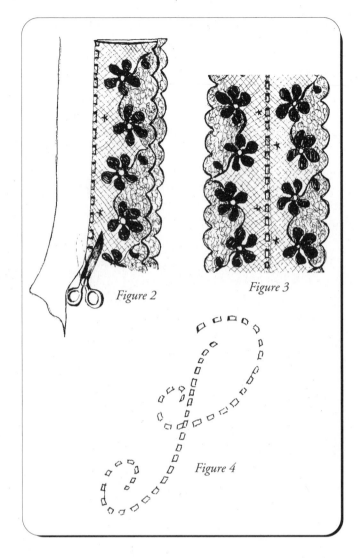

Figure 2

Figure 3

Figure 4

stitch straight (**fig.** 1). You can see that the entredeux stitching not only stitches in one of the most beautiful stitches, it also attaches the laces.

4. When you have finished stitching, tear away the stabilizer and turn each side of the lace back to carefully trim away the excess fabric (**fig.** 2).

5. Now it looks as if you have two pieces of lace with purchased entredeux stitched in between them (**fig.** 3).

Making Machine Entredeux, Embroidery Designs Or Initials

You can take almost any larger, plain embroidery design and stitch the entredeux stitch around it. You may find it necessary to put the design into an embroidery hoop for maximum effectiveness. I have some old handkerchiefs and some old tablecloths which actually look as if hemstitching has made the design. You can place several rows of entredeux stitching together to form a honeycomb effect which might be used to fill in embroidery designs.

Some of the prettiest monograms are those with hemstitching stitched around the letter. Once again, I think the liquid stabilizer and the embroidery hoop will be wonderful assets in doing this kind of wing needle work. Let your imagination be your guide when thinking of new and elegant things to do with these wonderful wing needle/entredeux stitches (**fig.** 4).

One of my favorite things to do with this entredeux stitch or pin stitch is simply to stitch it around cuffs, across yokes, around collars, down the center back or center front of a blouse. It is lovely stitched down both sides of the front placket of a very tailored woman's blouse. Some people love to machine entredeux in black thread on a black garment. The places you put this wing needling are endless. It is just as pretty stitched as a plain stitch as it is when it is used to stitch on laces. ▨

Puffing Techniques

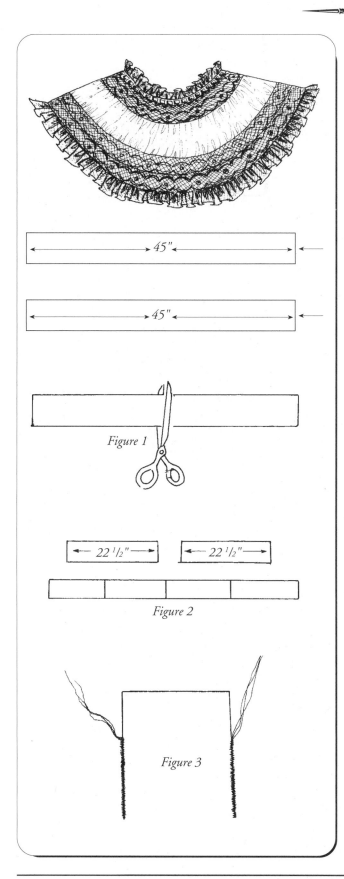

45"

45"

Figure 1

22 1/2"   22 1/2"

Figure 2

Figure 3

Puffing Method I
Gathering The Puffing Over A Quilting Thread Or Dental Floss

This method for making puffing simply rolls and whips the edges of the puffing strip by zigzagging over a quilting thread or dental floss. It has a finished edge which can be butted up to lace and zigzagged together. Although this is a good method for making puffing to curve around in a round portrait collar, I really do not believe that it is the easiest. Please read this method which is Puffing Method One. Then, if your machine has a gathering foot, read Puffing Method Two. Honestly, that is the easiest method. The choice is yours, of course.

1. Cut your puffing strip at lest two times the length of the finished round portion of the collar to which it is to be attached.

2. A suggested puffing length is to cut two strips of 45-inch fabric about 2 inches wide.

3. Cut one of them in two pieces. Stitch these pieces to either end of the long strip. You can put in a French seam or serge these seams together (**fig. 1**). You may press the puffing strip but **do not starch.** Starching will affect the gathers of the puffing.

4. This puffing strip will probably be a little long for the collar. I like to have too much puffing and lace when I am working at portrait collars rather than too little. Since I like full puffing, I usually use the whole fullness. If it is fuller than you want, then simply put in the fullness you want and cut off the back at both sides after you have shaped your puffing.

5. Mark the center of this puffing strip before you roll and whip the edge. The two quarter points are already marked with the two side strips (**fig. 2**).

6. Roll and whip the edges using quilting thread or dental floss. To do this, simply place the quilting thread or the dental floss on the very edge of both sides and zigzag it into place. Be careful not to catch the quilting thread or dental floss in the stitching (**fig. 3**). Zigzag the edge of the fabric using approximately a 2 1/2 to 3 1/2 width and a 1-1 1/2 length. You should zig going into the fabric and zag going all the way off of the fabric. The fabric will roll into a seam as you zigzag. The quilting thread will be rolled into that seam. Later you will use the very strong quilting thread to pull the gathers in your puffing (**fig. 4**).

7. **Note:** After you zigzag the quilting thread or dental floss into both sides of this puffing strip, you will probably see a few fuzzies and it may not look exactly perfect. This is normal because you used a relatively loose length (1-1 1/2) for

your zigzag. Using any tighter stitch tends to make the rolling and whipping too tight and makes the gathering of the puffing very difficult. Don't worry, when you zigzag your puffing to your lace, these fuzzies will go away.

8. Some sewing machines have a foot with a little hole in the center of the foot. If yours has this feature, put your quilting thread or dental floss in that little hole and your zigzagging will be perfectly in place and you won't have a chance of zigzagging through the quilting thread in the process of stitching.

9. After you finish your rolling and whipping on both sides, pull the gathering threads on both sides from both ends until it is gathered up to look like puffing (**fig. 4**).

10. Pin the puffing to the fabric board right through the tissue paper that you have already pinned your lace strips to, matching the center front of the collar with the center front of the puffing. Pin by "poking" the pins into your fabric board, on the bottom side of the puffing (**fig. 5**).

11. Keep on playing with the gathers until you have them evenly distributed. Then, pin the top side (the smaller side) of the puffing. You treat the puffing exactly like you treated the laces. Pin the larger side first and then pin the smaller side (**fig. 6**).

12. Press the puffing flat after spray starching it. **Note:** On any garment which will be washed, it is necessary to press the puffing flat because you will have to do this after it is washed anyway. A puffing iron is perfect for this job, depending on how wide the puffing is. I love flat pressed puffing and there really isn't much choice in leaving it unpressed unless it will go into a pillow to put on the bed and not wash for a very long time.

13. Playing with and distributing your gathers carefully usually takes a long time. Don't become impatient. Just keep fiddling with the puffing to be sure you have distributed it carefully. This is a good project to save for evening t.v. watching so you can really make it perfect. After you have pinned your puffing where it looks beautiful, carefully remove the "poked" pins and pin it flat to the tissue paper where the edge of the puffing on the top exactly meets the bottom edge of the lace row above it (**fig. 7**). Width=1 1/2 to 2 1/2: Length=1 to 2

14. You are now ready to take the tissue paper with its rows of lace insertion and rows of puffing over to the sewing machine to zigzag your row of puffing to the top row of lace. Stitch right through the tissue paper. Leave the pins in the puffing after you stitch around the top row because you are now ready to shape the next piece of lace to the collar just exactly like you did the others.

15. Continue adding lace rows to the portrait collar to make it as wide as you wish it to be.

16. If you choose, you can add more puffing rows in between the lace rows to put several puffing rows onto the collar.

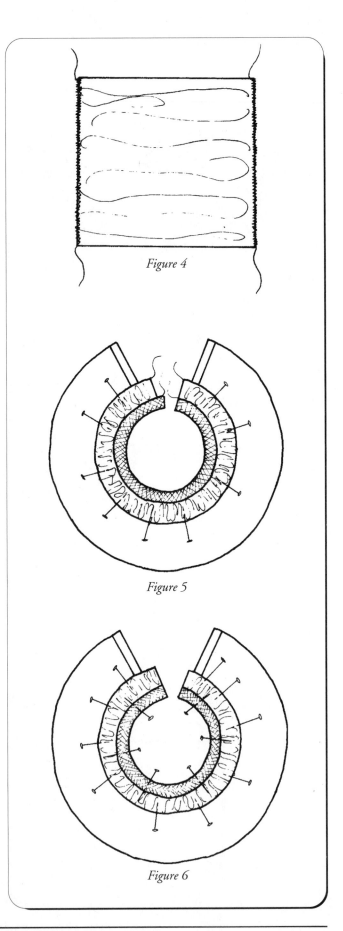

Figure 4

Figure 5

Figure 6

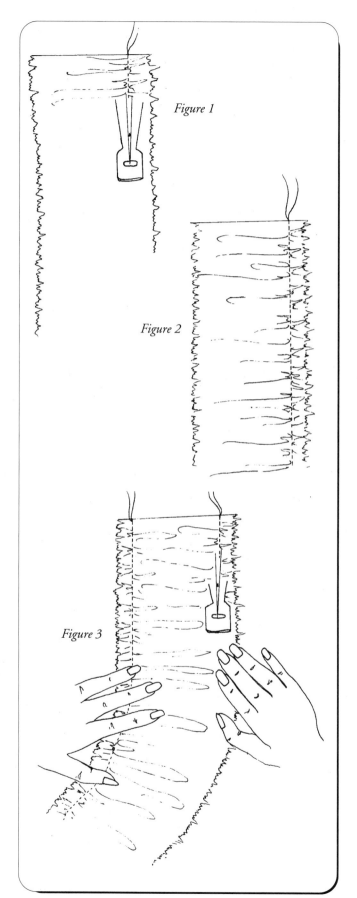

Figure 1

Figure 2

Figure 3

Gathering The Puffing Using The Gathering Foot On Your Machine

Two years ago, I wouldn't have told you that this was the easiest method of applying puffing into a round portrait collar. The reason being I didn't know how to make perfect puffing using the gathering foot for the sewing machine. I thought you used the edge of the gathering foot to guide the fabric underneath the gathering foot. This left about a 1/4-inch seam allowance. It also made the gathers not perfect in some places with little "humps" and unevenness on some portions. Therefore, I wasn't happy with puffing made on the gathering foot. When I asked my friend, Sue Hausman, what might be wrong, she explained to me that to make perfect gathering, you had to move the fabric over so that you would have at least a 1/2-inch seam allowance. She further explained that there are two sides to the feed dogs; when you use the side of the gathering foot, then the fabric only catches on one side of the feed dogs. It works like magic to move your fabric over and guide it along one of the guide lines on the sewing machine. If your machine doesn't have these lines, simply put a piece of tape down to make a proper guide line.

Making Gathering Foot Puffing

1. The speed of the sewing needs to be consistent. Sew either fast or slow but do not sew fast then slow then fast again. For the beginner, touch the "sew slow" button (if available on your machine). This will help to keep a constant speed.

2. The puffing strip should be gathered with a 1/2 seam allowance, with an approximate straight stitch length of 3, right side up (**fig. 1**). Remember that you can adjust your stitch length to make your puffing looser or fuller. Do not let the strings of the fabric wrap around the foot of the machine. This will cause to fabric to back up behind the foot causing an uneven seam allowance, as well as, uneven gathers. Leave the thread tails long in case adjustments are needed. One side of the gathering is now complete (**fig. 2**).

3. Begin gathering the second side of the strip, right side up. This row of gathering will be made from the bottom of the strip to the top of the strip. In other words, bi-directional sewing (first side sewn from the top to the bottom, second side sewn from the bottom to the top) is allowed. Gently unfold the ruffle with the left hand allowing flat fabric to feed under the foot. **Do not** apply any pressure to the fabric (**fig. 3**). **The** feeding must remain constant. Leave the thread tails long in case adjustments are needed. The puffing strip in now complete.

Placing Machine Gathered Puffing Into A Collar

1. Cut your strips of fabric.

2. Gather both sides of the puffing running the fabric under the gathering foot. Be sure you have at least a 1/2-inch seam allowance. When you use a gathering foot, the moveability of the puffing isn't as great as when you gather it the other way.

3. You, of course, have two raw edges when you gather puffing with the gathering foot (**fig. 8**).

4. Shape the puffing around the fabric board below the row of lace (or rows of lace) that you have already shaped into the rounded shape. Place the pins into the board through the outside edge of the puffing. Place the pins right into the place where the gathering row runs in the fabric (**fig. 9**).

5. Pull the raw edge of the machine puffed strip up **underneath the finished edge of the curved lace**, so that your zigzagging to attach the puffing will be on the machine gathering line. Put the rounded lace edge on top of the puffing. Pin the bottom edge of the puffing first so you can "arrange" the top fullness" underneath the curved lace edge which is already in place (the top piece of lace) (**fig. 9**).

6. It will be necessary to "sort of" arrange the machine gathered puffing, especially on the top edge which will be gathered the fullest on your collar, and pin it where you want it since the machine gathering thread doesn't give too much. After you have pinned and poked the gathering into place where it looks pretty on the top and the bottom, flat pin it to the tissue paper and zigzag the puffing strip to the lace stitching right on top of the lace.

    NOTE: You will have an unfinished fabric edge underneath the place where you stitched the lace to the puffing. That is o.k. After you have zigzagged the puffing to the lace, then trim away the excess fabric underneath the lace edge. Be careful, of course, when you trim this excess fabric, not to accidentally cut the lace.

7. If you have a machine entredeux/wing needle option on your sewing machine, you can stitch this beautiful stitch in place of the zigzagging. Since the fabric is gathered underneath the lace, you will have to be very careful stitching to get a pretty stitch.

8. Shape another piece of lace around the bottom of this puffing bringing the inside piece of curved lace exactly to fit on top of the gathering line in the puffing. Once again, you will have unfinished fabric underneath the place where you will zigzag the lace to the puffing collar. After zigzagging the lace to the puffing collar, trim the excess fabric away.

9. Continue curving the rest of the laces to make the collar as wide as you want it to be. ▨

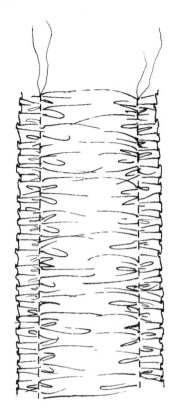

Figure 8

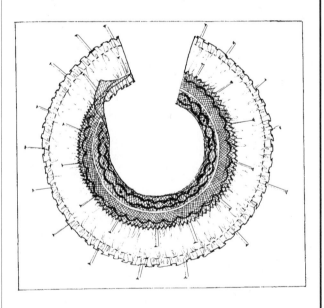

Figure 9

Basic Pintucking

Double Needles

Double needles come in different sizes. The first number on the double needle is the distance between the needles. The second number on the needle is the actual size of the needle. The chart below shows some of the double needle sizes. The size needle that you choose will depend on the weight of the fabric that you are pintucking (**fig. 1**).

Let me relate a little more information for any of you who haven't used the double needles yet. Some people have said to me, "Martha, I only have a place for one needle in my sewing machine." That is correct and on most sewing machines, you probably still can use a double needle. The double needle has only one stem which goes into the nedle slot; the double needles join on a little bar below the needle slot. You use two spools of thread when you thread the double needles. If you don't have two spools of thread of the fine thread which you use for pintucking, then run an extra bobbin and use it as another spool of thread. For most shaped pintucking on heirloom garments, I prefer either the 1.6/70, the 1.6/80 or the 2.0/80 size needle.

Fabric

a. 1.6/70 - Light Weight

b. 1.6/80 - Light Weight

c. 2.0/80 - Light Weight

d. 2.5/80 - Light Weight

e. 3.0/90 - Medium Weight

f. 4.0/100 - Heavy Weight

Pintuck Feet

Pintuck feet are easy to use and they shave hours off pintucking time when you are making straight pintucks. They enable you to space straight pintucks perfectly. I might add here that some people also prefer a pintuck foot when making curved and angled pintucks. I prefer a regular zigzag sewing foot for curved pintucks. Pintuck feet correspond to the needle used with that pintuck foot; the needle used corresponds to the weight of fabric. The bottom of these feet have a certain number of grooves 3, 5, 7, or 9. The width of the groove matches the width between the two needles. When making straight pintucks, use a pintuck foot of your choice. The grooves enable one to make those pintucks as close or as far away as the distance on the foot allows (**fig. 2**).

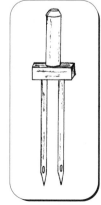

Preparing Fabric For Pintucking

Do I spray starch the fabric before I pintuck it? I usually do not spray starch fabric before pintucking it. Always press all-cotton fabric. A polyester/cotton blend won't need to be pressed unless it is very wrinkled. Tucks tend to lay flatter if you stiffen fabric with spray starch first; that is why I don't advise spray starching the fabric first in most cases. Pintuck a small piece of your chosen fabric with starch and one without starch, then make your own decision.

Straight Pintucking With A Pintuck Foot

Some of my favorite places places for straight pintucks are on high yoke bodices of a dress and along the sleeves. On ladies blouses, straight pintucks are lovely running vertically on the front and back of the blouse, and so slenderizing! One of the prettiest treatments of straight pintucks on ladies blouses is stitching about three to five pintucks right down the center back of the blouse. Tuck a little shaped bow or heart on the center back of the blouse; stitch several tiny pintucks and top them off with a lace shape in the center back. Horizontally placed straight pintucks are lovely running across the back yoke of a tailored blouse. Tucks are always pretty running around the cuff of a blouse. I love pintucks just about anywhere.

1. Put in your double needle. Thread machine with two spools of thread. Thread one spool at a time (including the needle). This will help keep the threads from becoming twisted while stitching the tucks. This would be a good time to look in the guide book, which came with your sewing machine, for directions on using pintuck feet and double needles. Some sewing machines have a special way of threading for use with double needles.

2. The first tuck must be straight. To make this first tuck straight, do one of three things: (**a.**) Pull a thread all the way across the fabric and follow along that pulled line. (**b.**) Using a measuring stick, mark a straight line along the fabric. Stitch on that line. (**c.**) Fold the fabric in half and press that fold. Stitch along that folded line.

3. Place the fabric under the foot for the first tuck and straight stitch the desired length of pintuck. (Length=1 to 2-1/2; Needle position is center) (**fig. 1**).

4. Place your first tuck into one of the grooves in your pintuck foot. The space between each pintuck depends on the placement of the first pintuck (**fig. 2**).

5. Continue pintucking by placing the last pintuck made into a groove in the foot.

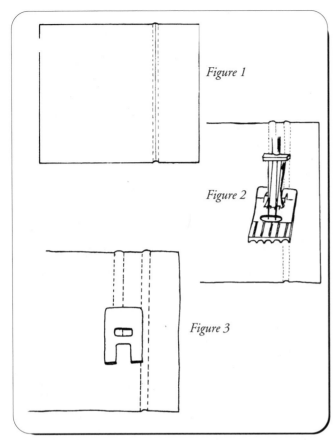

Figure 1

Figure 2

Figure 3

Straight Pintucking Without A Pintuck Foot

1. Use a double needle. Use your regular zigzag foot.

2. Thread your double needles.

3. Draw the first line of pintucking. Pintuck along that line. At this point you can use the edge of your presser foot as a guide (**fig. 3**).

NOTE: You might find a "generic" pintuck foot for your particular brand of machine.

Properly Tying Off Released Pintucks

A released pintuck is usually used to give fullness to a skirt. It is a perfectly elegant way to add detail to a garment which is easy to do using today's double needles. If you have a pintuck foot, please do use it for this treatment.

Straight pintucks that are made on a piece of fabric, cut out and stitched into the seams garment, do not have to be tied off. Why? When you sew the seam of the garment, the pintucks will be secured within that seam. Released pintucks stop at a designated point in the fabric. They are not caught in a seam and, therefore, have to be tied off. To make the most beautiful released pintuck possible, you must properly tie it off. If you want to take a short cut, then either back stitch on your machine or use the tie off feature that some of the modern machines offer. Please do not use a clear glue sold for tying off seams in sewing. One of my friends had a disastrous experience when making a lovely Susan York pattern featured in *Sew Beautiful* several years ago with over a hundred gorgeous released pintucks. She dabbed a little of this glue product at the end of each pintuck; when she washed and pressed the dress, each place on the Swiss batiste garment where that product had been touched on, turned absolutely brown. The dress with all of the money in Swiss batiste and French laces, had to be thrown away.

Properly tying off released pintucks is a lot of trouble. Remember, you can back stitch and cut the threads close to the fabric. The result isn't as pretty but it surely saves time. The choice, as always, is yours. If you are going to properly tie off those released pintucks, here are the directions.

1. End your stitching at the designated stopping point (**fig. 1**).

2. Pull out a reasonable length of thread before you cut the threads for this pintuck to go to the next pintuck. Five inches should be ample. You can use more or less.

3. Pull the threads to the back of the fabric (**fig. 2**). Tie off each individual pintuck (**fig. 3**).

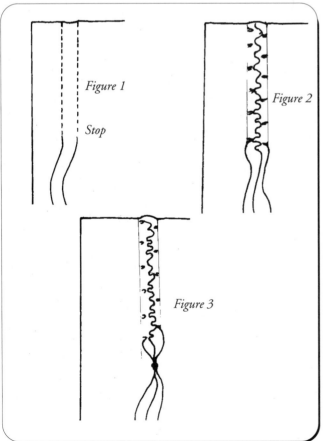

Figure 1

Stop

Figure 2

Figure 3

Bi-Directional Stitching Of Pintucks

The general consensus, when stitching pintucks, is to stitch down one side and back up the other side instead of stitching pintucks all in the same direction.

To prevent pintucks from being lopsided, stitch down the length of one pintuck, pull your sewing machine threads several inches, and stitch back up in the opposite direction (**fig. 4**).

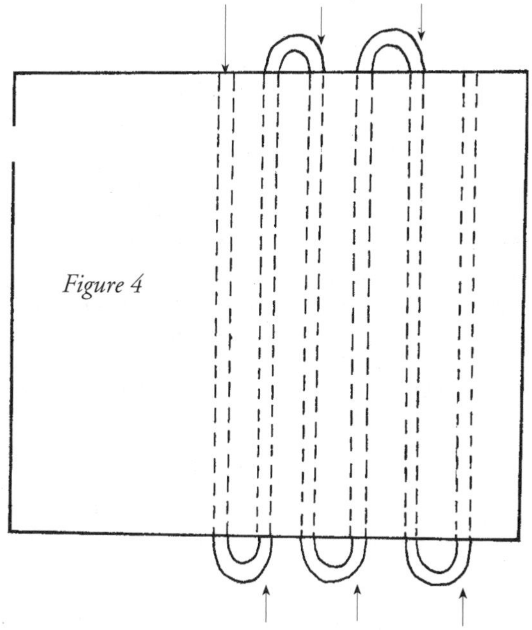

Figure 4

Making Waffle Pintucks

1. Stitch pintucks all in the same direction to the width you desire.
2. Stitch pintucks in the opposite direction (**fig. 1**).

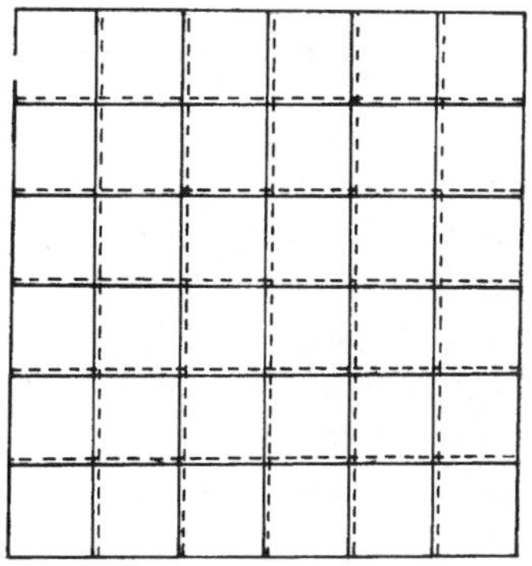

Figure 1

Cording Pintucks And Raised Pintucks

Cords make pintucks more prominent. Use Mettler gimp or #8 pearl cotton. Cording comes in handy when pintucks are being shaped. When pintucking across a bias with a double needle, you may get some distortion. The cord acts as a filler and will keep the fabric from distorting. Sometimes you might choose to use cording in order to add color to your pintucks. If you asked me, "Martha, do you usually cord pintucks? my answer would be no." However, just because I don't usually cord pintucks, doesn't mean that you won't prefer to cord them.

Some machines have a little device which sits in the base of the machine and sticks up just a little bit. That device tends to make the pintucks stand up a little more for a higher raised effect. Some people really like this feature.

1. If your machine has a hole in the throat plate, run the cord up through that hole and it will be properly placed without another thought (**fig. 2**).
2. If your machine does not have a hole in the throat plate, put the gimp or pearl cotton underneath the fabric, lining it up with the pintuck groove. Once you get the cording lined up under the proper groove, it will follow along for the whole pintuck.
3. You can stitch pintucks without a pintuck foot at all. Some sewing machines have a foot with a little hole right in the middle of the foot underneath the foot. That is a perfectly proper place to place the cord for shadow pintucks. Remember, if you use a regular foot for pintucking, you must use the side of the foot for guiding your next pintuck.

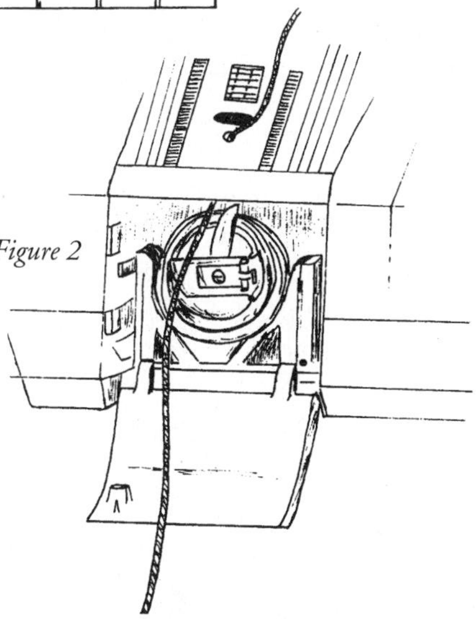

Figure 2

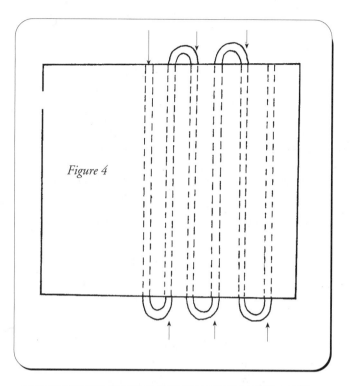

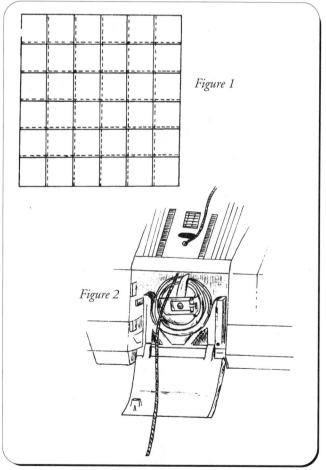

Pintucking Questions And Answers

Shadow Pintucks

Q. What is a shadow pintuck?

A. Shadow pintucks are pintucks with a touch of color showing through. Some people simply put a colored thread in the bobbin. You might want to try this to see if you like the effect. To properly shadow pintuck, you must use sheer fabric — batiste, organdy, or pastel silk.

1. Using the cording techniques found in this section, choose #8 pearl cotton in a color you would like to peek through the batiste or silk.

2. Pintuck, using thread that matches your batiste in the regular sewing machine hook-up, and colored pearl cotton for the shadow. However, I have seen pintucks with colored thread for the regular sewing machine thread and color for the cording. The choice is certainly yours.

Pintucking On The Sewing Machine

Q. What do I do about puckering when I pintuck straight strips of fabric?

A. There are several things that you can try. Sewing machine pintucks tend to pucker slightly. You can shorten your stitch length. You can pull the fabric from the front and back as you sew. You can lightly starch your fabric before you pintuck. You can loosen your bobbin tension. If you do any or all of these things, you may prevent your fabric from puckering, but you will also change the look of the pintuck. Try various techniques on your particular sewing machine. Actually, I don't mind the tiny puckers. They add texture to the garment and make the pintucks stand out.

Q. Would I ever want to use a cord enclosed in my pintucks?

A. Cords will keep the fabric from puckering so much. They also keep the pintuck from smashing flat when you press it. Some people absolutely love cords in their pintucks. In fact, all of the students I met while teaching in Australia use cords within their pintucks.

Cords are also used decoratively with a darker color of cord under white or ecru batiste. One of the dresses in the first *Sew Beautiful* Sweepstakes, had dark peach cording under ecru batiste pintucks; it was fabulous.

Q. Can pintucks be run any way on your fabric, or do they have to run vertically or parallel with the straight of grain?

A. Pintucks can be run in any direction. Consider scalloped pintucks. The ease or difficulty of making pintucks depends on the fabric you use. When making straight pintucks, I prefer to make them on the straight of the grain, parallel to the selvage.

Q. Are there any fabrics to completely avoid for pintucking?

A. Yes. Dotted Swiss is terrible. Printed fabrics, on which the design has been stamped, does not pintuck well. Resulting pintucks are uneven. Stiff fabrics do not machine pintuck well. You will end up with parallel stitching lines with no fabric pulled up between the stitching lines.

Q. What happens when I put a pintuck in the wrong place or my pintuck is crooked? Can I take it out?

A. Yes. Pintucks are easy to take out. Turn your fabric to the wrong side, and slide your seam ripper underneath the bobbin thread, which looks like a zigzag on the underside. The parallel top-stitching lines will just come right out after you slice the underside stitching.

Q. How do I press pintucks?

A. I prefer to spray starch a series of tucks before pressing it. Don't be afraid to starch and press pintucks. You might want to pin the edges of the pintucked fabric to the ironing board, stretching it out as far as you can. (This is nothing more than blocking your pintucked fabric.) Slide the iron in one direction to make all the pintucks lay in that one direction. Starch and press again. This will take out most of the puckers. Then, remove the pins from the ironing board. Flip over the pintucked piece you have just blocked and pressed, and press again. Not everyone prefers pintucks that lay in the same direction. For a less stringent appearance, lay your pintucked fabric piece face down on a terry cloth towel for the first and last pressing. ▧

Glass Head Pins Are Critical To Lace Shaping!

Purchasing GLASS HEAD PINS is one of the first and most critical steps to lace shaping. **All of this type of work has to be spray starched and pressed right on top of the pins.** Since plastic head pins melt, obviously they won't do. About nine years ago, a dear student came to my school and I hadn't made my self clear enough about the use of glass pins. I thought I had told everybody in no uncertain terms, but apparently I hadn't. After she had shaped a perfectly beautiful round portrait collar, she went to the ironing board to press her curved lace. In a few minutes she called to me with anxiety in her voice and said, "Martha, something is wrong." When I arrived to view the collar, little pink, red, blue, orange, purple, and black circles were embellishing this lovely French lace round collar. I apologized profusely for my not being clear in my instructions; my assistant quickly helped her begin another collar which would be minus those little creative melted points of color.

Metal pins such as the iris pins with the skinny little metal heads won't melt; however, when you pin hundreds of these little pins into cardboard, your finger will have one heck of a hole poked into it. Please purchase glass head pins and throw away your plastic head pins. How many times have I heard the question, "Martha, can you tell which are plastic and which are glass?" Well, I have to answer, "No, I can't until I put an iron to them. Then it is too late!" Get the proper pins, please. I also find that it is easier to get the pins one at a time if you have a wrist pin holder. Years ago when I lived in Charlotte, N.C. I used to sew for hours nearly every day. I went to the local grocery store so many times with my "fine wrist jewelry" in place, that they called me the "pin lady."

Please don't stick your hands into a pin box. More than one time I have brought my hand out with a pin stuck in my finger when I have attempted to do this. If you don't have a wrist holder, then scatter some pins out on your fabric board so you can see where you are picking them up. This might seem a little trite for me to be telling you this; however, you really don't know how many pins you will work with when you begin shaping laces.

Please Read This Before Learning Anything New!

I would like to share with you a life changing philosophy of education that was taught to me by Dr. Bill Purkey, one of my most important mentors, while I was in graduate school at the University of Florida. Since learning to sew is education, perhaps you will enjoy reading this section. He told us that he was going to blow an old American adage (or Australian, New Zealand, English, Canadian, or whatever). Everybody in your life taught you "When something is worth doing, it is worth doing right! or well." I'm telling you that there is no truth at all in that statement. Does that blow your mind? Well, I would like for each person reading this book to think of one thing that you do extremely well! I mean you are really good at this something. Then I would like for you to raise your hand if you did this thing well the very first time you ever did it. Isn't that funny? I bet 99% of you didn't raise your hand, did you? If you will let me rephrase the old American adage to read another way, I think it will make more sense for my life, and possibly for yours. "When something is worth doing, it is worth doing very poorly at first or very awkwardly. Only then, do you ever have a chance of doing it over and over again to make it better and perhaps eventually as perfect as it can be." Please think of something you really do well and think to yourself how long it took you to learn how to do that thing well. Then, please have patience with yourself and your family when you or they begin something new. I wish every teacher in the world working with children, would tell the class this adage. I think self concepts would be raised and little people would think that their first and awkward work was just the beginning of something wonderful after they practiced.

Drawing Shapes With Dots Rather Than A Solid Line

Margaret Boyles taught me years ago that it is simpler to draw your shapes on fabric by making dots about one half inch apart than it is to draw a solid line. This also means less pencil or marker to get out of the fabric when your lace shaping is finished (**fig. 1**).

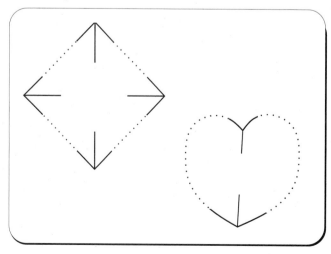

Please mark the turn around areas such as the center top and center bottom of the heart in a solid line. Also, make a solid line when marking the insides (bottom and top) of the heart where you will fold back your laces to make your fold back miter. When I am marking diamonds, I also make a solid line at the four angles of the diamonds. I make little dots as I travel around the straight sides. I also make a solid line into the center of the diamonds where I will pin at the top and at the bottom for my fold back miter.

Shish Kabob Sticks For Pushing And Holding Everything

When we teach in Australia we learn so much from the women there who are expert seamstresses. Actually we learn so much from students we teach all over the world. I have always said that learning from my students is the most exciting part of our education no matter where we go. I first learned about using wooden shish kabob sticks from some of the technical school sewing teachers in Australia. By the way, where does one get these wooden shish kabob sticks? At the grocery store! If you can only find the long ones, just break them in half and use the end with the point.

Nearly every woman in Australia uses a wooden shish kabob stick (about 5 or 6 inches long, not the super long ones) to push and to hold with her right hand as the sewing goes into the sewing machine. These sticks are used instead of the usual long pin or worse still, seam ripper that I have used so often. The sticks are wonderful for holding all fabrics, are inexpensive, have no sharp point to damage fabric or sewing machine needles and really are easy to hang on to. I shudder to think what would happen if sewing machine needle landed on a metal seam ripper as one was sewing one hundred miles per hour.

At several of our sewing seminars, we have handed out the wooden shish kabob sticks and the ladies have loved using them. The idea is that you can have something to hold your fabric or shaped lace on fabric as it feeds through the sewing machine which won't damage anything. Also, it keeps fingers away from the actual needle. Although I have never run a needle through my hand, I have certainly known of others who have done this. Using this stick is a safety technique as well as an efficient technique.

Making A Fabric Board

Fabric boards have become a must for lace shaping or any kind of working-in-the-round in heirloom sewing. They double as portable ironing boards also. At my School of Art Fashion in Huntsville, we make these boards in the double-wide version for collar classes and in the single-wide version for single lace shaping of hearts, diamonds, ovals, loops, and other shapes. Instructions for the double board follow, since it is the most convenient to have. You can also purchase a June Taylor Quilting Board for lace shaping also. We recommend that you make a little "sheet" just like a fitted sheet on your bed if you purchase this type of quilting board for your lace shaping. Since we use so much starch, the little sheet can be removed and washed and not ruin the surface of your quilting board. If you don't want to make this little sheet, then simply use a pillowcase over your June Taylor Board. Cardboard cake boards, covered with one layer of fabric or paper, also work well. You can also use just a sheet of cardboard. Another alternative is to go to any store which has old shipping boxes to throw away and cut the side out of a cardboard box. Cover the cardboard with paper or fabric and use this as your fabric board. One of my favorite lace shaping boards is a child's bulletin board. Another good one is a ceiling tile. Just staple or pin white typing paper or butcher paper over the board before you begin lace shaping.

One thing I don't particularly like in lace shaping is a padded board with a lot of bounce. I think it is easier to get the laces shaped properly without a lot of padding such as quilt batting. The simpler the better is my philosophy. ❈

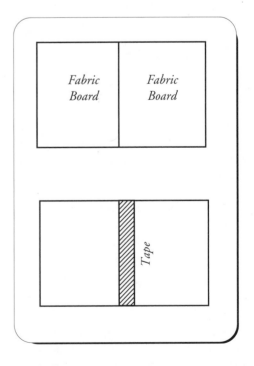

Shaping A Lace Scalloped Skirt

Shaping A Lace Scalloped Skirt

I have always loved scalloped skirts. The first one that I ever saw intimidated me so much that I didn't even try to make one for several years after that. The methods which I am presenting to you in this section are so easy that I think you won't be afraid to try making one of my favorite garments. Scallopping lace can be a very simple way to finish the bottom of a smocked dress or can be a very elaborate way to put row after row of lace scallops with curved pintucks in-between those scallops. Plain or very elaborate—this is one of my favorite things in French sewing by machine. Enjoy!

Preparing The Skirt For Lace Scallops

Before I give you the steps below, which is one great way to prepare scallops on a skirt, let me share with you that you can also follow the instructions found under the beginning lace techniques for scallops as well as diamonds, hearts, teardrops or circles. These instructions are that you can use any size scallop that you want to for any width skirt. How do you do that? Stitch or serge up one side seam of your whole skirt.

1. Pull a thread and cut or either tear your skirt. I usually put 88 inches in my skirt, two 44-inch widths - one for the front and one for the back. Make the skirt length the proper one for your garment (**fig. 1**).

2. Put in a French seam (or serge) one side seam only. You now have a flat skirt, which is approximately 88 inches wide (**fig. 1**). Probably by now you know that I really don't make French seams anymore; I use the rolled hem finish on the serger. It is beautiful, strong, and prettier than most French seams.

3. Fold the skirt in half at the seam line (**fig. 2**). Press. Fold it again (**fig. 3**). Press. Fold it again (**fig. 4**). Press. Fold it again (**fig. 5**). Press. When you open up your skirt, you have 16 equal sections (**fig. 6**). This is your guideline for your scallops. Each section is 5-1/2 inches wide.

4. You can make a template which fits between your folds by using a saucer, a dinner plate, an artist's flex-i-curve® or whatever has a curved edge. Make one template which has only one full sized scallop and the points of two more. Draw a straight line bisecting each top point of the scallop; make this line extend at least 2 inches above and below the point of the scallop (**fig. 7**). Make this template on a piece of paper so you can slip the bottom of the piece of paper along the bottom of the fabric and draw only one scallop at a time. You will slip this template between the folds that you made earlier by folding and pressing. This is the simplest way to get those scallops drawn on the whole skirt.

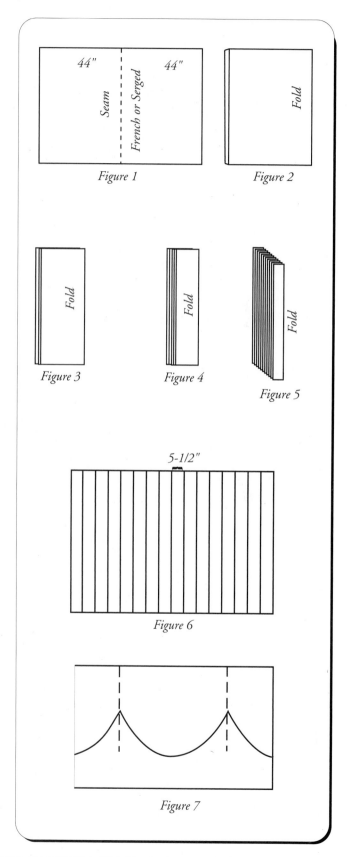

Figure 1

Figure 2

Figure 3

Figure 4

Figure 5

Figure 6

Figure 7

5. Draw your scallops between these folds or pressed in creases (**fig. 8**). You can place the scallops anywhere on the skirt bottom that you want to place them. For maximum use of the fabric, use the following guidelines for placing the scallops near the bottom of the skirt fabric. The bottom of the scallop (**Line A to B**) is at least 1-1/2 inches from the bottom of the skirt fabric (**fig. 9**).

6. Draw a line at the top of each scallop, bisecting the top of the scallop, approximately 2 inches tall. On **figure 9** the top of each scallop is **point C**; this 2-inch line extending above the scallop is **point D** (**fig. 9**). These bisecting lines going out of the top of each scallop are very important in the new fold back method of miters which follow.

Placing Your Skirt On The Fabric Board

1. Get a fabric board. This board is approximately 23 inches, which will allow you to work effectively with four scallops at one time. It does not matter how many scallops you work with at one time. The size of your board determines that.

2. Working from the left side of your skirt, place the left side of the skirt on the fabric board, right side up (**fig. 8**). If you are right handed, it is easier to work from left to right. You can also work from the right of the skirt or from the center of the skirt which has been French seamed or serged together.

Pinning The Lace Insertion
To The Skirt Portion On The Fabric Board

1. Cut enough lace insertion to go around all of the scallops on the skirt. Allow at least 16 inches more than you measured. You can later use the excess lace insertion in another area of the dress. If you do not have a piece of insertion this long, remember to piece your laces where the pieced section will go into the miter at the top of the scallop.

2. Pin the lace insertion to the skirt (one scallop at a time only) by poking pins all the way into the fabric board, through the bottom lace heading and the fabric of the skirt. Notice on (**figure 10**) that the bottom of the lace is straight with the pins poked into the board. The top of the lace is rather "curvy" because it hasn't been shaped to lay flat yet.

3. As you take the lace into the top of the first scallop, carefully place a pin into the lace and the board at **points C and D**. Pinning the D point is very important. That is why you drew the line bisecting the top of each scallop (**fig. 10**). Pin the B point at exactly the place where the flat lace crosses the line you drew to bisect the scallop.

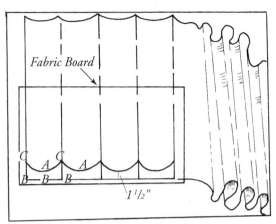

Figure 8

A = *Bottom Curve Of Scallop*
B = *Bottom Of Skirt Fabric*
C = *Top Of Scallop*
D = *Extended 2" Line Above Scallop*

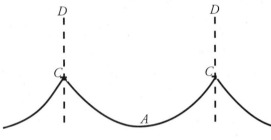

Figure 9

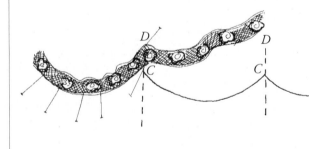

Figure 10

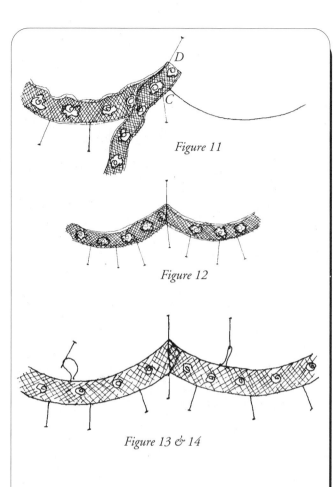

Figure 11

Figure 12

Figure 13 & 14

Pin Flat

Figure 15

Method Number One

Figure 16

4. Fold back the whole piece of lace onto the other side (**fig. 11**). Remove the pin at **C** and repin it to go through both layers of lace. Leave the pin at point **D** just as it is.

5. Then fold over the lace to place the next section of the lace to travel into the next part of the scallop (**fig.12**).

NOTE: If a little bit of that folded point is exposed after you place the lace into the next scallop, just push it underneath the miter until the miter looks perfect (**Fig. 13**). I lovingly call this "mushing" the miter into place.

6. To shape the excess fullness of the top of the scallop, simply pull a gathering thread at the center point of each scallop until the lace becomes flat and pretty (**fig. 14**).

7. Place a pin in the lace loop you just pulled until you spray starch and press the scallop flat. Remember, it is easier to pull the very top thread of the lace, the one which makes a prominent scallop on the top of the lace. If you break that thread, go in and pull another one. Many laces have as many as 4 or 5 total threads which you can pull. Don't worry about that little pulled thread; when you zigzag the lace to the skirt or entredeux stitch it to the skirt, simply trim away that little pulled thread. The heaviness of the zigzag or the entredeux stitch will secure the lace to the skirt.

8. Spray starch and press each scallop and miter after you finish shaping them.

9. After finishing with the section of scallops you have room for on that one board, pin the laces flat to the skirt and begin another section of your skirt (**fig 15**). You have the choice here of either zigzagging each section of the skirt as you complete it, or waiting until you finish the whole skirt.

10. If you choose to use a decorative stitch on your sewing machine (entredeux stitch with a wing needle) you will need to stitch with some sort of stabilizer underneath the skirt. Stitch 'n Tear is an excellent one. Some use tissue paper, others prefer wax paper or adding machine paper. Actually, the paper you buy at a medical supply store that doctor's use for covering their examining tables is great also. As long as you are stitching using a wing needle and heavy decorative stitching, you really need a stabilizer.

11. If you have an entredeux stitch on your sewing machine, you can stitch entredeux at both the top and bottom of this scalloped skirt (**fig. 16**). There are two methods of doing this:

Method Number One

12. After you finish your entredeux/wing needle stitching on both the top and the bottom of the scalloped skirt, trim away the fabric from behind the lace scallop.

13. Carefully trim the fabric from the bottom of the skirt also, leaving just a "hair" of seam allowance (**fig. 17**).

14. You are now ready to zigzag over the folded in miters (**fig. 18**). Use a regular needle for this zigzag.

15. Now zigzag the gathered laces to the bottom of this machine created entredeux.

Method Number Two

12. Machine entredeux the top only of the scallop (**fig. 19a**). Don't cut anything away.

13. Butt your gathered lace edging, a few inches at a time, to the shaped bottom of the lace scallop. Machine entredeux stitch in between the flat scalloped lace and the gathered edging lace, thus attaching both laces at the same time you are stitching in the machine entredeux (**fig. 19b**). Be sure you put more fullness in at the points of the scallop.

14. After the gathered lace edging is completely stitched to the bottom of the skirt with your machine entredeux, cut away the bottom of the skirt fabric as closely to the stitching as possible (**fig. 20**).

15. Zigzag over your folded in miters (**fig. 20a**).

16. If you are going to attach the lace to the fabric with just a plain zigzag stitch, you might try (Width=1-1/2 to 2, Length=1 to 1-1/2). You want the zigzag to be wide enough to completely go over the heading of the laces and short enough to be strong. If you are zigzagging the laces to the skirt, zigzag the **top only** of the lace scallops (**fig. 21**).

17. After you zigzag the top only of this skirt, carefully trim away the bottom portion of the fabric skirt trimming all the way up to the stitches (**fig. 21**).

18. Now you have a scalloped skirt. Later you might want to add entredeux to the bottom of the scalloped skirt. It is perfectly alright just to add gathered laces to this lace scallop without either entredeux or machine stitched entredeux. Just treat the bottom of this lace scallop as a finished edge; gather your lace edging and zigzag to the bottom of the lace (**fig. 22**).

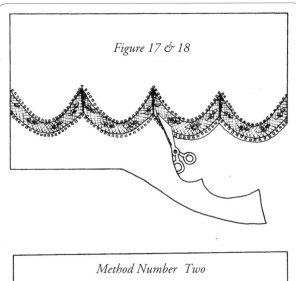

Figure 17 & 18

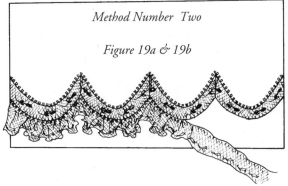

Method Number Two

Figure 19a & 19b

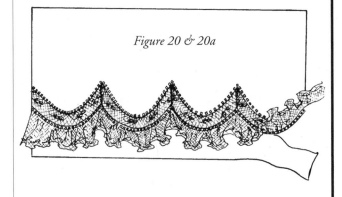

Figure 20 & 20a

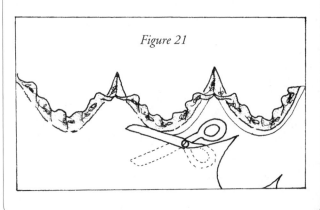

Figure 21

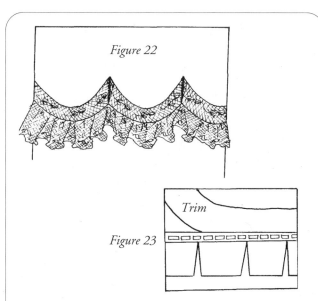

Figure 22

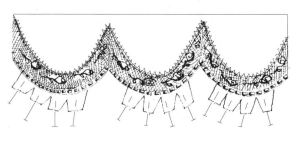

Trim

Figure 23

Figure 24

Figure 25

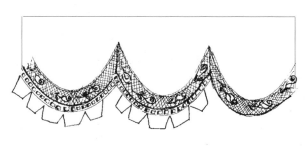

Figure 26

Finishing The Center Of The Miter

After Attaching It To The Skirt and Trimming Away The Fabric From Behind the Scallops

I always zigzag down the center of this folded miter. You can leave the folded lace portion in the miter to make the miter stronger or you can trim away the folded portion after you have zigzagged over the miter center. (**fig. 22**).

Shaping And Stitching Purchased Entredeux To Scallops

1. Trim off one side of the entredeux completely (**fig. 23**).

2. Slash the other side of the entredeux (**fig. 23**).

3. **You must pin, starch, and press the entredeux before sewing it to the scallops.** It won't hang right, otherwise.

4. Here is a great trick. In order to pin the entredeux into the points of the scallops most effectively, trim entredeux about 1-1/2 inches on either side of the point. This allows you to see exactly where you are placing the entredeux (**fig. 24**).

5. After pinning the entredeux into the points, starch, and press the entredeux into its shape.

6. Remove the pins from the skirt.

7. Zigzag the lace to the entredeux trying to go into one hole and off onto the lace (W=3, L=1-1/2).

8. As you go into the points with the entredeux, simply "smush" the entredeux into the point, stitch over it, and turn the corner (**fig. 25**).

9. There is an optional method for sewing entredeux on to scallops. Some people prefer to put entredeux on the bottom of a lace shaped skirt by using short pieces of entredeux which go only from top of the curve to top of the next curve (**fig. 26**). Treat it exactly as you did in steps 1-6 in this section. Overlap the trimmed edges in each point. When you attach the gathered laces by zigzagging, these cut points will be zigzagged together.

Adding Gathered Lace
To The Entredeux At the Bottom of Scallops

1. Measure around the scalloped skirt to get your measurement for the gathered lace edging you are going to attach to finish the skirt bottom.

2. Double that measurement for a 2-1 fullness. Remember that you can piece your laces if your piece of edging isn't long enough.

3. Cut your lace edging.

4. Using the technique "Sewing Hand-Gathered French Lace To Entredeux Edge" zigzag the gathered lace to the bottom of the entredeux (**fig. 27**).

5. You can also choose to use the method "Gathering French Lace By Machine, While Applying It To Trimmed Entredeux Edge" to attach this lace edging.

Gathering French Laces By Hand
Pull Thread In the Heading of Laces

On the straight sides of French or English cotton laces are several threads called the "heading." These threads serve as pull threads for lace shaping. Some laces have better pull threads than others. Before you begin dramatically-curved lace shaping, check to be sure your chosen lace has a good pull thread. The scallop on the top of most laces is the first pull thread that I pull. Most French and English laces have several good pull threads, so if you break the first one, pull another. If all the threads break, you could probably run a gathering thread in the top of the lace with your sewing machine.

1. Cut a length of lace 2-3 times the finished length to have enough fullness to make a pretty lace ruffle.

2. To gather the lace, pull one of the heavy threads that runs along the straight edge or heading of the lace (**fig. 28**).

3. Adjust gathers evenly before zigzagging.

Sewing Hand-Gathered French Lace To Entredeux Edge

1. Gather lace by hand by pulling the thread in the heading of the lace. I use the scalloped outside thread of the heading first since I think it gathers better than the inside threads. Distribute gathers evenly.

2. Trim the side of the entredeux to which the gathered lace is to be attached. Side by side, right sides up, zigzag the gathered lace to the trimmed entredeux (Width=1-1/2; Length=2). (**fig. 29**)

3. Using a wooden shish kabob stick, push the gathers evenly into the sewing machine as you zigzag. You can also use a pick or long pin of some sort to push the gathers evenly into the sewing machine.

Hint: To help distribute the gathers evenly fold the entredeux in half and half again. Mark these points with a fabric marker. Before the lace is gathered fold it in half and half again. Mark the folds with a fabric marker. Now gather the lace and match the marks on the entredeux and the marks on the lace (**fig. 30**) ▨

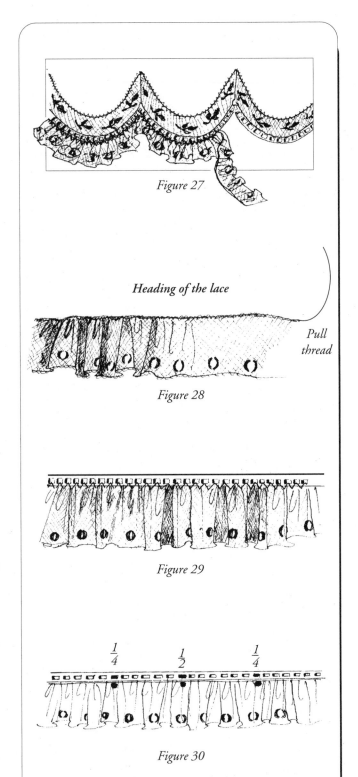

Figure 27

Heading of the lace

Pull thread

Figure 28

Figure 29

$\frac{1}{4}$ $\frac{1}{2}$ $\frac{1}{4}$

Figure 30

Shaping Lace Diamonds

Making Lace Diamonds

Lace diamonds can be used almost anywhere on heirloom garments. They are especially pretty at the point of a collar, on the skirt of a dress, at angles on the bodice of a garment, or all the way around a collar. The easiest way to make lace diamonds is to work on a fabric board with a diamond guide. You can make your diamonds as large or as small as you desire. I think you are really going to love this easy method of making diamonds with the fold back miter. Now, you don't have to remove those diamonds from the board to have perfect diamonds every time.

Making Lace Diamonds

Materials Needed

- ◆ Spray starch, iron, pins, fabric board
- ◆ Lace insertion
- ◆ Diamond guide

1. Draw the diamond guide or template (**fig. 1**).

2. Tear both skirt pieces. French seam or serge one side only of the skirt.

3. Working from the center seam you just made, draw diamonds all the way around the skirt. This way you can make any sized diamonds you want without worrying if they will fit the skirt perfectly. When you get all the way around both sides of the skirt you will have the same amount of skirt left over on both sides.

4. Simply trim the excess skirt away. Later you will French seam or serge the skirt on the other side to complete your skirt. This is the easy way to make any type of lace shaping on any skirt and it will always fit perfectly (**fig. 2**).

5. The guide or template, which you have just drawn, will be the outside of the diamond. Draw lines going into the diamond, bisecting each angle where the lace will be mitered. This is very important, since one of your critical pins will be placed exactly on this line. These bisecting lines need to be drawn about 2 inches long coming in from the angles of the diamonds (**fig. 3**). If you are making a diamond skirt, it is easier to draw your diamond larger and make your diamond shaping on the inside of the diamond. That way, the outside points of your diamond can touch when you are drawing all of your diamonds on the skirt.

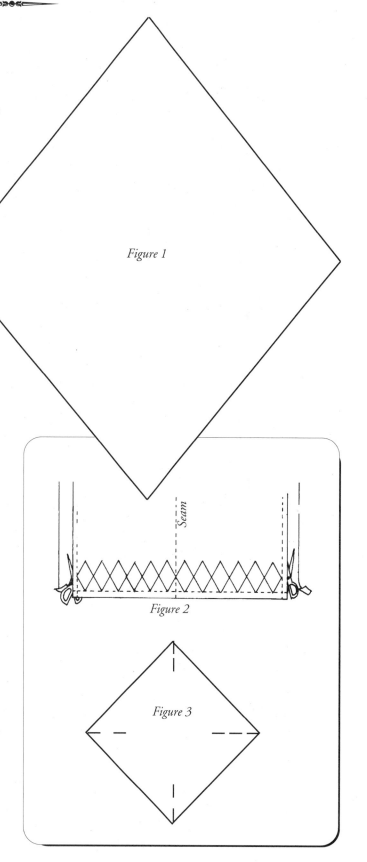

Figure 1

Figure 2

Figure 3

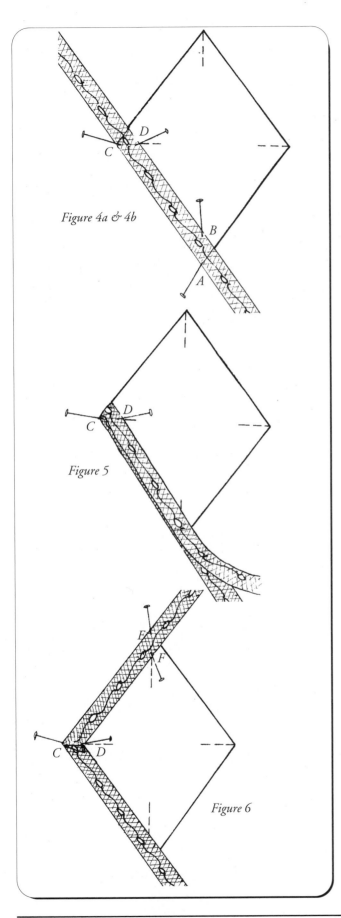

Figure 4a & 4b

Figure 5

Figure 6

6. As I said earlier, you can shape the laces for diamonds on either the outside or the inside of the template. I actually think it is easier to shape your laces on the inside of the template.

7. Place your skirt with the drawn diamonds on a fabric board.

8. Place the lace flat and guiding it along the inside of the drawn template, put a pin at **point A** and one at **Point B** where the bisecting line goes to the inside (**fig. 4a**). The pin goes through both the lace and the fabric into the fabric board.

9. Guiding the edge of the lace along the drawn template line, place another pin into the fabric board through the lace (and the fabric skirt) at **point C** and another one at **point D** on the bisecting line (**fig. 4b**).

10. Fold back the lace right on top of itself. Remove the pin from the fabric board at **point D**, replacing it this time to go through both layers of lace rather than just one. Of course, the pin will not only go through both layers of lace but also through the skirt and into fabric board (**fig. 5**).

11. Take the lace piece and bring it around to once again following the outside line. You magically have a folded miter already in place (**fig. 6**).

12. Guiding further, the edge of the lace along the inside of the drawn template line, place another pin into the fabric board through the lace at **point E** and another at **point F** on the bisecting line (**fig. 6**).

13. Fold the lace right back on top of itself. Remove the pin at **point F**, replacing it this time to go through both layers of lace rather than just one (**fig. 7**).

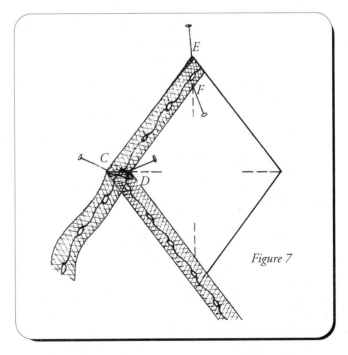

Figure 7

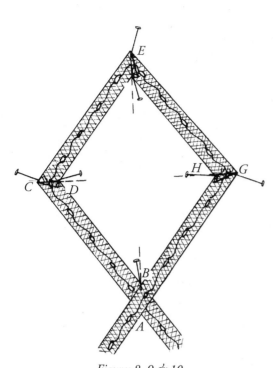

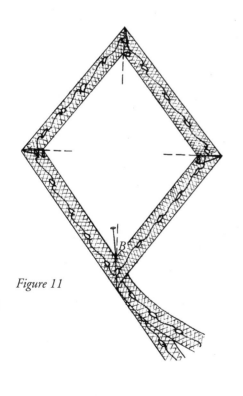

Figures 8, 9 & 10

Figure 11

14. Take the lace piece and bring it around to once again follow the outside line. You magically have a folded miter already in place (**fig. 8**).

15. Guiding further, the edge of the lace along the inside of the drawn template line, place another pin into the lace at **point G** and another pin at **point H** on the bisecting line.

16. Fold the lace right back on top of itself. Remove the pin at **point H**, replace it this time to go through both layers of lace rather than just one.

17. Take the lace piece and bring it around to once again follow the outside line. You magically have a folded miter already in place (**fig. 9**).

18. At the bottom of the lace diamond, let the laces cross at the bottom. Remove the pin at **point B** and replace it into the fabric board through both pieces of lace. Remove the pin completely at **point A** (**fig. 10**).

19. Taking the top piece of lace, and leaving in the pin at **point B** only, fold under and back the lace where it lays on top of the other piece of lace. You now have a folded in miter for the bottom of the lace.

20. Put a pin in, now, at **point B** (**fig. 11.**). Of course you are going to have to cut away this long tail of lace. I think the best time to do that is before you begin your final stitching to attach the diamonds to the garment. It is perfectly alright to leave those tails of lace until your final stitching is done and then trim them.

21. You are now ready to spray starch and press the whole diamond shape. After spray starching and pressing the diamonds to the skirt, remove the pins from the fabric board and flat pin the lace shape to the skirt bottom. You are now ready to zigzag the diamond or machine entredeux stitch the diamond to the garments. Suggested zigzag settings are Width=2 to 3, Length=1 to 1-1/2.

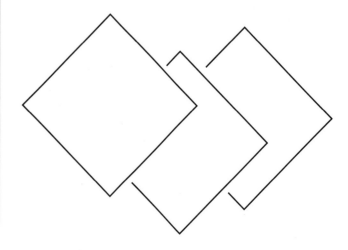

Finishing The Bottom Of The Skirt

These techniques are for finishing the bottom of a Diamond Skirt, a Heart Skirt, a Bow Skirt, or any other lace shaped skirt where the figures travel all the way around the bottom touching each other.

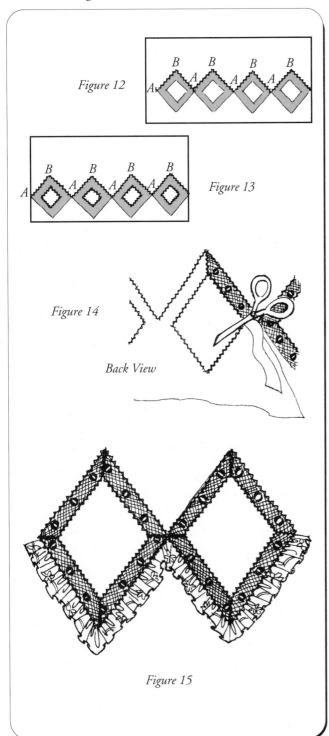

Figure 12

Figure 13

Figure 14

Back View

Figure 15

Method One

Using Plain Zigzag To Attach Diamonds (Or Other Shapes) To The Skirt.

1. First, zigzag across the top of the diamond pattern, stitching from **point A** to **point B** again to **point A** and finish the entire skirt (**fig. 12**). Your lace is now attached to the skirt all the way across the skirt on the top. If your fabric and diamonds have been spray starched well, you don't have to use a stabilizer when zigzagging these lace shapes to the fabric. The width stitch will be wide enough to cover the heading of the lace and go off onto the fabric on the other side. The length will be from 1/2 to 1, depending on the look that you prefer.

2. Zigzag all the diamonds, on the skirt, on the inside of the diamonds only (**fig. 13**).

3. You are now ready to trim away the fabric of the skirt from behind the diamonds. Trim the fabric carefully from behind the lace shapes. The rest of the skirt fabric will now fall away leaving a diamond shaped bottom of the skirt (**fig. 14**). The lace will also be see through at the top of the diamonds also.

4. If you are going to just gather lace and attach it at this point, then gather the lace and zigzag it to the bottom of the lace shapes being careful to put extra fullness in the points of the diamonds (**fig. 15**). If your lace isn't wide enough to be pretty, then zigzag a couple of pieces of insertion or edging to your edging to make it wider (**fig. 16**).

5. If you are going to put entredeux on the bottom of the shapes before attaching gathered lace to finish it, follow the instructions on attaching entredeux to the bottom of a scalloped skirt given earlier in this lace shaping section. Work with short pieces of entredeux stitching from the inside points of the diamonds to the lowe points of the diamonds on the skirt.

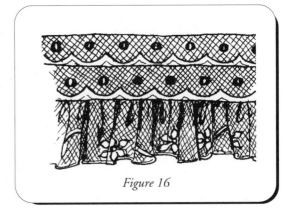

Figure 16

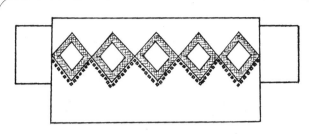

Figure 17

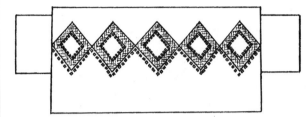

Figure 18

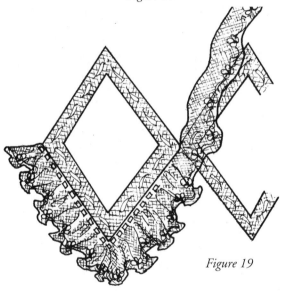

Figure 19

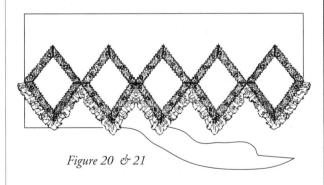

Figure 20 & 21

Using A Wing Needle Machine Entredeux Stitch To Attach Diamonds (Or Other Lace Shapes) To The Skirt

1. If you are going to use the wing needle/entredeux stitch on your sewing machine to attach your diamonds, or other lace shapes to the skirt, use the entredeux stitch for all attaching of the lace shapes to the skirt. Remember **you must use a stabilizer** when using the entredeux stitch/wing needle on any machine.

2. Place your stabilizer underneath the skirt, behind the shapes to be stitched. You can use small pieces of stabilizer which are placed underneath only a few shapes rather than having to have a long piece of stabilizer. Just be sure that you have stabilizer underneath these lace shapes before you begin your entredeux/wing needle stitching.

3. First, stitch the top side of the diamonds entredeux stitching from point A to point B all the way around the skirt. (**fig. 17**).

4. Secondly, stitch the inside of the diamonds using the entredeux stitch (**fig. 18**). Do not cut any fabric away at this point. Remember to continue using stabilizer for all entredeux/wing needle stitching.

5. You are now ready to gather your lace edging and machine entredeux it to the bottom of the skirt joining the bottom portions of the diamonds at the same time you attach the gathered lace edging. If your machine has an edge joining or edge stitching foot with a center blade for guiding, this is a great place for using it.

6. Gather only a few inches of lace edging at a time. Butt the gathered lace edging to the flat bottom sides of the diamonds.

7. Machine entredeux right between the gathered lace edging and the flat side of the diamond. Remember, you are stitching through your laces (which are butted together not overlapped), the fabric of the skirt and the stabilizer (**fig. 19**). Put a little extra lace gathered fullness at the upper and lower points of the diamonds.

8. After you have stitched your machine entredeux all the way around the bottom of the skirt, you have attached the gathered lace edging to the bottom of the skirt with your entredeux stitch.

9. Trim the fabric from behind the lace diamonds. Trim the fabric from underneath the gathered lace edging on the bottom of the skirt (**fig. 20**).

10. Either zigzag your folded in miters in the angles of the diamonds or simply leave them folded in. I prefer to zigzag them (**fig. 21**). You also have the choice of cutting away the little folded back portions of the miters or leaving them for strength.

Shaping Flip-Flopped Lace Bows

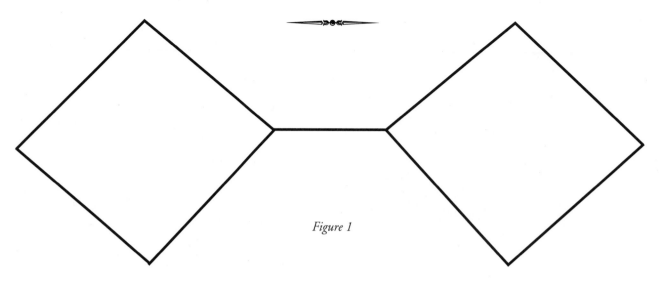

Figure 1

I make lace bows using a technique called "flip-flopping" lace — a relatively unsophisticated name for such a lovely trim. I first saw this technique on an antique teddy I bought at a local antique store. It had the most elegant flip-flopped lace bow. Upon careful examination, I noticed the lace was simply folded over at the corners, then continued down forming the outline of the bow. The corners were somewhat square. Certainly it was easier than mitering or pulling a thread and curving. I found it not only looked easier, it was easier.

Follow the instructions for making a flip-flopped bow, using a bow template. This technique works just as well for lace angles up and down on a skirt. You can flip-flop any angle that traditionally would be mitered. It can be used to go around a square collar, around diamonds, and around any shape with an angle rather than a curve.

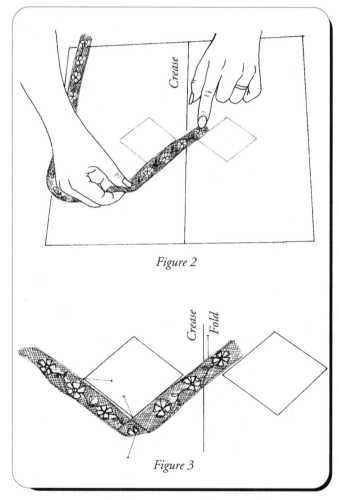

Figure 2

Figure 3

Flip-Flopping Lace

1. Trace the template onto the fabric exactly where you want to place bows (**fig. 1**). Remember, the easy way to put bows around a skirt is to fold the fabric to make equal divisions of the skirt. If you want a bow skirt which has bows all the way around follow the directions for starting at the side to make the bows in the directions given for a diamond skirt.

2. Draw your bows on your garment or on a skirt, where ever you want this lace shape.

3. Place your garment on your fabric board before you begin making your bow shapes. Beginning above the inside of one bow (**above E**), place the lace along the angle. The template is the inside guide line of the bow (**fig. 2**).

4. At the first angle (**B**), simply fold the lace where it will follow along the next line (**B-C**) (**fig. 3**). This is called flip flopping the lace.

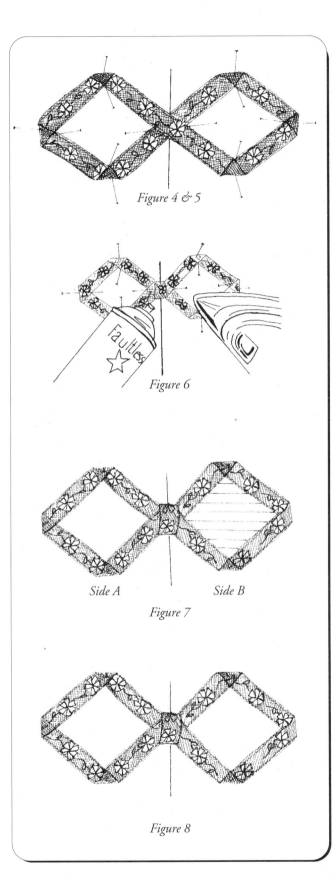

Figure 4 & 5

Figure 6

Side A   Side B

Figure 7

Figure 8

5. Place pins sticking through the lace, the fabric, and into the shaping board. I like to place pins on both the inside edges and the outside edges. Remember to place your pins where they lay as flat a possible.

6. The lines go as follows: A-B, B-C, C-D, D-A, A-E, E-F, F-G, G-H, H-E. Tuck your lace end under E, which is also where the first raw edge will end (**fig. 4**).

7. Cut a short bow tab of lace that is long enough to go around the whole tie area of the bow (**fig. 4**). This will be the bow tie!

8. Tuck in this lace tab to make the center of the bow (**fig. 5**). Another way to attach this bow tie is to simply fold down a tab at the top and the bottom and place it right on top of the center of the bow. That is actually easier than tucking it under. Since you are going to zigzag all the way around the bow "tie" it really won't matter whether it is tucked in or not.

9. Spray starch and press the bow, that is shaped with the pins still in the board, with its bow tie in place (**fig. 6**). Remove pins from the board and pin the bow flat to the skirt or other garment. You are now ready to attach the shaped bow to the garment.

10. This illustration gives you ideas for making a bow two ways. First, the "A" side of the bow has just the garment fabric peeking through the center of the bow. Second, the "B" side of the bow illustrates what the bow will look like if you put a pintucked strip in the center. Both are beautiful (**fig. 7**).

11. If you prefer the bow to look like side (A), which has the fabric of the garment showing through the middle of the bow, follow these steps for completing the bow. Zigzag around the total outside of the bow. Then, zigzag around the inside portions of both sides of the bow. Finally, zigzag around the finished bow "tie" portion (**fig. 8**). The bows will be attached to the dress.

12. If you prefer the bow to look like side (B), which will have pintucks (or anything else you choose) inside, follow the directions in this section. (These directions are when you have bows on areas other than the bottom of a skirt or sleeve or collar. If you have bows at the bottom of anything, then you have to follow the skirt directions given in the diamond skirt section.)

13. Zigzag the outside only of the bows all the way around. Notice that your bow "tie" will be partially stitched since part of it is on the outside edges.

14. I suggest pintucking a larger piece of fabric and cutting small sections which are somewhat larger than the insides of the bows (**fig. 9**).

15. Cut away fabric from behind both center sections of the bow. I lovingly tell my students that now they can place their whole fists inside the holes in the centers of this bow.

16. Place the pintucked section behind the center of the lace bows. Zigzag around the inside of the bows which will now attach the pintucked section. From the back, trim away the excess pintucked section. You now have pintucks in the center of each side of the bow (**fig. 10**).

17. Go back and stitch your sides of the bow "tie" down. After you have zigzagged all the way around your bow "tie" you can trim away excess laces which crossed underneath the tie. This gives the bow tie a little neater look.

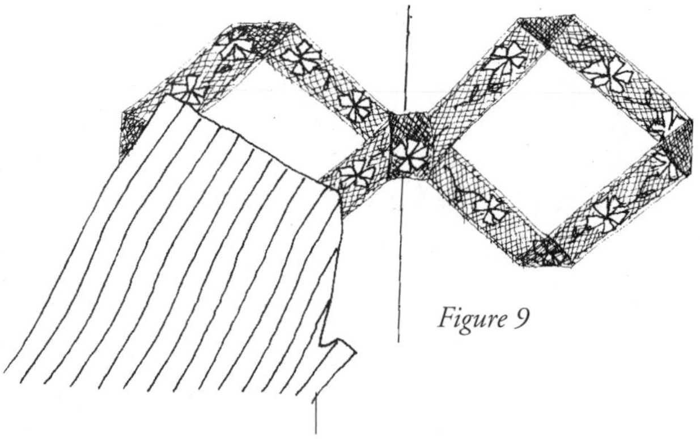

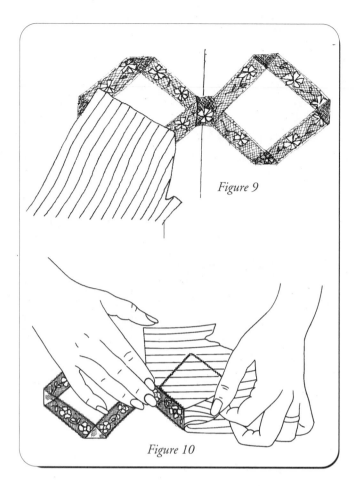

Figure 9

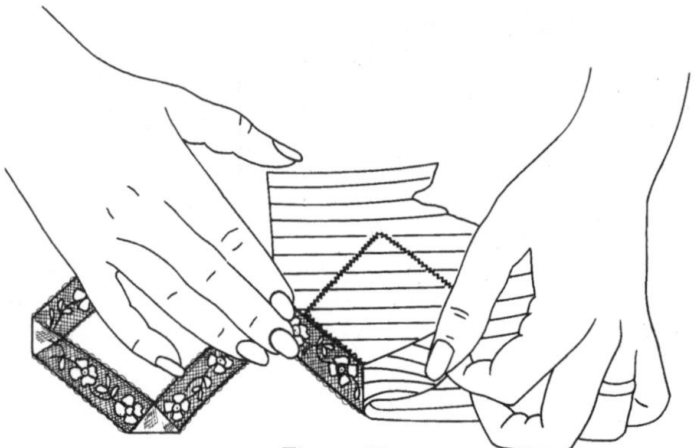

Figure 10

Tied Lace Bows

This method of bow shaping I saw for the first time years ago in Australia. It is beautiful and each bow will be a little different which makes it a very interesting variation of the flip flopped bow. Your options on shaping the bow part of this cute bow are as follows: **1.** you can flip flop the bow, or **2.** you can curve the bow and pull a string to make it round, or **3.** you can flip flop one side and curve the other side. Bows can be made of lace insertion, lace edging, or lace beading. If you make your tied lace bow of lace edging, be sure to put the scalloped side of the lace edging for the outside of the bow and leave the string to pull on the inside.

Materials Needed

✧ 1 yd. to 1 1/4 yds. lace insertion, edging or beading for one bow

Directions

1. Tie the lace into a bow leaving equal streamers on either side of the bow.
2. Using a lace board, shape the bow onto the garment using either the flip flopped method or the pulled thread curved method.
3. Shape the streamers of the bow using either the flip flopped method or the pulled thread method.
4. Shape the ends of the streamer into an angle.
5. Zigzag or machine entredeux stitch the shaped bow and streamers to the garment.

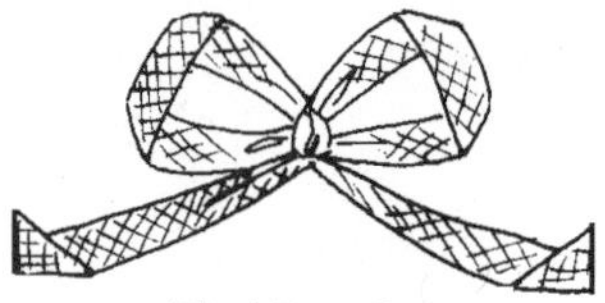

Tied Lace Bow

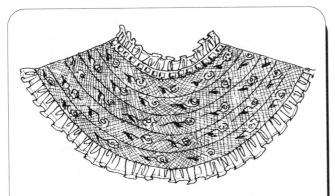

Round Portrait Collars

Materials Needed

❋ Sizes 4 and Under: 4 yards of 1/2-inch to 3/4-inch insertion; 2 yards of edging; 1-3/4 yards entredeux

❋ Sizes 5-12: 5 yards of 1/2-inch to 3/4-inch insertion; 2 yards of edging; 2 yards entredeux

❋ Adult: 6 or 7 yards of 1/2-inch to 3/4-inch insertion (This will depend on how wide you want to make your collar, of course.); 3 yards of edging; 2 1/2 yards entredeux

NOTE: If you are using wider insertion, you need less yardage. If you are using narrow insertion, you need more yardage. You may want your collar wider than the shoulder/sleeve point. Get more lace. And vice versa. There is really no exact lace amount.

❋ Glass head pins or Iris Super Fine Nickel-Plated Steel Pins.

NOTE: Do not use plastic head pins. They will melt when you press your laces into curves!

❋ Iron

❋ Magic Sizing or Spray Starch.

❋ Make a double-wide fabric board using the directions given earlier in this chapter. You can ask your fabric store to save two for you.

❋ Threads to match your laces

❋ A large piece of tissue paper like you use to wrap gifts

❋ Scissors

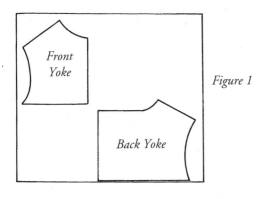

Front Yoke

Back Yoke

Figure 1

Making A Fabric Board

Use the directions found earlier in this guide.

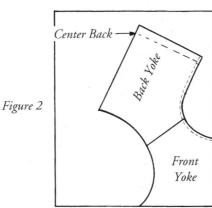

Center Back

Back Yoke

Front Yoke

Figure 2

Preparing The Paper Guide

1. Trace your collar guide onto a piece of tissue paper.

2. If your pattern doesn't have a collar guide, you can make one.

3. Cut out the front yoke and the back yoke of your paper pattern (**fig. 1**). Put the shoulder seams of your paper pattern together to form the neckline. Be sure to overlap the seam allowance to get a true seam line at the shoulder (**fig. 2**). Subtract the seam allowance around the neckline. This is the neck guide to use for your paper pattern. Trace the neckline off. Mark the center-back lines, which will be evident from your pattern pieces (**fig. 3**). As you look at **figure 3**, you will see that a large circle is on the outside of

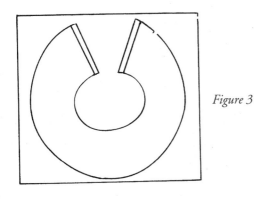

Figure 3

this pattern piece. You can draw this large circle on if you want to; however, you only need the neckline shape and the center back. You must draw the center back the length of your collar.

4. Mark the fold-back line. To get your fold-back line, measure the width of the gathered lace that will be used around the bottom of the collar and up the center back on both sides. Take that measurement off of the center-back point and mark the fold-back line (**fig 3**).

5. You will probably notice that the neckline isn't really round, but oval shaped. That is the true neckline on any pattern, not an exact circle. Use that shaped neckline as your neckline guide.

6. This neckline guide and the center-back line on the pattern are the only lines that you need to shape the circular laces around the collar. You will use the fold-back line after the lace shaping is done to finish the back of the collar. You only use the neckline guide for the first piece of lace. After that, you use the previously-shaped piece of rounded lace as your guide.

Making The First Two Rows Of Insertion

1. Shape the neckline row first. Then work from the neckline down to complete the collar width you want.

2. Cut your lace for the neckline or first row of your collar. **NOTE:** Cut extra. You will want to cut your laces longer than the center-back line of the collar you have marked. I suggest at least 3/4 inch to 1 inch longer than the exact center back.

3. Place the tissue paper guide on the fabric board.

4. Using your fabric board as your work base and your tissue paper collar guide, you are now ready to begin shaping your collar.

5. Pin the outside of the lace where the inside will touch the neck guide when it is pressed down. The outside lace will have the pins jabbing through the lace and the tissue paper, right into the fabric board. This outside line is not gathered at all. The inside will be wavy. At this point, the inside has no pins in it (**fig. 4**).

6. After you have pinned the outside of the lace onto the fabric board, gently pull the gathering string in the heading of the INSIDE of the lace. The lace will pull flat (**fig. 5**). Gently distribute the gathers by holding the lace down. Be certain that it is flat on the fabric board. You can pull your gathering rows from both ends. It is now time to put pins on the inside of the first row (**fig. 5**). Jab them into the fabric board. Spray starch lightly and steam.

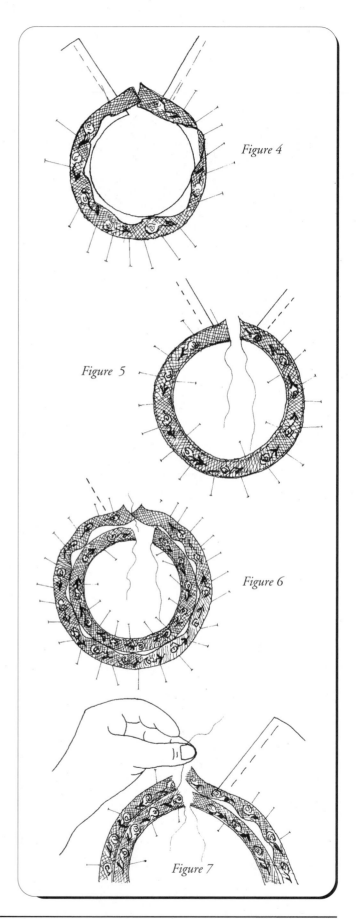

Figure 4

Figure 5

Figure 6

Figure 7

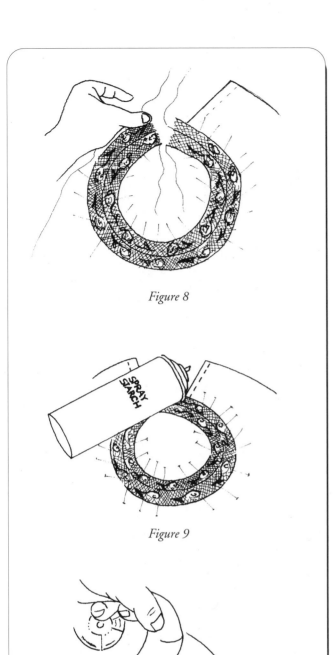

Figure 8

Figure 9

Figure 10

7. Now that the first row is pretty and flat, you are ready to do the same thing with the second row. Pin the OUTSIDE edge to the board by jabbing the pins, just like you did on the first row. Be sure the inside of the lace touches the first row when you press it down with your fingers (**fig. 6**). After you have gone all the way around with the second row of lace, pull from both ends to gather the inside row, just like you did the first row (**fig. 7**).

8. If you will remove the pins where the two rows butt (and where you will zigzag in a few minutes) and leave pins on the two outside rows, you will find it easier to press them.

9. Spray starch the two rows (**fig. 8**). Don't worry if spray starch gets on the tissue paper, because when you spray the two rows, it naturally gets on the tissue paper. It looks a little soggy; however, it will dry nicely with a hair dryer.

10. Using a hair dryer, dry the starch and the tissue paper where the starch made it wet. If you do not dry the paper before you steam the laces, the paper will tear easily. If your tissue paper tears anytime during the process of making this collar, simply put another piece of tissue paper behind the whole collar and stitch through two pieces.

11. After you have dried the starch, press and steam the laces right on the paper (**fig. 9**).

12. Remove the jabbed pins, one at a time, and flat pin the lace to the paper on both rows. Pin with the points toward the neckline. This makes it a lot easier when you stitch your collar, because when the pins are in this position, you can pull then out as you zigzag. If they are pinned the other way, it is difficult to remove the pins as you stitch. Never sew over pins, please! It is easier to remove the pin than it is to replace the needle (**fig. 10**).

13. (Stitch right through the tissue paper and the lace. Later, you will tear away the tissue paper.) Move to your sewing machine, and zigzag (Width=1-1/2 to 2, Length=1-1/2 to 2) (**fig. 10**). This width and length are just suggestions. Actually, the width and length will depend on the width of the laces in the heading of your particular lace. The length stitch will depend upon your preference. If you like a heavier, closer together look, make your stitch length shorter. If you like a looser, more delicate look, make your stitch length longer.

14. The first two rows should now be zigzagged together.

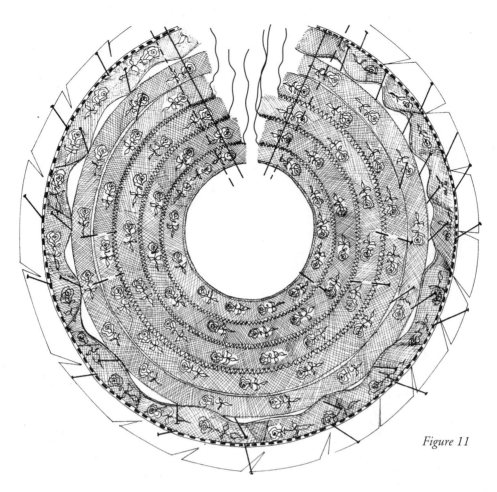

Figure 11

Making The Rest Of The Rows Of Insertion

1. Following the directions given for applying the second row, pin, and stitch the rest of the rows that you want to have on your collar. Make the collar as wide as you want it (**fig. 11**).

2. Here is a little trick that I have learned through experience. After you have pinned, pressed, starched, pressed, and zigzagged your first two rows together, the remaining rows can be made on the paper pattern at the same time. You don't have to stitch each row of insertion right after shaping it (**fig. 11**). You might choose to stitch after each row of shaping. The choice is yours.

3. Shape the laces on the rest of the collar by pinning, pressing, starching, pressing, and letting dry (**fig. 11**).

4. After all the lace rows are shaped and the tissue paper is completely dry, pin them flat, remembering to place the pins with the points toward the neckline and the heads away from the neckline (**fig. 11**). Zigzag the laces together.

5. Cut a piece of entredeux with enough length to go completely around the outside row of lace insertion, allowing for plenty of excess. You don't want to run out.

6. Trim off one side of the entredeux completely and slash the other row so it will curve easily (**fig. 11**).

8. Pin the entredeux around the outside row of lace, jabbing pins into the holes of the entredeux about every 2 inches or so. After the entredeux is all the way around the curved lace collar, press, starch, press again, and allow to dry. You can always dry it with a hair dryer if you want to begin stitching immediately (**fig. 11**).

9. Pin the entredeux to the tissue paper at several places. You are now ready to begin stitching the first row of lace insertion that is not already stitched. Remember, if you have chosen to stitch each row of insertion after it was shaped, you might have already stitched all of your laces at this time.

10. Stitch each row, starting with the unstitched one closest to the neckline. Move outward with each row for your stitching. Remove the pins, one at a time, as you are stitching.

11. With each successive row, carefully remove the pins, and be sure to butt the lace edges exactly as you stitch around the collar.

12. The entredeux to the last row of insertion may or may not be the last row that you will stitch, while the tissue paper is still on the collar. You will have to make a decision concerning whether you want to use Method I or Method II a little later on in the instructions.

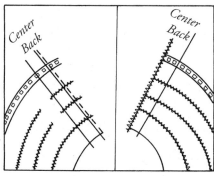

Figure 1b   Figure 1a

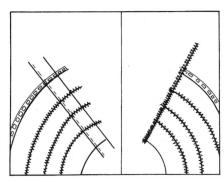

Figure 2a   Figure 2b

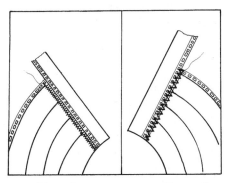

Figure 3a   Figure 3b

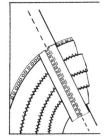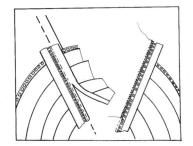

Figure 1   Figure 2   Figure 3

— Using The Center Back Of The Collar —

Check The Fold Back Line

1. The center back of a garment is just that - where the backs meet. This collar will not end at the center back point unless you are not putting laces up the center back of the collar.

2. You can choose to put no laces and no entredeux up the center back. In this case, you will work on the center back line. The best way to finish the back of the collar, if you make this choice, is to serge or overlock the collar just outside of the center-back line (**fig. 1a**). Then fold your serged seam to the back, and straight-stitch it to the collar (**fig. 1b**). That leaves just a finished lace edge as the center back.

3. If you are adding lace edging and entredeux up the back of the collar, you will have to use the fold-back line you made in the beginning on your pattern. Laces don't need to overlap at the center back, but meet instead. Check to be sure that your fold-back line is as wide as your lace edging is from the center-back line on your pattern.

— Method I For Adding Entredeux —

1. Make a straight row of stitching on the fold-back line. You are still stitching through the tissue paper.

2. Trim away the laces, leaving about 1/8 inch of raw lace edge (**fig. 2a**).

3. Zigzag very tightly (Width=1-1/2, Length=1/2) to finish the lace edge (**fig. 2b**). You can also serge the back of the collar to finish it.

4. Butt the entredeux to the finished edge (**fig. 3a**) and zigzag, going into the holes of the entredeux and off (**fig. 3b**).

— Method II For Adding Entredeux —

1. Using the technique "Entredeux To Flat Fabric," attach the entredeux to the back of the collar. Stitch in the ditch (**fig. 1**), trim (**fig. 2**), and zigzag (**fig. 3**).

2. You have two options when finishing this straight line of stitching. Either serge or zigzag along this line. You will make the decision in the next section. For right now, don't trim away any laces along the foldback line; just leave the collar like it is.

3. Trim away the other side of the entredeux. It is now ready for gathered lace to be attached to it. ❈

Method I

For Attaching Gathered Lace To Entredeux On The Outside Edge of the Collar With Tissue Paper

Question: When would you use Method I?

For some, this method is the easiest for distributing lace evenly because you can put the quarter points exactly where you want them and control the fullness. If you have a machine which isn't up to par, stitching laces on tissue paper is easier than working without it. So, for some people the method of stitching the gathered lace on while tissue paper is still attached is the easiest.

1. Cut lace edging to be gathered around the bottom and up the back of the collar. Use a 1-1/2 - 1 fullness or a 2 - 1 fullness, depending on the amount of lace desired.

2. After cutting your lace, (allow about 2 inches to turn each back corner and about 10 inches to gather and go up each back of the collar) fold the rest of the lace in half, and mark the center of the lace. Fold once again, and mark the quarter points. This will allow you to distribute the fullness accurately.

3. Pull the gathering thread in the top of the edging. Pin the center of the lace to the center of the entredeux edge of the collar. Pin the quarter points of the lace to the approximate quarter points of the collar. You should have about 12 inches of lace on each end to go around the corner of the collar and to gather it up the back of the collar. After figuring out these measurements, begin to distribute and pin the gathered lace to the bottom of the collar entredeux. Distribute the gathers carefully. Pin all the way around.

4. Stitch the gathered lace (Width=1-1/2 to 2, Length=1/2) to the entredeux, still stitching through the tissue paper. You are only going to stitch around the bottom of the collar. Leave the laces unattached at this point, coming up the center back.

5. Carefully tear away the tissue paper from collar.

6. If you are not going to use a serger, trim away the lace ends 1/4 inch away from the fold-back line of the collar where you have stay-stitched. This 1/4 inch gives you a seam allowance to zigzag to finish. If you plan to serge the outside of this line, you do not have to trim away the lace since the serger does this for you.

7. Zigzag tightly over this stay-stitched line (Width=1 to 2, Length=1/2).

8. If you have a serger, serge this seam rather than zigzagging over it.

9. If you serged this seam, fold back the serged edge, and straight-stitch it down.

10. If you zigzagged over this seam, use this rolled and whipped edge as the finished edge of this seam.

Finishing The Application

Of Entredeux and Gathered Lace Edging

1. Now that your fold-back line is finished, you are ready to finish gathering the lace edging and zigzag it to the back of the collar.

2. Trim the other side of the entredeux up the back of the collar.

3. Put extra gathers in the lace edging when going around the corner. This will keep it from folding under.

4. After gathering the lace edging, butt the gathered laces to the trimmed entredeux and zigzag to the collar.

5. Fold down the top of the lace edging before completely zigzagging to the top of the collar. That way you have a finished lace edge on the top of the collar.

Method II

For Attaching Gathered Lace To The Entredeux of the Collar Without Tissue Paper

Question: When would you use Method II?

If the tension is good on your sewing machine, use Method II. If you don't mind the laces not being exactly the same gathering all the way around, use Method II. By the way, the laces won't be distributed evenly using Method I either. I haven't found a way to perfectly distribute and gather laces and attach them using any method, including hand sewing! However, Method II is the easiest.

1. Tear away the tissue paper from your collar.

2. Cut the lace edging, which will be gathered around the bottom of the collar and up the back of the collar. You can use a 1-1/2 - 1 fullness or a 2 - 1 fullness. It really depends on how much lace you wish to use.

3. Now that your fold-back line is finished, you are ready to finish gathering the lace edging and zigzag it to the back of the collar.

4. Trim the other side of the entredeux.

5. Using the techniques found in "Gathering French Lace By Machine, While Applying It To Trimmed Entredeux Edge," attach your lace to the bottom of the collar and up the back edges. ▨

Round Portrait Collar Variations

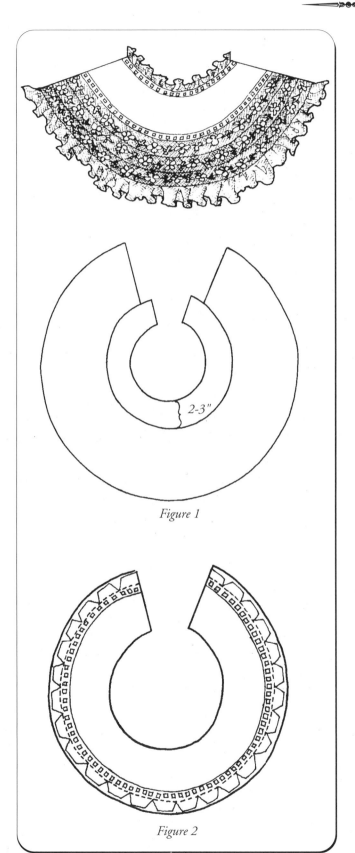

Figure 1

Figure 2

Adding A Fabric Neckline Piece

Portrait collars are lovely when they start with a fabric circular piece finished with entredeux at the bottom. After your entredeux is attached, then complete the portrait collar exactly as you would if the fabric weren't there. If you are adding a fabric neckline piece, **You must use the actual dress or blouse pattern to make your round portrait collar guide.** If you are making a lace only portrait collar, you can use a general neckline guide since lace can be shaped to go into many shapes. For the fabric neckline, you must make an exact pattern to fit the neckline of the garment.

Materials Needed

✻ Laces and entredeux for portrait collar given in the portrait collar section

✻ 1/3 yard batiste for adult collar

✻ 1/4 yard for infant or small child's collar

✻ 1 extra yard of entredeux for use at the bottom of the fabric portion of the collar (Optional if you have a machine which makes machine entredeux with a wing needle.)

1. Refer to the directions for Preparing The Paper Guide which tells you how to get your neckline curve for your actual garment. If you are putting in this fabric around the neckline, you must cut an actual pattern by the neckline of the garment to which it will be attached.

2. Be certain when you cut the collar fabric piece that you mark in a seam allowance exactly like the one on the garment neck edge.

3. Cut out a circular neckline piece extending beyond the center back neck edge. You're not going to use this excess, it is only for security in case you want to make the center backs a little wider after you try on the collar! Also, when you zigzag entredeux and laces together, sometimes the fabric shrinks up just a little because of all of that heavy stitching (**fig. 1**).

Method I

Purchased Entredeux Added To Bottom Of Fabric Collar

4. Cut enough entredeux to go around this curve with a little excess on either side. Trim one side only of the entredeux. Slash the other side so it will curve around the neckline edge.

5. With the slashed side of the entredeux meeting the cut curved edge of the collar, pin, using the fabric board, the entredeux around the outside edge of this fabric neck line piece (**fig. 2**).

6. Spray starch and press.

7. Using the method, entredeux to flat fabric (stitch in the ditch, trim and zigzag or serge the whole thing with a rolled hem), stitch the entredeux to the outside edge of the curve. You can also serge this curved entredeux onto the collar. I suggest that first before you serge the entredeux on, you straight stitch in the ditch to be sure that it is perfectly placed. Then, using your rolled hemmer, serge it to the collar.

8. Press the entredeux down. You now have completed the fabric circle with the trimmed entredeux already attached. You have a trimmed entredeux edge to shape the laces onto with the first row of shaped laces which will come next (**fig. 3**).

9. Place this fabric/entredeux piece on the piece of tissue paper which you also drew to match this neckline edge. You are now ready to shape the laces and finish the collar following all directions in the Making A Round Lace Portrait Collar section.

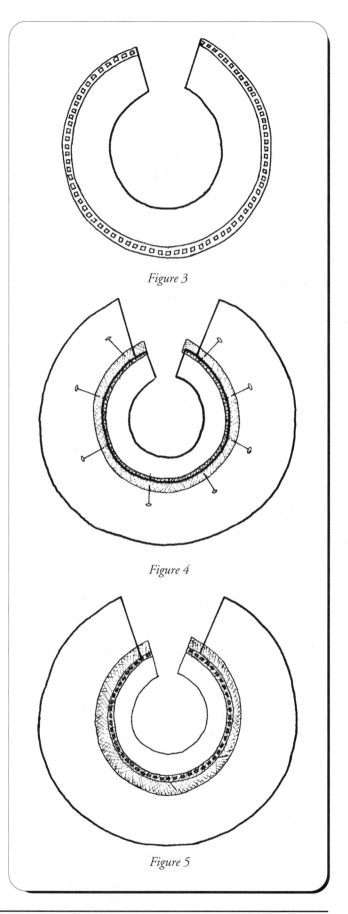

Figure 3

Figure 4

Figure 5

Method II

Stitching The First Row of Laces To The Collar Using Machine Entredeux Stitch And Wing Needle

10. Skip the entredeux altogether. Shape the first row of laces overlapping the raw edge of the fabric portion of the collar by about 1/4 inch; you can choose to overlap more if you want to (**fig. 4**).

11. After pinning and shaping the first row of rounded laces to overlap this fabric collar, stitch a row of machine entredeux stitching at the seam line. Now, it looks as if you have entredeux on your collar and if was so much easier than actually applying entredeux. If you have excess fabric underneath your stitching, simply trim away this excess fabric from your collar after the whole collar is finished (**fig. 5**).

12. To finish the collar, simply follow all directions in the Making A Round Lace Portrait Collar section. ❈

Curving Lace

Since many heirloom sewers are also incurable romantics, it's no wonder hearts are a popular lace shape. Hearts are the ultimate design for a wedding dress, wedding attendants' clothing, or on a ring bearer's pillow. As with the other lace shaping discussed in this chapter, begin with a template when making hearts. When using our heart template, we like to shape our laces inside the heart design. Of course, shaping along the outside of the heart design is permitted also. Whatever is easiest for you.

With the writing of the *Antique Clothing* book, I thought I had really figured out the easy way to make lace hearts. After four years of teaching heart making, I have totally changed my method of making hearts. This new method is so very easy that I just couldn't wait to tell you about it. After shaping your hearts, you don't even have to remove them from the skirt to finish the heart. What a relief and an improvement! Enjoy the new method of making hearts with the new fold back miters. It is so easy and you are going to have so much fun making hearts.

1. Draw a template in the shape of a heart. Make this as large or as small as you want. If you want equal hearts around the bottom of a skirt, fold the skirt into equal sections, and design the heart template to fit into one section of the skirt when using your chosen width of lace insertion.

2. Draw on your hearts all the way around the skirt if you are using several hearts. As always, when shaping lace, draw the hearts onto the fabric where you will be stitching the laces.

3. Draw a 2-inch bisecting line at the top into the center and at the bottom of the heart into the center (**fig. 1**).

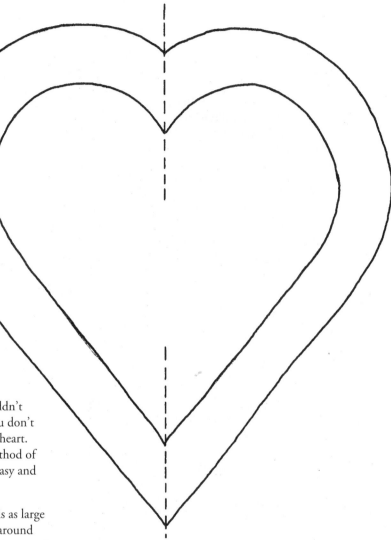

NOTE: I would like to refresh your memory on lace shaping along the bottom of a skirt at this time. You make your hearts (or whatever else you wish to make) above the skirt while the skirt still has a straight bottom. Later after stitching your hearts (or whatever else) to the skirt, you cut away to make the shaped skirt bottom .

4. Lay the fabric with the hearts drawn on top, on top of the fabric board. As always, pin the lace shaping through the lace, the fabric and into the fabric board.

5. Cut one piece of lace which will be large enough to go all the way around one heart with about 4 inches extra. Before you begin shaping the lace, leave about 2 inches of lace on the outside of the bottom line.

6. Place a pin at **point A**. Beginning at the bottom of the heart, pin the lace on the inside of the heart template. The pins will actually be on the outside of the lace insertion; however, you are shaping your laces on the inside of your drawn heart template.

7. Work around the heart to **point C**, placing pins at 1/2-inch intervals. Notice that the outside will be pinned rather tightly and the inside will be curvy. **Note:** One of our math teacher students told me years ago, while I was teaching this lace shaping, a very important fact. She said, "Martha did you know that a curved line is just a bunch of straight lines placed in a funny way?" She said this as I was trying to explain that it was pretty easy to get the straight lace pinned into a curve. Since I remembered as little about my math classes as possible, I am sure that I didn't know this fact. It makes it a lot easier to explain taking that straight lace and making a curve out of it to know that fact.

8. After finishing pinning around, to the center of the heart, place another pin at **point D** (**fig. 2**).

9. Lay the lace back on itself curving it into the curve that you just pinned (**fig. 3**). Remove the pin from **Point D**, and repin it this time pinning through both layers of lace.

10. Wrap the lace to the other side and begin pinning around the other side of the heart. Where you took the lace back on itself and repinned, there will be a miter which appears just like magic. This is the new fold-back miter which is just as wonderful on hearts as it is on diamonds and scalloped skirts.

11. Pin the second side of the lace just like you pinned the first one. At the bottom of the heart lay the laces one over the other and put a pin at **point B** (**fig. 4**).

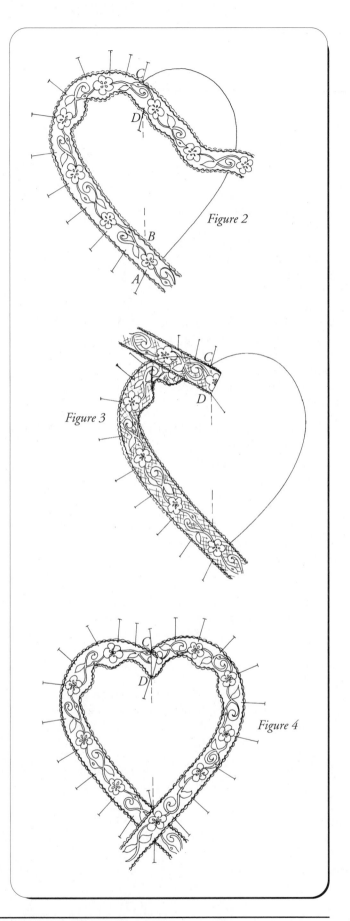

Figure 2

Figure 3

Figure 4

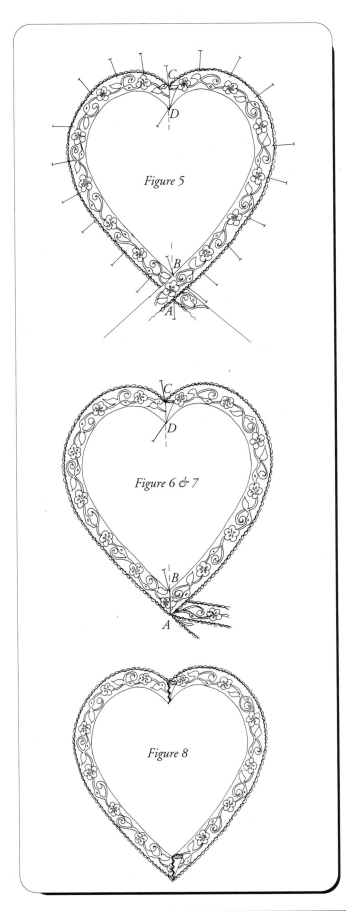

Figure 5

Figure 6 & 7

Figure 8

12. It is now time to pull the threads to make the curvy insides of the heart lay flat and become heart shaped. You can pull threads either from the bottom of the heart or threads from the center of each side of the heart. I prefer to pull the threads from the bottom of the heart. Pull the threads and watch the heart lay down flat and pretty. (**fig. 5**).

After teaching literally hundreds of students to make hearts, I think it is better to pull the thread from the bottom of the heart. You don't need to help the fullness lay down; simply pull the thread. On other lace shaped curves such as a scalloped skirt, loops, or ovals, you have to pull from the inside curve.

13. Spray starch and press the curves into place.

14. To make your magic miter at the bottom of the heart, remove the pin from **Point A**, fold back the lace so it lays on the other piece of lace, and repin **Point A**. You now have a folded back miter which completes the easy mitering on the heart (**fig. 6**). You are now ready to pin the hearts flat onto the garment and remove the shaping from the fabric board.

15. You can trim these bottom "tails" of lace away before you attach the heart to the garment or after you attach the heart to the garment. It probably looks better to trim them before you stitch (**Fig. 7**).

16. You can attach the hearts just to the fabric or you can choose to put something else such as pintucks inside the hearts. If you have hearts which touch going all the way around a skirt, then follow the directions for zigzagging which were found in the diamond section

17. If you have one heart on a collar or bodice of a dress, then zigzag the outside first. If you choose to put something on the inside of each heart, cut away the fabric from behind the shape after zigzagging it to the garment. Then, put whatever you want to insert in the heart behind the heart shape and zigzag around the center or inside of the heart. Refer to the directions on inserting pintucks or something else in the center of a lace shape in the flip flopped bow section.

18. You can certainly use the entredeux/wing needle stitching for a beautiful look for attaching the hearts. Follow the directions for machine entredeux on the lace shaped skirt found in the diamond section of this lace shaping chapter.

19. After you cut away the fabric from behind the hearts, go back and zigzag over each mitered point (**fig. 8**). You then have the choice of either leaving the folded over section or of cutting it away. Personally, I usually leave the section because of the strength it adds to the miters. The choice is yours. ※

Shaping Curves And Angles With Pintucks

Pintucks are inexpensive to make. They add texture and dimension without adding cost to the dress. They're rarely found on store-bought clothing. One of my favorite things in the whole world to do is to follow pintucked shapes with lace insertion or decorative stitches on your machine for an enchanting finish. Simply use your template and pintuck, then use the insertion like you would use any Swiss handloom. For threads, use white-on-white, ecru-on-ecru, or any pastel color on white or ecru.

The effect of shaped pintucks is so fabulous and so interesting. Virtually everybody is afraid that she doesn't know how to make those fabulous pintucks thus making a garment into a pintuck fantasy. It is so easy that I just can't wait to share with you the tricks. I promise, nobody in my schools all over the world ever believes me when I tell them this easiest way. Then, everybody, virtually everybody, has done these curved and angled pintucks with absolute perfection. They usually say, "This is really magic!"

The big question here is, "What foot do I use for scalloped pintucks?" For straight pintucks, I use a pintuck foot with the grooves. That foot is fine for curved or scalloped pintucks also, but I prefer either the regular zigzag foot or the clear applique foot, which is plastic and allows easy "see through" of the turning points. Try your pintuck foot, your regular sewing foot, and your clear applique foot to see which one you like the best. Like all aspects of heirloom sewing, the "best" foot is really your personal preference. Listed betlow are my absolute recommendations for curved and angled intucks.

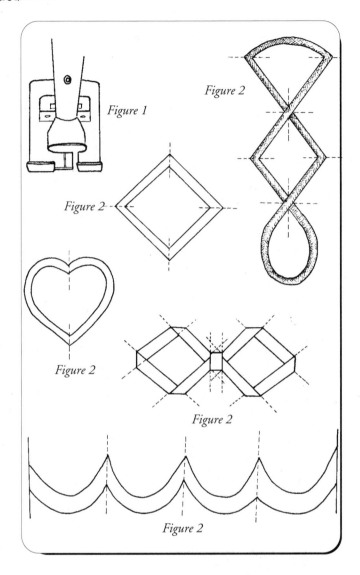

Figure 1

Figure 2

Figure 2

Figure 2

Figure 2

Figure 2

Martha's General Rules Of Curving And Angling Pintucks

1. Use a regular zigzag foot, or a pintuck foot (**fig. 1**).

2. Either draw on your pintuck shape, or zigzag your lace insertion to the garment. You can either draw on pintuck shapes or follow your lace shaping. My favorite way to make lots of pintucks is to follow lace shaping which has already been stitched to the garment.

3. Using a ruler, draw straight lines with a fabric marker or washable pencil, bisecting each point where you will have to turn around with your pintuck. In other words, draw a line at all angles where you will have to turn your pintuck in order to keep stitching. This is the most important point to make with curved and angled pintucks. When you are going around curves, this bi-secting line is not necessary since you don't stop and pivot when you are turning curves. Everywhere you have to stop and pivot, these straight lines must be drawn (**fig. 2**).

4. Use a 1.6 or a 2.0 double needle. Any wider doesn't curve or turn well!

5. Set your machine for straight sewing, W=1.5. Notice this is a **very short stitch**. When you turn angles, this short stitch is necessary for pretty turns.

6. Press Needle Down on your sewing machine if your machine has this feature. This means that when you stop sewing at any time, your needle will remain in the fabric.

7. Stitch, using either the first line you drew or following around the lace shaping which you have already stitched to your garment. The edge of your presser foot will guide

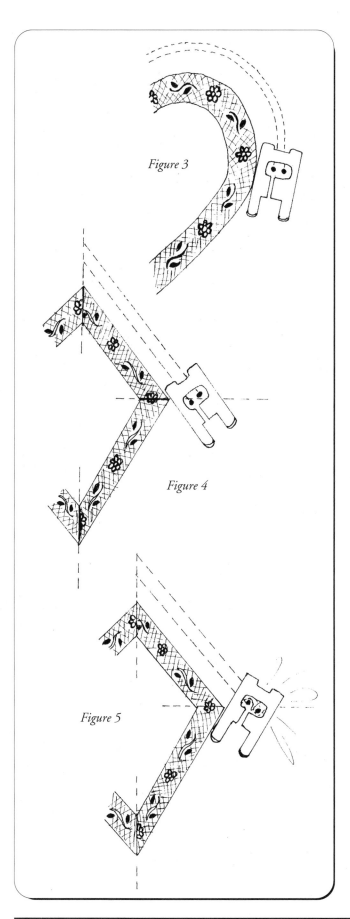

Figure 3

Figure 4

Figure 5

along the outside of the lace shape. When you go around curves, turn your fabric and keep stitching; do not pick up your foot and pivot. This makes the curves jumpy, not smooth (**fig. 3**).

8. When you come to a pivot point, let your foot continue to travel until you can look into the hole of the foot, and see that your double needles have **straddled the line you drew on the fabric.** Remember your needles are **in the fabric** (**fig. 4**).

9. Sometimes, the needles won't exactly straddle the line exactly the way they straddled the line on the last turn around. Lift the presser foot. (Remember, you needles are still in the fabric.) Turn your fabric where the edge of the presser foot properly begins in a new direction following your lace insertion lace shaping or your drawn line, lower the presser foot, and begin sewing again (**fig. 5**).

10. Wait A Minute! Most of you are now thinking, "Martha You Are Crazy. There are two major problems with what you just said. You said to leave the double needles in the fabric, lift the presser foot , turn the fabric, lower the presser foot and begin sewing again. If I do that I will probably break my double needles, and there will be a big wad or hump of fabric where I twisted the fabric to turn around to go in a new directions. That will never work!" I know you are thinking these two things because everybody does. Neither one of these things will happen! It is really just like MAGIC. TRY THIS TECHNIQUE AND SEE WHAT I AM SAYING. Ladies all over the world absolutely adore this method and nobody believes how easy it is.

11. After you get your first row of double needle pintucks, then you can use the edge of your regular zigzag sewing machine foot guiding along the just stitched pintuck row as the guide point for more rows. The only thing you have to remember, is to have made long enough lines to bisect each angle that you are going to turn. You must have these turn around lines drawn so you can know where to stop sewing, leave the needles in the fabric, turn around, and begin stitching again. These lines are the real key.

Making A Skirt For Curved Pintuck Scallops Or Other Fancy Design

I always like to give the easiest way to do anything. Probably most of you know that by now! To divide any garment piece (skirt, bodice, collar or whatever) into equal parts, fold it in half. This marks the half-way point. Continue to fold in halves until the piece is divided the way you want it. If you are to mark the bottom of a skirt, seam (French seam, flat lock or rolled serger hem) one side seam first so that you can work on the entire skirt (**fig. 1**).

If you want to use this skirt for curved pintucks only, that is great. If you want to use the drawn scallop to make a scalloped piece of lace insertion, then you will guide your regular zigzag sewing machine foot with the double needles along the scalloped lace insertion later for your curved pintucks. Remember, those bisecting straight lines are the most significant part of making pintucks turn around properly at angles.

1. Take your skirt, sleeve, bodice, or pattern part and fold it in half. Press (**fig. 2**).

2. Fold that in half again. Press. If you have a skirt with the front and back already stitched together on one side, you now have it folded in quarters. The seam will be on one side. Press on that seam line.

3. Fold in half again. Press. Your piece is now divided into eighths (**fig. 3**).

4. Repeat this process as many times as necessary for you to have the divisions that you want.

5. Open up your garment part. Use these fold lines as your measuring points and guide points (**fig. 4**).

6. It is now time to make one template which will fit between the scallops. Using this illustration make one template, only, with partial scallops on either side of this template. Use a piece of typing paper or notebook paper (**fig. 5**). You can go to the cupboard and get a dinner plate, a saucer, or a coffee can or whatever to draw your one scallop which goes between the folds. Measure up evenly on each side of the scallop before you make this one pattern. Where the curve of the scallop meets the folded line of the skirt must be evenly placed on either side. After you have made your one pattern, you are ready to trace the first row of scallops on the skirt.

7. Make the template pattern where the bottom of the piece of paper lines up with the bottom of the skirt. Each time you move the paper over to mark a new scallop you can always line up the bottom of this template with the bottom of the skirt. Draw the scallops and the dotted A-B lines also.

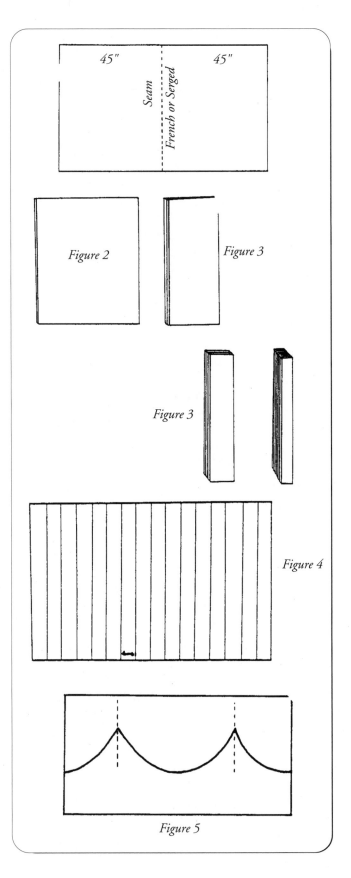

Figure 2

Figure 3

Figure 3

Figure 4

Figure 5

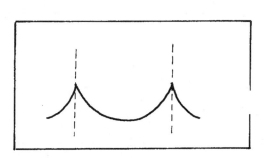

Figure 5

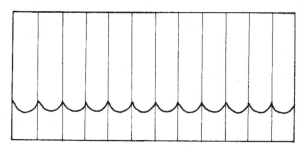

Figure 6

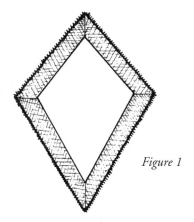

Figure 1

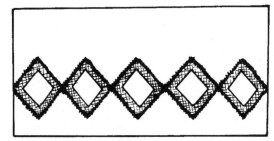

Figure 2

8. Draw dotted lines bisect the tops and bottoms of the scallops (**fig.** 5). Make these lines as tall as you want your pintuck sets to go. These lines serve as the turn around points for all of your pintucks. **They are absolutely necessary for correct turning around at the angles. These lines are the real keys to perfect sets of pintucks traveling in any angle and turning around at the proper point.**

9. Trace with a fabric marker the scallops between the fold lines (**fig.** 6). Since you made your pattern where the bottom of the piece of paper follows along the bottom of the skirt, your scallops will be equally spaced and be properly aligned with the bottom of the fabric. You will move your template from fold to fold marking the whole scallop and a part of the next one. Mark the straight up and down lines bisecting each scallop. These lines will be along the fold lines. When you move your template over to the next fold to mark the next scallop you will line up three things: the last piece of the scallop which overlaps, the straight lines, and the bottom of your template along the bottom of the skirt.

10. Use the curved lines for making only the first row of machine pintucks. After that you can use the edge of your sewing machine foot for guiding the next row of scallops.

11. Follow directions from "Martha's General Rules Of Curving And Angling Pintucks," page 255.

Making Strips Of Pintucking To Insert In Center Of Lace Shapes

One of the prettiest things to do in lace shaping is to make a strip of double needle pintucks and insert these pintucks behind the center of a heart, a diamond, a bow, or an oval. There are several methods of inserting this pintucked strip behind a lace shape. I think the one below is the easiest.

1. Make your heart, diamond, or bow and zigzag or machine entredeux stitch (**outside only**) to the garment skirt, collar, bodice, or whatever. In other words, make all of the shapes that you are going to make and zigzag the outside only to the garment (**fig.** 1). Note: If you are making a heart, diamond, oval or bow skirt, go ahead and stitch all the hearts around the skirt (**outside stitching only**) **fig.** 2. Trim away the inside fabric of the diamonds, several at a time. Stitch the pinstitching in each of those trimmed hearts before trimming the inside fabric of the next hearts.

2. Make a straight strip of machine pintucks longer that the actual insides of the shapes, and a little bit taller also (**fig.** 3).

3. After zigzagging or machine entredeux stitching the **outside only, of the lace shape** (diamond, heart, bow, loop or whatever) to the garment, cut away the whole fabric inside of the lace shape. It is alright to cut almost to the stitching since the heavy stitching of a heavy zigzag or the

machine entredeux stitching has hundreds of stitches holding the shape to the garment (**fig. 3**). **Note:** If you are making a heart, diamond, oval or bow skirt, go ahead and stitch all the hearts around the skirt (**outside stitching only**). Trim away the inside of the hearts several at a time. Stitch the pinstitching in each of those trimmed hearts before trimming the inside fabric of the next hearts.

4. Place the pintucked strip behind one shape at a time. Stitch around the inside of the shape attaching a portion of the pintucked strip (**fig. 4**). You can either zigzag , machine entredeux stitch or machine pin stitch.

5. Trim away the pintucked strip very close to the zigzag zagging from behind lace heart, diamond, bow or oval.

Stitching One Or Two Rows Of Pintucks Inside A Fancy Lace Shape

Unlike inserting a strip of pintucks into a lace shape, when you want to stitch only one or two rows of pintucks following the shape within a heart, bow, diamond, oval or whatever, you do not have to cut away the fabric. You will use your double needles, a regular zigzag foot , and the drawn lines bisecting each turn around point.

1. Make your desired lace shape such as a heart, bow, diamond, oval or whatever. Attach to garment.

2. After shaping your desired lace shape, simply draw the bisecting lines to intersect the turn around points. Draw the lines only to the inside of the shape if you are only going to put pintucks on the inside of the shape (**fig. 1**).

3. Using your regular zigzag foot and your 1.6 or 2.0 pintuck double needles, travel around the inside of the lace shape using the edge of the zigzag foot to guide alone your lace shapes. Use a needle down position and a straight stitch with a length=1.5.

4. Using the directions for making curved and angled pintucks, stitch within the figure.

Making Double Needle Shadow Embroidery Designs

When I was in Australia, one of my students who is a sewing teacher in New Zealand asked me if I had ever made shadow embroidered double needle designs. I replied that I hadn't but that I was certainly interested. She then painted on liquid stabilizer, let it dry and placed this piece of fabric in an embroidery hoop. She then drew a shadow work design from my shadow work embroidery book, put in 2.0 double needles, white thread, and proceeded to stitch all the away around that shadow work bow simply straight stitching with a short stitch (1.5 length) and made a perfectly acceptable looking shadow embroidered bow. She used a regular zigzag sewing foot not a

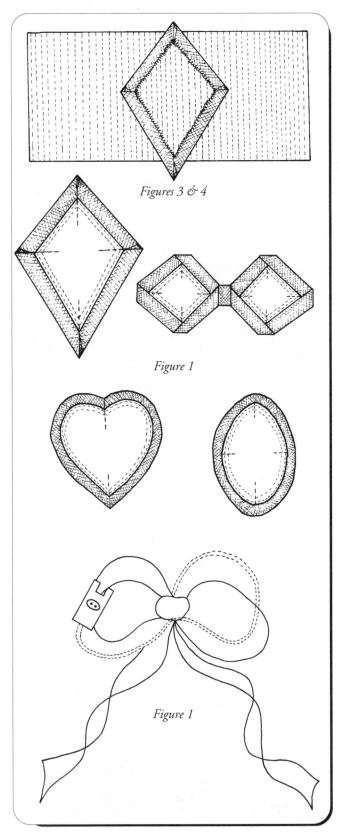

Figures 3 & 4

Figure 1

Figure 1

pintuck foot with her double needles. Now, shadow work embroidery, it isn't; however, it is very lovely and very quick. You might want to try it (**fig. 1**). ▓

Advanced Techniques

Shaped Puffing

Narrow puffing strips can be shaped in many of the same ways in which wide lace insertion can be shaped. This technique for puffing should be used only for decorative effects, and not on sleeve cuffs, for yoke-to-skirt attachments, or any place where there is stress on the fabric, because it is not as strong as puffing made with entredeux. It is a lovely treatment for skirts or collars. The loops and teardrops shown here have a little Swiss embroidered motif in the center; however, you could use lace insertion or a lace rosette in the center.

Puffing Directions

1. On paper, trace around the Swiss motif. Draw another line the width of the insertion away from the motif outline. Draw another line 1" (or desired width of puffing) beside 2nd line. Draw another line the width of insertion outside the 3rd line. Draw lines at the bottom to continue into smooth scallops (**fig. 1**).

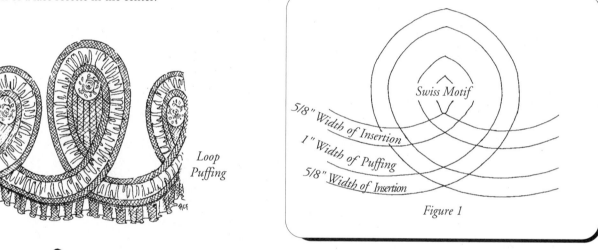

5/8" Width of Insertion

1" Width of Puffing

5/8" Width of Insertion

Swiss Motif

Figure 1

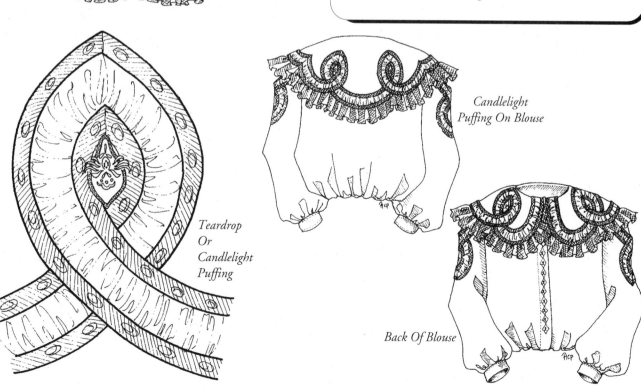

Loop Puffing

Teardrop Or Candlelight Puffing

Candlelight Puffing On Blouse

Back Of Blouse

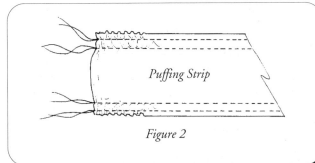

Puffing Strip

Figure 2

2. Cut lots of puffing strips 3/4" wider than your finished puffing. Run gathering threads 1/8" and 1/2" from each long edge. Use cotton covered polyester thread, loosened top tension, stitch length 2.5, stitch with bobbin thread on right side of strips (**fig.** 2).

3. Gather puffing strip to approximately 2:1 fullness and distribute gathers evenly. Place puffing strip over fabric (over fabric board), and pin in place as you would shaped insertion. Pull up gathering threads on inner curves to make puffing lay flat, just as you would pull the thread in the heading of lace insertion. Use your fingernail to distribute gathers (**fig.** 3).

4. Baste or pin puffing in place close to raw edges. Shape insertion along drawn lines. Remove pins from fabric board. Zigzag in place except for very center of loop (**fig** 4). Trim all layers from behind lace and puffing.

5. Place Swiss motif in center of loop and zigzag to lace.

Narrow Puffing With A Gathering Foot

You can use the gathering foot on your sewing machine to make this narrow puffing around the curves. Carefully place the inside gathers with your fingers. Then, pin. It really does work! ▓

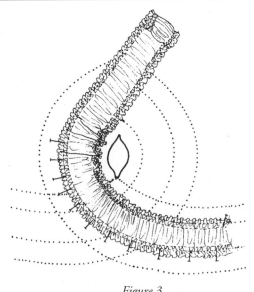

Figure 3

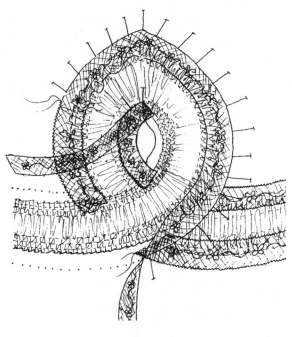

Figure 4

Celtic Lace Designs

Quilting designs take on many different shapes and forms. Celtic quilting is the use of narrow bias strips of fabric used to create a design. These designs, inspired by Celtic art, are put in template form and traced on the fabric. The bias strips are then shaped over the template designs thus creating the Celtic quilting technique. Celtic lace shaping is simply replacing the bias strips of fabric with lace insertion. The lace insertion is shaped over the Celtic design template traced on the fabric. The lace is then stitched in place, creating a beautiful, intricate lace design. The fabric can then be cut away from the lace or the fabric can be left behind the lace.

An infinite number of Celtic designs would be possible for the person with the patience to imagine and draw them. In addition to Celtic designs, a lot of other quilting designs can be the inspiration for creative lace shaping.

I think very narrow lace insertion (less than 1/2 inch wide) will be best in nearly all situations. As I look through quilting design books lots and lots of designs stand out in my mind as being lovely to interpret into lace shaping. I love the Hawaiian, shell, scallops, leaves, flowers, baskets, Virginia Reel, Grandmother's Flower Garden, hearts, gladioli, crazy quilt, wedding ring, lots of applique designs, tulips, sunflowers, daisies, forget-me-not, or wild rose. The possibilities are absolutely endless.

Several years ago I wouldn't have said that geometric designs are suitable for lace shaping. One summer at our school, a lady modeled the most beautiful linen dress with geometric quilting designs done in laces. It was very tailored and very lovely. So, the sky is really the limit when using quilting designs for lace shaping.

Lace Requirements

• Every line on the lace motif should be continuous.

• No more than two lines should cross at any intersection.

Lace Requirements

1. The insertion needs to be very narrow (3/8 inch or less) to be shaped into the tight curves and loops in these designs.

2. The lace must be woven in an "over, under, over, under" (weaving) manner. There should not be two overs and two unders next to each other.

3. Divide the template into sections or continuous loops (from one "under" to another "under"). The lace pieces will be easier to "weave" if the lace pieces are of shorter

measure. Use a tape measure to determine the length of each continuous loop of lace, cut lace a few inches longer than these measurements.

Celtic Lace Shaping Rules

1. Start at an "under."

2. Allow the raw end of the lace to extend 1/4 inch.

3. Patiently shape the lace directly onto the fabric, shaping all curves and mitering corners.

4. Follow the "over" and "under" markings, gently weaving the insertions under the sections of lace already pinned down at the appropriate points.

5. You should end each section at the same "under" at which you started. Shape and pin the lace on the entire motif before you do any sewing. Starch and press.

Stitching Celtic Design In Place

1. Use a small pin stitch if possible to stitch if possible to stitch the insertion down, or a zigzag if you machine does not do a pinstitch.

2. Begin stitching at an "under," and end the stitching by backstitching when you come to an "under."

3. Continue in the manner until all the insertion is stitched down.

4. Rinse the fabric in warm water to remove all the markings, and press to dry.

5. Using a very small, very sharp scissors, carefully trim away all fabric from behind the insertion. Also trim away the lace on the underside of the intersections to enhance the woven appearance of this technique. ▧

Using The Patterns

Each applique design can be dissected into smaller pieces. Some of the applique pieces may extend under other applique pieces. Some applique designs are drawn with a dotted line extending from the appliqued piece. This shows that the fabric extension is under another piece. When dissecting these designs, watch for these dotted lines. When you are tracing your pattern which will later be used for cutting out your applique fabric, include the dotted extension as a part of your pattern.

For example, on the coal car of the train, the coal pattern piece extends under the body of the car and the body of the car extends under the wheels (**fig. 1**). This is the applique design. Here are the dissected pieces.

Some applique patterns have a definite right and left side (**fig. 2**). For example, letters of the alphabet (B, E, R), or a clown holding balloons with his left hand (**fig. 3**). Other patterns do not, such as the letter A (uppercase) or O. Keep this in mind when following the directions below.

1. Tracing Pattern On Bonding Agent

If Wonder Under™ or another paper-backed bonding agent is used, **trace each individual pattern piece on paper backing**, with a permanent fine-tip marker. Since the pattern is placed on the wrong side of the fabric, and if it has a definite right and wrong side, the pattern should be traced in reverse. Any design traced exactly as it is featured in this book will appear in reverse on the project.

Take the clown applique as an example. If the clown were holding balloons in his left hand and that is how you want it to look on the garment, the design would need to be traced in reverse. If the balloons on the completed project need to be in the clown's right hand, trace as is. All samples in this book were traced in reverse first.

Tracing A Pattern In Reverse Image

1. Photocopy or trace the design from this book.

2. Hold the design to a window with the design facing outside.

3. Trace the design on the back of the paper.

4. This newly traced design is your reverse image.

2. Roughly Cut Pattern

Roughly cut out pattern pieces to separate, leaving about 1/4 inch to 1/2 inch around pattern lines. **Do not cut** pattern on cutting lines at this time (**fig. 4**).

Figure 1

Figure 2

Figure 3

Figure 4

3. Fusing

Follow the bonding agent instructions and fuse to the wrong side of a square of applique fabric. Be sure the bonding agent does not extend past the edges of the fabric to be appliqued (**fig. 5**).

4. Cutting Out Applique

Cut out applique pieces along cutting lines. Remember to use the dotted extensions where indicated as the cutting lines.

* **Fine Fuse™ or Stitch Witchery™ (fig. 6)**

a. An applique pressing sheet is required. Plastic coated freezer paper or lightweight iron-on stabilizer is also needed.

b. Trace pattern pieces onto paper side of freezer paper or stabilizer with a fine- tip permanent marker. Since the pattern is placed on the right side of the fabric the pattern should be traced as is, no reversal is necessary.

c. Press to right side of applique fabric.

d. Fuse bonding agent to wrong side of fabric using the pressing sheet between bonding agent. Iron according to manufacturer's instructions.

e. Peel off pressing sheet. Cut out pattern pieces along lines traced on the stabilizer. There will be paper on the right side and the bonding agent on the wrong side of each piece.

5. Placing Applique Pieces

a. Place pattern pieces on base fabric in desired position, fitting pieces together as you would a puzzle. Remember when putting the pieces together, the background pieces may extend under foreground pieces (designated by dotted lines). This will help you to see how the final design will look, as well as decipher where each piece will be fused (**fig.** 7).

b. Slide applique to the side, away from placement of design. While looking at the total design, remove paper backing from first piece to be fused. If paper is difficult to remove try scratching an X or a line in the paper backing with a straight pin or needle. This will help release the paper from the applique piece.

c. Fuse in position. Repeat in order for other pieces. Fusing order instructions are given for each design. **Note:** The background pieces are fused first, layering perspectively to the foreground to complete the fusing of the design.

6. Stabilizer

Place stabilizer under base fabric in the area of the applique (**fig. 8**).

7. Stitching

Satin stitch each piece, background to foreground. Satin stitch maneuvers, including straight lines, curves, corners, and points will be discussed in the section, *Stitch Maneuvers.*

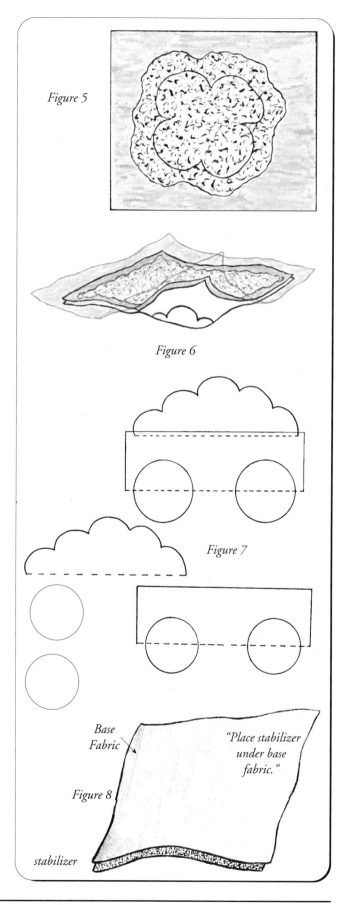

Figure 5

Figure 6

Figure 7

Base Fabric

"Place stabilizer under base fabric."

Figure 8

stabilizer

Applique Stitch Maneuvers

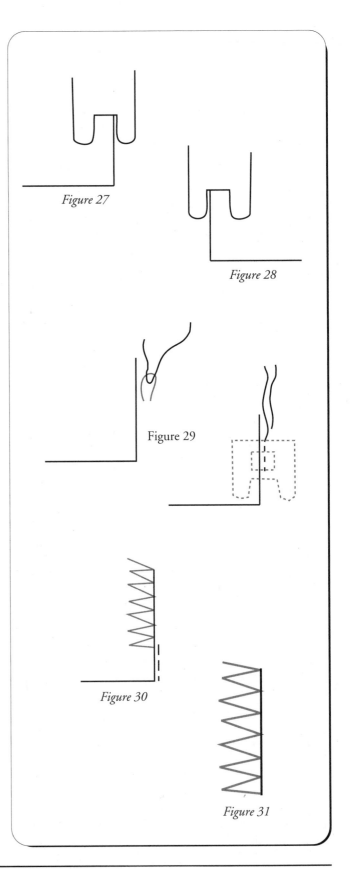

Figure 27

Figure 28

Figure 29

Figure 30

Figure 31

General Directions

1. Never start stitching at a corner or point; start at a straight side or curve.

2. Preferably, the applique piece should be positioned so that the left swing of the needle (zig) stitches on the applique piece and the right swing of the needle (zag) stitches off the applique piece (**fig. 27**). **All stitch maneuver directions are given with applique piece positioned on the left needle swing unless otherwise indicated.** Sometimes the applique piece should be placed on the right needle swing (**fig. 28**). Applique piece position is provided in such maneuvers.

3   **Tie-On** (**fig. 29**). Using a short straight stitch, take one complete stitch on the fabric right next to the applique. Pull gently on the top thread, bringing the bobbin thread to the top side of the fabric. Place threads under and behind foot. Take several straight stitches on base fabric just off applique.

4. Set machine to desired zigzag width and length. (Note the stitch width, length and tension of practice pieces in *Machine Settings - Tension*) If "needle down" is available on your machine, it will be helpful in satin stitching and pivoting. Reposition applique so that zigzag stitches are placed mostly on the applique but extend completely off the edge of the applique. This will stitch the applique piece on in a neat fashion encasing the raw edges of the applique. If the entire stitch is taken on the applique, fuzzy may occur on the edge of the applique piece. If you don't stitch enough on the applique fabric, the applique may pull from the stitching.

5. Take all stitches perpendicular to the edge of the applique.

6. Stitch individual pieces and detail lines (that identify arms, legs, flower petals, etc.), working background to foreground.

7. Do not push or pull but simply guide the fabric through the machine. Let the machine do the work. A gentle nudge may be required when crossing over previous stitching.

8. **Tie-Off** (**fig. 30**). Change to a short straight stitch, reposition applique, and take several straight stitches just beside the satin stitch.

9. Cut threads very close to the stitching.

10. Complete design using steps 1-8 on this page.

11. With a water-soluble marker, transfer any straight stitch detail not previously satin stitched (eyes, mouth, hair, nose, glasses). These will be stitched using *Free-Motion Embroidery*.

Straight Lines

Follow steps in General Directions (**fig. 31**).

Outside and Inside

1. Zigzag along the applique as described in steps 1 - 7 of the *General Directions*. While stitching along a curve, the stitching will fail to be perpendicular to the applique, therefore pivoting is required. There is more area to cover along the outside edge of the curve, so the pivot must be taken with the needle down at this outside edge (**fig. 32**).

2. To pivot on a curve, leave the needle in the **outside edge of the curve** (not specifically on the zig or the zag). Raise the foot and pivot very slightly, keeping the stitches perpendicular to the edge of the applique. It is better to pivot too often than not often enough. If the needle is left in the inside edge of the curve while pivoting, a V will occur in the stitching.

Note: When stitching around a curve, the tendency is to force the stitching without pivoting. This will cause the applique edge to be wavy, therefore pivoting is very important!

Pivoting Rule For Curves: To pivot on an outside curve, the needle is left in the fabric right next to the applique piece. To pivot on an inside curve the needle is left in the applique piece itself.

Corners

Block Corners

Any zigzag sewing machine will accomplish this very simple method of turning corners.

Outside Block Corners
Method 1

1. Zigzag along the applique as described in steps 1 - 7 of the *General Directions*.

2. Stitch down first side to corner, stopping with the needle down at the point of the corner (**fig. 33**).

3. Pivot 90° (**fig. 34**). Walk the machine by using the fly wheel to take the first stitch that should be placed in the edge of the previous stitching.

4. Continue stitching along the second side (**fig. 35**). Some machines may need a little push to begin satin stitching the second side at the corner. To keep the machine from bogging down at this point, push gently by placing fingers along the sides of the foot to help move the stitching over the previous satin stitch at the corner.

Outside Block Corner
Method 2

1. Zigzag along the applique as described in steps 1 - 7 of *General Directions*.

2. Stitch down first side to corner, stopping with the needle down on the left swing [not on the point of the corner (zag) but on the other side (zig)] (**fig. 36**).

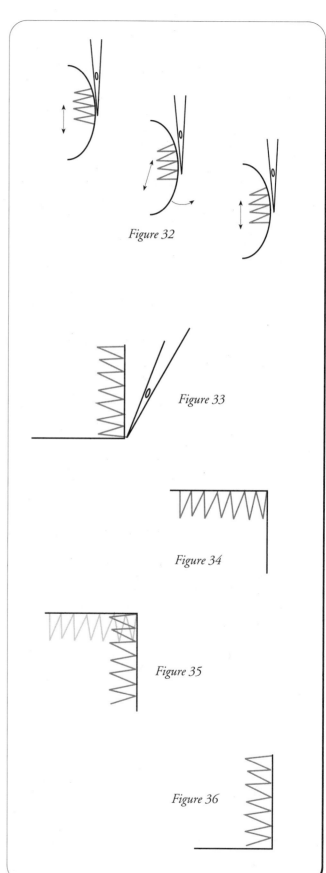

Figure 32

Figure 33

Figure 34

Figure 35

Figure 36

3. Pivot 90°. Raise needle out of fabric, raise presser foot, and reposition so that the needle pierces the same hole of the last stitch before the pivot (**fig. 37**). Lower foot.

4. Continue stitching.

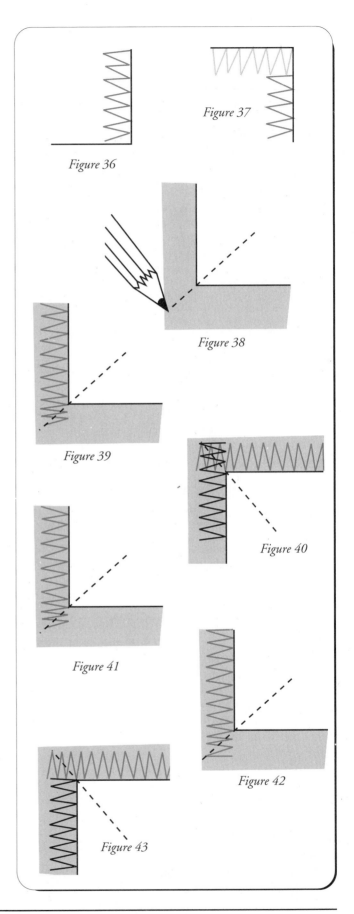

Figure 37

Figure 36

Inside Block Corner
Method 1

1. Bisect corner using a water-soluble marker (**fig. 38**).

2. With applique on left needle swing, zigzag along the applique as described in steps 1 - 7 of the General Directions. Continue stitching until the left needle swing hits the drawn line (**fig. 39**).

3. With needle in fabric, raise foot, pivot 90°, walk the machine by using the fly wheel to take the first stitch that should be placed in the edge of the previous stitching (**fig. 40**), lower foot and continue stitching along the second side.

4. Some machines may need a little push to begin satin stitching the second side at the corner. To keep the machine from bogging down at this point, push gently by placing fingers along the sides of the foot to help move the stitching over the previous satin stitch at the corner.

Figure 38

Inside Block Corner
Method 2

1. Bisect corner using a water-soluble marker (**See fig. 38**).

2. With applique on left needle swing, zigzag along the applique as described in steps 1 - 7 of the General Directions.

3. Continue stitching until the left needle swing hits the drawn line (**fig. 41**).

4. On the next stitch, leave the needle down on the right swing (**fig. 42**). Raise foot, pivot 90°, lower foot, raise needle out of fabric, raise presser foot, and reposition so that the needle pierces the same hole of the last stitch before the pivot (**fig. 43**).

5. Continue stitching along the second side.

Figure 39

Figure 40

Figure 41

Mitered Corners

Before beginning the maneuvers of miters and points it will be helpful to practice on stabilized scrap fabric, increasing and decreasing the stitch width with the right hand while guiding fabric with the left. Watch where the needle is stitching, not the stitch width knob or lever. Also practice this stitching method using right and left needle position, if available.

Mitering corners can be done if your machine has the capability of changing needle positions (right, left or both) and being able to change the stitch width while stitching in any of these needle positions. Note: Once the needle position is changed, it may stay in that position to continue stitching until the next maneuver (corner or point) is reached.

Figure 42

Figure 43

Sewing Machines with Right and Left Needle Position Outside Corner

1. Place applique pieces on the left swing of the needle.

2. Zigzag along the applique as described in steps 1 - 7 of the General Directions.

3. Stitch down first side to corner, stopping with the needle down at the point of the corner (**fig 44**).

4. Pivot 90° (**fig. 45**). Lower the foot. Note the stitch width used.

5. Raise needle from fabric, change to right needle position and a 0 stitch width. Reposition so that the needle pierces the same hole of the last stitch before the pivot.

6. Guide the fabric with the left hand while gradually increasing stitch width with the right hand, stopping at the original width setting. Changing the width from 0 to the original width should be completed when the edge of the previous stitching of the first side is reached (**fig. 46**). It will be helpful to watch where your needle is stitching, not the stitch width knob or button.

Inside Corner

1. Place the applique pieces on the left swing of the needle.

2. Bisect inside corner with water-soluble marker (**fig. 47**).

3. Zigzag along the applique as described in steps 1 - 7 of the General Directions.

4. Stitch down first side until the left swing of the needle intersects drawn line (**fig. 48**).

5. Leaving the needle down, raise the foot, pivot 90° (**fig. 49a**), lower foot. Note the stitch width being used.

6. Raise needle from fabric. Change to left needle position and a 0 stitch width. Reposition so that the needle pierces the same hole of the last stitch before the pivot.

7. Guide the fabric with the left hand while gradually increasing stitch width with the right hand, stopping at the original width setting. Changing the width from 0 to the original width should be completed when the edge of the previous stitching of the first side is reached. It will be helpful to watch where your needle is stitching, not the stitch width knob or button (**fig. 49b**).

Sewing Machines with Right Needle Position Only Outside Corner

Refer to Mitered Corners - Outside Corners.

Inside Corner

1. Refer to Mitered Corners - Inside Corner. However, applique piece must be positioned on the right needle swing.

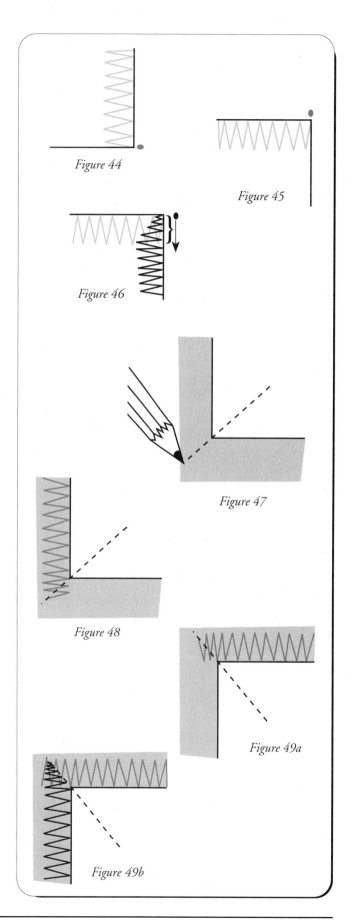

Figure 44

Figure 45

Figure 46

Figure 47

Figure 48

Figure 49a

Figure 49b

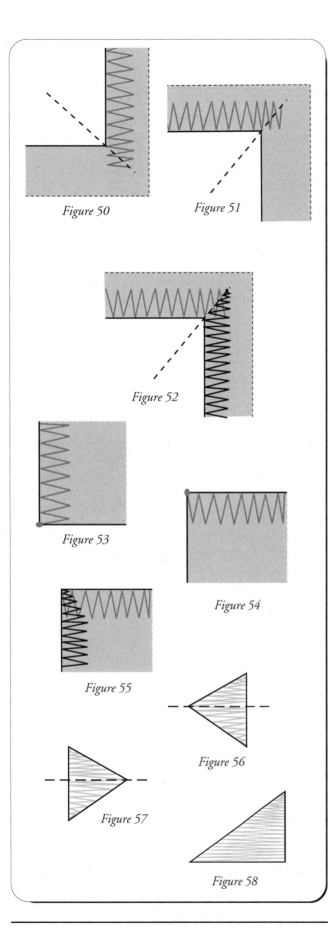

Figure 50

Figure 51

Figure 52

Figure 53

Figure 54

Figure 55

Figure 56

Figure 57

Figure 58

2. Stitch until the right swing of the needle intersects the drawn line leaving the needle down (**fig. 50**).

3. Raise the foot, pivot 90°, lower foot (**fig. 51**).

4. Note the stitch width being used. Raise needle from fabric. Change to right needle position and a 0 stitch width.

5. Reposition so that the needle pierces the same hole of the last stitch before the pivot.

6. Guide the fabric with the left hand while gradually increasing stitch width with the right hand, stopping at the original width setting. Changing the width from 0 to the original width should be completed when the edge of the previous stitching of the first side is reached (**fig. 52**). It will be helpful to watch where your needle is stitching, not the stitch width knob or button.

Sewing Machines with Left Needle Position Only Outside Corner

1. Applique piece must be positioned on the right needle swing.

2. Stitch down first side to corner, stopping with the needle down at the point of the corner (**fig. 53**).

3. Raise foot, pivot 90°, lower foot. Note the stitch width being used. Raise needle from fabric, change to left needle position and a 0 stitch width. Reposition so that the needle pierces the same hole of the last stitch before the pivot (**fig. 54**).

4. Guide the fabric with the left hand while gradually increasing stitch width with the right hand, stopping at the original width setting. Changing the width from 0 to the original width should be completed when the edge of the previous stitching of the first side is reached (**fig. 55**). It will be helpful to watch where your needle is stitching, not the stitch width knob or button.

Inside Corner

The inside corner directions are the same directions given under *Mitered Corners - Right and Left Needle Position - Inside Corners.*

*Optional Decorative Stitch Used for Mitered Corners

There are several machines that have a solid triangle as a decorative stitch. All or part of this stitch can be used to miter a corner. On a stabilized scrap fabric, work one complete pattern starting at the beginning of the pattern.

- If the pattern looks like (**fig. 56**), only half of the pattern will be used and it is in right needle position.

- If the pattern looks like (**fig. 57**), only half of the pattern will be used and it is in left needle position.

- If the pattern looks like (**fig. 58**), it is stitching in a right needle position and the entire pattern is used.

- If the pattern looks like (**fig. 59**), it is stitching in left needle position and the entire pattern is used.

- If your machine has mirror image this pattern can be stitched in either right or left needle position.

Follow directions above for appropriate needle position through the pivot.

Directions For Built In Decorative Stitch Triangle

1. Stitch down first side to corner stopping with the needle down at the point of the corner (**fig. 60**).

2. Raise foot, pivot 90°, lower foot. Note the stitch width and length being used.

3. Raise needle and engage decorative stitch matching the length and width of the original satin stitch. Stitch pattern through widest point (**fig. 61**).

4. Raise needle. Engage original satin stitch taking the first stitch by re-entering the hole of last stitch. Continue (**fig. 62**).

Points

All points are stitched in center needle position.

Outside Point

1. Applique piece on left needle swing.

2. Zigzag along the applique as described in steps 1 - 7 of the General Directions. Zigzag toward point until needle is stitching off both sides of the applique piece. Leave needle down on left side (**fig. 63**).

3. Raise foot, pivot so that point is directly toward you (**fig. 64**).

4. Note stitch width. Continue stitching to the point guiding the fabric with your left hand, while decreasing stitch width with your right hand to cover applique piece.

   a. For a sharp point it will be necessary to take the stitch width down to 0 (**Fig. 65**).

   b. For a blunt point, taking the width to 0 is not necessary (**fig. 66**).

5. Lower needle, raise foot, pivot 180° (the point of the applique piece is pointed away from you) (**fig. 67**).

6. Lower foot, raise the needle and reposition so that the first stitch will re-enter the hole of the last stitch.

7. Continue stitching away from the point, guiding the fabric with your left hand, while increasing the stitch width with your right hand to the original width. Continue stitching (**fig. 68**), pivoting as necessary to keep the satin stitches perpendicular to the applique edge.

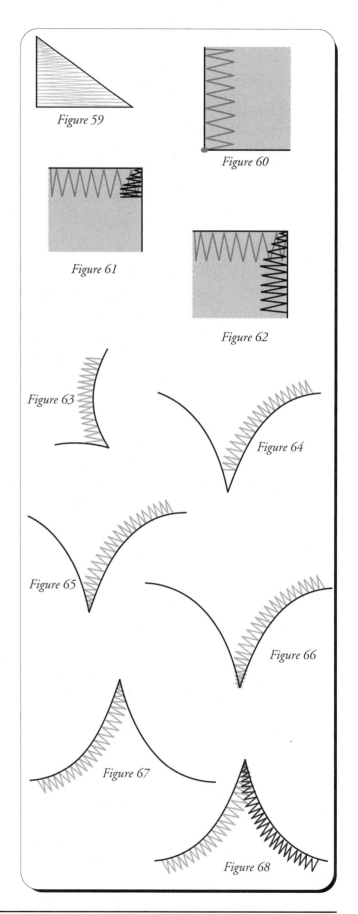

Figure 59

Figure 60

Figure 61

Figure 62

Figure 63

Figure 64

Figure 65

Figure 66

Figure 67

Figure 68

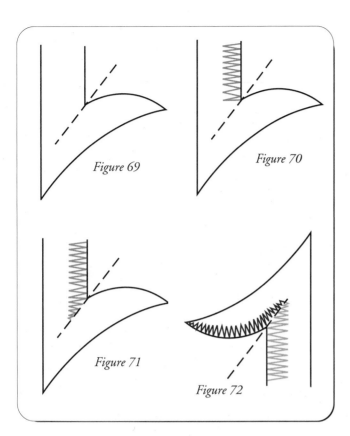

Figure 69

Figure 70

Figure 71

Figure 72

Inside Point

1. Applique piece on left needle swing.

2. Bisect the point using a water-soluble pen (**fig 69**).

3. Zigzag along the applique as described in steps 1 - 7 of the General Directions. Continue stitching until the right swing of the needle is off the applique at the point (**fig. 70**).

4. Note original stitch width. Guide the fabric with your left hand, so that the right needle swing hits the bisected line as you decrease stitch width gradually to 0 (**fig. 71**).

5. With the needle down, raise the foot, pivot approximately 180° positioning unstitched edge of applique under the foot. Lower the foot and continue stitching as you gradually increase the stitch width to the original width keeping the right needle swing butted up against the edge of the previous stitching. Continue stitching (**fig. 72**), pivoting as necessary to keep the satin stitches perpendicular to the applique edge. ▩

Detail Lines

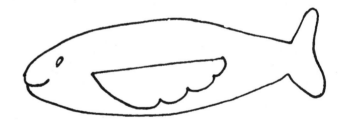

Detail Lines- (eyes, mouth, fins and fin lines)

After completing applique, stitch detail lines using straigh stitches, zigzag stitches or decorative stitches. Detail lines can also be stitched by hand.

← *Detail lines*

Shadow Applique

Different colored fabrics can be applied to the wrong side of a sheer fabric to give a shadow effect. This simple technique can be applied to collars, blouse fronts, cuffs, and skirt hems. An open zigzag, blanket stitch or other decorative stitch can be used to apply the colored fabrics to the base fabrics.

Supplies

- ❈ Sheer Base Fabric (blouse, collar, etc.)
- ❈ Bright or Dark Appliqué Fabric
- ❈ Open Toe appliqué foot
- ❈ Machine Embroidery Thread
- ❈ Size 70 to 80 Needle
- ❈ 6" to 8" Hoop (Wooden machine embroidery or spring tension)
- ❈ Marking Pens or Pencils, Water or Air Soluble
- ❈ Small, Sharp Pointed Scissors
- ❈ Appliqué Scissors

Shadow Applique Fabrics

1. Base Fabric

The base fabric should be a sheer fabric so that the fabric appliqué will show through from the wrong side. If a fabric other than white is used, experiment to see how it will change the color of the appliqué fabric. The appliqué will show more distinctly after it is lined.

2. Appliqué Fabric

The appliqué color should be bright enough to show through base fabric. Some colors will look "muddy" under the base fabric. Always test appearance of color by placing a single layer of appliqué fabric between two layers of the base fabric.

General Shadow Appliqué

Directions

1. To determine the size of base fabric to be shadow appliqued, consider the position of the appliqué. The fabric should extend beyond the appliqué design in all directions, so that it may be placed in the hoop. For example, when doing shadow appliqué on a pocket edge, even though the pocket pattern itself is small, you must start with a piece of fabric large enough to fit in the hoop (**fig. 1**). Another example would be when placing shadow appliqué near the edge of a collar, the base fabric must be large enough to contain the whole collar pattern plus enough fabric on the edges to hold in the hoop (**fig. 2**).

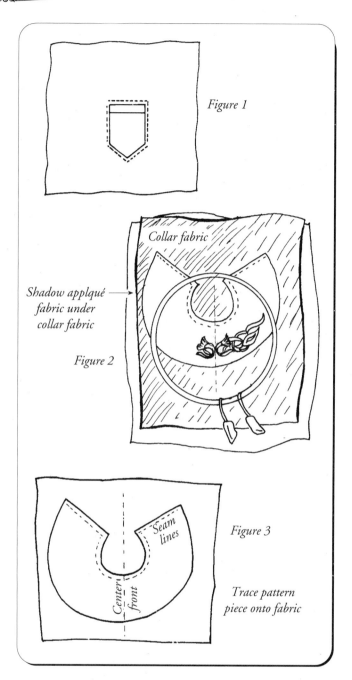

Figure 1

Collar fabric

Shadow applqué fabric under collar fabric

Figure 2

Seam lines

Center front

Figure 3

Trace pattern piece onto fabric

2. Press and starch the pretreated fabric to remove all of the wrinkles and give the fabric some body. Several applications of starch can be used.

3. Trace the pattern piece (cutting lines, seam lines and center front line and all other necessary markings) (**fig. 3**). Trace the design, within the pattern stitching lines, to the base fabric in the desired position (**fig. 4**). When tracing, especially the design for the appliqué, maintain as fine a line as possible since you will be stitching ON this line. A

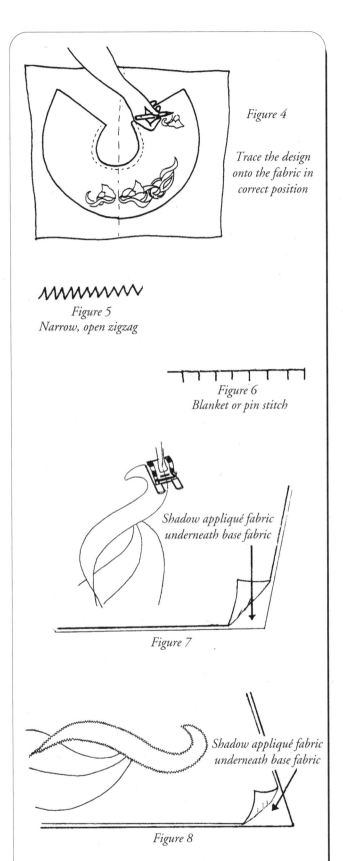

Figure 4

Trace the design onto the fabric in correct position

Figure 5
Narrow, open zigzag

Figure 6
Blanket or pin stitch

Shadow appliqué fabric underneath base fabric

Figure 7

Shadow appliqué fabric underneath base fabric

Figure 8

washable marking pencil with a sharp point is helpful. To trace the design, place the base fabric in a hoop large enough to encompass the design, this will help to hold the fabric flat and keep it from shifting while tracing (don't pull fabric too tight in hoop).

4. To determine the thread color to use, place a piece of each of the appliqué fabrics between two layers of base fabric. Match the thread to the color that shows through the base fabric. It will be lighter than the actual appliqué fabric. Use this color for the top thread. White or base fabric color thread can be used in the bobbin throughout the project.

   The upper thread tension should be loosened so that the bobbin thread will pull the top thread to the wrong side. It should not be so loose that the bobbin thread forms a straight line on the wrong side. Test to make correct adjustments.

5. Decide what stitch to use to attach the appliqué fabric to the base fabric. There are several choices.

   A narrow open zig zag can be used, a stitch width of about 1 mm and a length of 1 mm (**fig. 5**). This is not a satin stitch, but a short, narrow zig zag stitch.

   A pin stitch or blanket stitch can also be used if your machine has this capability (**fig. 6**). The pin stitch generally has a heavier look than the blanket stitch. The stitch width should be narrowed to about 1 mm and the length may also need to be adjusted. Test on a sample to make adjustments.

6. With machine shadow appliqué, the appliqué fabric is placed to the wrong side of the base fabric and you must work from foreground to background (opposite from regular machine appliqué). Place both fabrics in a hoop, layered with the right side of the appliqué fabric to the wrong side of the base fabric. When learning to do shadow appliqué by machine, have the appliqué fabric large enough to be placed in the hoop with the base fabric. As you become more accustomed to this technique it is not necessary to place the fabrics in a hoop (**fig. 7**). When the stitching is done, care should be taken to keep the appliqué fabric from shifting or wrinkles being stitched in. Pin in place if necessary or use a touch of water soluble glue stick to hold the fabric in place. Spray starching the appliqué fabric again will help it to remain flat.

   Decide on the starting point, generally not a corner or a point. Pull up bobbin thread and tie on by taking several tiny straight stitches on the drawn line of the appliqué pattern. Stitch on design line to completely enclose area in that color (**fig. 8**). When using the pin stitch or blanket stitch, the straight part of the stitch should be on the design line and the "fingers" part or "ladder steps" of the stitch

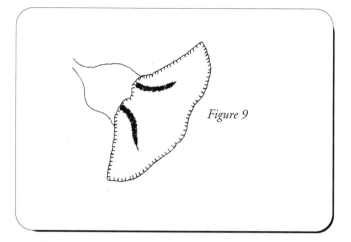

Figure 9

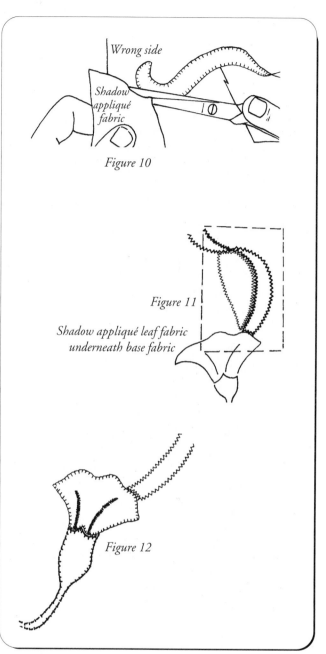

Wrong side

Shadow appliqué fabric

Figure 10

Figure 11

Shadow appliqué leaf fabric
underneath base fabric

Figure 12

should be INTO the appliqué (**fig. 9**). You may need to engage "mirror image" if your machine has this capability or stitch in the opposite direction to place the stitch correctly.

6. Trim the <u>appliqué</u> fabric close to the stitching lines, being careful not to cut the stitches (**fig. 10**). If both the base fabric and the appliqué fabric are in the hoop, remove the hoop, and re-hoop just the base fabric. Trimming will be easier if the base fabric remains in the hoop.

7. Working foreground to background, place the next color to be appliqued under the base fabric as above and stitch. For areas that touch each other, the stitching must be done on BOTH sides of the appliqué (**fig. 11**) Allow the regular zigzag stitches to just touch each other (not overlap) or the straight part of the pin or blanket stitch to be beside each other (**fig. 12**).

8. Continue in this manner until all of the appliqué pieces are attached and trimmed.

9. Wash fabric to remove all of the markings.

10. Press with the right side down on a towel. ▓

Maderia Appliqué

Madeira applique originated on the island of Madeira in Portugal. It involves stitching a fabric onto another fabric. By hand, the raw edges are turned under and the folded edge is stitched down using the Point de Paris stitch. Here, we have changed it so that it can be done on the sewing machine. This technique can be used for applying borders to collars, cuffs, etc. or used to apply shapes to collars, cuffs or garments.

Supplies:

- ❧ Base fabric
- ❧ Appliqué fabric
- ❧ Water soluble stabilizer
- ❧ Fine weight thread, machine embroidery
- ❧ Water and/or air soluble marking pens
- ❧ Trimming scissors
- ❧ Wing or large size needle for entredeux or pin stitch

Optional Supplies:

- ❧ Light box
- ❧ Temporary water-soluble, spray-on adhesive (KK-200)
- ❧ Water soluble glue stick
- ❧ Point Turner

General Madeira Appliqué
Directions

1. Pretreat all fabric since WSS will need to be rinsed away when finished.

2. Trace the appliqué pattern to the right side of a block of the appliqué fabric or on the WSS.

3. Layer the WSS to the right side of the appliqué fabric.

4. Stitch completely around the design with a short, straight stitch (1 to 1.5 mm) (fig. 1).

5. Trim the seam allowance to 1/8 inch. Clip and notch curves as needed.

6. Press flat on the fabric side.

7. Slit the WSS in the center (fig. 2)

8. Turn the WSS to the wrong side of the appliqué, which turns the seam allowance to the wrong side.

9. Press to form a sharp crease at the stitching line (fig. 3).

10. Place the appliqué piece with the turned under seam allowance in position on the base fabric. Pin or glue stick in place (fig. 4).

11. Use an entredeux, pin stitch or other desired stitch to stitch the edge of the appliqué to the base fabric (fig. 5). Adjustments in width and/or length may be required to achieve the desired look. Use of a wing or large size needle will create a more obvious hole for the entredeux or pin stitch. Always test on excess fabrics to achieve the desired effect.

12. Rinse to remove the WSS that is under the appliqué.

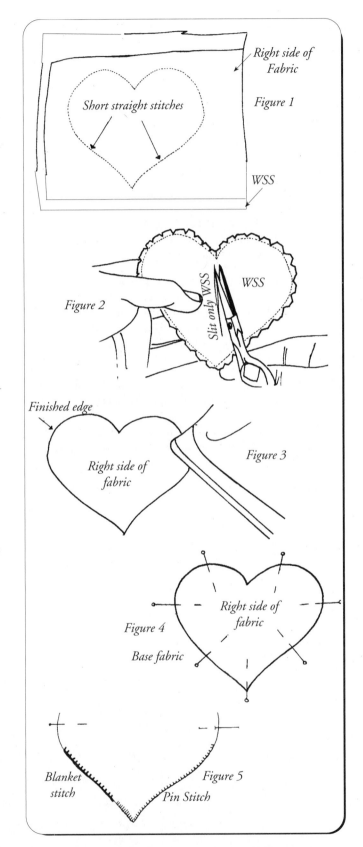

Short straight stitches

Right side of Fabric

Figure 1

WSS

Figure 2

Slit only WSS

WSS

Finished edge

Right side of fabric

Figure 3

Right side of fabric

Figure 4

Base fabric

Blanket stitch

Figure 5

Pin Stitch

Madeira Appliqué Borders

Supplies:

- ♣ Base fabric (collar, etc.)
- ♣ Appliqué fabric for border
- ♣ Water soluble stabilizer
- ♣ Fine weight thread, machine embroidery
- ♣ Water and/or air soluble marking pens
- ♣ Trimming scissors
- ♣ Wing or large size needle for entredeux or pin stitch

Optional Supplies:

- ♣ Light box
- ♣ Temporary water-soluble, spray-on adhesive (KK-200)
- ♣ Water soluble glue stick
- ♣ Point Turner

Method I

1. Pretreat all fabric since WSS will need to be rinsed away when finished.

2. Starch and press both base fabric and border fabric.

3. Trace border stitching lines onto a block of border fabric using water or air soluble pen (the inside and outside edges) (**fig. 1**).

4. Place a block of WSS to the right side of the border fabric on top of the traced stitching lines. Use of KK 200 will keep the WSS from shifting.

5. Stitch around the inside edge of the border using a short straight stitch (1 to 1.5 mm stitch length) (**fig. 2**).

6. Press along stitching on the fabric side.

7. Trim the excess fabric and WSS to 1/8 inch from stitched line. Clip and/or notch the seam allowance close to stitching (**fig. 3**).

8. Turn the WSS to the wrong side and press on the fabric side forming a sharp crease. The WSS will form a facing and keep the seam turned to the wrong side. The WSS can be pressed, but a **lower temperature** and **no steam** are required. Use a point turner for any points (**fig. 4**).

9. Cut out the pattern from the base fabric and mark border placement lines (**fig. 5**).

10. Lay the right side of the border fabric to the wrong side of the base fabric, matching the design lines. Pin in place (**fig. 6**).

11. Stitch the outside edge of the design, base fabric on top, using a short straight stitch as above (**fig. 7**). Press flat.

12. Trim seam allowance to 1/8 inch, clip or notch all curves (**fig. 8**).

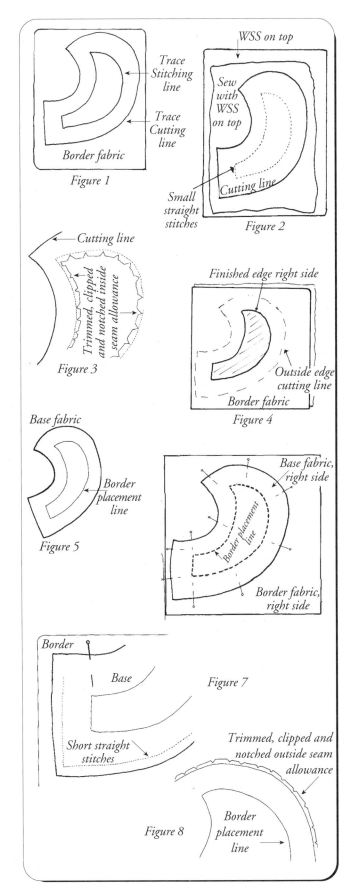

WSS on top

Trace Stitching line

Trace Cutting line

Border fabric

Figure 1

Sew with WSS on top

Small straight stitches

Cutting line

Figure 2

Cutting line

Trimmed, clipped and notched inside seam allowance

Figure 3

Finished edge right side

Outside edge cutting line

Border fabric

Figure 4

Base fabric

Border placement line

Figure 5

Base fabric, right side

Border placement line

Border fabric, right side

Border

Base

Figure 7

Short straight stitches

Trimmed, clipped and notched outside seam allowance

Figure 8

Border placement line

13. Turn the border fabric to the right side of the base fabric. Use a point turner to get sharp points.

14. Press flat to achieve a sharp crease.

15. Use an entredeux, pin stitch or other desired stitch to stitch the loose (inside) edge of the border fabric to the base fabric (**fig. 9**). Adjustments in width and/or length may be required to achieve the desired look. Use of a wing or large size needle will create a more obvious hole for the entredeux or pin stitch. Always test on excess fabrics to achieve the desired effect.

16. Rinse well to remove all of the markings and WSS caught under the border fabric.

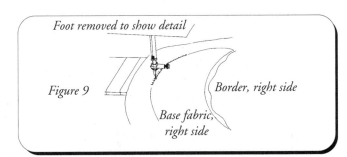

Figure 9

Foot removed to show detail

Border, right side

Base fabric, right side

Method II

1. Pretreat all fabric since WSS will need to be rinsed away when finished.

2. Starch and press both base fabric and border fabric.

3. Cut out the pattern from the base fabric and the border fabric. Mark the border placement line on the base piece and the stitching line on the border piece (**fig. 1**).

4. Place a piece of WSS to the right side of the border fabric and stitch the inside edge of the border as described above. Trim the WSS to match the outside edge (**fig. 2**).

6. Place the right side of the border fabric (border fabric has been stitched on the inside seam line, but NOT trimmed) to the wrong side of the base fabric, matching cut edges.

7. Stitch the outside edges together (**fig. 3**).

8. Lift up the border fabric (with WSS) from the base fabric. Trim the WSS and border fabric along the inside edge of the border to 1/8 inch, clipping or notching curves as needed (**fig. 4**).

9. Pull or cut WSS from lower seam. Flip WSS to the wrong side of the border, making a facing, which will turn trimmed edge to the wrong side. Press to form a sharp crease (**fig. 5**).

10. Trim the outside edge of the border fabric and the base fabric to 1/8 inch, clipping and notching as needed (**fig. 6**).

11. Turn the border fabric to the right side of the base fabric, press to form a sharp crease, use point turner as necessary (**fig. 7**).

12. Stitch the inside edge of the border to the base fabric with the desired stitch (**fig. 8**).

13. Rinse well to remove all of the markings and WSS caught under the border fabric. ▨

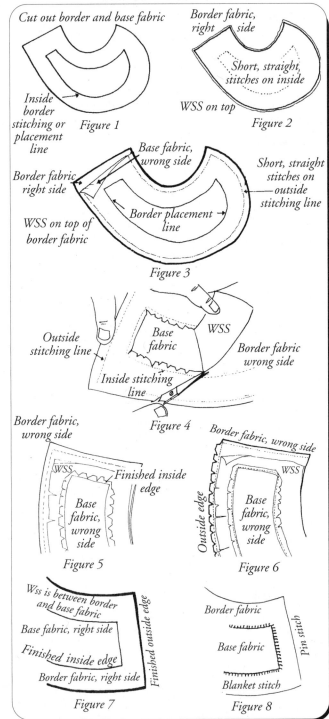

Cut out border and base fabric

Inside border stitching or placement line

Figure 1

Border fabric, right side

Short, straight stitches on inside

WSS on top

Figure 2

Base fabric, wrong side

Border fabric, right side

WSS on top of border fabric

Short, straight stitches on outside stitching line

Border placement line

Figure 3

Outside stitching line

Base fabric

WSS

Border fabric wrong side

Inside stitching line

Figure 4

Border fabric, wrong side

WSS

Finished inside edge

Base fabric, wrong side

Figure 5

Border fabric, wrong side

WSS

Outside edge

Base fabric, wrong side

Figure 6

Wss is between border and base fabric

Base fabric, right side

Finished inside edge

Border fabric, right side

Finished outside edge

Figure 7

Border fabric

Base fabric

Pin stitch

Blanket stitch

Figure 8

Shark's Teeth Technique

One afternoon while browsing in an antique store here in Huntsville, I saw a petticoat which absolutely winked at me. I had to take it home. Later that day I called my incredibly talented friend, Sue Pennington, to ask her if she could unravel the techniques which were used in making this breathtaking petticoat. Sue and her family began to call this petticoat, the shark's teeth garment because sharks have rows and rows of white triangular teeth.

Since the technique and the original Sue Pennington garments appeared in *Sew Beautiful*, Summer 1991 magazine, the response has been unbelievable. Most readers love the tailored look of this type of French sewing. Don't be afraid of making shark's teeth. They are very easy to make especially if you use glue stick to hold the points into place while you sew. By the way, you can make a shark's teeth panel to insert into any portion of any garment. Just make the panel larger than your pattern piece, and after completing the shark's teeth treatment, cut out your garment.

The fabric used to make shark's teeth must be lightweight and closely woven. Polyester-cotton blends would be difficult to work with because they do not hold a sharp crease. Heavily starched light weight cottons work beautifully. This technique is not difficult, although accuracy in marking, pressing, cutting and stitching is necessary. The results are well worth the effort.

Materials Needed

* 100% cotton fabric
* Dixon pencil or quilter's pencil
* Fabric glue stick
* Sharp scissors

Template and Tucking Guide

* Template
* *Tucking Guide*

1. Using the tucking guide on page 311 mark tucking lines across fabric using a Dixon pencil or quilter's pencil. The marking device must be easily removed after ironing. I usually mark tucking lines using dots or short lines. Mark tucks lightly, just enough for you to see. These tucking lines are 1-5/8 inch apart (**fig. 1**).

2. Fold fabric along these lines, wrong sides together and press (**fig. 2**).

3. Stitch 1/2 inch from the fold of the fabric. This creates a tuck (**fig. 3**).

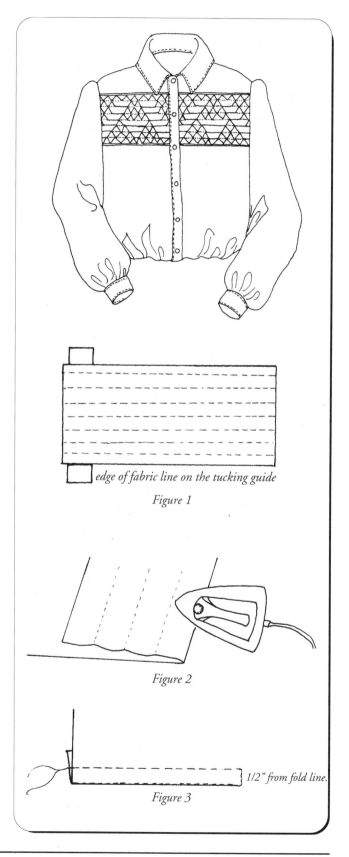

edge of fabric line on the tucking guide

Figure 1

Figure 2

1/2" from fold line.

Figure 3

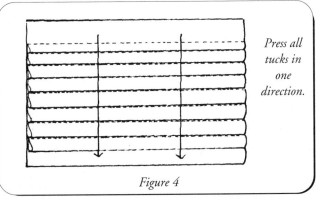

Press all tucks in one direction.

Figure 4

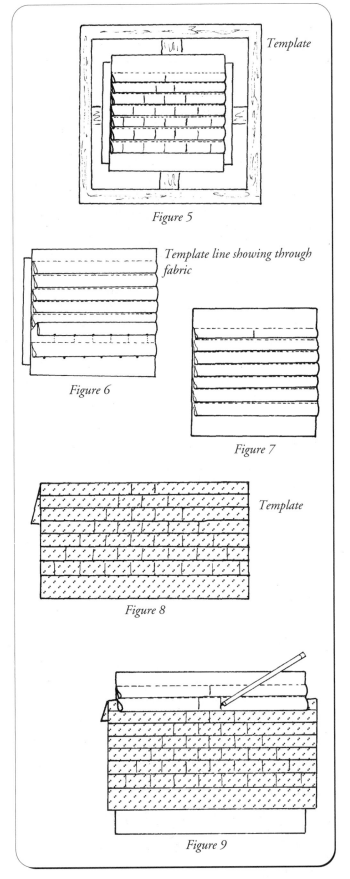

Template

Figure 5

Template line showing through fabric

Figure 6

Figure 7

Figure 8

Template

Figure 9

4. Place the tucked piece on the ironing board, tuck side up, and slide the iron over the tucks in one direction.

5. Turn the piece over, tucked side down, starch and press again. Now starch and press one more time with the tucks right side up. The tucks should almost touch (**fig. 4**).

6. With the tucks pointing at you, place the Shark's Teeth template (pyramid) centered under the tucked panel with the widest part of the template (pyramid) closest to you and the top of the template (pyramid) at the first tuck. Transferring the marks to the top of the tucks can be done using three different methods, all methods will have the same end results.

I. Window Method

To see the marks through three fabric layers hold the template and tucked fabric to a window and transfer the marks of the pyramid to each tuck. The first tuck will have one mark, the second tuck - two marks, the third tuck - three marks, etc. Once marking is started be careful not to let the template slip. Template marks are equally spaced on each side of the mark above (**Fig. 5**).

II. Lift And Mark Method

Lift the tuck to allow you to see the template through one fabric layer but transfer the mark to the fold of the tuck with a dot (**fig. 6**). Repeat transfer for the other pleats.

III. Folding The Template Method

7. Mark the first tuck in the center. This represents the first mark of the template (**Fig. 7**).

8. Fold the template so that the second row of marks is at the top of the paper (**fig. 8**).

9. Place template under the second tuck and center these two marks with the first mark of the first tuck. Transfer these two marks on the second tuck (**fig. 9**).

10. Fold the template so that the third row of marks is at the top of the paper.

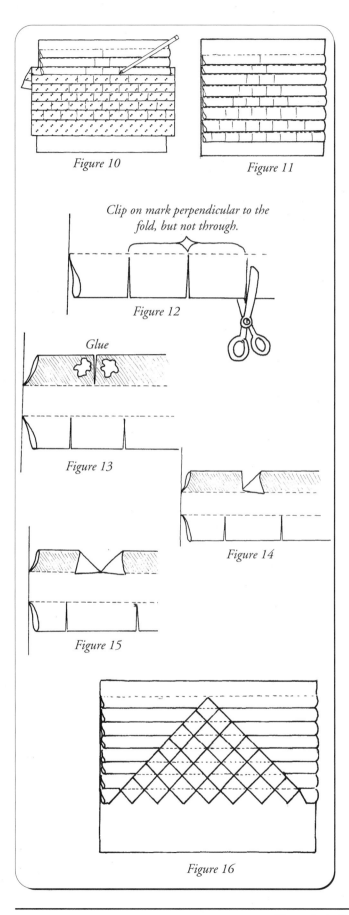

Figure 10

Figure 11

Clip on mark perpendicular to the fold, but not through.

Figure 12

Glue

Figure 13

Figure 14

Figure 15

Figure 16

11. Place the template under the third tuck and center these three marks with the two marks of the tuck above (**fig. 10**).

12. Transfer all marks using the preferred transfer technique (**fig. 11**).

13. Clip perpendicular to the fold of the tuck, through the two layers of the tuck. Clip to, but not through the stitching line of the tucks (**fig. 12**).

14. Flip the first tuck up, at the clip, so that you can see the underside and place a small amount of fabric glue on each side of the clip (**fig. 13**).

15. Fold the cut edges of the clip to the underside of the tuck just over the stitching line (**fig. 14**). These fabric angles should hide the stitching line of the tuck and create the angular opening in the first tuck (**fig. 15**).

16. Repeat for all clips.

17. Starch and press tucks back toward you hiding all the folded corners (**fig. 16**).

18. Top stitch just under the stitching line of the tuck with a tiny zigzag (3/4 length and 1 width). This stitching will be made through the two layers of the tuck and the base fabric (**fig. 17**). Instead of a zigzag, a decorative stitch can be used (**fig. 18**). This zigzag or decorative stitch should catch all the clipped edges of fabric (**fig. 19**).

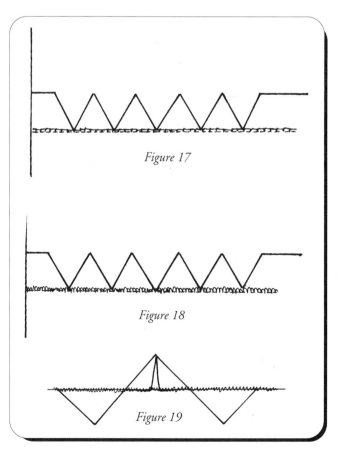

Figure 17

Figure 18

Figure 19

Adding Shark's Teeth To Your Pattern

Shark's teeth can be added to a pattern by working with a block of tucks the length and width of the pattern piece. Cutting lines for the open angles of the sharks teeth can then be placed appropriately and construction of the sharks teeth completed as stated above.

1. Measure the pattern piece for your shark's teeth at the widest point and the longest point (**fig. 20**).

2. Using the longest length, multiply this measurement by two. This will give you the number of 1/2-inch tucks required for this pattern piece. Each of these tuck will take up 1 inch   of the fabric. Now to find the length to cut the fabric, add the length of the pattern plus the number of tucks required. The width will remain the same. Cut a piece of fabric to this measurement plus 2 inches extra in length and width (to be on the safe side) (**fig. 21**).

3. Mark for the tucks by starting 1-1/2 inch from the bottom edge of your fabric with your first fold mark. Mark the entire piece (**fig. 22**).

4. Tuck the fabric as described in Step 2 and 3. Starch and press tucked piece as described in Step 4. Trace pattern piece on tucked piece using a fabric marker (**fig. 23**).

5. Decide where to put the open angles of the shark's teeth design. The pyramid shape is the most common design but others may be used. Mark tucks for cutting (**fig. 24**).

6. Follow Steps 5 through 11 to complete shark's teeth. Cut out along pattern lines and construct garment according to directions.

Shark's Teeth Insertion

1. When making a shark's teeth insertion, decide on the number of tucks desired. Use the following formula for cutting the width of the insertion fabric: 1-5/8 inch multiplied by the number of tucks plus 1 inch (extra fabric top and bottom for space and seam allowance). For Sue's dress, three tucks were used. Therefore the formula for the width of the fabric is 1-5/8 inch x 3 = 4-3/4 inch +1 inch = 5-3/4 inch. The length of the fabric will depend on where the insertion is used. Sue's dress took approximately two 45-inch lengths for the front panel. Dress bottoms would take approximately two 45-inch lengths. Cut fabric for tucked piece.

2. Start marking the first tucking line in the center of the fabric. Measure above and below this fold line 1-5/8 inch (**fig. 25**).

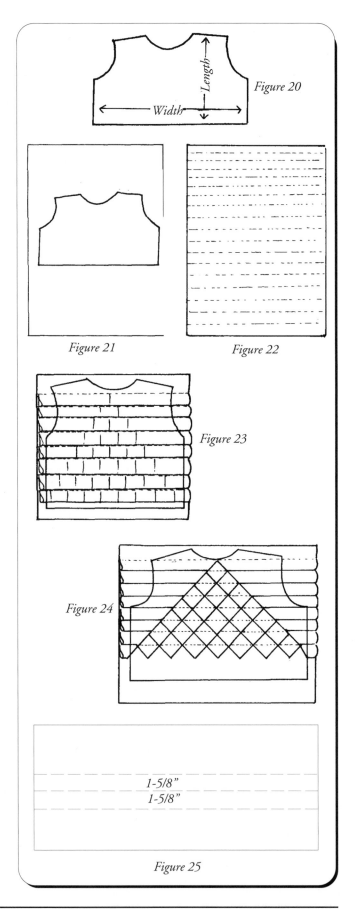

Figure 20

Figure 21

Figure 22

Figure 23

Figure 24

1-5/8"
1-5/8"

Figure 25

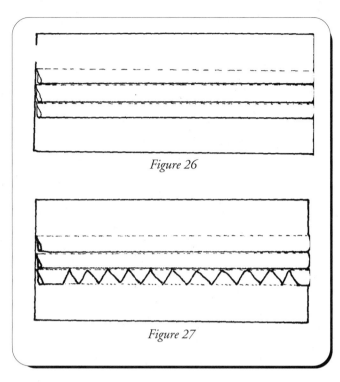

Figure 26

Figure 27

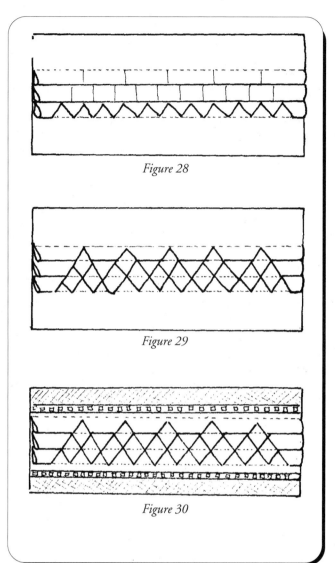

Figure 28

Figure 29

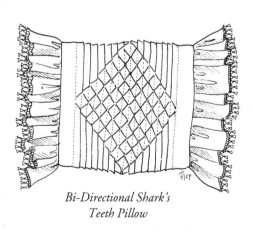

Figure 30

3. Tuck fabric using general directions step 2 and 3. Starch and press using General Directions step 4 (**fig. 26**).

4. Mark the bottom tuck with parallel lines 7/8 inch apart. Cut along these lines for open angles of the teeth (**fig. 27**). Place the template under the remaining tucks to complete the pyramids (**fig. 28**). Mark the cutting lines   and complete the shark's teeth using the General Directions steps 5 - 11 (**fig. 29**).

5. Use completed strip as insertion attaching entredeux, laces, etc to the shark's teeth insertion piece (**fig. 30**). ❖

Shark's Teeth Doll Dress

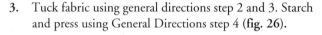

Bi-Directional Shark's Teeth Pillow

Australian Windowpane

This technique is achieved by stitching a block of sheer fabric on top of the background fabric in the desired design. The background fabric is then cut away within the design, leaving the sheer fabric on top. The excess sheer fabric is cut away from the front and a satin stitch is applied. This gives a similar appearance to cutwork, but the sheer fabric supports the opening.

Supplies

❀ Base Fabric

❀ Australian Windowpane Fabric; Netting or Sheer Fabric

❀ Machine Embroidery Thread to Match Project

❀ Size 70 (10) Sewing Machine Needles

❀ Water or Air Soluble Markers or Pencils

❀ Water Soluble Stabilizer (WSS)

❀ Machine Embroidery or Spring Tension Hoop

❀ Sharp Pointed, Trimming Scissors

❀ Open Toe Appliqué Foot

Optional:

❀ Spray Starch

❀ Appliqué Scissors

Directions

1. Pretreat the fabrics since you will need to rinse the WSS away when finished.

2. Press the fabric to remove all wrinkles. Spray starch the fabric to add body. Several applications of spray starch may be used.

3. Trace the pattern piece to a square of base fabric. Mark the cutting and seam lines and the center front or other important marking lines (**fig.** 1). Trace the design in the desired position on the traced pattern. Placing the fabric in a hoop for tracing will help to minimize shifting while tracing (**fig.** 2).

4. Layer in the hoop:

    a. base fabric with design, right side up

    b. square of WSS, large enough to fit in hoop

    c. square of windowpane fabric, right side up, large enough to fit in hoop (**fig.** 3)

See Machine Embroidery, "Placing Fabric in the Hoop"

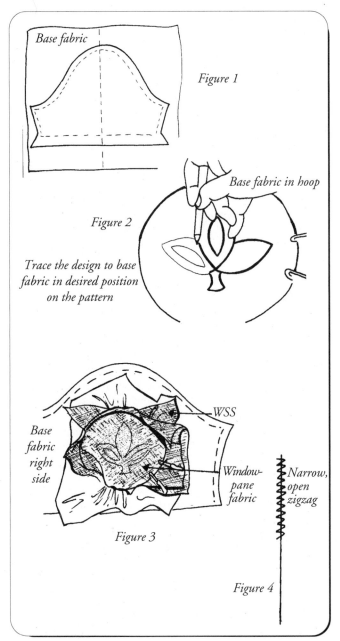

Base fabric

Figure 1

Figure 2

Base fabric in hoop

Trace the design to base fabric in desired position on the pattern

Base fabric right side

WSS

Window-pane fabric

Narrow, open zigzag

Figure 3

Figure 4

Note: For small, simple designs it is not necessary to place these fabrics in a hoop. Care should be taken to keep all layers from shifting. This can be done using pins or fabric glue stick.

5. Place the open toe appliqué foot or appliqué foot and a new, size 70 (10) needle on the machine. Thread the machine with matching thread, top and bobbin. Loosen top thread tension slightly.

6. Set the machine for a narrow, open zigzag, about .5 to 1 mm width and a 1 mm length. This is not a satin stitch (**fig.** 4).

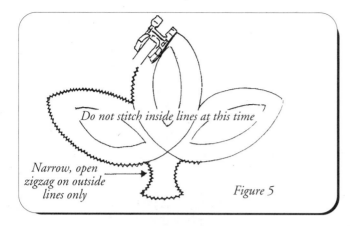

Do not stitch inside lines at this time

Narrow, open zigzag on outside lines only

Figure 5

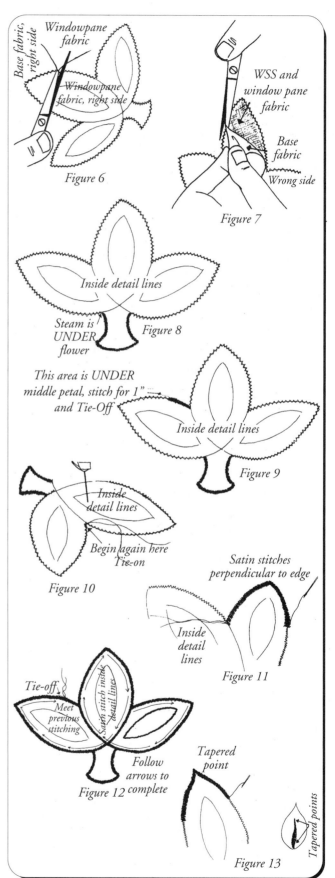

Base fabric, right side

Windowpane fabric

Windowpane fabric, right side

Figure 6

WSS and window pane fabric

Base fabric

Wrong side

Figure 7

Inside detail lines

Steam is UNDER flower

Figure 8

This area is UNDER middle petal, stitch for 1" and Tie-Off

Inside detail lines

Figure 9

Inside detail lines

Begin again here Tie-on

Figure 10

Satin stitches perpendicular to edge

Inside detail lines

Figure 11

Tie-off

Satin stitch inside detail lines

Meet previous stitching

Follow arrows to complete

Figure 12

Tapered point

Tapered points

Figure 13

7. Stitch around the design on the **OUTSIDE** edges (**fig. 5**).

8. Remove the fabrics from the hoop, if a hoop were used.

9. On the **RIGHT** side, trim the windowpane fabric close to the stitching without cutting the stitching (**fig. 6**).

10. From the **WRONG** side, trim the base fabric from the inside of the design allowing the netting or sheer fabric to show through as a single layer. The layer of WSS is between the fabric layers and will aid in the trimming without cutting the net or sheer fabric (**fig. 7**).

11. Place fabric and WSS back in the hoop, if desired.

12. Set the machine up for a narrow to medium satin stitch (width of 1.5 to 2.5 mm, length of approximately .5 mm).

13. Working on the right side, satin stitch the design, working from background to foreground (stem first, then flower) (**fig. 8**). Any inside design lines, as the veins of leaves or individual flower petals are also worked background to foreground. The vein lines may need to be stitched before the outline of the leaves. Part of one area may need to be stitched before the entire design is stitched. In this design, satin stitch about 1" on the left petal and tie-off since it is under the middle leaf (**fig. 9**). The satin stitch will encase all of the raw edges from the right and wrong sides. The general rules for Machine Appliqué are follows:

   a. Pull up the bobbin thread and tie on at the beginning of stitching (**fig. 10**).

   b. Work background to foreground.

   c. Keep the satin stitches perpendicular to the design lines, pivoting as necessary (**fig. 11**).

   d. Tie off before moving from one area to another. To tie off, change stitch width to "0" and take several tiny straight stitches along the edge of the satin stitches (**fig. 12**).

14. The satin stitch width can be tapered for the veins and the top of the leaves (**fig. 13**). As you stitch, increase and decrease the width for the tapered appearance. Practice to achieve a smooth increase and decrease. ▨

Shadow Diamonds

I fell in love with shadow diamonds with the purchase of the Ladies Shadow Diamond Skirt, featured in my *Antique Clothing, French Sewing by Machine* book. From all over the world ladies have enjoyed making shadow diamonds for collars, skirts, bodices and sleeves. One morning as we were working on this book in the studio, our friend Gail Settle came up the stairs. She had a bag with a real surprise in it which she felt we would want to see. It was the sweetest antique apron that I have ever seen with these baby shadow diamonds on the front of the skirt of the apron and on the ties. What an incredible amount of work for an apron! Immediately we asked if we could include this template and technique for baby diamonds in the new book. Gail agreed. This technique would be so sweet in the princess curved front christening gown or on a high yoke bodice of another gown. Enjoy this technique. Please work slowly because it is tedious!

Materials Needed

✧ X-acto knife and cutting mat or small pair of very sharp scissors

✧ Suggested fabrics: Linen, Swiss Batiste, Victorian batiste or any other fabric that holds a crease.

✧ Dixon pencil or regular pencil

✧ Thread, iron, ironing board and starch

✧ Baby Shadow Diamond Template

General Directions

Two pieces of fabric will be required to complete this technique. The top layer will have the diamond shapes cut into the fabric. This cut layer will be the outside of the garment. The second layer will be placed behind the diamond cut outs to shadow through.

1. Trace lightly, using a Dixon pencil or pencil, the shadow diamond template on the wrong side of the fabric (**fig. 1**). The template can be extended to cover more area or squares can be arranged to form shapes.

2. Using and X-acto knife and cutting mat or small pointed scissors cut, very carefully, along solid lines of the + (**fig. 2**).

3. Working from the wrong side of the fabric, pull the center points at the middle of the "X's" that you have just cut, to the back creating an open diamond (**fig. 3**). Finger press in place. This should hold the folded pieces enough for you to then press with an iron.

4. Press folds in place.

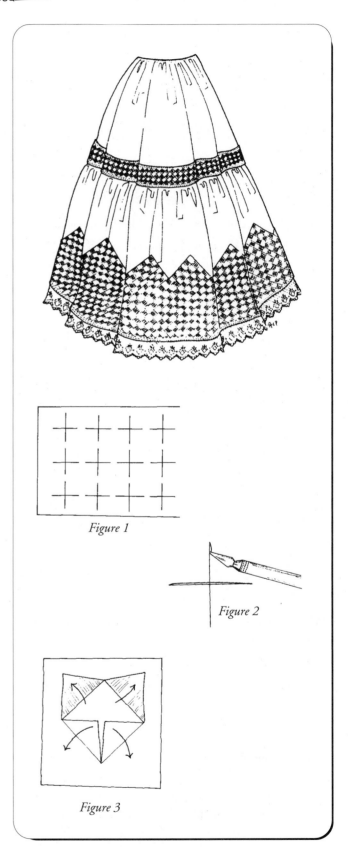

Figure 1

Figure 2

Figure 3

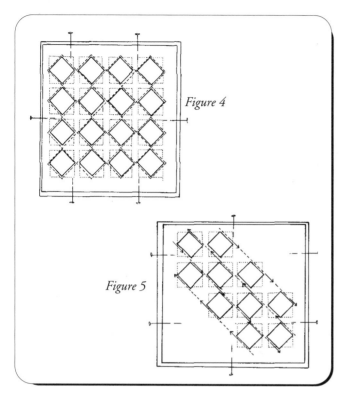

Figure 4

Figure 5

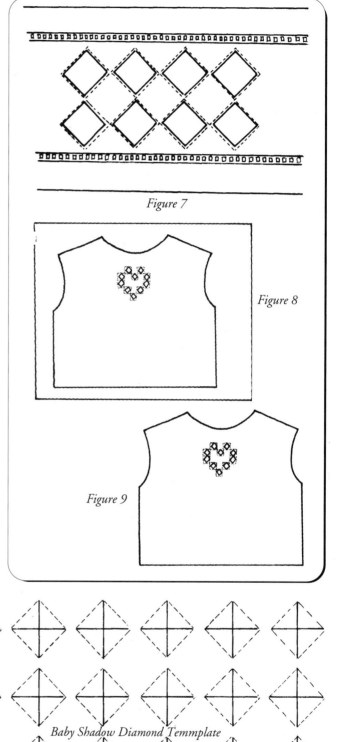

Figure 7

Figure 8

Figure 9

Baby Shadow Diamond Temmplate

5. Place second layer of fabric over the folded angles. The second layer of fabric will show through the holes. Pin the two layers of fabric together and straight stitch along the folds in a diagonal pattern (**figs. 4 and 5**) or straight stitch around the edges of the square to hold the fabric angles in place (**fig. 6**). This stitching will hold folded edges in place.

Shadow Diamonds Insertion

Cut a strip of the fabric the length and width of the desired insertion piece. Trace, cut and press open diamonds. Place second layer of fabric cut the same width and length as the first. Place on top of the cut diamonds and stitch in place as described in step 5 of the General Directions. Continue adding laces, entredeux, etc. to the shadow diamond insertion treating the two layers of fabric as one layer (**fig. 7**).

Shadow Diamond Yoke Or Bodice

Cut two rectangles of fabric larger than the yoke or bodice. Trace the pattern on the top rectangle using a fabric marker. Trace the shadow diamond template in desired position. Cut and press folds of diamonds in place. Place second layer of fabric which is cut the same width and length as the first on top of the diamonds and stitch in place as described in step 5 of the General Directions. Straight stitch just inside the pattern line (**fig. 8**). Cut pattern from fabric and stitch two layers of fabric as one layer (**fig. 9**). ▓

Easy Shadow Diamonds

Easy shadow diamonds are just that, very easy. The strip or pattern piece has two layers of fabric. The top layer is organdy or other see-through fabric and the bottom layer is an opaque fabric. The see-through fabric will remain on top of the bottom layer of fabric, in other words the see-through fabric is not cut away.

Materials Needed

Organdy or other see-through fabric to fit pattern piece or shadow diamond strip.

Directions

1. Cut organdy and fabric to fit pattern piece or shadow diamond strip.

2. Trace shadow diamond template on the organdy (**fig. 1**).

3. Place the organdy on top of the fabric. Pin the two layers in place matching any pattern lines. Stitch around the diamond shape using a hem stitch or zigzag (**fig. 2**).

4. Trim the fabric from the back of the diamond (**fig. 3**). This creates the shadow diamond. ❁

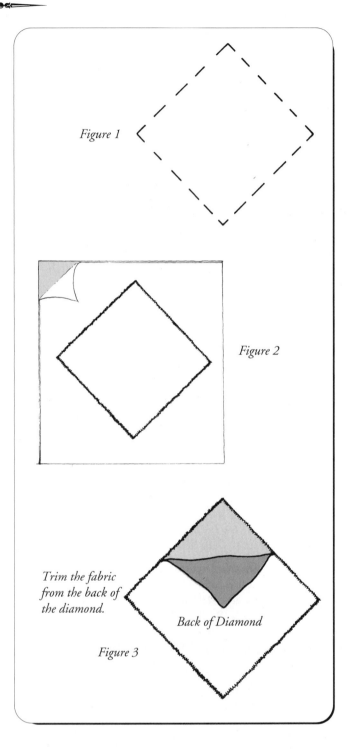

Figure 1

Figure 2

Trim the fabric from the back of the diamond.

Back of Diamond

Figure 3

With this method, you embroider from the wrong side of the fabric. When the fabric is loaded into the hoop, the wrong side of the fabric will be facing out. The design is traced onto that side. The stitches, a closed herringbone, are rather like "sewing" with a bite taken out of the top of the design and a bite taken out of the bottom. I prefer this method more than working from the front, because it is easiest.

1. Trace your design onto the wrong side of the fabric. If you are using an alphabet, be sure that the letters are properly reversed (**fig. 1**). An easy way to reverse letters or a design onto the wrong side of the fabric is to use a photocopy machine. Copy the design onto a clear plastic sheet like you would use for an overhead projector. This is called a transparency. Flip the transparency over. Run a copy on paper this time. It will be reversed properly.

Figure 1

2. Insert the fabric into the embroidery hoop.

3. Cut a piece of embroidery floss approximately 18 - 22 inches long (**fig. 2**). Remember to knot the cut end, although you will later cut that knot away.

4. There are two ways of placing the loose end (the knotted end of the floss) while you stitch your shadow embroidery.

   a. Lay the end of the floss (rather a long one) outside the embroidery hoop and close the hoop over it. This gives you plenty of floss to later weave into the completed design (**fig. 3**).

   b. Bring your knot up through the circle of fabric as far away from your first stitch as possible.

   Note: Sometimes there is not enough embroidery floss "tail" to easily weave into the completed design.

   Following the illustrations given, using the leaf shape (**fig. 4**), begin your stitching.

5. With the thread below the needle, bring the needle down at (A) (**fig 5**) and up at (B) (**fig. 6**). Pull through.

7. Move down. Thread above the needle, put your needle down at (C) (**fig. 7**) and up at (B) (**fig. 8**). Move into the exact same hole as your needle made on the first bite at (B).

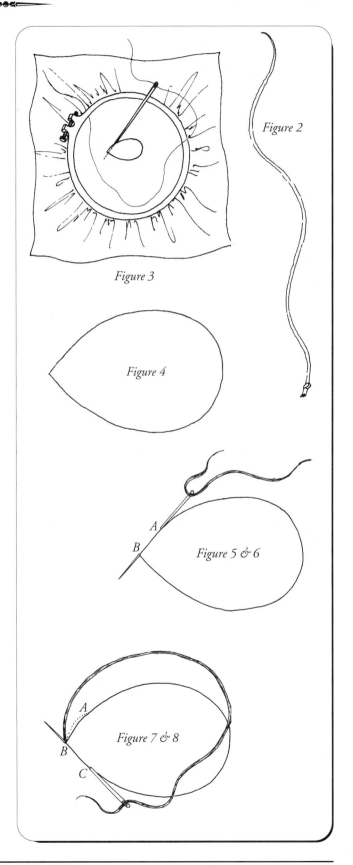

Figure 2

Figure 3

Figure 4

Figure 5 & 6

Figure 7 & 8

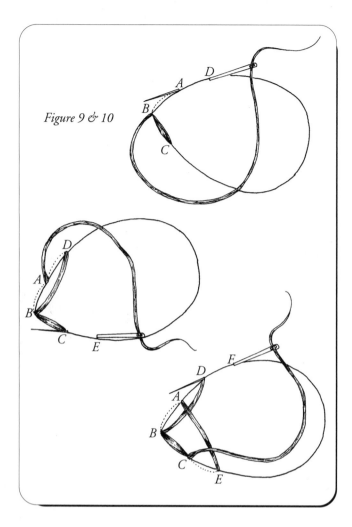

Figure 9 & 10

Figure 15 & 16

Figure 17 & 18

Figure 19 & 20

Figure 21 & 22

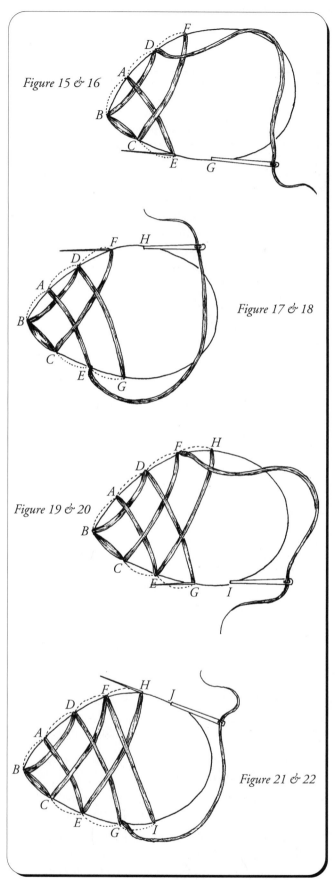

Note: In order to easily remember whether the thread is above or below the needle, see the "Cat And The Courthouse Story" in the **Smocking Techniques** chapter.

8. With the thread below the needle, bring the needle down at (D) (**fig. 9**) and up at (A) (**fig. 10**).

9. With the thread above the needle, bring the needle down at (E) (**fig. 11**) and up at (C) (**fig. 12**).

10. When you come to a large curve, make your outside stitches (on the largest part of the curve) larger. Make the inside stitches closer together. You may find it necessary, sometimes, to go in one hole twice on the inside area. Finish the design according to (**figures 13 - 30**).

11. Keep turning your work so that the portion of the design you are currently working on is horizontally in front of you and so that you are working from left to right.

12. When you have finished your work, weave the tail of the thread through the stitching on the sides. As with most needlework, never knot your thread. Just weave it.

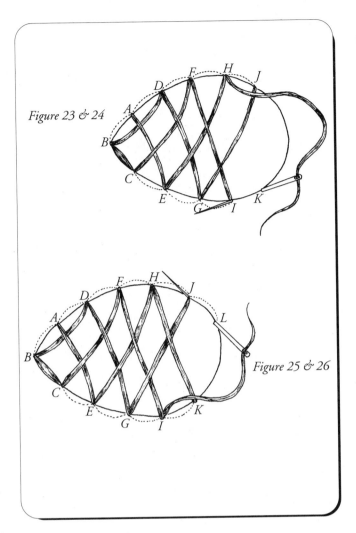

Figure 23 & 24

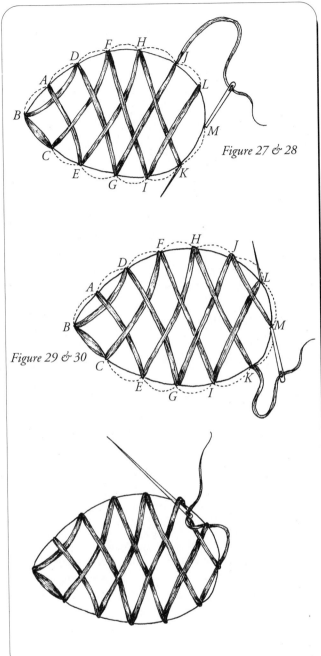

Figure 27 & 28

Figure 25 & 26

Figure 29 & 30

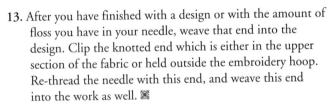

13. After you have finished with a design or with the amount of floss you have in your needle, weave that end into the design. Clip the knotted end which is either in the upper section of the fabric or held outside the embroidery hoop. Re-thread the needle with this end, and weave this end into the work as well. ▩

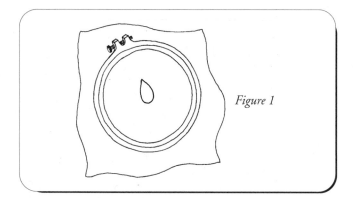

Figure 1

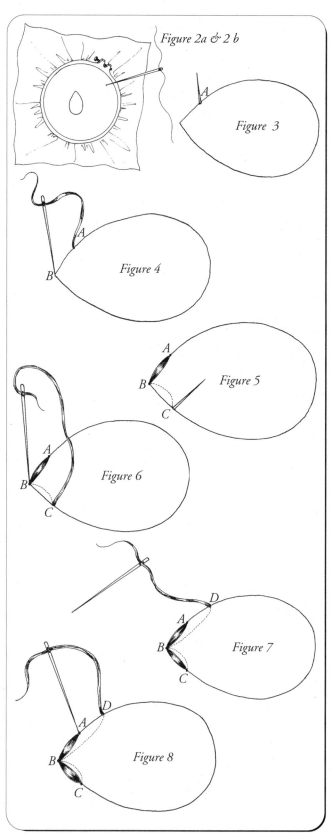

Figure 2a & 2 b

Figure 3

Figure 4

Figure 5

Figure 6

Figure 7

Figure 8

1. Trace the design you would like to shadowwork on the right side of the fabric (**fig. 1**).

2. Place the fabric into them embroidery hoop centering the design to be stitched. The right side of the fabric will be facing you.

3. Cut a piece of embroidery floss approximately 18 - 22 inches long. Separate the strands of floss. Thread one strand of floss through your favorite shadowwork needle. I suggest using a 10 sharp, 10 Crewels, or a 26 tapestry needle. Remember to knot the cut end of the floss, although you will later cut that knot away.

4. Securing the thread.

   Method 1. Place the knot on the wrong side of the fabric between the hoop and the fabric. Close the hoop (**fig. 2a**).

   Method 2. Place the needle in the right side of the fabric as far away from your first stitch as possible. The knot will end up on the right side of the fabric (**fig. 2b**).

   Either of these methods will put the needle/ thread on the back side of the fabric. Note: This thread tail will need to be long enough to weave back through the stitching after the design is complete.

5. Bring the needle to the right side of the fabric at the beginning point (A) (**fig. 3**).

6. To make the first stitch, take the needle down at point (B) to the wrong side of the fabric (**fig. 4**).

7. Move to the other side of the design and bring the needle up at (C) (**fig. 5**) and back down at (B) (**fig. 6**). Pull gently.

8. Bring the needle up from the backside at (D) (**fig. 7**) and back down at (A) (**fig. 8**).

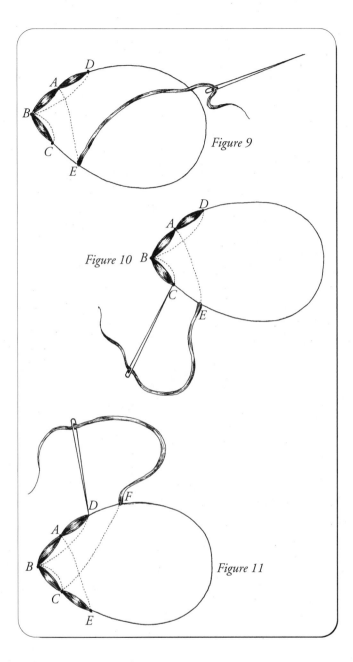

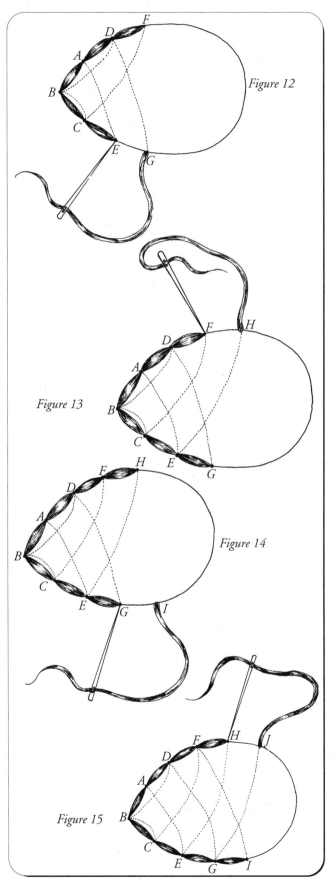

Figure 9

Figure 10

Figure 11

Figure 12

Figure 13

Figure 14

Figure 15

9. Move down to the other side and come up through (E) (**fig. 9**) and go back down at (C) (**fig. 10**).

10. Move to the other side and come up at (F) and back down at (D) (**fig. 11**).

12. Move to the other side and come up through (G) and down at (E) (**fig. 12**).

13. When you come to large curve, make your outside (on the largest part of the curve) larger. Make the inside stitches closer together. You may find it necessary to go in one hole twice on the inside area. Finish the design according to (**figures 13 - 20**).

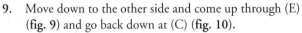

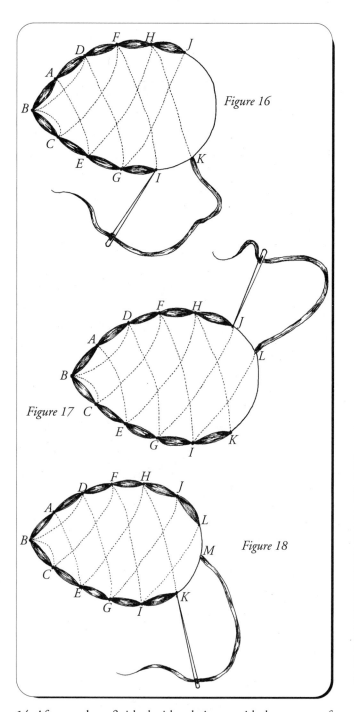

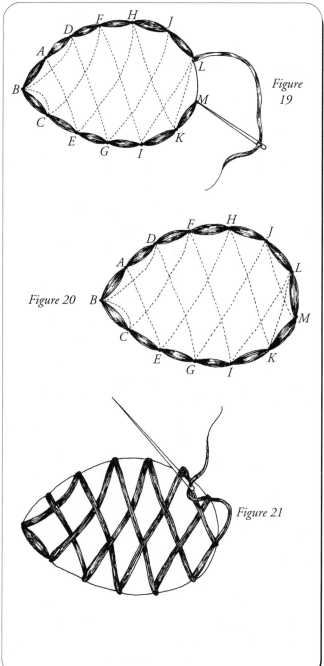

Figure 16

Figure 17

Figure 18

Figure 19

Figure 20

Figure 21

14. After you have finished with a design or with the amount of floss you have in your needle, weave that end into the design. Clip the knotted end which is either in the upper section of the fabric or held outside the embroidery hoop. Rethread the needle with this end, and weave this end into the work as well (**fig. 21**). ▨

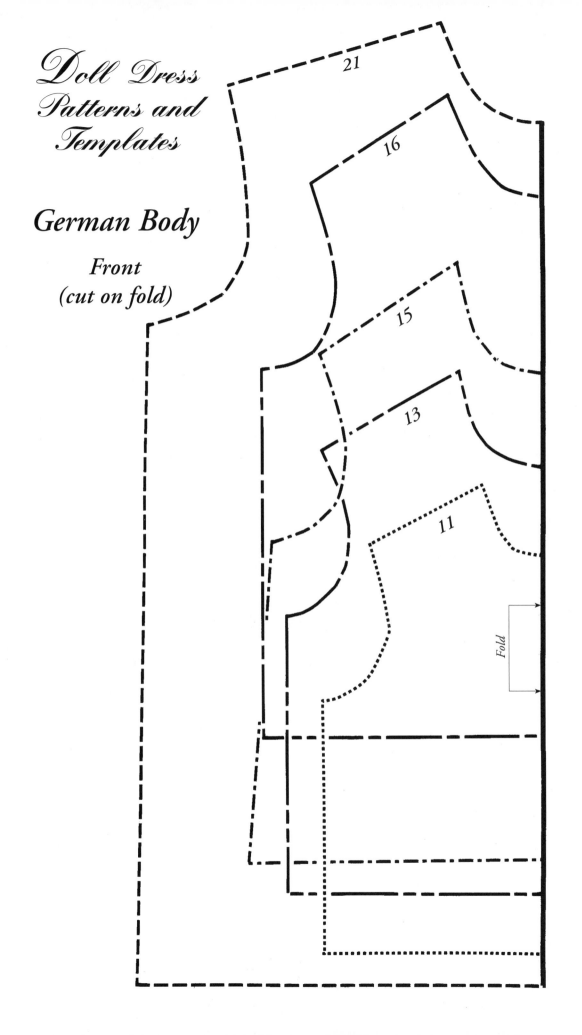

Doll Dress
Patterns and
Templates

German Body

Front
(cut on fold)

21

16

15

13

11

Fold

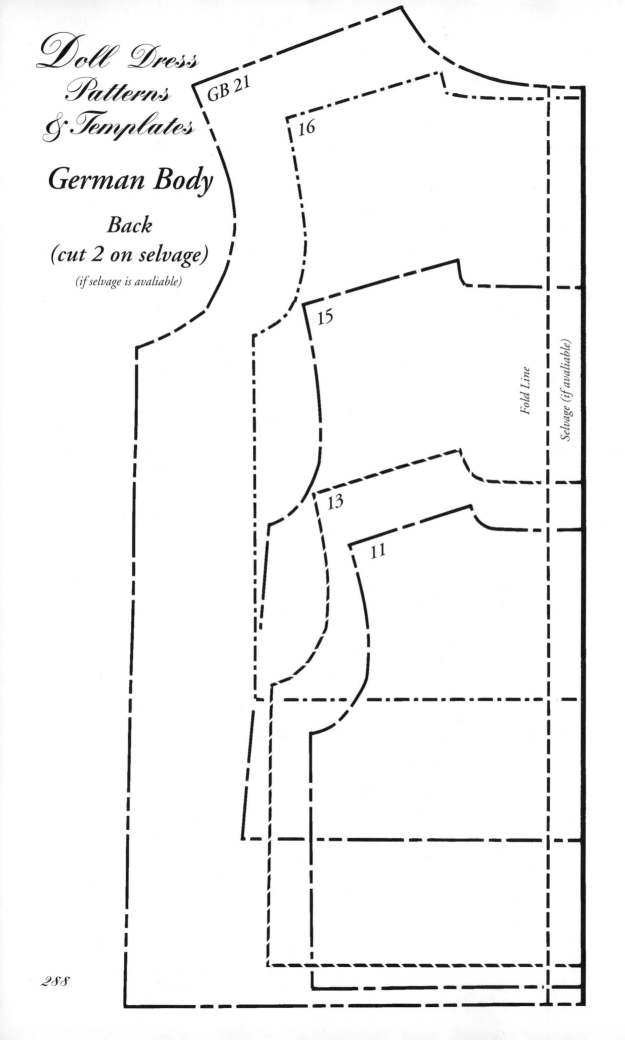

Doll Dress
Patterns
& Templates

German Body

Back
(cut 2 on selvage)

(if selvage is avaliable)

GB 21

16

15

13

11

Fold Line

Selvage (if avaliable)

288

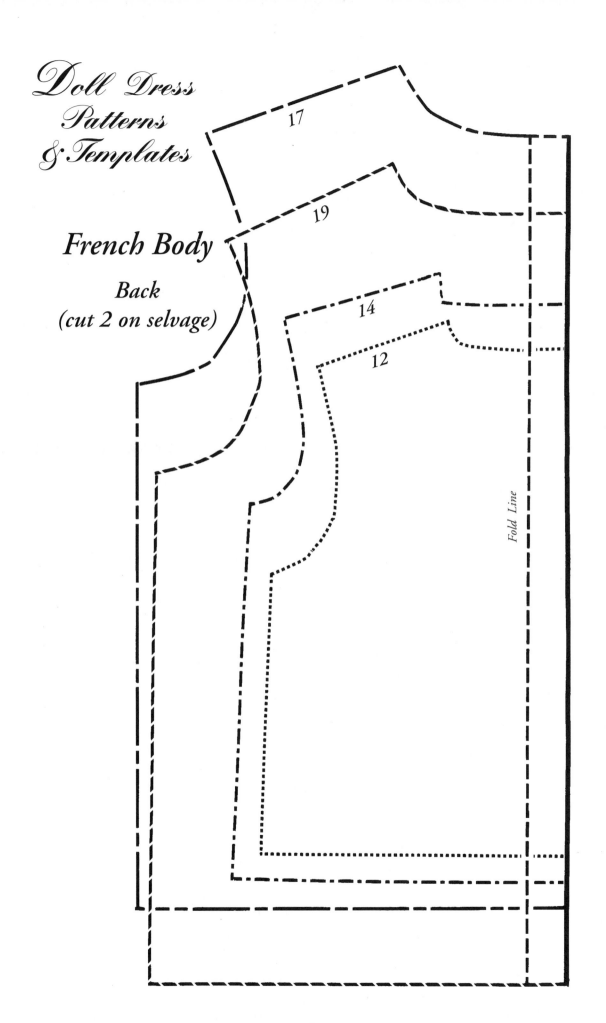

Doll Dress
Patterns
& Templates

French Body

Back
(cut 2 on selvage)

17

19

14

12

Fold Line

289

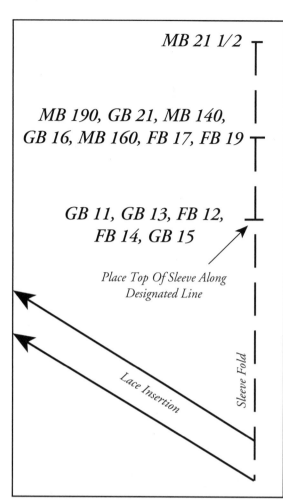

MB 21 1/2

MB 190, GB 21, MB 140,
GB 16, MB 160, FB 17, FB 19

GB 11, GB 13, FB 12,
FB 14, GB 15

*Place Top Of Sleeve Along
Designated Line*

Sleeve Fold

Lace Insertion

Sleeve Template for
Heart Dress on page 52.

French Body

Front (cut on fold)

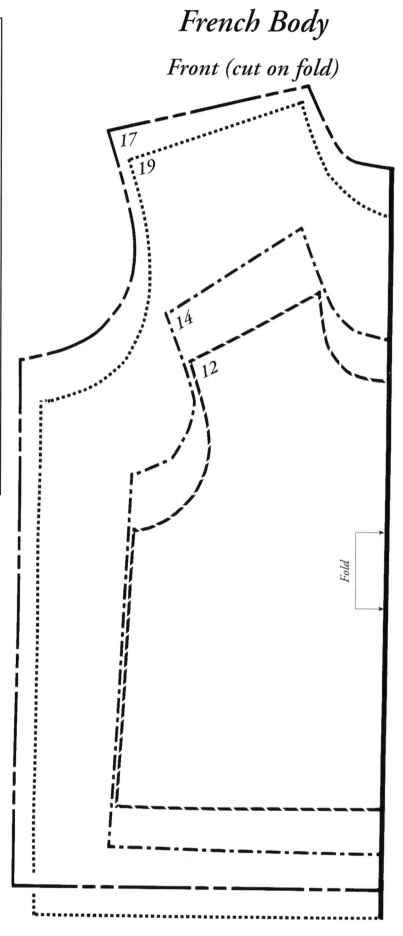

17

19

14

12

Fold

*Doll Dress
Patterns
& Templates*

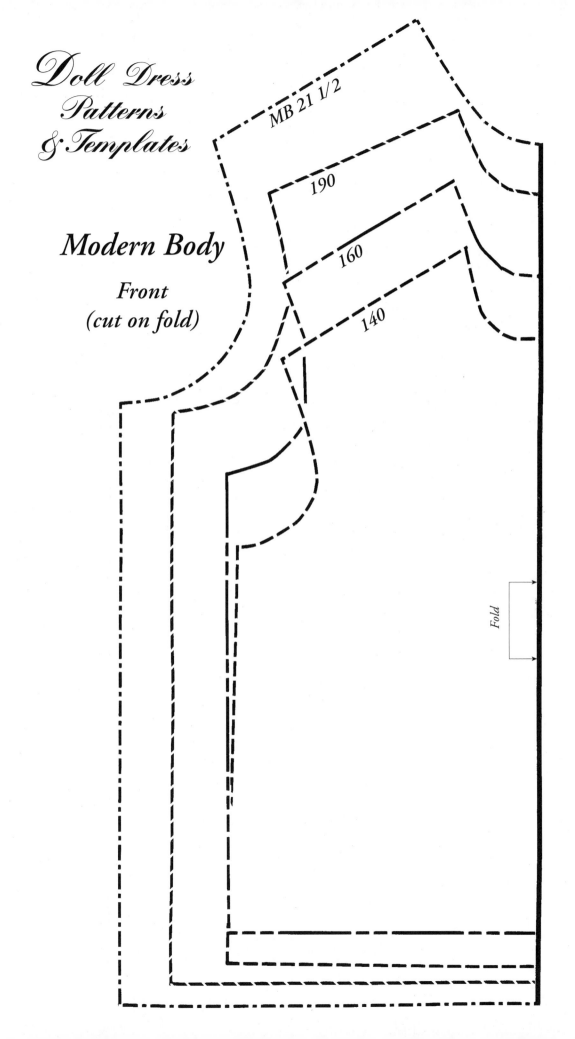

*Doll Dress
Patterns
& Templates*

Modern Body

*Front
(cut on fold)*

MB 21 1/2

190

160

140

Fold

291

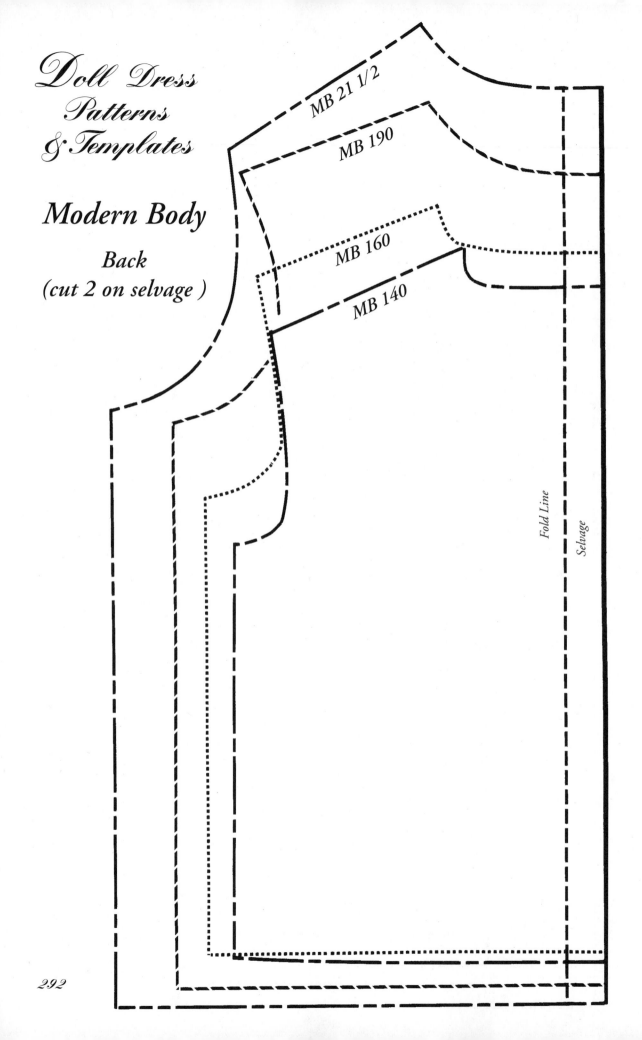

*Doll Dress
Patterns
& Templates*

Modern Body

*Back
(cut 2 on selvage)*

MB 21 1/2

MB 190

MB 160

MB 140

Fold Line

Selvage

292

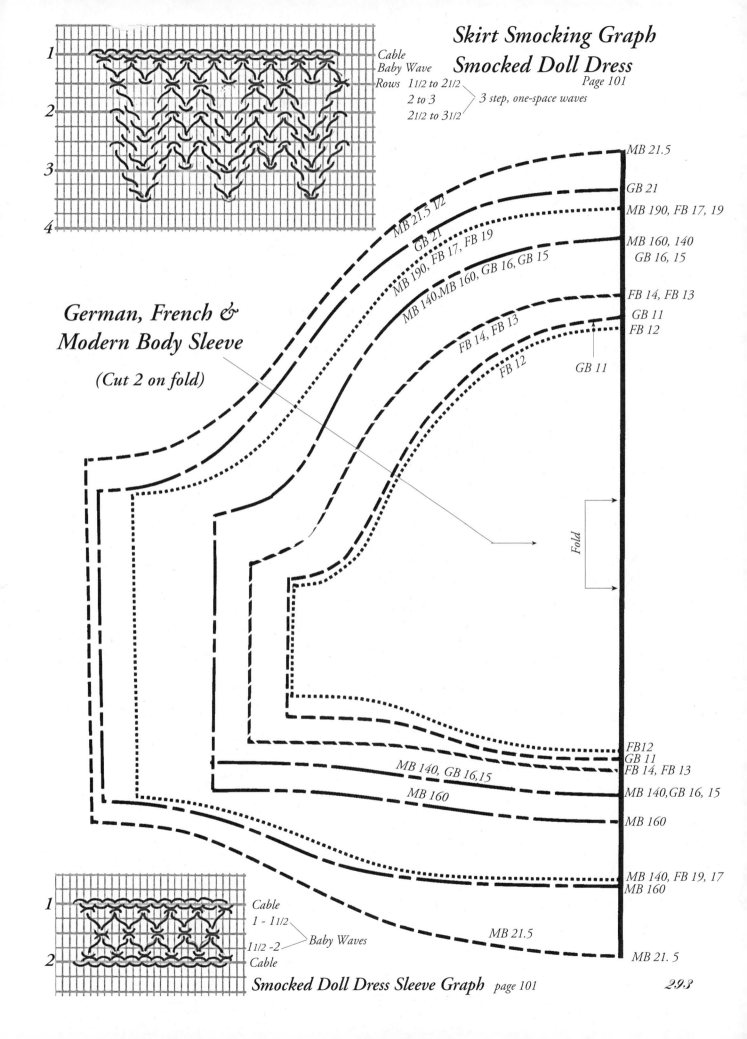

Skirt Smocking Graph
Smocked Doll Dress
Page 101

Cable
Baby Wave
Rows 11/2 to 21/2
2 to 3   3 step, one-space waves
21/2 to 31/2

MB 21.5

MB 21.5 1/2
GB 21
MB 190, FB 17, FB 19
MB 140, MB 160, GB 16, GB 15
FB 14, FB 13
FB 12
GB 11

GB 21
MB 190, FB 17, 19
MB 160, 140
GB 16, 15
FB 14, FB 13
GB 11
FB 12

German, French &
Modern Body Sleeve

(Cut 2 on fold)

Fold

FB12
GB 11
FB 14, FB 13

MB 140, GB 16,15
MB 160

MB 140, GB 16, 15

MB 160

Cable
1 - 11/2
Baby Waves
11/2 -2
Cable

MB 140, FB 19, 17
MB 160

MB 21.5

MB 21. 5

Smocked Doll Dress Sleeve Graph page 101

293

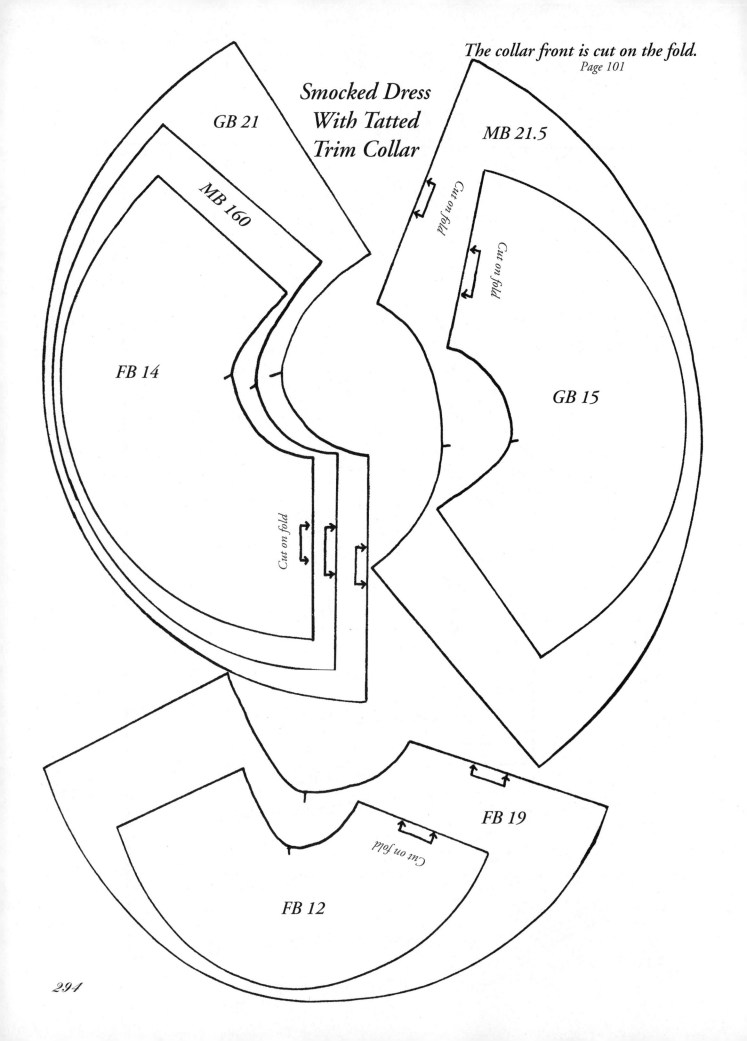

The collar front is cut on the fold.
Page 101

Smocked Dress
With Tatted
Trim Collar

GB 21

MB 21.5

MB 160

Cut on fold

Cut on fold

FB 14

GB 15

Cut on fold

FB 19

Cut on fold

FB 12

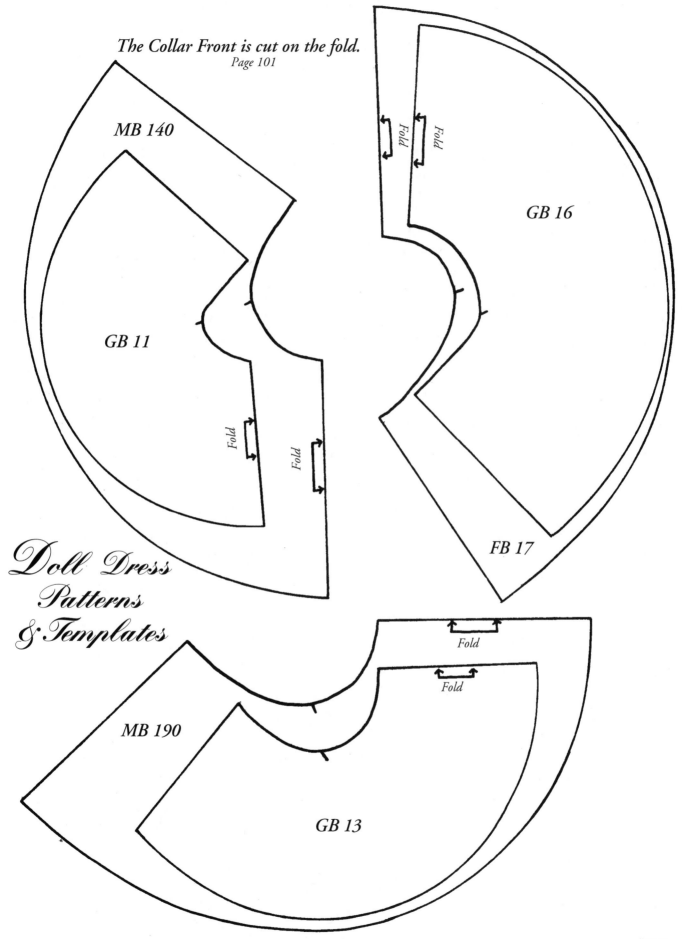

The Collar Front is cut on the fold.
Page 101

MB 140

GB 16

Fold

Fold

Fold

GB 11

Fold

Fold

FB 17

*Doll Dress
Patterns
& Templates*

Fold

Fold

MB 190

GB 13

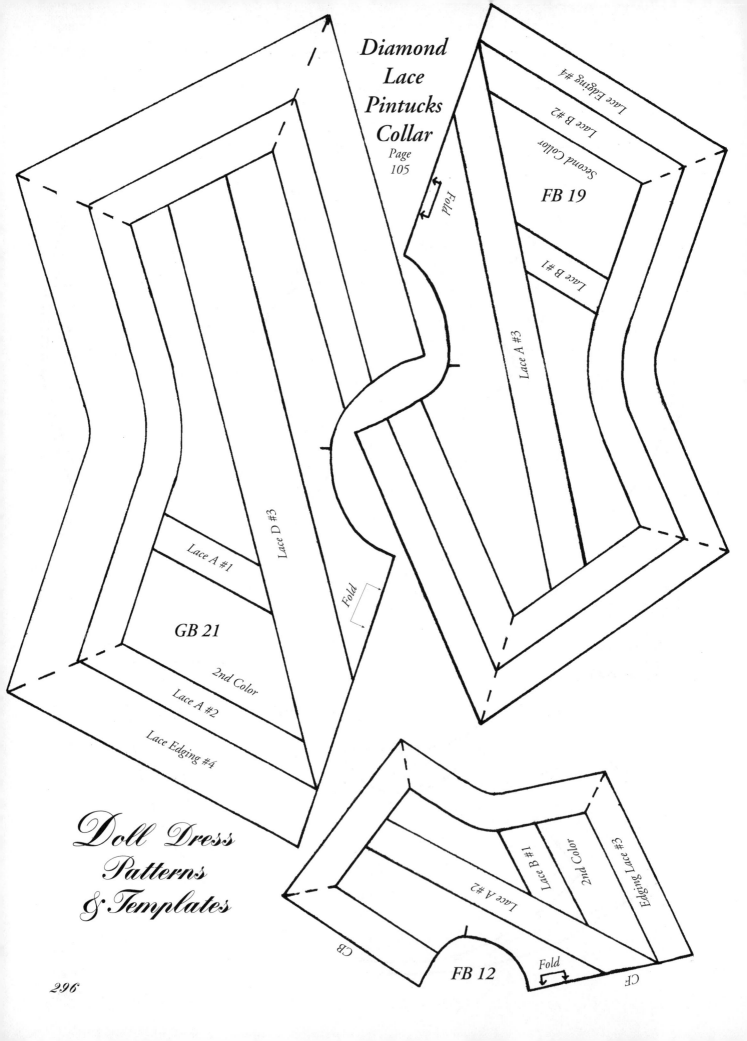

Diamond
Lace
Pintucks
Collar
Page
105

Fold

FB 19

Second Collar

Lace Edging #4

Lace B #2

Lace B #1

Lace A #3

GB 21

Lace A #1

Lace D #3

2nd Color

Lace A #2

Lace Edging #4

Fold

Lace A #3

Lace A #2

Lace B #1

2nd Color

Edging Lace #3

CB

Fold

CF

FB 12

Doll Dress
Patterns
& Templates

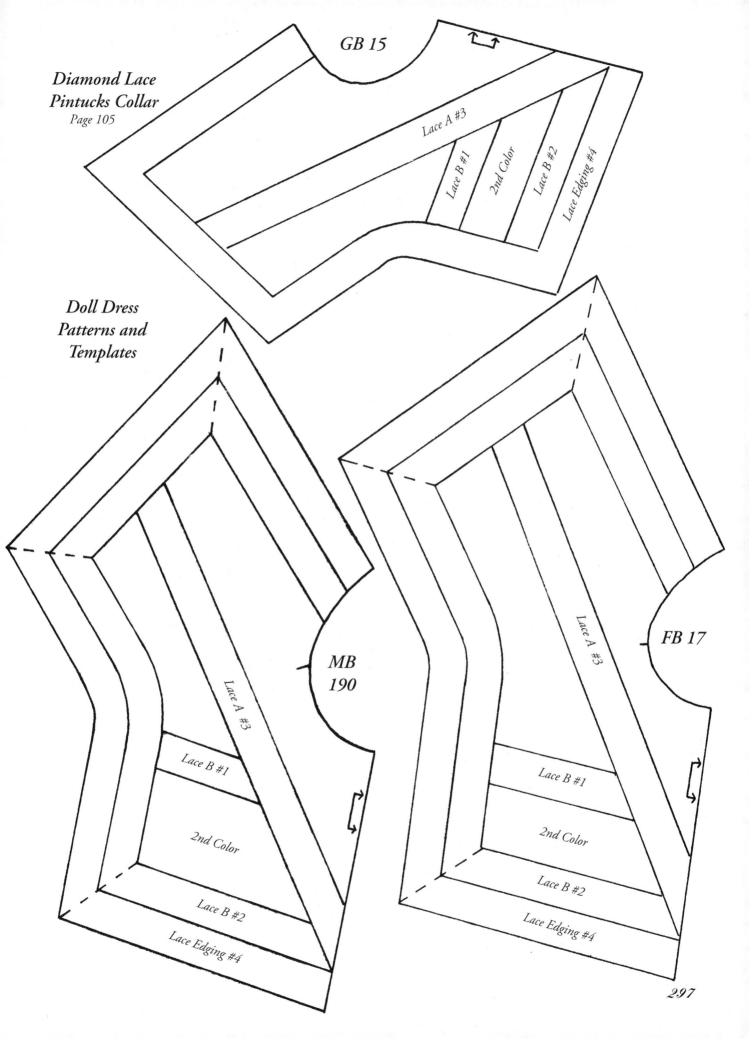

GB 15

*Diamond Lace
Pintucks Collar*
Page 105

Lace A #3
Lace B #1
2nd Color
Lace B #2
Lace Edging #4

*Doll Dress
Patterns and
Templates*

Lace A #3

Lace B #1

2nd Color

Lace B #2

Lace Edging #4

*MB
190*

Lace A #3

FB 17

Lace B #1

2nd Color

Lace B #2

Lace Edging #4

297

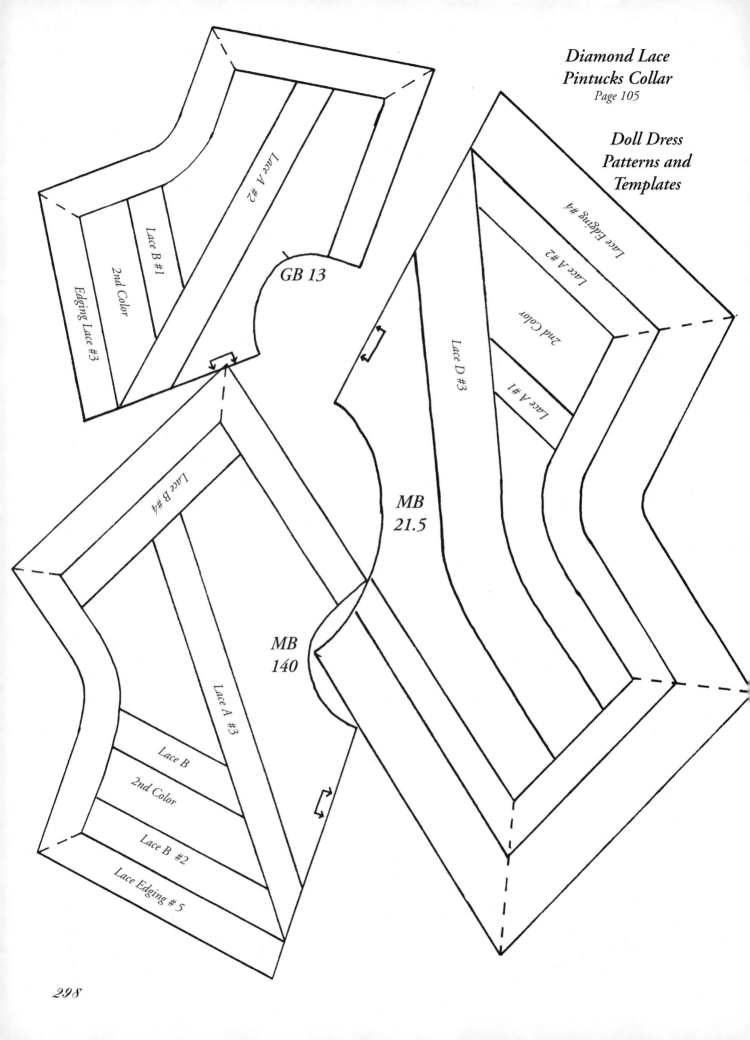

Diamond Lace
Pintucks Collar
Page 105

Doll Dress
Patterns and
Templates

GB 13

Lace A #2

Lace B #1

2nd Color

Edging Lace #3

Lace Edging #4

Lace A #2

2nd Color

Lace A #1

Lace D #3

MB
21.5

MB
140

Lace B #4

Lace A #3

Lace B

2nd Color

Lace B #2

Lace Edging # 5

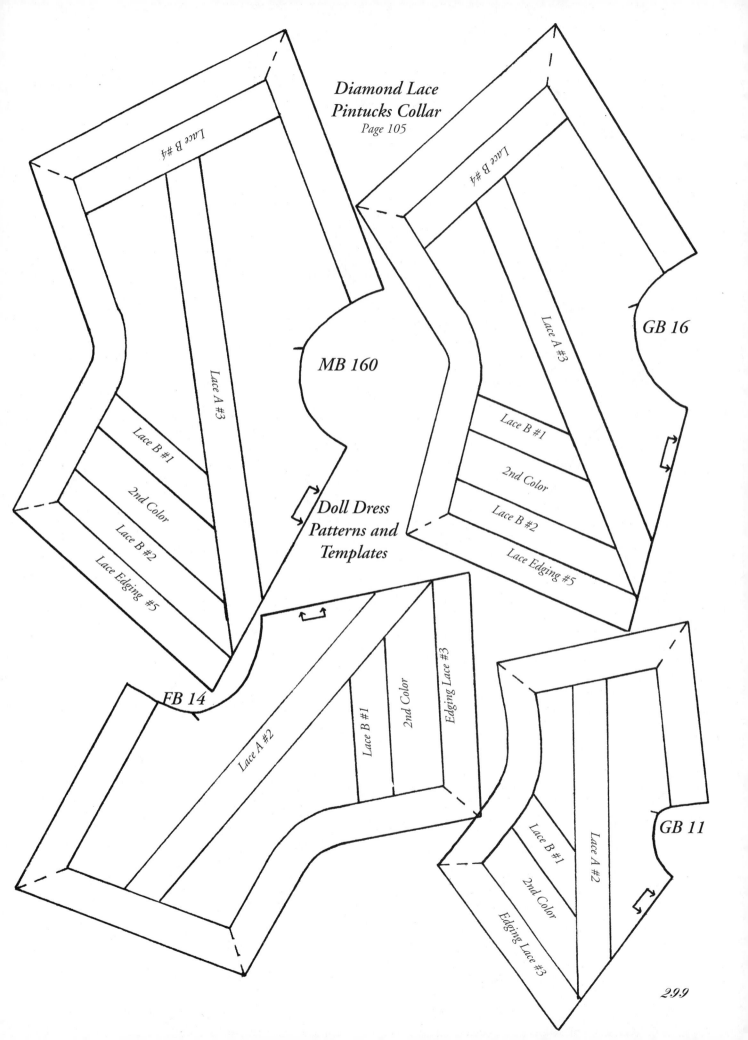

Diamond Lace
Pintucks Collar
Page 105

Lace B #4

Lace A #3

MB 160

Lace B #1

2nd Color

Lace B #2

Lace Edging #5

*Doll Dress
Patterns and
Templates*

Lace B #4

Lace A #3

GB 16

Lace B #1

2nd Color

Lace B #2

Lace Edging #5

FB 14

Lace A #2

Lace B #1

2nd Color

Edging Lace #3

GB 11

Lace B #1

Lace A #2

2nd Color

Edging Lace #3

299

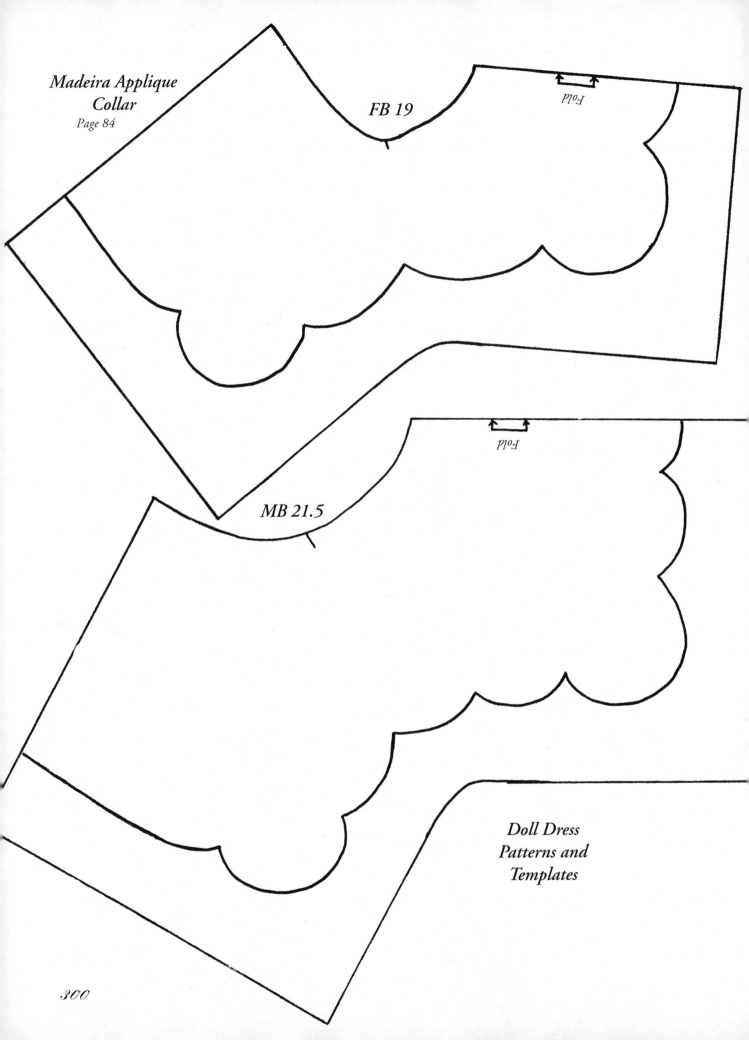

Madeira Applique
Collar
Page 84

FB 19

Fold

MB 21.5

Fold

Doll Dress
Patterns and
Templates

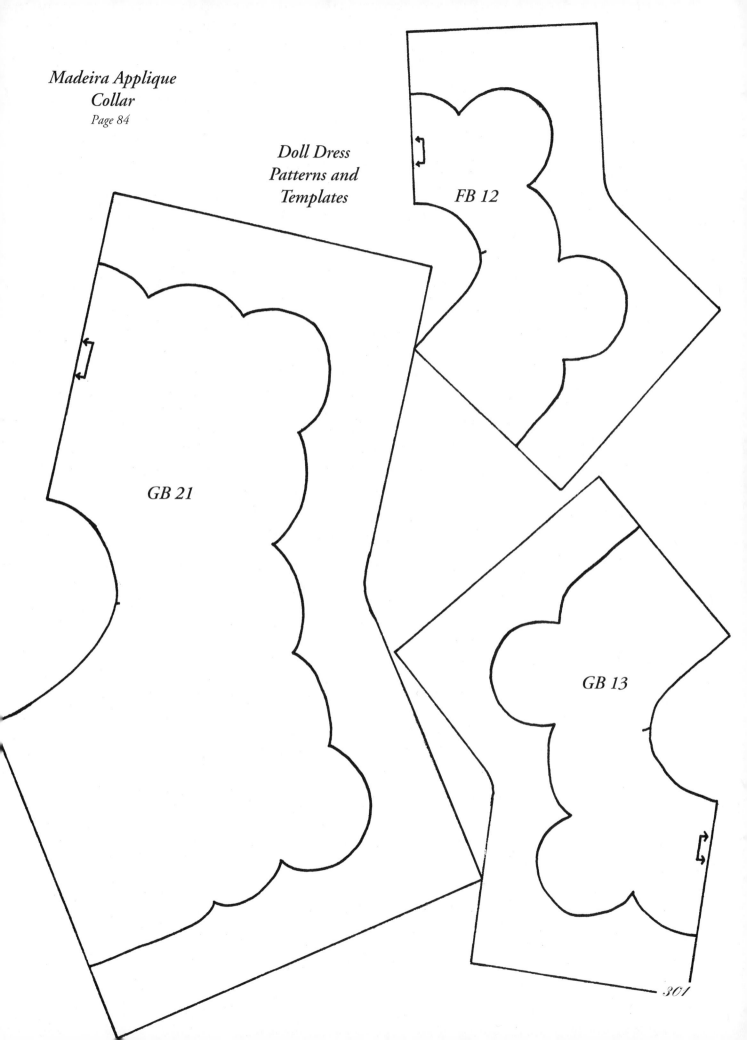

Madeira Applique
Collar
Page 84

Doll Dress
Patterns and
Templates

FB 12

GB 21

GB 13

301

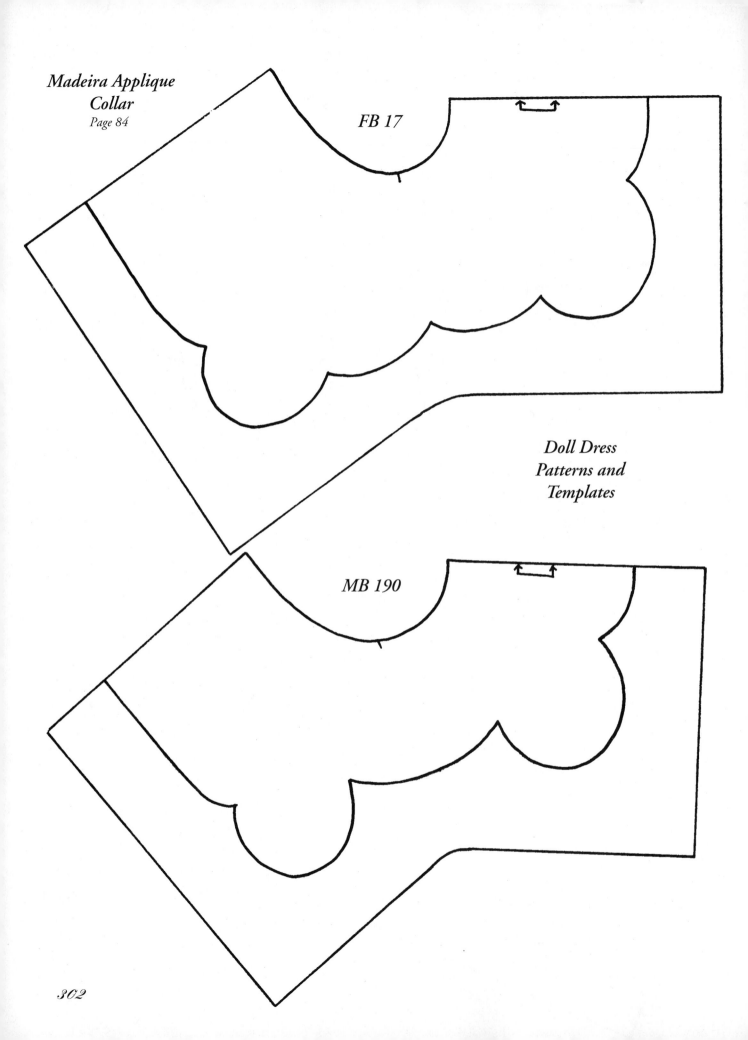

Madeira Applique
Collar
Page 84

FB 17

Doll Dress
Patterns and
Templates

MB 190

302

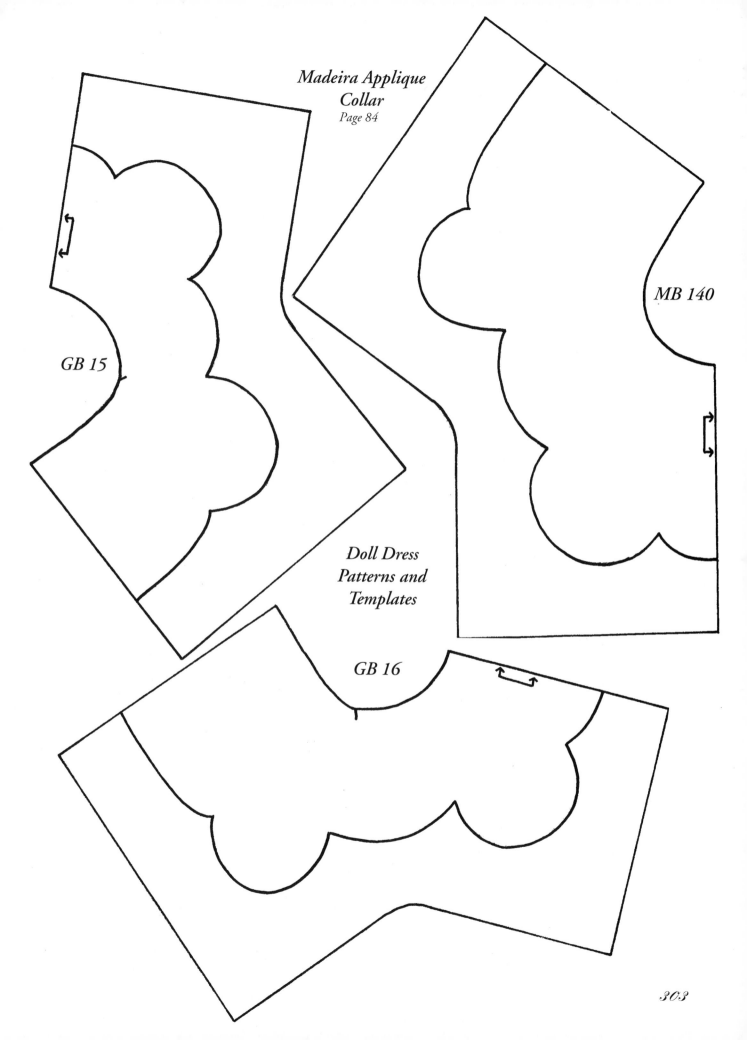

Madeira Applique
Collar
Page 84

MB 140

GB 15

Doll Dress
Patterns and
Templates

GB 16

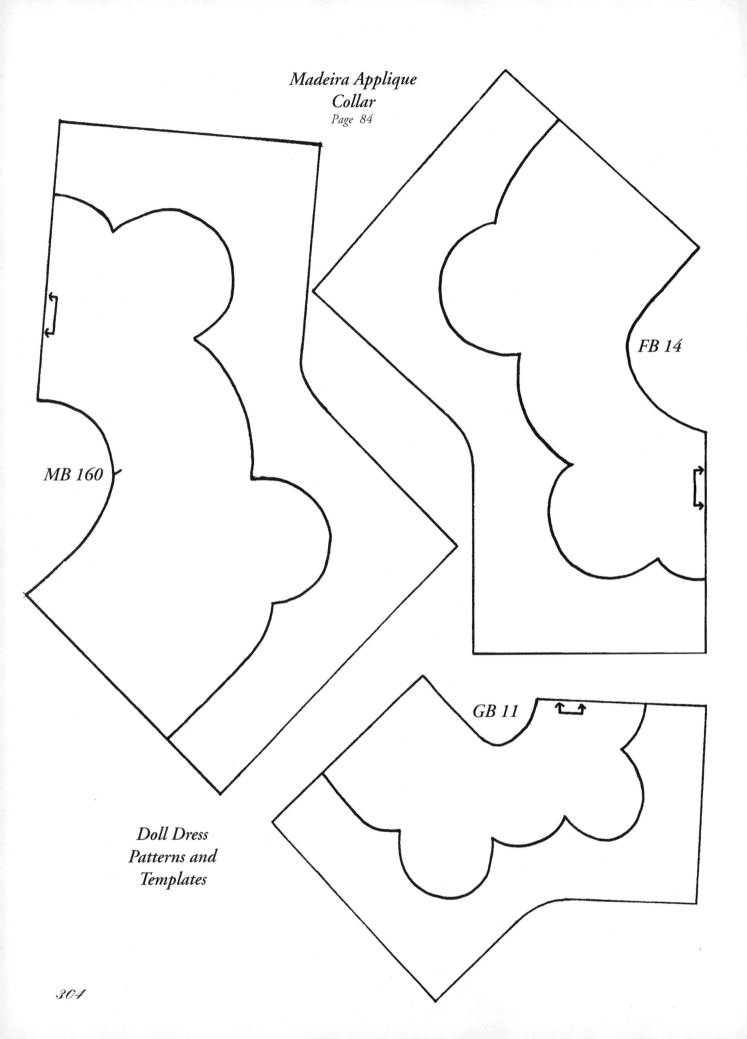

*Madeira Applique
Collar*
Page 84

FB 14

MB 160

GB 11

*Doll Dress
Patterns and
Templates*

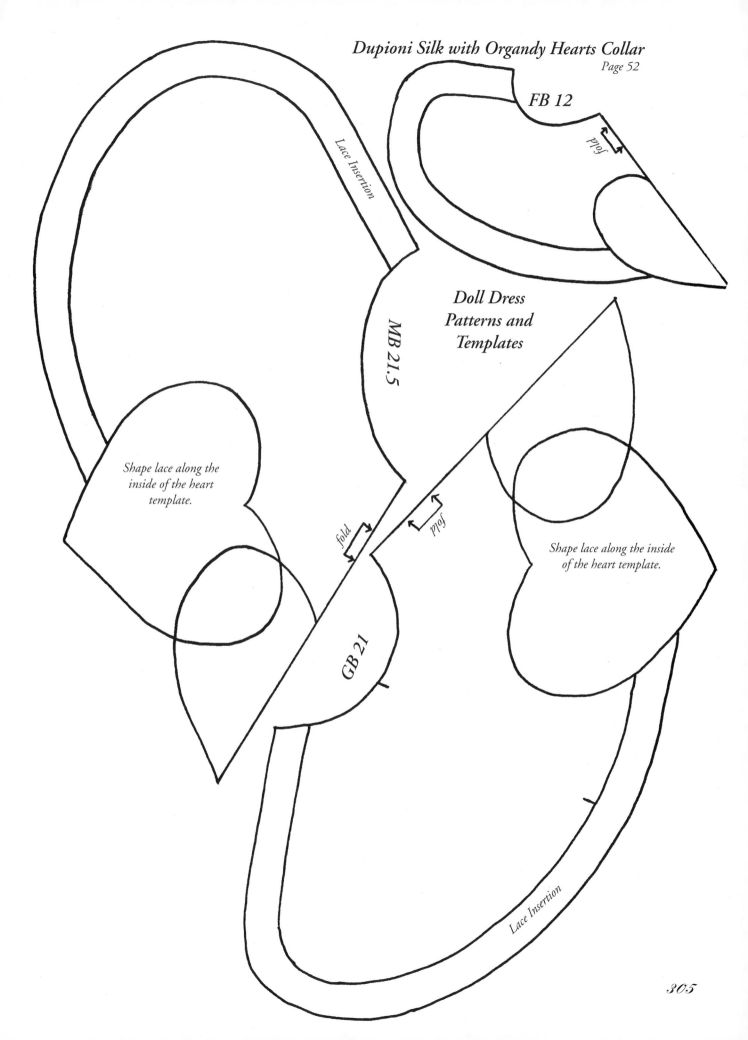

Dupioni Silk with Organdy Hearts Collar
Page 52

FB 12

fold

Lace Insertion

MB 21.5

Doll Dress Patterns and Templates

Shape lace along the inside of the heart template.

fold

fold

Shape lace along the inside of the heart template.

GB 21

Lace Insertion

305

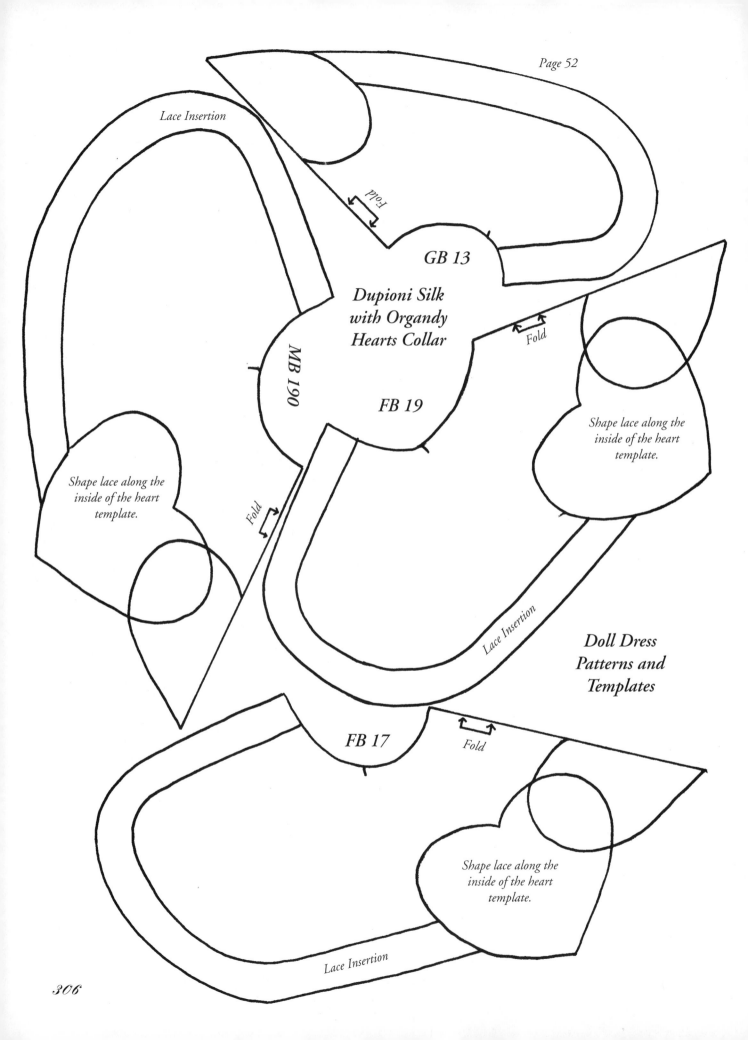

Lace Insertion

Fold

GB 13

**Dupioni Silk
with Organdy
Hearts Collar**

MB 190

FB 19

Fold

*Shape lace along the
inside of the heart
template.*

*Shape lace along the
inside of the heart
template.*

Fold

Lace Insertion

**Doll Dress
Patterns and
Templates**

FB 17

Fold

*Shape lace along the
inside of the heart
template.*

Lace Insertion

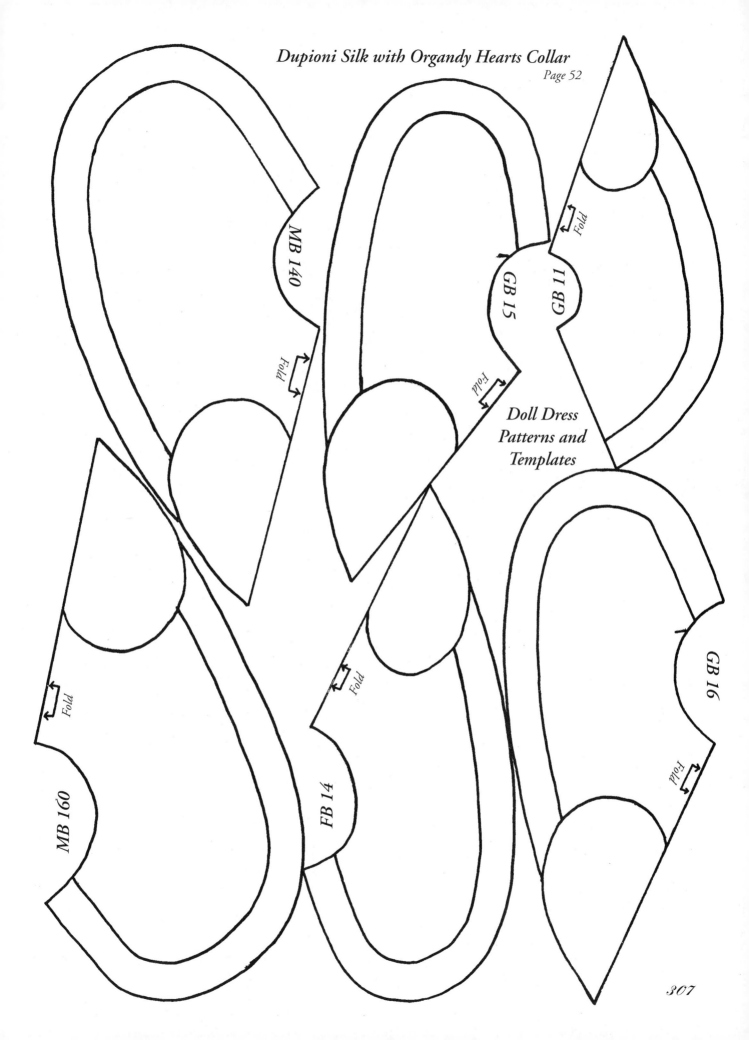

Dupioni Silk with Organdy Hearts Collar

Page 52

MB 140

GB 15

GB 11

Fold

Fold

Doll Dress
Patterns and
Templates

MB 160

Fold

FB 14

Fold

GB 16

Fold

307

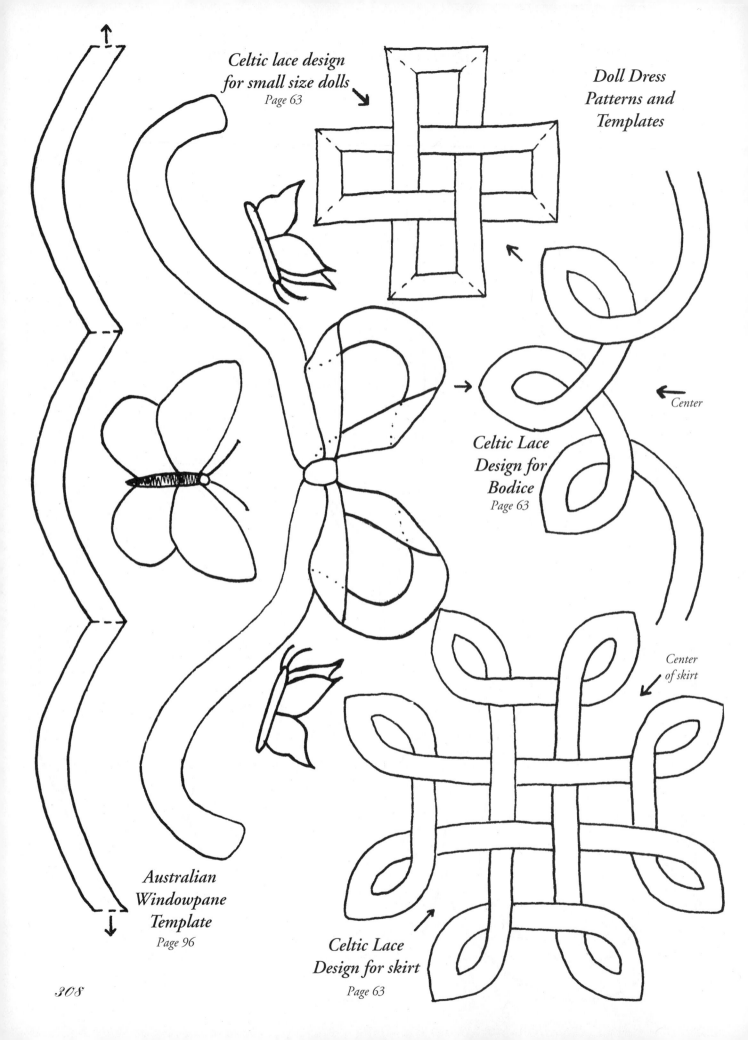

Celtic lace design
for small size dolls
Page 63

Doll Dress
Patterns and
Templates

Center

Celtic Lace
Design for
Bodice
Page 63

Center
of skirt

Australian
Windowpane
Template
Page 96

Celtic Lace
Design for skirt
Page 63

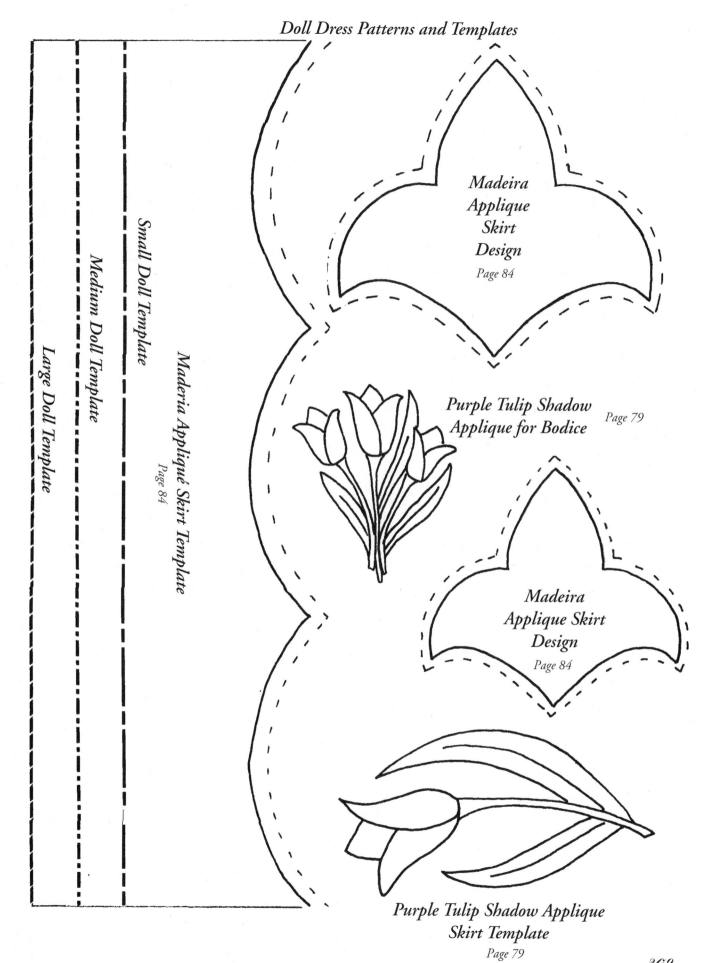

*Madeira
Applique
Skirt
Design*

Page 84

*Purple Tulip Shadow
Applique for Bodice*   Page 79

*Madeira
Applique Skirt
Design*

Page 84

Small Doll Template

Medium Doll Template

Large Doll Template

Maderia Appliqué Skirt Template
Page 84

*Purple Tulip Shadow Applique
Skirt Template*

Page 79

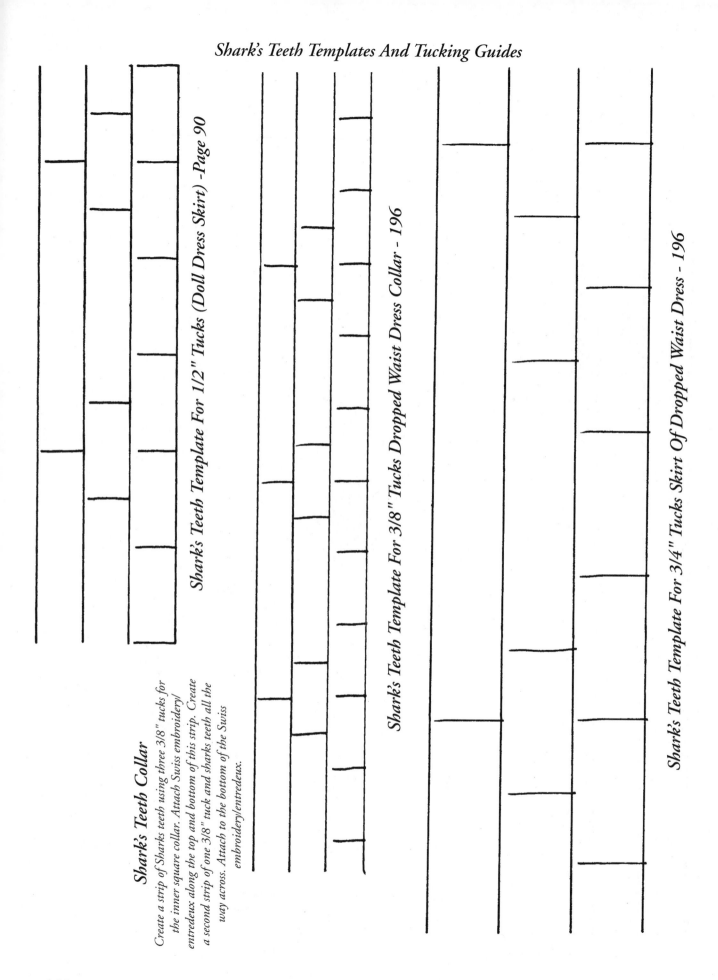

Shark's Teeth Collar

Create a strip of Shark's teeth using three 3/8" tucks for the inner square collar. Attach Swiss embroidery/entredeux along the top and bottom of this strip. Create a second strip of one 3/8" tuck and shark's teeth all the way across. Attach to the bottom of the Swiss embroidery/entredeux.

Shark's Teeth Template For 1/2" Tucks (Doll Dress Skirt) -Page 90

Shark's Teeth Template For 3/8" Tucks Dropped Waist Dress Collar - 196

Shark's Teeth Template For 3/4" Tucks Skirt Of Dropped Waist Dress - 196

Shark's Teeth Tucking Guide

Page 196 Child's Skirt

3/4" Tucking Guide

Top

Page 90 Doll Skirt

1/2" Seam

Top

Page 196 Child's Collar

3/8" Tucks

Top

1

2

3

Bottom

Bottom

Bottom

General Shark's Teeth
Template

#1

#2

#3

#4

#5

#6

#7

#8

Center Tucking Guide in the center of the fabric. Repeat Tuck Lines Below.

Fold

Fold

Fold

Fold

Shark's Teeth
Tucking Guide-

Page 153 - Quilt - Mark 4 tucks each side of center
Page 31 — Pillow - Mark 8 tucks each side center
— Pillow Repeat for 4 more tucks   Stitching Line

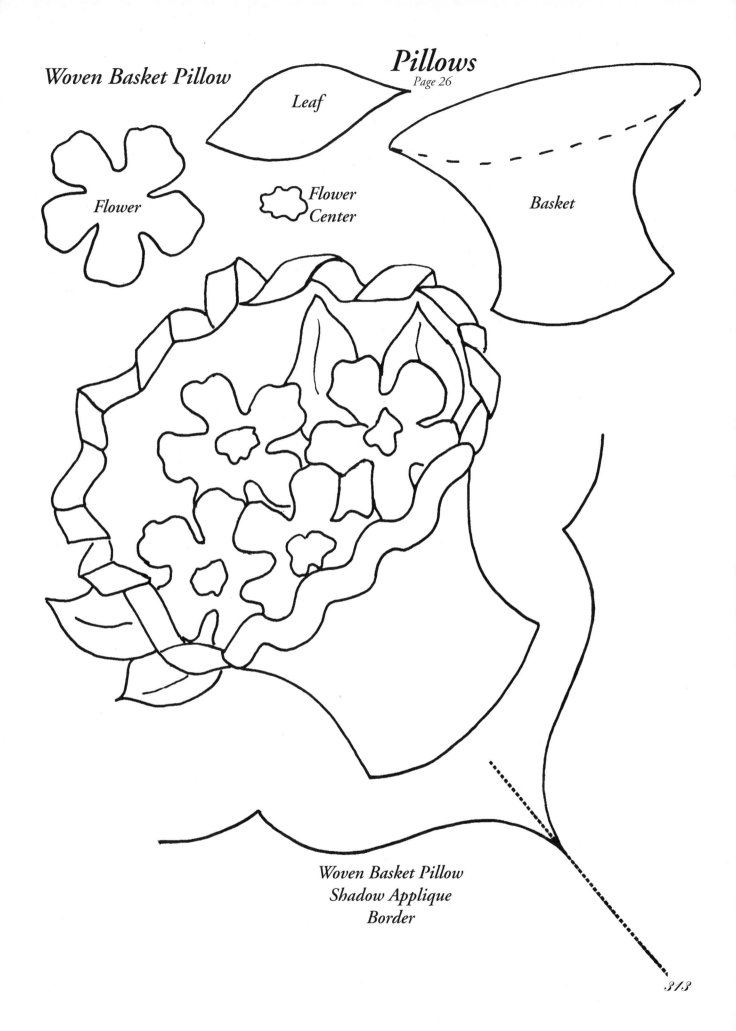

Woven Basket Pillow

Leaf

Flower

Flower
Center

Basket

Woven Basket Pillow
Shadow Applique
Border

313

Pillows

Page 24

Appliqued Rose Pillow

Rose Piece 1

Petal 2

Rose
Piece 2

Rose Piece 3

Petal 1

2

3

1

314

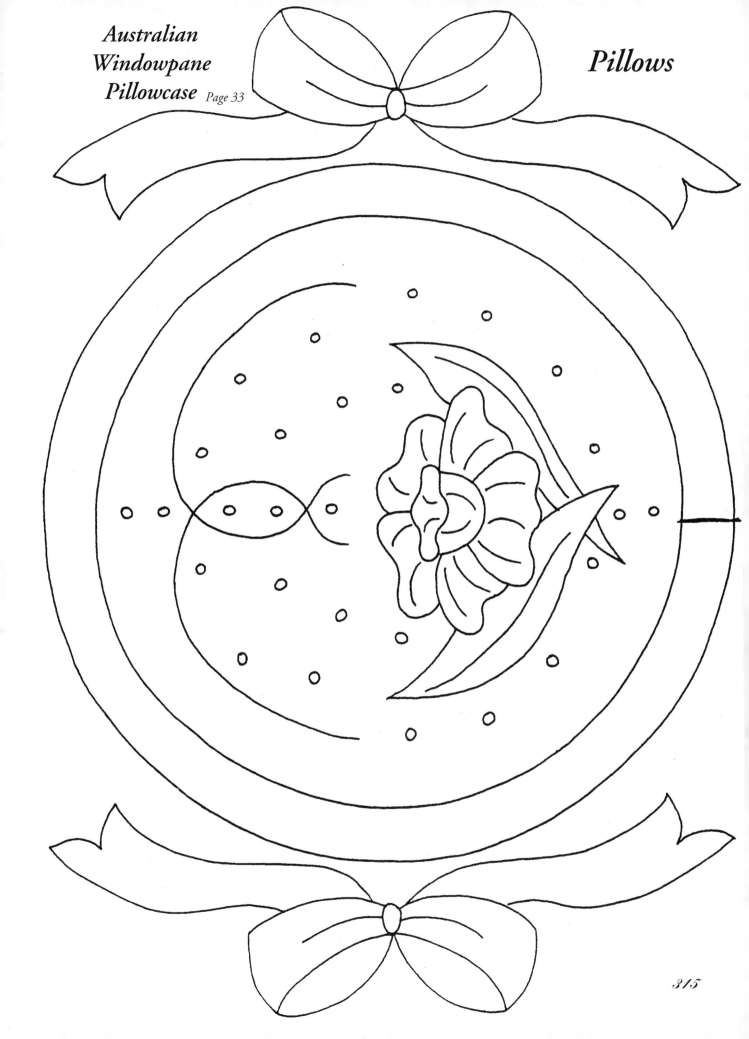

Pillows

Lace Shaped Baby
Pillow Template
Page 40

Baby

Diamond
Template for
Diamond Braid
Pillow
Page 42

Madeira Applique
Pillow Template
Page 28

Pillow Celtic Lace Pillow Template

Crazy Patch Baby Pillow Center Template

Page 14

Baby

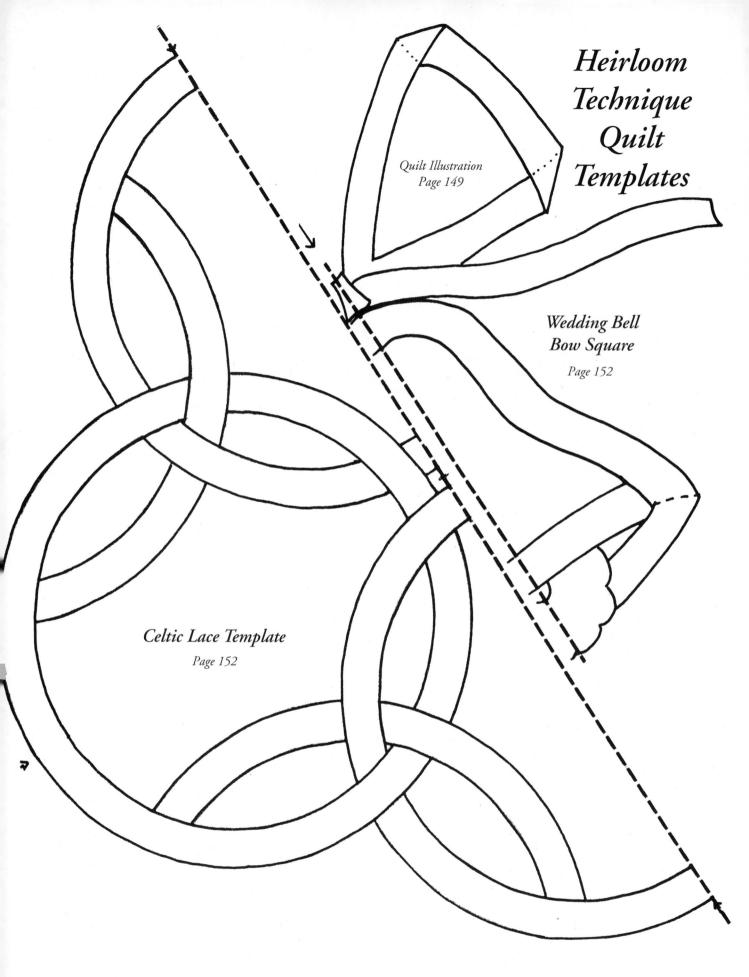

*Heirloom
Technique
Quilt
Templates*

*Quilt Illustration
Page 149*

*Wedding Bell
Bow Square*

Page 152

Celtic Lace Template

Page 152

318

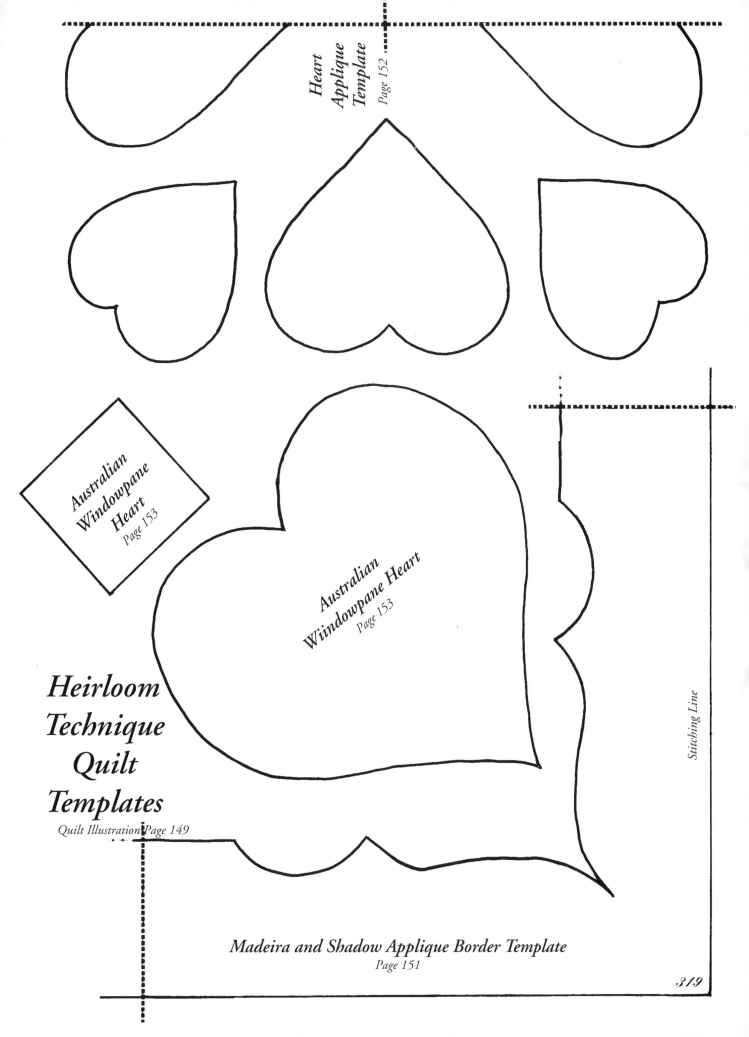

Heart
Applique
Template
Page 152

Australian
Windowpane
Heart
Page 153

Australian
Wiindowpane Heart
Page 153

Heirloom
Technique
Quilt
Templates

Quilt Illustration Page 149

Stitching Line

Madeira and Shadow Applique Border Template
Page 151

319

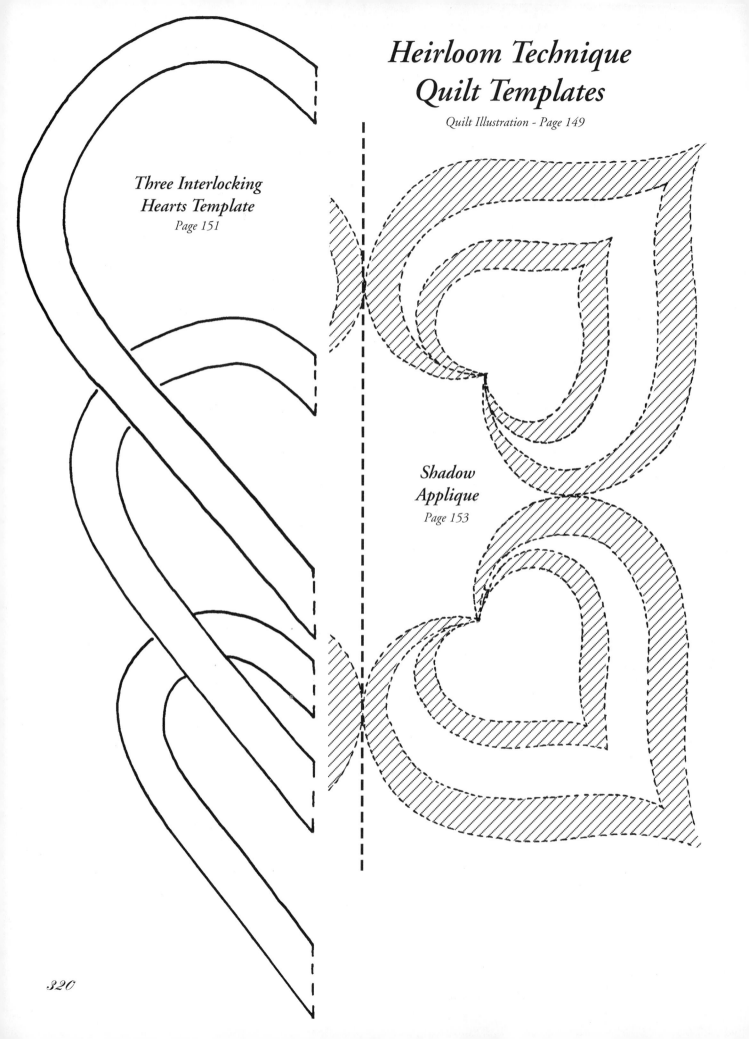

Heirloom Technique Quilt Templates

Quilt Illustration - Page 149

**Three Interlocking
Hearts Template**
Page 151

*Shadow
Applique*
Page 153

Heirloom Technique
Quilt Templates

Quilt Illustration on page 149

Lacy Pocket Template
Page 150

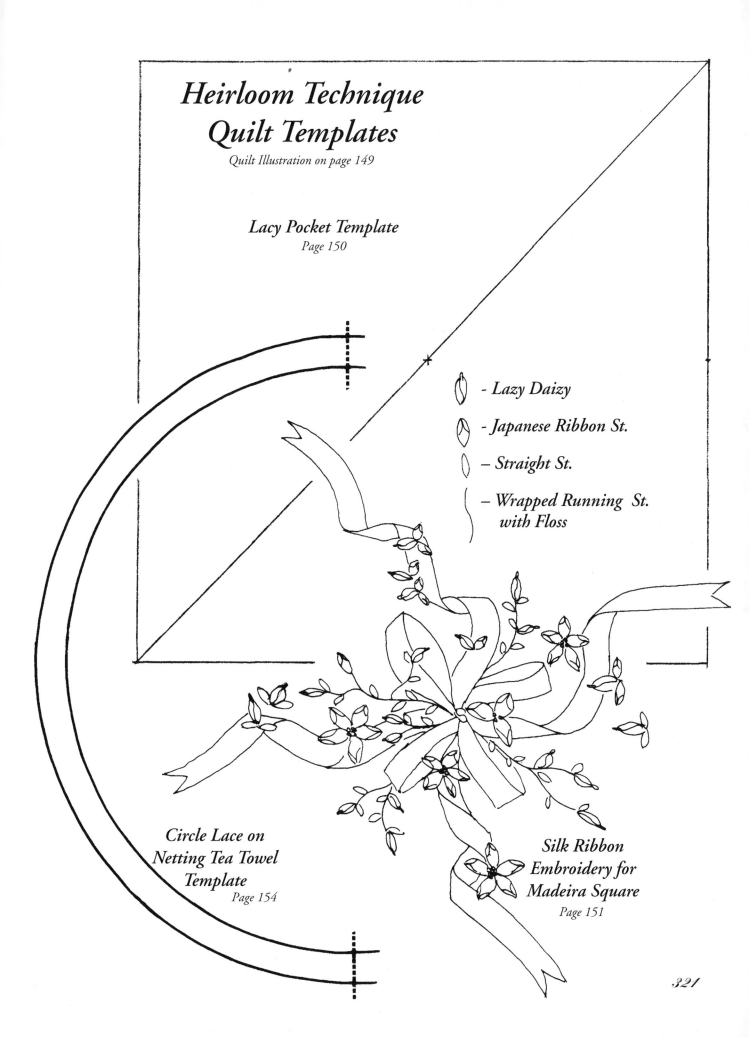

- Lazy Daizy

- Japanese Ribbon St.

- Straight St.

- Wrapped Running St.
  with Floss

Circle Lace on
Netting Tea Towel
Template
Page 154

Silk Ribbon
Embroidery for
Madeira Square
Page 151

ABCDEFGH
IJKLMNOP
QRSTUVXY
WZ abcdefgh
ijklmn opqrs
tuvw xyz

Applique Quilt Alphapet   *Page 157*

First Day at School

Flowers used to decorate words. Use if desired.

322

Applique
Quilt
Page 157

First Word

First Party

da
da

First Prom

First Haircut

323

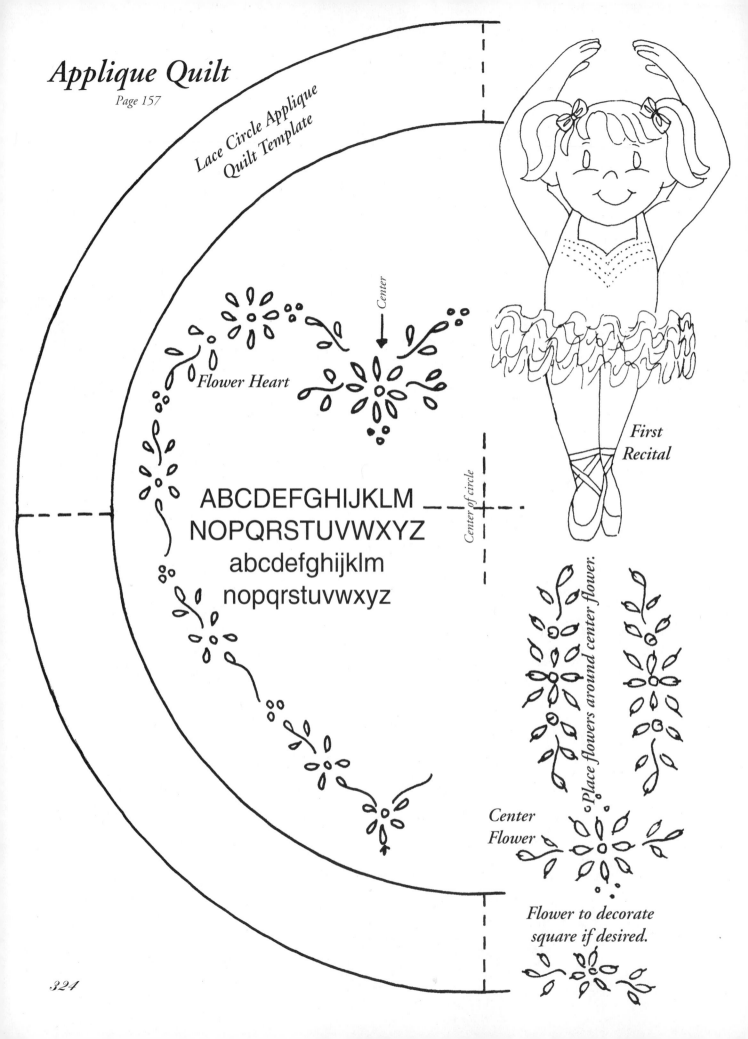

Applique Quilt

Page 157

Lace Circle Applique Quilt Template

Center

Flower Heart

Center of circle

ABCDEFGHIJKLM
NOPQRSTUVWXYZ
abcdefghijklm
nopqrstuvwxyz

First Recital

Place flowers around center flower.

Center Flower

Flower to decorate square if desired.

Applique Quilt

Page 157

First Spend The Night

PJ's

First Tooth

center

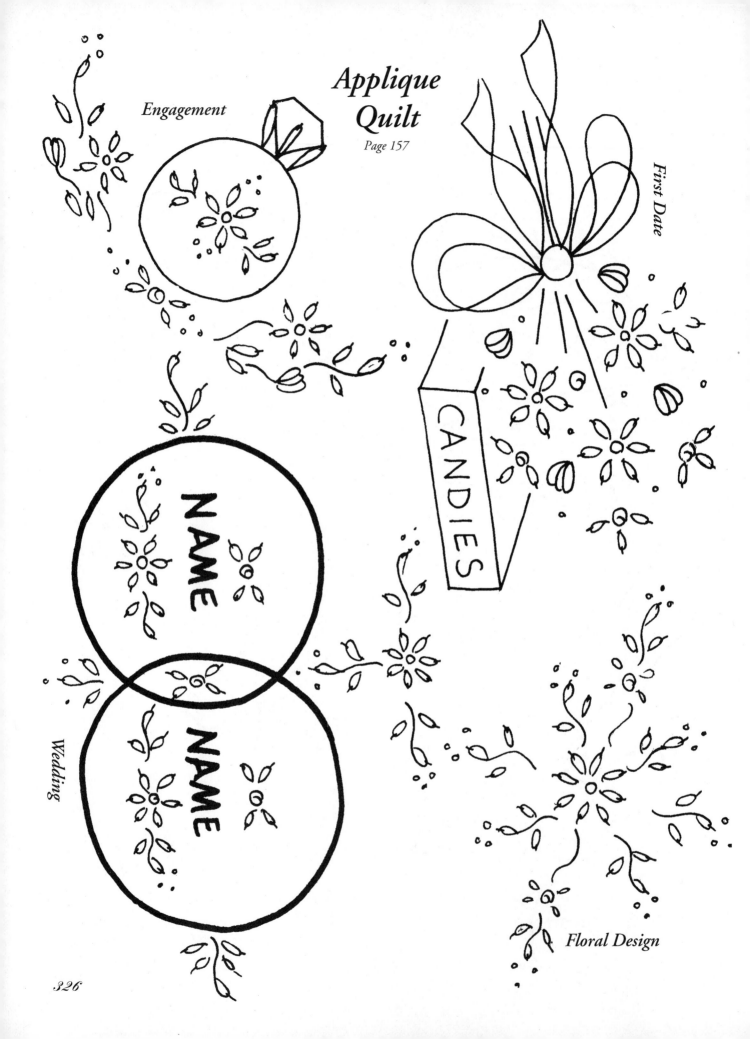

Engagement

Applique Quilt
Page 157

First Date

CANDIES

NAME

NAME

Wedding

Floral Design

326

Applique Quilt
Page 157

First Step

Graduation

First Birthday

Baptism

327

Index

Show Index Program Guide 200

About The Author

 artha Campbell Pullen, a native of Scottsboro, Alabama, is an internationally-known lecturer and author in the heirloom sewing field. After graduating with a degree in speech and English from the University of Alabama, she taught those subjects at almost every level of middle school and high school. Later, her studies led to receiving a Ph.D. in educational administration and management from the University of Alabama.

Her love of sewing and children's clothing encouraged the opening of Martha Pullen's Heirloom Shop in Huntsville, Alabama, August 1, 1981. Two months later, she opened Martha Pullen Company, Inc., the wholesale division. She has served on the board of directors of the Smocking Arts Guild of America and has presented workshops on French sewing by machine throughout the United States, Australia, England, and New Zealand. Books she has written and published include *French Hand Sewing by Machine, A Beginner's Guide; Heirloom Doll Clothes; Bearly Beginning Smocking; Shadow work Embroidery; French Sewing by Machine: The Second Book; Antique Clothing: French Sewing by Machine; Grandmother's Hope Chest; Applique, Martha's Favorites; Heirloom Sewing For Women; Joy of Smocking; Martha's Sewing Room and Victorian Sewing and Crafts.*

Martha is also the founder and publisher of a best-selling magazine, *Sew Beautiful,* which is dedicated to heirloom sewing. The publication charms more than 80,000 readers worldwide. She has just completed a television series for public television entitled, *"Martha's Sewing Room."*

She is the wife of Joseph Ross Pullen, an implant dentist, mother of five of the most wonderful children in the world, and grandmother of the six most beautiful, intelligent, precious and adorable grandchildren in the world. She participates in many civic activities and is an active member of her church. She also volunteers with the Southern Baptist Foreign Mission Board.